Th Feminist Critique of Language:
A Reader

'Since publication, the first edition of *The Feminist Critique of Language* has been a cornerstone of courses on language, gender and power. The revisions and updates new edition ensure that it will continue to be indispensable for studen scholars alike. ... Overall, the project is fresh and well conceived, and of erable importance as a roadmap through the convoluted terrain of langua ender studies.'

Mary Bucholtz, *University of California, Berkeley*

The Feminist Critique of Language is both an established guide to the major debates and directions in current feminist thinking about language and a digest of the history 20th-century feminist ideas about language.

The new edition has been thoroughly updated and expanded to take account of new developments in feminist debates about language, such as the acknowledgement of differences that exist within the group 'women' and subsequent avoidance of ethnocentric and class-biased generalizations. It also includes new material on sexist language and political correctness.

The Reader brings together some of the most thought-provoking and controversial key texts by such writers as Luce Irigaray, Otto Jespersen, Cora Kaplan, Robin Lakoff, Trinh T. Minh-ha, Dale Spender, Deborah Tannen and Virginia Woolf.

The Feminist Critique of Language is divided into three parts: *Speech and Silence: the quest for women's voices in culture; Representations: sexist language and sexist discourse; Talking Gender: dominance, difference, performance*. Each section is then subdivided to make explicit the different strands within the debate. New editorial material and further reading sections have been added.

This Reader is ideal as a core text for courses in Language, Literature, Women's Studies and Gender Studies.

The Feminist Critique

of Language:

A Reader

Second edition

Edited, with an introduction
by

Deborah Cameron

London and New York

First published 1998
by Routledge
11 New Fetter Lane, London EC4P 4EE

Simultaneously published in the USA and Canada
by Routledge
29 West 35th Street, New York, NY 10001

Typeset in Perpetua by
Florencetype Ltd, Stoodleigh, Devon

Printed and bound in Great Britain by
TJ International Ltd., Padstow, Cornwall

British Library Cataloguing in Publication Data
A catalogue record for this book is available from the British Library

Library of Congress Cataloguing in Publication Data

The feminist critique of language : a reader / [edited by] Deborah
    Cameron. – 2nd [rev.] ed.
        p.   cm.
    Includes bibliographical references (p.) and index.
    ISBN 0–415–16399–4 (hardcover). – ISBN 0–415–16400–1 (pbk.)
    1. Language and languages–Sex differences.   2. Sexism in language.
3. Women–Language.   I. Cameron, Deborah, 1958–   .
P120.S48F46   1998
408'.2–dc21   97–23068
                                                                            CIP

ISBN 0–415–16399–4 (hbk.)
ISBN 0–415–16400–1 (pbk.)

Contents

PART THREE
Talking gender: Dominance, difference, performance

CONTENTS

Preface to the second edition

THE FEMINIST CRITIQUE OF LANGUAGE was originally part of a
series called *Word and World*, addressed to students of literature. The idea
behind the series was that literary texts cannot be studied in isolation from
broader theoretical and cultural debates; this volume presented a selection
of materials dealing with feminist debates on language. It turned out however
that the materials were of interest not only to literature students, but to a
wider and more diverse audience. In this extensively revised edition I have
taken more account of that diversity, and set out to make the book more
useful to more readers. I have also, of course, updated it to reflect the feminist debates of today, as opposed to the debates of ten years ago when I was
preparing the first version.

Not everything about the book has changed. The overall goals remain
the same as they were before: to illustrate the diversity and complexity of
feminist ideas about language, to trace the evolution of important debates
over time, and to make texts available in their original forms, as opposed to
paraphrasing and summarizing in the manner of a conventional textbook. But
if my aims as an editor have not changed, the body of material that might
have some claim to be included in this book has changed quite a lot. This is
not only (though it is partly) because of the accumulation of more and more
relevant publications. Since I made my original selections, theoretical debates
have moved on, new questions have been raised, and priorities have shifted.
The cultural and political context for the feminist critique of language is
different now from what it was ten years ago.

Such changes are to be expected, but they make an editor's task more
difficult: the more there is to choose from, the harder the choices. I am
pleased that I have been able to increase the overall amount of reprinted
material; at the same time I am sorry that I have had to exclude material

that would certainly have appeared if space were unlimited.[1] I have been obliged to make choices about which of the original pieces to retain, which to replace with newer contributions and which contributions those should be. Here I want to say something about the principles that have guided me, and in the process to answer some frequently asked questions posed by users of the first edition.

To begin with, I have prioritized *feminist* work. Some readers have suggested including non-feminist/anti-feminist contributions, to make clear what feminist arguments are directed against. In fact this is the reason why I originally included, and have retained, Otto Jespersen's pre-feminist (1922) essay 'The Woman'. It is important to have some idea what discourse about language and gender was like before there was a feminist critique. By contrast, I suspect that today's reader needs no potted summary of the views of today's anti-feminists, and therefore I have not included any (unless you count Douglas Hofstadter's 'Person Paper', a satirical tour of anti-feminist clichés). The point I am more concerned today's reader should appreciate — for often it is obscured by the simplistic presentations of feminism that dominate mainstream culture — is that feminism itself encompasses a considerable range of intellectual and political views. Since the mid-1970s, the most important debates have been internal ones.

A second point about the selection I have made is that it is not intended to function as a survey of empirical research findings on language and gender. For one thing, such surveys date very quickly; for another, compiling a reader is an unnecessarily cumbersome way of presenting the information. Surveys are better suited to the summarizing approach of the textbook or the review article in a scholarly journal.[2] This book is aiming for a different balance between breadth and depth of coverage. It is offered as an informed guide to some major debates and directions in current feminist thinking about language, and also to some extent as a digest of the history of feminist ideas about language in the twentieth century.

The first of these aims is obvious enough, but the 'historical' aim may need more justification. Readers might well ask: 'why include old texts advancing ideas that have now been superseded?'. My answer to this would be that a 'deep' understanding of any field of intellectual inquiry relies partly on being able to place its concerns in historical context. Unless you know how, and from what, a field's current preoccupations have developed, you cannot properly assess the validity and significance of new research findings. That said, I have tried to strike a balance between looking back to the 'classic' discussions of language and gender, and looking towards newer work which will shape the discussion in future. Some texts really are classics; others, including a few which were included in the first edition of this Reader, were important for a certain period of time, but they no longer have the kind of influence which would justify their (re)inclusion here.

When it comes to selecting new pieces, I have had to make choices of both a practical and a more theoretical kind. Other things being equal, I have preferred to reprint pieces that are relatively hard for students to get hold of, rather than pieces – however excellent in themselves and however well they might fit – that are already accessible in other anthologies. One effect of this choice has been to shift the balance of this volume's content away from 'literary' sources. Feminist literary theory, which includes quite a lot of writing about language and gender from a poststructuralist perspective, is now well represented in a number of texts and anthologies for students, and I have not felt it necessary or desirable to duplicate these sources (I have mentioned some of the most accessible ones in the 'Further reading' section at the end of Part 1).

On the more theoretical side, I have tried to engage with what I referred to earlier as the 'theoretical movements' and 'shifting priorities' within feminist language studies. One theme here is the growth of what might be called feminist critiques of (earlier) feminist critiques. As one would expect, the concepts which served feminists well enough twenty years ago – 'women's language' and 'sexist language' are obvious cases in point – have since been subjected to critical scrutiny from within.

This brings me to what is probably *the* most frequently asked question about my selections in the original edition of this book, a question about the representation of *differences* among women. An important reason why feminists are now critical of much earlier work is that so much of it focused narrowly on a particular (straight, white and middle-class) version of femininity. In the study of language and gender as in feminist studies generally, most scholars today are careful to acknowledge the differences that exist within the group 'women' and to guard against ethnocentric and class-biased (over)generalizations. There has been a growth of interest in the complex interactions between different aspects of an individual's or a group's identity, and in the equally complex interactions between different kinds of power relations. Sexism does not work in exactly the same way for rich and poor women or white and black women; conversely, the experience of poverty and/or racism is in some respects gendered, taking different forms and having different meanings for women and for men. It is not just a question of adding up how many separate forms of oppression someone faces, but of recognizing differences in the structuring of oppression, and real conflicts of interest and perception between differently positioned women as a consequence of that.

The theme of diversity, difference and conflict among women is a significant one in current feminist debates and my selection of recent work is intended to reflect that. However, I have made certain choices about *how* to reflect it and some readers may be critical of those choices. This volume as a whole is still dominated by the voices and ideas of women who are, among other things, white, highly educated, native and probably monolingual speakers of English, and born before 1970. It is not a coincidence that these are the women who have typically gained most from the social changes associated with recent feminism and it is important to ask how and to what extent that has affected the shape of the feminist critique of language. But as I will argue in more detail in a new section of the introduction ('The feminist critique of language and the politics of identity'), the question is not a simple one and the answers are not always clear-cut. Here I will confine myself to encouraging the reader to pay attention to the issue, not only in relation to contributions by 'minority' women but in relation to *every* contribution – including, of course, my own editorial contributions.

The section of this book that has been expanded most significantly is Part 2, 'Representations: sexist language and sexist discourse'. There are two reasons for this. One is that the need for accessible feminist material is greater in this area. By comparison, the other main area of work in feminist linguistics – the speech styles of women and men – is better represented in existing publications aimed at students. The other reason is that debates on 'sexist language' and other aspects of representation have been changed significantly by certain developments of the last few years. The controversy about so-called 'political correctness' has reignited public arguments about a lot of well-worn questions, as well as raising some new ones. My selections in the 'representations' section respond to the changed cultural context in two ways. In some cases, they talk directly about the 'political correctness' debate. In other cases they are meant to fill a gap that the debate has made all too apparent: public commentary on the 'PC' issue has often proceeded from crude preconceptions, and there is a need for wider awareness of more sophisticated arguments about how and why language matters. Since feminists have been talking about this for more than twenty years (whereas the 'PC' bandwagon only really started rolling in the early 1990s), it is not surprising that feminist work has much to offer in this regard.

The job of an editor not only involves selecting material, it also involves deciding how to present it so that the reader derives maximum benefit. This is another area in which I have made changes. While this edition retains the three-part structure of the original, I have subdivided each main section to make explicit the different strands within the debate. I have also provided more by way of editorial material, introducing and contextualizing the selections, and providing a 'further reading' section, in each part. (I have made more detailed suggestions on how to find your way around in a separate note on 'Using this book', p.xvii.)

If these are, as I hope, improvements from the reader's point of view, I have been able to make them largely because of feedback supplied by users of the original edition. I have benefited in particular from the questionnaires returned to the publisher by teachers who used the book with their students, from the comments of the anonymous readers who assessed the proposal for a revised edition, and from discussions with friends and colleagues. In the last category, special mention must be made of Kay Richardson and Zoë Wicomb, to whose detailed and incisive comments this book is much indebted.

In addition I am grateful to Miranda Filbee and Louisa Semlyen at Routledge for their help with numerous practical tasks, as well as their support for the project as a whole. A less obvious debt, but in my own estimation a major one, is to my sister-editors on the feminist journal *Trouble & Strife*. Not least among the things I have learnt from working with them is that editing is a hard job to do well. It is for readers to judge how well or badly I have done it in this case; but to all those who have helped me do it better than I might have done otherwise, I offer my sincere appreciation and my thanks.

Notes

1   Reviewers of collections like this one often devote a lot of attention to the editor's selections/omissions, and these are invariably discussed as if the editor had total control over them. In the interests of demystification, let me point out that often s/he does not! Constraints of space and budget rule some choices out; some authors decline, as is their privilege, to have their work reprinted in a different context (and sometimes a slightly different, e.g. shortened, form) from the one they originally intended. I'm sure readers will share my gratitude to those who have generously allowed me to reprint and so recontextualize their writing. I hope readers will recognize, too, that editing a collection like this always involves a certain amount of compromise. No single book can be a substitute for wide reading, and at various points in this volume I have tried to direct readers to the breadth and variety of sources this collection alone cannot provide.

2   A review article dealing with recent developments in feminist language studies (at least, they are recent at the time of this writing) is my own 'Gender, language and discourse: a review' in the feminist journal *Signs* (Cameron 1998). For suggestions on accessible textbooks, see the 'Further Reading' section at the end of Part 3.

Acknowledgements

The editor and publishers would like to thank the following copyright holders for permission to reprint material:

Maria Black and Rosalind Coward, 'Linguistic, social and sexual relations: a review of Dale Spender's *Man Made Language*', *Screen Education*, 39 (1981), pp. 69–85.

Ann Bodine, 'Androcentrism in prescriptive grammar', from *Language in Society*, 4 (1975), by permission of Cambridge University Press.

Deborah Cameron, 'Lost in Translation,' from *Trouble & Strife*, 32 (Winter 1995/96) by permission of the author.

Kate Clark, 'The linguistics of blame', from *Language, Text and Context*, edited by Michael Toolan, London: Routledge (1992), by permission of Routledge.

Jennifer Coates, 'Thank God I'm a woman', from *Woman Talk*, by permission of Blackwell Publishers and Jennifer Coates.

Margaret Doyle, Introduction to *The A–Z of Non-Sexist Language*, first published by The Women's Press Ltd (1995) by permission of The Women's Press Ltd.

Susan Ehrlich and Ruth King, 'Gender-based language reform and the social construction of meaning', from *Discourse and Society*, 3, pp. 1515–66. Reprinted by permission of Sage Publications Ltd and the authors.

Pamela Fishman, 'Conversational insecurity', from *Language: Social Psychological Perspectives*, edited by H. Giles, W. Robinson and P. Smith, Oxford: Pergamon Press (1980) by permission of Dr H. Giles.

Kira Hall, 'Lip Service on the Fantasy Lines', from *Gender Articulated*, edited by Kira Hall and Mary Bucholtz, London: Routledge (1995) by permission of Routledge Inc.

Douglas Hofstadter, 'A person paper on purity in language', from *Metamagical Themas*, New York: Basic Books (1985); Harmondsworth: Penguin (1986). By permission of Penguin Books Ltd.

Luce Irigaray, 'Linguistic sexes and genders', translated by Alison Martin from *Je tu Nous*, by permission of Routledge Inc.

Otto Jespersen, 'The woman', from *Language: Its Nature, Development and Origin* (1922), by permission of Routledge.

Cora Kaplan, 'Language and gender', from *Sea Changes*, London: Verso (1986), by permission of Verso.

Robin Lakoff, extract from *Language and Woman's Place*, New York: HarperCollins (1975), by permission of HarperCollins Publishers.

Sally McConnell-Ginet, 'The sexual (re)production of meaning: A discourse-based approach', Reprinted by permission of the Modern Language Association of America from *Language, Gender and Professional Writing*, edited by Francine W. Frank and Paula A. Treichler.

Sara Mills, 'The gendered sentence', from *Feminist Stylistics*, by permission of Routledge and Sara Mills.

Trinh T. Minh-ha, 'Difference: "a special Third World women's issue",' from *Woman, Native, Other*, by permission of Indiana University Press.

Felly Nkweto Simmonds, 'Naming and identity', from *Reconstructing Womanhood*, edited by Delia Jarret-Macauley, by permission of Routledge.

Dale Spender, extracts from *Man Made Language*, by permission of HarperCollins NY.

Deborah Tannen, 'The relativity of linguistic strategies: rethinking power and solidarity in gender and dominance', from *Gender and Conversational Interaction*, edited by Deborah Tannen, by permission of Oxford University Press and Deborah Tannen.

Aki Uchida, 'When "difference" is "dominance"', from *Language in Society* 21:547–68, by permission of Cambridge University Press.

Virginia Woolf, 'Women and fiction', from *The Essays of Virginia Woolf: Volume II 1912–1918*, by permission of the Estate of Virginia Woolf and Chatto & Windus.

Every effort has been made to obtain permission to reproduce copyright material. If any proper acknowledgement has not been made, or permission not received, we would invite copyright holders to inform us of the oversight.

Using this book

THE DIFFERENCE BETWEEN A Reader and a textbook is that the latter has only one authorial voice, whereas the former presents a diversity of voices, each one speaking for herself and in her own original words.[1] It is, however, the job of an editor to ensure that polyvocality ('many-voicedness') does not turn into cacophony: that the various voices can be understood, and that the whole adds up to at least the sum of its parts. Like the chair at a meeting or the MC at a variety show, the editor must periodically intervene to keep order and/or inform the audience of what is about to happen.

I have provided a general introduction, the purpose of which is to place what follows – that is, the entire book – in some kind of historical, intellectual and political context. What is the feminist critique of language? Or, as I have put it in the title of my introduction, 'Why is language a feminist issue?' My answer is framed in quite general terms; it does not go into detail about the articles which make up the bulk of this volume, but rather seeks to provide a framework in which those articles will make sense. However, I have also provided editorial material which does deal more specifically with the particular writings I have chosen to include.

Those writings have been grouped in three main sections or parts, and each part is further divided into subsections. The editorial material I have added to help readers work through the book has a matching structure. Each main part is preceded by an introduction which contextualizes its concerns and discusses each of the pieces, in the order in which they come (part of the point being to show how they relate to one another). This introduction is divided up by headings that correspond to the subsection divisions.

The arrangement just described is one I find preferable to giving each piece its own, shorter introduction. I did try out the latter approach, but the effect was 'bitty' and obscured the connections and/or contrasts between different pieces. Having decided not to treat each piece as an isolated atom, however, I have tried to organize the editorial material so it is (a) structured in a way that is easy to find your way through and (b) compatible with a range of different reading strategies. For example, the reader who wishes to orient herself in a general way before she focuses on anything specific could read the introductory material straight through before embarking on any of the articles in a given part. A reader who is more concerned with a specific question could read just that section of the introduction that relates to the relevant article(s), though she might want to read the whole thing later. Alternatively, such a reader could plunge straight into the article(s) of her choice and come back later to the introduction for additional information, either reading it all or skipping to the heading that matches what she has just been reading. Or she could use some combination of these possibilities.

At the end of each part there is a section called 'Further reading' which suggests additional sources of material for readers who are interested in following up particular issues and topics. This section picks out references I think are especially useful to readers of his volume; but these selected references need to be used in conjunction with the bibliography at the very end of the book, since that is the only place where full publication details appear.

Note

1   In some cases, however, not all of them. I have made cuts for reasons of space to some contributions, and this is indicated by the insertion of [. . .] in the text. Some footnotes have also been cut. The original source is given in every case for readers who wish to consult the full, uncut version.

Introduction:

WHY IS LANGUAGE A FEMINIST ISSUE?

WHY IS LANGUAGE a feminist issue? To readers well versed in modern literary and social theory, the question might seem naive, the answer obvious; others may find the whole issue obscure, or consider it a distraction from 'serious' politics. Yet what cannot be disputed is that contemporary feminisms (I use the plural advisedly) have placed language on the political agenda. A 'feminist critique of language' now exists; its influence on public and academic discourse is such that it cannot just be dismissed. Rather its meaning has to be grasped and its implications assessed.

Feminist views on language are diverse. This reflects both the political differences that have always existed within feminism, and the great proliferation of 'discourses' – intellectual traditions, theoretical frameworks, academic disciplines – in which language itself is discussed. Although I have titled this volume *The Feminist Critique of Language*, the ideas that go under that heading are not homogeneous, and not static. In this selection – and it *is* a selection, with all the non-neutrality the word implies – I want to show that feminist views on language are complex, and to guide the reader through that complexity. This introduction will suggest some frameworks, theoretical, historical and thematic, in which we can order and make sense of different feminist views.

Critique

To begin with, what is a 'feminist critique of language'? What, for that matter, is a critique of anything? It may sound like fancy jargon, but I am

1

using the term *critique* deliberately because it has two meanings, and both are relevant.

The first meaning is the more familiar. Nowadays the term *critique* is often used as a synonym for the related word *criticism* as most of us understand it, that is, negative assessment or evaluation. That is apposite, because feminists are indeed critical of language as we know it. Language, for women, is not good enough, and one constant theme of the feminist critique is the need to change it and make it fitter for our use. Readers will be acquainted with some of the ways in which feminist activists have challenged, and to a certain extent changed, conventional English usages like generic *he* and *man*, and titles that mark women's marital status. They may also have encountered the idea of women's dissatisfaction with language as an expressive medium: the quest for new images and ways of writing which represent women's bodies and lives as conventional language allegedly cannot. All this implies a negative assessment of existing linguistic practice, a critical approach to the way language has been, and still is, used.

But *critique* also has a more specialized meaning. In philosophy, to undertake a critique of something is to examine the conditions on which it exists, calling into question the assumptions it is based on. Some strands of feminism can fairly be said to have produced a critique of language in this second sense as well. Feminists have come up with novel theories and perspectives on language as a social and cultural institution, questioning, for instance, the assumption that the two sexes share a common language, and reviving an old debate about linguistic determinism – the question being how far language underpins as opposed to just reflecting our perceptions of the world.

In putting this collection of writings together I have tried to do justice to both kinds of feminist critique. I have included not only theoretical writings but more personal reflections, as well as practical or polemical manifestos. But to list these different types of writing is not enough to unravel the complexities of feminist debate. Within the categories of theory or polemic (and the boundaries are often blurred in any case) there are differing approaches and concerns which need to be distinguished and placed in context. I could have organized the book around the identification of theoretical currents and political tendencies, but in the end I decided against it. Apart from being dry, the result would have been to obscure what the currents and tendencies have in common. And in spite of everything, I believe they have much in common. From different perspectives and preconceptions, feminist writers on language return, insistently, to the same major themes.

I have structured this volume around three main themes: the theme of silence and exclusion, which also raises the question of women finding an authentic voice in which to speak and write; the theme of representation, in which the cultural meaning of gender is constructed and contested, and the theme of how and to what end we become gendered through our linguistic behaviour. Each theme occupies a part of the book, and the pieces I have chosen to exemplify each one show that themes come with many variations. At many points, I have selected and organized the material so that it can be read as a debate between differing positions: one of the things I want to emphasize is that feminists are not only in dialogue or conflict with non- or anti-feminists, but also, often, with one another. Mapping the feminist critique in detail is, accordingly, a complicated task. Here I want to sketch in some rough outlines to prepare the reader for what lies ahead. I will therefore introduce the three main themes in turn.

Speech and silence

'Speech' and 'silence' have been powerful *metaphors* in feminist discourse, used to figure all the ways in which women are denied the right or the opportunity to express themselves freely. Because the terms are so often used metaphorically, it is not always easy to pin down what concrete conditions they allude to. A claim that women are 'silent' or 'silenced' cannot mean that they are always and everywhere *literally* silent, nor that they lack the capacity to use language, which is the inalienable birthright of every human being. It cannot even mean that there are no linguistic activities associated with women more than with men, for in fact there are many: in the culture I belong to, 'gossip', keeping teenage diaries, and writing letters or cards to family members are among those that come to mind.

But this listing of genres associated with women gives a clue to one possible meaning of women's silence. For the genres are not prestigious, and some (e.g., gossip) are actually disparaged. They are *private* uses of language, confined to the space of home, family and immediate community. In the public domain, and especially the domain of official culture (by which I mean a society's representation of itself in rituals, codified knowledge and creative art), the genres associated with women have little currency.

It has been argued (e.g., Kaplan, this volume) that the silence of women is above all an absence of women's voices from high culture. If we look at a society's most valued linguistic registers — religious ceremonial, political rhetoric, legal discourse, science, poetry — we find women for the most part silent and in many cases silenced: it is not just that women do not speak, they may actually be prevented from speaking, whether by explicit taboos and restrictions or by the more genteel tyrannies of custom and practice. Even where it seems women could participate if they chose to, the conditions under which they are obliged to live their lives may make this a difficult or dangerous choice. Silence can also mean censoring yourself for fear of being ridiculed, attacked or ignored.

How is silencing done? At its most extreme (and literal), it operates through overt prohibitions and taboos. In some societies, there are rules forbidding women to speak outside their houses or in the presence of super-ordinates. There are also elaborate restrictions on women in certain communities uttering the names of their husbands' kin, and any words that happen to sound like these forbidden names. This does not render women unable to speak at all, but it does compel them to resort to circumlocution (Jespersen, this volume, discusses the phenomenon; more recent discussions include Bodine 1975, and Kimenyi 1992). It may be thought that modern western cultures impose no comparable restrictions, but even if it is not formulated as a taboo, there is certainly hostility towards women engaging in certain linguistic practices. There is still, for example, a widespread unease about women using obscene language, and about men using it in women's presence. Women who take up the role of public orator, priest or even the less exalted role of stand-up comic will find that, in some quarters at least, this presumption is met with an irrational loathing. Public oratory and saying the liturgy were, until recently, quite explicitly forbidden to women (the latter still is forbidden in some religious traditions). Even our secular rituals – wedding receptions for example – typically allot the speaking roles to men.

All that said, it is necessary to make at least two qualifications to global and pessimistic generalizations about women's 'silence'. In a footnote to her essay 'Speech and silence', the anthropological linguist Susan Gal (1991:426) reminds her readers: 'the fact that social science has neglected women makes women of the past and other cultures *seem* silent, when in fact the silence is that of current western scholarship'. The generalization that women across cultures are excluded from public and highly valued forms of speech (for example, ritual, verbal art performance) has been contested in recent feminist scholarship, and on this subject there is much still to know.

Gal also notes in the body of her essay that the *meaning* of silence is more complicated than the simple equation of it with powerlessness suggests. Sometimes – in situations where one is required to 'confess all' by a priest, therapist or officer of the law, for instance – silence is a strategy of resistance to oppressive power. Conversely, it can be a weapon of the powerful: the taciturnity associated with some forms of masculinity (cf. the stereotype of the 'strong, silent man') is part of *male* power, rendering men emotionally distant or unavailable. Gal argues that women's relatively powerless position may in fact be what impels them to develop distinctive verbal skills, such as the ongoing attentiveness and ability to adjust to others in conversation, marked by features like politeness, well-timed supportive minimal responses, style shifting and code-switching, which have been noted by many language and gender researchers.

Literacy practices

Writing is a somewhat different case from speech (though the 'speech and silence' metaphor often encompasses both). Here a recurring theme is the exclusion of women from the skills needed to write at all, for writing is a technology and has been monopolized, like most technologies, by relatively privileged people. Lack of literacy is often the consequence of lacking access to schooling, which is itself usually a consequence of poverty. But there have been cases where literacy was specifically forbidden. Alice Walker asks (1984:233–4):

> What did it mean for a black woman to be an artist in our grand-mothers' time? In our great-grandmothers' day? It is a question with an answer cruel enough to stop the blood. ... How was the creativity of the black woman kept alive, year after year and century after century, when for most of the years black people have been in America it was a punishable crime for a black person to read and write?

For a slave to read and write, and for anyone to teach him or her to do so, was not merely unlikely given the conditions of enslavement, it was specifically criminalized. This was not just one more petty humiliation inflicted by the master, but a calculated act of self-protection on his part. Powerful groups often fear that the ability to read and write, should it spread among the powerless, will give uncontrolled access to subversive ideas, and so facilitate critical thought, opposition and finally rebellion. This is not only a question of gender, of course: the prohibition Alice Walker notes applied equally to black slaves of both sexes, and in other contexts the same fear has been expressed about working-class literacy. But in a similar way, organizers of women's literacy projects today have reported cases where men express fears that the ability to read and write will make their wives, sisters and daughters too independent, too critical.

Women in the industrialized (or post-industrial) west no longer lack access to print literacy; in some ways, indeed, this has come to be perceived as a female domain (I am thinking about the fact that many clerical jobs are also women's jobs, while in Britain, at least, it is constantly reported that girls do better than boys in school subjects where reading and writing are central). But as many scholars have pointed out, literacy is not one undifferentiated thing, and it cannot be reduced to the decoding of print on a page (or a computer screen). Researchers today are more apt to discuss 'literacy practices' than simply 'literacy', meaning that there are different things one can do with reading and writing, and different meanings one can attach to them. Even in societies where literacy is the norm, literacy *practices* may not be distributed evenly across all social groups.

A much-discussed example of uneven distribution concerns the rapidly-evolving literacy practices of computer mediated communication (CMC) via the Internet. It is frequently suggested that the virtual world, like the real one, is male dominated, while women remain second-class 'netizens' as measured by their overall rates of active participation (posting) in many discussions. If this is true (the qualification is because the nature of the net makes solid statistics difficult to come by) it is not only because women have less access than men to the technology needed to participate in CMC, or to the skills needed to make use of that technology. These are no doubt factors, but it is also important to consider the social context in which net users operate.

For instance, active participation in a virtual community requires leisure time, a commodity of which some people have more than others (again, gender is not the only relevant factor, but there is certainly a sexual division of leisure as well as labour – the two go together). Feminists also pose questions about how 'woman-friendly' an environment cyberspace is. The posting of aggressive or abusive messages is common enough to have its own label among net-users ('flaming'); it has been argued that this particular practice is more off-putting to most women than to most men. It has also been reported that in some contexts, especially if they try to pursue feminist arguments, women are more likely to be flamed (see Herring, *et al.* 1995). Practices which, if they occurred in the real rather than the virtual world, we would call sexual harassment and stalking, have also been encountered by more than a few women net-users. Some have responded by deliberately constructing male or ambiguous identities. This strategy may bring relief from offensive communications, but it silences women in the sense that it conceals and so negates their presence *as* women.

If flaming and harassment deter women from participating in CMC, and place restrictions on those women who do participate, the conditions are in place for a communicative practice originally dominated by men for material reasons (e.g., better access to technology) to go on being dominated by men for social reasons even after material conditions have changed. Some feminist writers, such as Dale Spender in her book about CMC, *Nattering on the Net* (1996), see parallels between what is happening in this new communication medium and what happened historically with the technology of printing, and the publishing industry to which it gave rise.

Illiteracy and lack of education were not the only obstacles to women writing for publication. As Virginia Woolf pointed out in *A Room of One's Own* (also briefly in 'Women and Fiction', this volume), until recently even women of the privileged classes typically lacked the economic independence and the time needed for sustained literary effort. Some writers have talked about the practical and psychological problems of writing while caring for young children. There is, still, an assumption that women's time and energy are endlessly available for ministering to the needs of others. Male writers have benefited from the devotion of wives, sisters and daughters; it is rare by contrast for a woman writer to receive comparable support from anyone.[1]

Here we might pause to consider Alice Walker's point that different women are differently positioned: many have faced, and some have over-come, obstacles that seem far more insurmountable than the ones Virginia Woolf discusses. It is salutary, for instance, to place alongside Woolf's famous *Room of One's Own* a short story by the South African writer Gcina Mhlophe, 'The Toilet'. The black woman factory worker protagonist of this story not only has no 'room of her own', she is illegally sleeping in the room allotted to her sister, a maid in a white household. To avoid discovery she must leave the house hours before her shift begins. Killing time, she discovers a public toilet which has been left unlocked and in this unpromising space she begins to write. At the end of the story she finds the toilet locked, but resolves to go on writing nevertheless. Another, nonfictional case which comes to mind is that of Anne Frank, whose famous diary was written in hiding from the Nazis. Frank, like Mhlophe's protagonist, had neither the material nor the mental freedom which Virginia Woolf speaks of as desirable for writers; in one way it is remarkable that such women wrote even so, but in another way it might suggest that writing itself can offer the individual a means for transcending extreme and oppressive circumstances. This too is surely part of the story of women's writing.

Literary culture has often been patronizing or unfriendly to those women who were able to enter it. As is well known, many women writers in the nineteenth century adopted male pen names to ensure their work would receive serious critical attention, and to escape the charge of coarseness or inde-cency which fell on women dealing with the literary themes of sexuality and passion. Women writers have faced a double bind: their work could be crit-icized as 'unfeminine' or, conversely, as 'too feminine', not the work of a 'real' writer but merely of a 'woman writer'.

Writing and 'difference'

One strand in the feminist critique of language has posed the question: in these cultural conditions, how can women write 'authentically'? Is it enough for women to be able to write as men do? If we are 'allowed in' to litera-ture and culture only on condition that we accept the traditional (masculine) norms regarding what is worth writing about and how, are we not simply exchanging one kind of silencing for another? Some feminists would answer the last two questions 'no' and 'yes' respectively. They advocate that women should find ways of writing that acknowledge and attempt to express women's *difference*. This means not only writing *about* different things, but for some critics, radically remaking literary style, or even language itself. Writing in

1975 about the developments that were later to be called in shorthand the 'new French feminisms', the critic Shoshana Felman emphasized the radical nature of their linguistic project:

> The challenge facing the woman today is nothing less than to reinvent language ... to speak not only against but outside the structure ... to establish a discourse the status of which would no longer be defined by the phallacy of male meaning.

The ways in which conventional language silences and marginalizes women have been extensively discussed by feminists from a number of theoretical perspectives (see contributions to this volume by Spender and Irigaray); and debate continues on the subject of what a 'feminine writing' or 'women's language' might be (see the contributions by Woolf and Mills).

The idea of (re)inventing an 'authentic' women's writing as an antidote to 'silencing' is not, however, without its feminist critics. Elaine Showalter, for example, acknowledges that silencing is a problem, but has argued that language itself is not what silences women; rather it is the restrictions placed on women's ability or entitlement to use it:

> The appropriate task for feminist criticism is to concentrate on women's access to language ... on the ideological and cultural determinants of expression. The problem is not that language is insufficient to express women's consciousness but that women have been denied the full resources of language and have been forced into silence, euphemism and circumlocution.
>
> (Showalter 1981: 193)

Another, and increasingly powerful, line of feminist argument against the notion of an authentic women's writing criticizes the *essentialism* of the underlying notion of women's 'difference' – that is, their supposed difference from *men*. It has been pointed out, for instance, that many of the qualities of language proposed by certain feminists as authentically 'feminine' look suspiciously like the qualities associated with femininity in the most un-reconstructedly *anti-feminist* discourse: thus feminine writing is said to be closer to the body, less rational and structured on less linear principles. (Which might suggest that women have bodies rather than minds, cannot think rationally and have a poor grasp of time and space!) Both Sara Mills and Trinh Minh-ha (this volume) point to problems with any uncritical attempt by feminists to reclaim such ideas of sexual difference. Trinh also points out forcefully the dangers inherent in making the concept of difference a unitary one, polarizing masculine and feminine while glossing over the multiple differences that exist among women (or men). Since there are differences within the category 'women', when 'women' speak in one voice, the inevitable if paradoxical result is to silence many women, to speak for them and so prevent them speaking for themselves.

A further objection to notions like 'feminine writing' and 'women's language', which is particularly salient for linguists, is their utopianism and ahistoricism: although the conventions of language-use change (indeed, feminism has to some extent changed them), there is no potential for 'reinventing' language from scratch in the literal sense some feminists seem to be advocating. On the one hand, language depends on innate cognitive faculties which constrain the form a human language can take. On the other hand, and perhaps even more significantly from a feminist viewpoint, language-using is a *social* practice, grounded in history and in the conditions of its users' lives. Individual acts of will do not, on their own, change it, and where we do collectively succeed in changing it, it still bears the traces of what has gone before. One cannot speak 'outside the structure', either of language or society. Feminists can, however, struggle, from the inside, to speak *against* the structure, by contesting/critiquing the representation of women in language and discourse. That is the second main theme of this book.

Representations: sexist language and sexist discourse

Language is a major component of any human culture. It encodes a culture's preoccupations and its values; it is one of the main means whereby these are transmitted to children and other incomers to the community. Many strands in the feminist critique of language have concerned themselves with what languages tell their users and their learners about gender and about women.

On the whole, feminists have concluded that our languages are sexist. They represent or 'name' the world from a masculine viewpoint and in accordance with stereotyped beliefs about women, men and the relationship between them. Some feminists have argued (see, for example, Spender, this volume) that this comes about because, like Adam naming God's creation in the Book of Genesis, men have had a monopoly of naming; and the consequences are serious, because names are not just reflections of pre-existing realities, nor arbitrary labels with no relation to reality, but a culture's way of fixing what will *count* as reality in a universe pregnant with a multitude of possible realities.

This is not an idea that feminists invented. The question of how names relate to things is ancient (in the western tradition it goes back to Plato), but the specific question of whether language reflects or determines what we perceive as real (or salient, or significant) is most often associated with two US linguists of the early twentieth century, Edward Sapir and Benjamin Lee Whorf. Students of Amerindian languages, they — especially Whorf —

discussed how far apparent differences in the perceptions of Native American peoples and Europeans might be related to fundamental differences in the grammatical and semantic structure of Amerindian and European languages. One of their aims in raising this possibility was to question the 'natural' assumption of Europeans that their way of looking at the world was either the only way or the best way. Sapir and Whorf were opposed, in other words, to assumptions of cultural superiority that we would nowadays characterize as racist. There is a certain logic in some feminists' having appropriated their ideas for use in a critique of sexism, the main claim being that many languages have an underlying pattern whereby 'male' is positive and 'female' negative, and because this is part of the code it also becomes part of what users of the language take for granted as reality.

The Sapir–Whorf hypothesis continues to generate controversy among linguists. Most reject strong versions as theoretically flawed and lacking good supporting evidence, but less strong claims are still of interest to some scholars (see Gumperz and Levinson 1995; Lee 1992). One problem in assessing the arguments is that the versions of Whorf's ideas that most commonly circulate are crude: some critics charge that they are also quite patronizingly racist. For example, the linguist Geoff Pullum (1993) has commented scathingly on the now-familiar observation that Eskimos have a lot of words for snow, so they can discern more different types of snow than people who have fewer words. Pullum disputes whether the claim about Inuit people having an elaborate snow vocabulary is true to begin with; but even if it *were* true, he points out, there would be nothing remarkable or profound about it. If someone were to observe that printers have a lot of words for fonts, no one would suggest that their perceptions or mental processes were in any way different from non-printers': we would simply suppose that, as a consequence of being professionally concerned with fonts, they had acquired a specialist technical vocabulary most of us lack. The difference is, printers do not belong to a culture we regard as strange and exotic. Our stance on the 'Eskimos and snow' issue betrays our patronizing and credulous attitude to those we categorize as 'other', different from ourselves.

Comparably crude feminist versions of Whorfian ideas are, similarly, open to criticism. Whatever the effects of, say, the English generic *man* on English-speakers' perceptions, it is clear we are not so constrained in our worldview by our language as to be incapable of reflecting on the implications of words: if we were, it would not be possible to frame arguments against sexist language. Distinguishing generic uses of *man* from specifically masculine ones is not impossible just because the same word is used in both cases (the problem is rather what the conflation of 'male' and 'human' symbolizes). If I see a banner saying 'All men are equal' I know I can join the demonstration; if I see the word MEN on the entrance to a public lavatory, I know I am not supposed to enter. Words on their own are not everything.

Nor is the way words acquire meaning a straightforward matter of someone deciding on a definition. Dale Spender's account of 'man made language' sometimes conjures up implausible scenarios of elite men at some point in the history of humanity sitting down to formulate the semantic rules that relegate women to 'negative semantic space'. (When did this happen, and in what language did the men pass the resolution?)

But you do not have to be a Whorfian to accept that languages can be sexist, and that this matters. Even if the assumptions that inform sexist language are not created by language, to the extent that our lives are carried on in language (which is to a considerable extent, for most of us), the sexism of language must constantly re-enact and reinforce the commonsense 'normality' of sexist assumptions. Indeed, the more banal the enactment – and a lot of our linguistic interactions are nothing if not banal – the more difficult it is to challenge. To challenge someone who hurls sexist abuse at you is one thing, but who has the gall, or the time, to challenge an inter-locutor every few words in the course of a perfectly ordinary conversation?

Beyond 'naming'

What *are* the assumptions that conventional language reinforces? There is a certain imprecision about many uses of the term 'sexist language'; the term homogenizes, and this can disguise the fact that sexist assumptions enter into language at various levels, from morphology (for example suffixes like -ess) to the stylistic conventions of particular registers and fields of discourse, such as 'love poetry' or 'rape reporting'. In my own view, sexist language is not best thought of as the naming of reality from a single, male perspective. It is a multifaceted phenomenon, taking different forms in different representational practices, which have their own particular histories and characteristics.

The representation of sexual violence against women is a case in point (and one of considerable concern to feminists: it is touched on in contributions to this volume by Ehrlich and King and McConnell-Ginet, and is discussed in detail by Kate Clark). Consider the following two newspaper reports of an incident involving a married couple. The first comes from a 'quality' newspaper, The *Daily Telegraph*, the second from a popular tabloid, The *Sun*. I reproduce them both to show that we are not dealing with the idiosyncrasy of a single journalist or newspaper but with an institutionalized set of conventions.

> A man who suffered head injuries when attacked by two men who broke into his home in Beckenham, Kent early yesterday, was pinned down on the bed by intruders who took it in turns to rape his wife. (*Daily Telegraph*)

> A terrified 19-stone husband was forced to lie next to his wife as two men raped her yesterday. (*Sun*)

My interpretation of what is happening in these reports is that the act of rape is being represented as a crime against a man rather than a woman. Rape was originally synonymous with theft: to rape a woman was to rob her father or husband of her value by rendering her unchaste – hence the fact that a man who raped a virgin might be compelled to marry her as a punishment. This view of rape is supposed to have been supplanted by a more modern view of it as an assault on a woman's bodily integrity: it is a crime against the person rather than a property crime. Yet these reports suggest that old prejudices die hard.

The interpretation I have just outlined is supported by several features of the language. In both reports, the experience of the man is foregrounded. He is the theme, the first person to be mentioned, and the grammatical subject of the main clause. He is also the subject of the verbs *suffered* and *was forced*. The woman by contrast – always referred to as 'his wife' – only appears at the end of a long, complex sentence. Her rape is mentioned in a dependent clause. In the first report it is third in order of importance, behind the man's head injuries and the violation of 'his home' (not hers, apparently). In the second report a similar ordering of events gives the impression that the really appalling thing was less the rape *per se* than the fact that the man was forced to witness it.

Among the things this analysis might make us think about are the limitations of considering sexist representations exclusively in terms of a set of expressions that are always and everywhere objectionable. Apart from the asymmetry between *man* and *wife* in the first report there is nothing here for a conventional critique of sexist language to get hold of: no generic masculines, no overtly derogatory descriptions of the woman (indeed, the most overtly derogatory description is the *Sun*'s apparently gratuitous mention of the man's weight), just a set of choices that add up to an androcentric and sexist view of the incident being related.

By far the most important among these choices are *grammatical* ones, whereas the most familiar analyses of sexism in language focus on *words*. Examples like this cast doubt on the centrality of 'naming' in the feminist critique of language. A theory that reduces language to names simply does not get to grips with what is offensive about these reports. Similarly, as Black and Coward (this volume) argue forcefully in relation to Dale Spender's work, a global claim that language-in-general is sexist and man-made is too unspecific to capture exactly what it is we should be criticizing in particular practices of representation; the sexism of rape reporting is not the same as the sexism of, say, job advertisements or children's reading books.

Changing our practice

One way in which Dale Spender's notion of man-made language *is* helpful is in recognizing the agency of human language users in constructing and changing linguistic practice. A lot of ways of talking about language portray it as a sort of organic growth: in popular cliché, 'language is a living thing'. But as James Milroy (1992) has pointed out, this is a misleading image, as senseless as saying that birdsong is a living thing or swimming is a living thing. These are, rather, the activities of living things (in the case of language, of human beings). If we are concerned with the representation of gender, it is far more helpful to consider languages as cultural edifices, regulated by the norms we find in dictionaries, grammars and stylebooks. One could, as does Ann Bodine (this volume) make an argument that historically, the norm-makers have been men (conservative ones at that), and this has affected what the norms are. On the other hand, as Bodine also notes, language is not just a cultural edifice but also an everyday practice; and experience shows we should not overestimate the ability of norm-makers to dictate the terms of everyday usage.

The reason for insisting on these points is that to detach language-using from its historical, cultural and social context and to place it, instead, in the 'natural' realm of 'living things', is a recipe for political inertia. One of the most persistent lines of opposition to feminist critiques of language, and one that has acquired renewed vigour in recent debates about 'political correctness', is the idea that nothing can, or should, be done about sexism; it has been entrenched since time immemorial, it is just part of the language, and attempts to get rid of it are futile if not positively dangerous. Some commentators counsel feminists to be patient: in time language will change of its own accord. This extends the 'living thing' metaphor by suggesting that language is subject to the evolutionary process of natural selection. It may seem a plausible enough argument, but it overlooks the fact that *language* does not change (for language as such cannot 'do' anything, any more than birdsong or swimming can): it is *speakers* who change their behaviour (or not, of course, as the case may be). Change is not always, admittedly, the result of organized campaigns like the ones feminists have waged on the issue of sexist language. It can be unplanned, disorganized and patchy. But by acknowledging that conventions of representation have been historically and socially constructed, we are also suggesting they can be de- and re-constructed: organizing to bring about change is not a futile activity, whereas waiting for 'the language' to change itself *is*.

Feminist activity over the past twenty-five years has, at the very least, sensitized language-users to the non-neutral nature of linguistic representation. What was previously unquestioned or indeed unnoticed in our usage is now the site of a struggle for meaning, in which our notions of what is natural and normal, masculine or feminine, elegant or offensive, can be argued about. This has in fact led to observable changes (or more accurately, to significant variation in usage where previously there was little or none). But the opening up of arguments, however contentious and unresolved, is an achievement in its own right.

Talking gender

The third set of debates I want to look at concerns the styles of speech that researchers have claimed as characteristic of women and men. This is in some ways a more specialized area of discourse than those discussed above: though there is considerable interest in the topic, not only among feminists but among the public at large, the social scientific research at issue in discussions of it is not always accessible to the average person with no background in the relevant disciplines (e.g. linguistics and social psychology). This is also, arguably, the area where the debate among feminists themselves has been most heated. The first thing I need to say as I attempt to put the arguments in context is that feminist scholars have real and serious disagreements about the nature and significance of gendered styles of speaking.

One disagreement centres on the question of how far we should frame this field of study as being about differences between men's and women's ways of speaking. The sex difference approach, which compares some aspect of the behaviour of women and men and then proposes an explanation of any differences that emerge (typically there is less concern about discovering or explaining similarities), is part of our intellectual inheritance from pre-feminist scholarship (as is illustrated by Jespersen, this volume). It is also extremely persistent in 'folklinguistic' discourse: as an academic known to be interested in language and gender, I receive at least one call every month from a journalist or a researcher for a TV programme, and the caller invariably begins by telling me, 'I want to do something about men and women using language differently.' I find this problematic, and later on I will say why, as well as explaining how the topic of gendered speech could be approached from some other angle.

Given that much feminist research *has* in fact focused on the issue of male–female differences, and has found quite a number of them, a major disagreement among feminists has been about the best way of explaining the differences. Many surveys of this debate have distinguished three explanatory frameworks used by feminists, labelling them 'deficit', 'dominance' and 'difference'.

Deficit, dominance, difference

A deficit framework suggests that women's ways of speaking are, whether by nature or nurture, deficient in comparison to men's. In its nurture variant this is the idea that often underpins, for example, the provision of assertiveness training to women (see Crawford 1995 for a full discussion): assertiveness is conceived as something women lack, and the lack is conceived as disadvantageous to them. A dominance framework suggests that women's ways of speaking are less the result of their gender *per se* than of their subordinate position relative to men: the key variable is power (as is argued, for instance, by Fishman, this volume). Finally, a difference framework suggests that women's ways of speaking reflect the social and linguistic norms of the specifically female subcultures in which most of us spend our formative years. (Analogously, men's ways of speaking reflect the norms of male subcultures.) The difference between women and men is like the difference between speakers from two cultures who are not well acquainted with one another's customs and may often, therefore, misunderstand one another.

While few feminist linguists now (if any) would wish to endorse the deficit framework, there has been, and still is, considerable debate on the competing claims of the dominance and difference frameworks. Dominance researchers have been criticized for making simplistic assumptions both about men's intention to dominate women in conversation and about the relationship of linguistic strategies to power or powerlessness (see Tannen, this volume; also Gal's remarks on the variable meanings of silence, cited above). Difference researchers on the other hand have been criticized for failing to distinguish questions about the intentions of individual men to dominate individual women from questions about the social structure, in which men as a gender occupy the dominant position; and also for giving too little weight to the ways in which, to quote Aki Uchida (this volume), '"difference" *is* "dominance"' (my emphasis). In other words, it can be argued there is a non-arbitrary coincidence between the gender-differentiated traits we call masculinity and femininity and the status-marked traits we call powerful and powerless.

The dominance/difference debate is not, however, the only arena where feminists are engaged in arguments with one another. Researchers in both frameworks have attracted criticism from the increasingly prominent anti-essentialist current in feminist linguistics.

Essentialism and anti-essentialism

Essentialism is one of those words that comes with a lot of baggage, is used differently by different writers, and, like *chauvinism* or *anarchism*, has acquired negative connotations whose connection with the technical meaning may not be immediately obvious. I will define it initially as 'belief in essences', that is, the conviction that there is some essential, fundamental and fixed property or set of properties which all members of a particular category must share, and by which they are distinguished from the members of other categories. In the context of this discussion, the relevant categories are women and men.

The most obvious and familiar kind of essentialism in relation to women and men is *biological*, and the term *essentialist* is sometimes used as if it meant 'believing that differences between women and men are biological/innate'. Deborah Tannen, for instance, has defended herself against charges of essentialism by pointing out, with justification, that she has never

15

suggested the differences she identifies in male and female conversational styles have anything to do with biology (see the introduction to Tannen 1994). It is important to grasp, however, that when feminists talk about essentialism, they do not always – or even often, nowadays – mean the biological kind. When one feminist is labelled essentialist by another, the intended criticism is more likely to be that she treats women as being (*a*) in some fundamental way all the same as each other, and (*b*) fundamentally different from men. Essentialism means assuming, in other words, that there is some crucial characteristic that all women have in common, and on the basis of which we can classify them as women.

If this quality is not biological, what is it? Among the suggestions that have been made, arguably the most influential have been about children's psychological development in the context of family relationships. Some feminists have suggested that as a consequence of being cared for and having their primary relationship with an adult of the same gender, usually their mother, girls develop a more relational sense of self than boys, who are both more driven and more easily able to differentiate themselves from their mothers. This kind of selfhood is fundamental to femininity and distinguishes it from masculinity.

This is an argument about gender (socially constructed) rather than sex (biological). Conventional parenting and childcare arrangements are not straightforwardly about biology, they are to a large extent social; but this theory says they nevertheless produce systematic and stable differences in the psychological dispositions of girls and boys. (Here it should perhaps be pointed out that saying something is 'socially constructed' does not imply that it is a figment of the imagination, or that we could simply wish it away. How much I get paid is socially constructed – there is no law of nature which dictates my value on the labour market – but it still has real, material consequences for whether I can pay my bills at the end of the month, and I can't change it unilaterally.)

Feminist anti-essentialism distrusts all attempts to locate gender in fixed and fundamental qualities instilled in women or men, whether by nature or nurture. It disputes that there is *one* version of femininity or masculinity, and that any single story (e.g., the one about how girls relate to their mothers) can encompass the experience of every woman. More radically, some anti-essentialists dispute that we have a fixed gender identity at all. They prefer to talk about 'doing' or 'performing' gender, which implies that gender is not a thing but a process, and one which is never finished. It also implies that in principle we may 'do' or 'perform' gender differently in different contexts – even at the level of the individual woman or man, there is not necessarily any core of gendered behaviour that cannot vary and change.

Most feminists today are anti-essentialist in the sense of accepting that we cannot talk about gender in the universal or global terms which were common in the past. In practice that usually meant talking about the experience of the most privileged women as if it were shared by all women, when clearly it is not. Differences, indeed conflicts, between women must be acknowledged and theorized. The more radical ideas just mentioned, however, are also more controversial. Some feminists are troubled by the implication that there is no level at which women as a category have anything in common, since this seems to undermine the possibility of coherent feminist analysis: for instance, the *content* of the sexual division of labour differs in different communities, but is it illegitimate to make the *formal* generalization that all communities have one? Many are troubled by the implication in some postmodernist theoretical discussions that gender divisions have no material basis, and that the very term 'women' is an essentializing fiction which should now be laid to rest. Pointing to such persistent phenomena as unequal pay, sexual harassment, rape and domestic violence, these feminists feel it is too soon to celebrate what Stevi Jackson (1992) has sardonically dubbed 'the amazing deconstructing woman'.

In feminist *linguistics,* the most obvious effect of anti-essentialism has been to call into question the idea of what Robin Lakoff called 'women's language', for any such idea begs the question: which women do you mean? Global or universalizing claims about what characterizes the linguistic behaviour of women and distinguishes it from that of men have not ceased altogether, but they are regularly criticized for ignoring or downplaying the heterogeneity of the group women even within a single society, let alone worldwide. While it could be said in response to this criticism that the question 'Can we make cross-cultural generalizations about "women's language"?' is at bottom an empirical one, the onus is on anyone who wishes to investigate it to be clear about her motives: it is no longer seen simply as the obvious question to ask. Nor is it taken as obvious that the answer will be 'yes' (though Janet Holmes (1993) lists a number of findings that are potential universals, in the sense that they have recurred in very different societies). In linguistics as in other disciplines, feminists are now interested in what divides women as well as in what they might have in common; they are not looking for the linguistic manifestations of femininity, singular, but for femininities, plural.

They are also interested in the idea of gender as something people 'do' or 'perform' as opposed to something they 'have'. The traditional assumption in sociolinguistics was that women and men used language in characteristically different ways *because* they were gendered. I am a woman: therefore I speak like one. The 'performance' approach suggests instead that women and men use language as they do *in order to be, and be perceived as, gendered.* Researchers who adopt this approach (for example, Jennifer Coates and Kira Hall, both this volume) note that people can perform gender differently in different contexts. It is not suggested that we are necessarily conscious of 'putting on a performance' (once again, to say something is 'constructed' does not mean it isn't also *real*); though some researchers have been particularly interested in cases where the performance *is* conscious and deliberate, as with people who 'pass' for the opposite sex, or the telephone sex workers discussed by Hall.

The feminist critique of language and the politics of identity

There is a complicated relationship between feminist anti-essentialism and the tendency in feminism (and other contemporary social movements) known as 'identity politics', in which political claims are formulated and validated on the basis that those making the claims share a certain social identity and location as, say, 'lesbians', 'women with disabilities', 'older women', 'black women', 'Jewish women', 'working-class women' and so on. One of the things this tendency is saying is the same as one of the things the anti-essentialist tendency says: that we must attend to differences and conflicts among women far more carefully than we – or some of us – did in the past. Women are not all the same, and to speak of 'women' when really you are only talking about white middle-class heterosexual women, say, is an exclusionary and oppressive act on a par with men talking about 'man' or 'people' and meaning only themselves. (It also leads to a basic descriptive inadequacy: feminists must reject any account of gender relations that cannot deal with *all* the forms we know those relations take.) At the same time, there is a sense in which identity politics is in contradiction with anti-essentialism. Anti-essentialism questions the idea of authentic, fixed identities; identity politics, as the label suggests, centres on precisely that idea.

Since I edited the first edition of this book, identity politics has entered more deeply into the feminist critique of language, in two main ways. One is in relation to the debate on 'political correctness'. In some respects, though not all, the practices which are glossed as 'PC' could be seen as linguistic reflexes of identity politics (feminist and otherwise); the main thing at issue in the linguistic element of the debate is the labelling of socially salient differences (such as those of gender, race/ethnicity, sexuality and (dis)ability), and who gets to make rules about it. Increasingly, the feminist critique of sexist language (see above) has been subsumed into this wider debate on the representation of groups who have traditionally been defined as other (and by others).

One sign of this is the fact that institutions which once had only guidelines about 'nonsexist language' are increasingly producing broader guidelines on 'inclusive' or 'nondiscriminatory' language that take in such matters as ethnicity and disability. This particular practice is modelled on the more narrowly feminist one. Indeed, one could argue that it is at least partly because of the *success* of the feminist critique in raising consciousness and affecting practice that the politics of language and labelling are no longer seen as being only a feminist issue. Yet the question could be asked: is this apparent broadening in some ways taking us back to the narrow and super-ficial focus on 'naming' that many feminists have criticized (see above)? The 'PC' debate on language is basically nomenclatural; important lessons from the experience of feminist reformers and campaigners appear not to have been learned (see contributions to this volume by Ehrlich and King, and Clark).

The second way in which identity politics has affected the feminist critique of language is more relevant to the sociolinguistic study of gendered verbal behaviour. As I noted above, the critique of essentialism has made many researchers sceptical about monolithic male and female speech styles, and reluctant to look for some globally-conceived 'women's language'. But whereas some researchers have moved towards a more fluid (some would say, too fluid) notion of gender under the influence of anti-essentialism, there is also a tendency, influenced more by identity politics, to move towards a notion of gender that is not so much fluid as *fragmented*: instead of one women's language we get a multiplicity of them, each associated with a particular group of women who share an identity as, say, 'lesbians' or 'African-American women'. Just as the pioneers of the feminist critique started by posing the question: How are women different, linguistically, from men?', so some feminists today are posing questions like: 'How are black women different, linguistically, from white women?' or 'How are lesbians different, linguistically, from straight women?' (In this case, actually, the question is just as likely to be how gay men and lesbians differ from straight people, with gender a secondary consideration. For a survey of the emergent field of lesbian and gay sociolinguistics see Jacobs 1996, and for examples of recent research in this area, Livia and Hall 1997).

It is clear that questions of identity and difference, diversity and conflict among women are an important strand in current feminist debates about language, and this book should represent that. But while I have tried to select contributions that take up issues of identity and diversity in various ways (see especially Trinh, Uchida and Hall), I have not tried to ensure, as an iden-tity politics approach might suggest I should, that as many kinds of previously marginalized feminist identity as possible (for example, black, Asian, Latina, Irish, working-class, lesbian) are represented by an author who explicitly claims that identity for herself and her work. This decision reflects my own view that *identity is not, in and of itself, politics*. There is a difference between terms like 'women', 'lesbians', 'black women', 'white middle-class women', etc., which are identity labels, and 'feminist', which denotes a set of *political* positions. In titling this volume *The* Feminist *Critique of Language* I am signalling a concern with political positions and arguments rather than with the identities or social locations of the authors whose work I include.

At this point it might be asked, is there not a causal connection between the two things, identity/location and political position? My answer is 'yes and no'. While I do accept that your history and social location are likely to affect what you believe to be politically important (thus black women are less likely than white women to 'forget' to consider the intersections of sexism and racism), I also think feminists must avoid making crude assumptions about the relationship of someone's identity or experience to her politics: there is more to our political analyses and commitments than our demographic profiles in terms of race, ethnicity, class and sexuality.

Feminist identity politics seems at times to reduce the former to the latter. As Liz Kelly, Sheila Burton and Linda Regan put it, there is an assumption that 'critical awareness and understanding are inscribed on a person through forms of oppression, [whereas] such awareness is inaccessible to those who have not '"lived" such experience' (Kelly, Burton and Regan 1992). But as Kelly *et al*. go on to argue, this assumption is suspect. If it *could* be assumed that 'living' oppression automatically produced a critical analysis of it, then all women would be feminists (which plainly they are not), and there would be no political disagreements among feminists whose life experiences are similar (which plainly there are). This provides a further reason for resisting the notion that the question of diversity is best answered by finding someone to represent 'the black perspective', 'the lesbian perspective' and so on: there is no single, generic black or lesbian perspective, any more than there is a single, white heterosexual one. That is certainly not a justification for leaving considerations of race and sexuality out of feminist discussion; rather it is an argument against simplistic ideas about what it *means* to consider these matters seriously, and about *who* is entitled/ qualified/obliged to consider them. If *all* feminists are not obliged to develop a critical politics around race and sexuality, then there is very little hope for the feminist critique and the feminist movement.

Finally, at least for the moment, I think it remains possible to defend some notion of *the* feminist critique of language – which is not to say that feminists engaged in this project agree with one another, for I hope I have made clear there is significant *dis*agreement, but rather to say that they are still in productive dialogue with one another. Even strong disagreements (for example, the dominance/difference debate, or the arguments around diversity and identity) continue to be framed by some sense that we share common concerns and address similar questions. It is my hope that this volume will help readers new to the feminist critique of language to understand both the shared concerns and the differing positions feminists can take up in relation to them. It is also my hope that the writings collected here will help to explain why so many feminists have been so fascinated, engaged and excited by the problems and the possibilities of language.

Note

1   A noteworthy exception is the contemporary British writer Jeanette Winterson, about whom it has been widely reported that women friends and admirers take care of her domestic and other mundane arrangements. What's noteworthy is that this is often cited with evident disapproval, contributing to an image of Winterson as conceited, selfish and pretentious. Whatever one may think of this particular case, it bears pointing out that *not* doing your domestic labour has been the norm for most comparable men, and even today dedications of books to the proverbial 'wife without whom . . .' occasion no disapproving comment.

Speech and silence: The quest for women's voices in culture

Introduction to part one

PART ONE OF THIS BOOK presents a number of approaches to what has been called the silencing of women in and by language and culture – a well-established theme of feminist writing across many disciplines. I have divided the material into two sections: the first, 'Identities', dealing with general issues of cultural identity and self-definition, the second, 'Gender, language and literature' dealing more specifically with questions about women's literary production.

Though shorter than the others, this part of the book is, deliberately, wide-ranging and heterogeneous. I have included contributions by women who represent a number of different disciplinary or intellectual, as well as experiential and political, perspectives, and which treat language less as an end in itself than as a point of entry to the larger terrain of culture, identity and history. These subjects have fascinated many different kinds of writers, and lent themselves to different kinds of writing, to more personal reflections as well as conventionally academic discussions, or texts that weave the two together.

Identities

The main focus of this section, 'Identities', is on the various labels we apply to ourselves and each other. It is not that I think identity is merely a question of labels (on the contrary) but if one considers identity from the point of view of the feminist critique of *language*, the subject of labelling is clearly of some importance. One of the things language is – though not the only thing – is a powerful device for labelling and categorizing. Accordingly, when feminists have discussed the links between language and identity it is often labels, their implications and their limitations, that discussion has revolved around.

I don't think it is a coincidence that so many of the most illuminating feminist writings on questions of language, identity and labels are by women who have a personal or family history of migration (and/or racism), who have access to more than one linguistic and cultural tradition, and whose relationship to the dominant *feminist* tradition is not an untroubled one. Both contributors to this section fall into this category (as would some white European migrant women; see the further reading suggestions at the end of this Part). I take it, however, that their writings are illuminating for every reader, not just those who share the authors' particular histories (which are, of course, different from one another).

The first piece reprinted here, Felly Nkweto Simmonds's 'Naming and identity' (1995) discusses a type of identity-label which seems so obvious that its complexity and significance can easily be overlooked: the personal name. Simmonds's reflections on her own names provide an elegant demonstration of the point that personal names are not *only* personal: in her family's choice of names for her, and later on in her own choices (of a saint's name at confirmation and then of her husband's last name on marriage) there is a whole history and politics – in this case, a story of imperialism (political, economic, cultural and religious), of migration to Europe and of racism and ethnocentrism encountered there. Patriarchal assumptions are also an inseparable part of the story, from the disruption of pre-colonial woman-centred naming practices to the Roman Catholic ideals of womanly virtue as reflected in the saints' names available for girls.

What is 'silenced' by the naming traditions most readers of this book will be most familiar with – that is, patriarchal ones, in which family names pass down the male line – is women's history and female ancestry. Where a woman takes her husband's name at marriage, the continuity of her own identity over time is also disrupted. Even when individuals enter into them willingly, such practices symbolize the traditional view of women as a kind of property that passes from one male-headed household to another. Not surprisingly, then, naming practices have been questioned by feminists in practice as well as theory, whether by asserting the right of married women to keep their own names – though this still usually means keeping names inherited from one's forefathers rather than one's foremothers – or by inventing entirely new names on a non-patriarchal model, as has been done for instance by the feminist linguists Julia Penelope and Birch Moonwomon – though this strategy comes at the cost of disconnecting you from your ancestry and history: too high a cost, perhaps, for diaspora women like Felly

Nkweto Simmonds. Simmonds's discussion underlines how the complicated choices women are now enabled or perhaps even obliged to make about what names to use in what contexts, reflect the complexity and multifacetedness of identity itself.

Questions of identity, labelling and self-definition are also foregrounded in the extract reprinted here from Trinh T. Minh-ha's *Woman, Native, Other* (1993). The extract comes from a chapter titled 'Difference: "a special Third World women issue"'. Trinh's discussion does not, however, take any of these terms ('difference', 'Third World', 'women') for granted: on the contrary, she questions the apparent simplicities of 'identity' and 'difference', in part by engaging in critical scrutiny of the language feminists commonly use to talk about them. Her chapter title is ironic: she is saying that difference is *not* a special Third World women's issue, but an issue for all feminists.

Trinh points out there are connections to be made between some uses of *Third World* and some uses of *women*. For instance, both can be used as modifiers ('women writers', 'Third World writers') which underline the definition of a group as 'other' (by contrast we do not usually talk about 'men writers' and 'First World writers'). The word *woman* itself, in much (white or 'First World') feminist discourse, has had the same weaselly, ambiguous and finally exclusionary quality as the word *man* in non-feminist discourse. *Man* purports to include women but on inspection usually does not. *Women*, similarly, purports to refer to all women, but as Trinh says, it 'tends to efface difference within itself'. The generic woman denoted by *women* is rarely from the so-called Third World. 'Minority women' (itself perhaps a curious expression given that in global terms the women it refers to are the numerical majority – compare the use of the term 'minority' to refer to women as a group in contrast to men)– still face the same problem as the nineteenth-century black American anti-slavery activist Sojourner Truth, who had to persuade her white audience that she really was a woman. One questioner suggested that she prove it by exposing her breasts. Trinh observes that both sexism and racism take *bodily* identity and difference – genitals, skin colour – as their bottom line. The forms of feminism with which she takes issue are those which follow a similar logic, seeking to ground some general account of women's nature, identity or essence in their (single, sexual) *difference* from men.

Obviously, Trinh is not only addressing linguistic issues here. The primary target of her critique is not language *per se* but essentialism, the quest to define the true nature of women or natives by pinning down what makes them different from men or Europeans. Her discussion does, however, illustrate an important development in the feminist critique of language, which was always in fact latent within it. When feminists undertake a critique of 'man-made language' or 'masculine discourse', they open up the possibility that the same critical methods will be turned on them as well. Having pointed out the gaps, silences, elisions and exclusions in malestream discourse on women, it is difficult for (white, First-World) feminists to resist the logic of the argument when similar things are pointed out in their own discourse. Yet to accept the logic of the argument is to raise new political problems. If feminism is a movement that presses the claims of women, but at the same time 'women' is not a unitary category or a single interest group, then for whom does feminism speak and with what authority? If it truly acknowledges difference – not in the essentialist and hierarchical sense criticized by Trinh but in the sense of multiplicity – can feminism, or women, speak at all?

Gender, language and literature

The second section in this part of the book examines the nature of and reasons for women's silence in the domain of literature: their virtual absence from that domain before about the seventeenth century, and their apparent preference thereafter for particular genres and styles (novels rather than essays or poetry, for example).

Virginia Woolf's 'Women and fiction', written in 1929, stresses the material and social constraints on women who might have aspired to write up until her own time: their lack of education, their domestic responsibilities, the social disapproval of 'unwomanly' activities and ambitions, the restricted experience even privileged and relatively well-educated women had to draw on. Obviously there were great women novelists writing in English before the 1920s; many of Woolf's observations are not so much about why women couldn't write at all, as about why fiction, and the novel in particular, would offer women the most congenial form in which to write. This is partly a question of the pervasive division between public and private spheres, which were (and to some extent still are) understood as, respectively, masculine and feminine. Though all published writing is in one sense public, the novel as a genre deals with private and domestic concerns. As Woolf points out, it is far less likely that women who had not even been allowed to vote until 1928 would find it obvious or relevant to write in more public sphere-oriented genres like political satire.

Cora Kaplan has a somewhat different explanation of women's exclusion from poetry in particular. In 'Language and gender' (1986, though written originally ten years before that) Kaplan acknowledges the material constraints discussed by Woolf, but takes a psychoanalytic approach to the 'silencing' of women. She argues that, as the most concentrated form of symbolic language, poetry is forbidden to women at a deeper level than lack of access to the supports (social, economic or educational) needed to write it. Hence the ambivalence or defiance which she points to as a recurring feature in the work of early women poets. Whereas Woolf hints that women writers of this century have at least partly resolved their relationship to language and literary discourse – an argument that might seem even more plausible seventy years on – Kaplan sees this troubled relationship as integral to patriarchal cultures, reproduced in each generation through the processes whereby our psychic identities are formed. Language, she says, 'remains [women's] as a consequence of being human, and at the same time not theirs as a consequence of being female'.

One of the observations in 'Women and fiction' that has continued to reverberate in discussions of language and gender is the remark Woolf makes that 'the very form of the sentence does not fit [the woman writer]'. Both in Woolf's remarks and in much writing within the theoretical current of feminist criticism represented by Cora Kaplan, we find the assertion, or the assumption, that women either do write differently, or freed from patriarchal restraints, *would* write differently, from men. And the difference is conceived not only as a question of subject matter and viewpoint, say, but also and more fundamentally as a question of linguistic form, of words and sentences.

Sara Mills's 'The gendered sentence', which has been excerpted from the chapter with that title in her book *Feminist Stylistics* (1995), discusses in detail the claim that there is something distinctive linguistically about writing produced by women, surveying the empirical work that has been carried out in an effort to support or disprove the hypothesis, and commenting on the assumptions which underlie this kind of research, as well as the conclusions one might reasonably draw from it. Mills's title 'The gendered sentence' alludes to a remark Virginia Woolf made in a 1923 review of a novel by her contemporary Dorothy Richardson, that the latter 'has invented, or if she has not invented, developed and applied to her own uses, a sentence which we might call the psychological sentence of the feminine gender'.

It might well be objected that empirical stylistic analysis – the counting of adjectives, the taxonomizing of verbs – is an extremely blunt and inappropriate instrument for pursuing the idea Woolf was getting at: no wonder, a sceptical critic might say, if 'scientific' investigation has failed to uncover any well-defined object corresponding to that idea. However, one of the virtues of Mills's discussion, from the point of view of what I am attempting to do in this part and in this volume as a whole, is that it exposes the real disagreements, or perhaps one might better say blank incomprehensions, among feminist scholars who approach language with the assumptions of different academic disciplines. From a linguist's perspective, proposals about 'the feminine sentence' which cannot be related to the nitty-gritty of sentence structure in real texts are easily dismissed as meaningless hot air.

How should these disagreements among feminists be approached? One could reframe the question, as Sara Mills does in some places, as 'why do people believe there is a "feminine sentence" and in what do they take its difference to consist?' One could also ask in what ways and to what extent beliefs a scientist might dismiss as empirically unfounded are nevertheless productive for feminist understanding and, perhaps even more significantly, for feminist interventions in literary practice. The kind of writing that is sometimes called *écriture feminine* ('feminine writing'), for instance, may be based on specious claims about women's 'natural' ways of expressing themselves; yet this discourse on women's writing has facilitated the creation of a new and distinctive literary practice, and to some extent changed the *value* accorded to certain putatively feminine qualities in writing.

There is plenty of room for debate on whether this particular development is a good or a bad thing, but the more general point is that concepts of dubious empirical status, like 'the feminine sentence', are not necessarily ineffectual just because they are imaginary rather than 'real'. On the contrary, imagination must rank among the most powerful political weapons in feminism's armoury; it is a necessary political resource, since there are no 'real' models, either historical or extant, for the kind of society feminists want. It is at least partly for that reason that literature – an art form that harnesses the power of language to the power of the imagination – has been accorded such importance in feminist struggles.

Identities

Chapter 1

Felly Nkweto Simmonds

NAMING AND IDENTITY

M Y PATERNAL GRANDPARENTS named me Nkweto wa Chilinda. But the name arrived too late. Time had moved on. This was the middle of the twentieth century. The modern age. Modernity had implications for my very identity in colonial central Africa, what is now Zambia.

When I was born, my parents also gave me a name, as they waited for the ancestors to grant me life. This was taking time. Messages and letters took weeks to get to my grandparents' village and back. I had to be called something and my father found an English name for me from a book that he was reading. Nora. In my father's house I'm still called Nora.

In terms of names, I was born at the wrong time. The postwar colonial African society into which I was born was having a crisis of identity. A separation of the old order from the new. Families were literally torn apart, separated by the idea of progress itself. Having an English name was symbolic. It was one way that you could show you were of the modern world . . . could speak English. Many English names were literally invented and appropriated for whatever was the immediate need . . . registering for a job in the mines, registering for school . . . for the future that was beckoning so tantalizingly in the shape of crowded towns, shanty towns, badly paid jobs. . . . The resulting names were fantastic. Any English word could be and *was* used as a name, producing names that exposed the very idea of progress as a sham, a pantomime, a charade – the modern world was a game, you took on a role and a name . . . Cabbage, Spoon, Pelvis, Loveness. . . .

But there were some of us who played this game too seriously. We were pawns in a game whose rules we didn't know. Our names symbolized another existence. A God beyond our imagination. A Christian God . . . Mary, Joseph, James . . . Felicitas. At the appointed time I became Felicitas, and joined the world of rosary beads, holy water, saints, a virgin, confession . . . hellfire and damnation . . . a very modern world.

I now had three names. This is the order in which they came to me: Nora Nkweto (wa Chilinda) Felicitas. And my father's clan name, Mfula — rain. We are of the rain clan.

Nora Nkweto Felicitas Mfula. My friends call me Felly.

There are many things wrong with the way I was named. The first being that I shouldn't carry a name from my father's family at all. As AbaBemba we are matrilineal. The maternal spirits of the ancestors should be passed on to the child through the given name. This does not imply a female name, but a maternal ancestor, female or male. Names are not gendered. My mother's grandmother delivered me. By ancestral right she should also have named me. That was my first loss, the first confusion in my identity. I was born at a time when AbaBemba men were acquiring authority over their wives and children based on the new ways of the modern world. The loss of the right to name me was a loss for my mother and all our foremothers, and a loss for me, who carries my father's people's spirit, I who am denied a continuation of the female line.

However, I carry an important name. Nkweto wa Chilinda. Apparently he was my great-grandfather — and who am I to doubt it, although of course as one who has studied history there is a clash of truths even in the name I carry. The Bemba historian P. B. Mushindo claims to be unable to trace Nkweto wa Chilinda's descendants after he and his wife '. . . left home, possessions, their high position, subjects, slaves, etc. for love of their child. . . .' A child that they had only been able to have because of the medical skills of strangers who came into his country: '. . . the Ng'alang'asa . . . who had a great knowledge of medicine . . .' to whom they had promised the first child born to them. *Ulupangi lwatamfishe Nkweto mu Chilinda*, '. . . a vow drove Nkweto out of Chilinda. . . .'

If he was never heard of again, how come his name lives on?

My grandfather was known as *umwana wa MuSukuma*, '. . . a child of the Sukuma. . . .' The Sukuma live on the shores of Lake Victoria, several thousand miles north of where Chilinda would have been, but easily accessible to traders who came down the Rift Valley, along Lake Tanganyika.

Are the Ng'alang'asa and the Sukuma related in some way?

The name was important enough for my grandfather. In it there is a message for me. Now, as an adult, I find the further I am from home, not just in distance, but also in time, the more I need to reclaim this name, and the position I have in LuBemba history. It is then I recognize that Nkweto wa Chilinda's spirit and I are one — strangers in strange lands — but also guardians of our past.

Chilinda is the verb for one who guards (*ukulinda*), a guardian (*chilinda*).

The second thing wrong with my naming was the very order in which the names came to me. I was Nora first. My family still call me Nora. Also my parents' friends. I can tell how long people have known me (and in what space) by the name they call me. Nkweto as a name stood no chance against progress. My grandmother, my father's mother, was the only one who always called me Nkweto – and sometimes the full name, Nkweto wa Chilinda, when she wanted to make me feel very special. She has a special place in my heart.

At the age of ten, I named myself . . . Felicitas.

Felicitas . . . Felly. There is a whole lot wrong with this name that I still carry as the ultimate symbol of my confused identity. I no longer have a reason to carry it. I'm no longer a Catholic, which was the only reason I took the name in the first place! I had been in my Catholic convent school for a full year before I was baptised. It was a terrible year. I had arrived with names that were not acceptable. Nora Nkweto Mfula. At least Nora was an English name. Nkweto I dropped, completely. It was a shameful name, a pagan name – even a man's name – how could I live with it? And in any case, we were not allowed to use African names – except as surnames – so that we couldn't be confused with 'white' men's children – 'coloureds', as they were called, in the Southern African way. This was, of course, not a realistic fear. We didn't come in contact with 'white' children, in their posh convent in the town, and as for 'coloured' children, 'white' men's children with African women, they were out of sight (out of mind) in special schools, usually in the middle of nowhere, looked after by nuns . . . hiding one of the 'white' man's fears in Africa. Miscegenation.

It wasn't just the fact of not having an appropriate English name that was the problem. It had to be a saint's name. The saint was your guardian, could mediate on your behalf – a short cut to God, or even better still to the Virgin Mary. . . . *She* was amazing . . . The Mother of God. In a society that values motherhood, no one could hold a candle to this woman. She was to be the ultimate Role Model with an in-built contradiction – we couldn't be mothers *and* remain virgins. It was a terrible situation to be in, and encouraged us to dedicate many rosaries to the Virgin Mary to help us live this contradiction as chastely as possible. We were constantly reminded that our biggest enemy was the desire for men . . . and that it was the men themselves who inevitably, in the end, would lead us into temptation.

I remember with absolute clarity, sitting on the school veranda with two of my friends on the Saturday afternoon, the day before I was baptised, trying to select a name. The book of saints' names also gave a summary of the saint's life and how she/he achieved sainthood.

Saint Laeticia and Saint Felicitas. Saint's Day 6 March (near my birthday, 26 February). Felicitas was the African slave woman to a Roman woman,

Laeticia. They both converted to Christianity and were fed to the lions. Actually I don't really know if that *is* how they died, but my imagination has always been fired by the idea of being eaten by a lion, a common threat to naughty children in my grandmother's village. This sounded right. Also there was no other Felicitas in my school, so there wasn't to be much competition for favours from Saint Felicitas. She would be my own special saint. Even at that age I liked the idea that Felicitas was an African.

Felicitas . . . Latin for happiness.

And I was happy. At last my soul had been cleansed of Original Sin. The only thing between me and eternal life in Heaven was myself . . . temptation, sinning. . . . For the next eight years I tried as best as I could to be good. In the end the modern world defeated me in the shape of Karl Marx (a Dead 'white' Man) and real live men. By then I had shortened my name to Felly . . . (and had forgotten what happens to naughty girls. After all 'white' hunters had as near as possible wiped out all the lions.)

So now I carry a man's name as well. A 'white' name! Simmonds. Apparently there is Dutch blood somewhere on his father's line. The Dutch blood that is so afraid of African blood in Africa.

My National Insurance papers and my driving licence are the only documents as far as I know that carry all my names. Felicitas Nora Nkweto Simmonds.

Often I drop Nora, it is the name I least relate to, unless I'm in Zambia, which is not often these days. I haven't been there since my mother died three years ago. Sometimes I feel that I can't go back. However, these days Nkweto is with me now in a way that I haven't felt before. It could be because of my mother's death. I need to feel close to her spirit, through my own spirit, Nkweto wa Chilinda. Recently I've used it when I write poetry, when I write from my soul, when I'm saying something that touches my very core.

In public, at conferences, for example, I insist that my full name appears on my name tag. In a society that cannot accommodate names that come from 'other' cultures, this can be a frustrating exercise. It is no wonder that many Black children will Anglicize their names to avoid playground taunts . . . and much worse. We are still fighting colonialism.

Friends ask me why I don't just drop my non-African names. It would be a good idea, but not a practical one. In reality, my reason has nothing to do with practicality, it has to do with my own identity. For better, for worse, my names locate me in time and space. It gives me a sense of my own history that I not only share specifically with a generation of people in Africa but also with all Africans in the Diaspora.

I belong to a time. The twentieth century. A time of fragmentation, a time of rebirth. I need to understand and know myself from that position. It is the only position I have, wherever I am. In both my private space and my public life. I'm also lucky. Naming myself differently to suit the occasion allows me the space to experience all my subjective realities and identities (we all have many) in a way that does not imply fragmentation, but coherence.

I also know I belong and simultaneously don't belong either to the time or the space I occupy. I carry my history and that of my people. As I experience life, all that I experience is also in readiness for those who come after me, those who will carry my name and my spirit. That is my identity.

Three summers ago, in New York, at an international women's conference, I *really* experienced being an African woman in the Diaspora as I sat with Joselina and Sueli from Brazil. It was hard to accept that these women were strangers to me . . . I was also freaked by the many times women came to talk to me, thinking that they knew me from somewhere. To make sense of this experience I wrote this poem for Sueli, with whom I could only communicate through Joselina.

Coming to America

I am here,
To feed my fragmented self.
I am here,
To see my other self.
When you ask me —
Have I seen you before?
Why do I say
No, this is my first crossing of the Atlantic.
You have seen me before.
I am your sister.
The sister, whose memory three hundred years of separation
   cannot wipe out,
Even though you speak Portuguese now.
And I, English . . .
You are my sister,
I know you,
And you know me.
You are the sister that I lost so many centuries ago . . .
But still pined for,
   Just to see you
   and smile at you,
   and, maybe talk to you.
   And if lucky,
   Hold your hand.
   Hold you in my arms.
   After all these years.

Reprinted from Delia Jarrett-Macaulay (ed.), Reconstructing womanhood, Reconstructing feminism. (London: Routledge, 1995).

Chapter 2

Trinh T. Minh-ha

DIFFERENCE: 'A SPECIAL THIRD WORLD WOMEN'S ISSUE'

The female identity enclosure

DIFFERENCE AS UNIQUENESS or special identity is both limiting and deceiving. If identity refers to the whole pattern of sameness within a human life, the style of a continuing me that permeates all the changes undergone, then difference remains within the boundary of that which distinguishes one identity from another. This means that *at heart*, X must be X, Y must be Y, and X *cannot* be Y. Those who run around yelling that X is not X and X *can* be Y usually land in a hospital, a 'rehabilitation' center, a concentration camp, or a res-er-va-tion. All deviations from the dominant stream of thought, that is to say, the belief in a permanent essence of wo/man and in an invariant but fragile identity, whose 'loss' is considered to be a 'specifically human danger,' can easily fit into the categories of the 'mentally ill' or the 'mentally underdeveloped.' It is probably difficult for a 'normal,' probing mind to recognize that to seek is to lose, for seeking presupposes a separation between the seeker and the sought, the continuing me and the changes it undergoes. What if the popularized story of the identity crisis proves to be only a story and nothing else? Can identity, indeed, be viewed other than as a by-product of a 'manhandling' of life, one that, in fact, refers no more to a consistent 'pattern of sameness' than to an inconsequential process of otherness? How am I to lose, maintain, or gain an (fe/male) identity when it is impossible to me to take up a position outside this identity from which I presumably reach in and feel for it? Perhaps a way to portray it is to borrow these verses from the *Cheng-tao-ke*:

You cannot take hold of it,
But you cannot lose it.
In not being able to get it, you get it.
When you are silent, it speaks:
When you speak, it is silent.

Difference in such an insituable context is *that which undermines the very idea of identity*, deferring to infinity the layers whose totality forms 'I.' It subverts the foundations of any affirmation or vindication of value and cannot, thereby, ever bear in itself an absolute value. The difference (within) between *difference* itself and *identity* has so often been ignored and the use of the two terms so readily confused, that claiming a female/ethnic identity/difference is commonly tantamount to reviving a kind of naïve 'male-tinted' romanticism. If feminism is set forth as a demystifying force, then it will have to question thoroughly the belief in its own identity. To suppose, like Judith Kegan Gardiner, that 'the concept of female idenity provides a key to understanding the *special qualities* of contemporary writing by women . . ., the diverse ways in which writing by women *differs* from writing by men,' and to 'propose the preliminary metaphor "female identity is a process" for the most fundamental of these differences' does not, obviously, allow us to radically depart from the master's logic. Such a formulation endeavours to 'reach a theory of female identity . . . that *varies from the male model*,' and to demonstrate that:

> primary identity for women is more flexible and relational *than for men*. Female gender identity is *more* stable *than male gender identity*. Female infantile identifications are *less* predictable *than male ones* . . . the *female counterpart* of the male identity crisis may occur more diffusely, at a different stage, or not at all. (1981: 353 my italics)

It seems quite content with reforms that, at best, contribute to the improvement and/or enlargement of the identity enclosure, but do not, in any way, attempt to remove its fence. The constant need to refer to the 'male model' for comparisons unavoidably maintains the subject under tutelage. For the point is not to carve one's space in 'identity theories that ignore women' and describe some of the faces of female identity, saying, like Gardiner: 'I picture female identity as typically less fixed, less unitary, and more flexible than male individuality, both in its primary core and in the entire maturational complex developed from this core,' but patiently to dismantle the very notion of core (be it static or not) and identity.

Woman can never be defined. Bat, dog, chick, mutton, tart. Queen, madam, lady of pleasure. MISTRESS. *Belle-de-nuit*, woman of the streets, fruitwoman, fallen woman. Cow, vixen, bitch. Call girl, joy girl, working girl. Lady and whore are both bred to please. The old Woman image-repertoire says She is a Womb, a mere baby's pouch, or 'nothing but sexuality.' She is a passive substance, a parasite, an enigma whose mystery proves to be a snare and a delusion. She wallows in night, disorder, and immanence and is at the same time the 'disturbing factor (between men)' and the key to the beyond. The further the repertoire unfolds its images, the more entangled it gets in its attempts at capturing Her. 'Truth, Beauty, Poetry – she is All: once more all under the form of the Other. All except herself', Simone De Beauvoir wrote. Yet, even with or because of Her capacity to embody All, Woman is the lesser man, and among male athletes, to be called a woman is still resented as the worst of insults. 'Wo-' appended to 'man' in sexist contexts is not unlike 'Third World,' 'Third,' 'minority,' or *color* affixed to *woman* in pseudo-feminist contexts. Yearning for universality, the generic 'woman,' like its counterpart, the generic 'man,' tends to efface difference within itself. Not every female is 'a real woman,' one knows this through hearsay . . . Just as 'man' provides an example of how the part played by women has been ignored, undervalued, distorted, or omitted through the use of terminology presumed to be generic, 'woman' more often than not reflects the subtle power of linguistic exclusion, for its set of referents rarely includes those relevant to Third World 'female persons.' 'All the Women Are White, All the Blacks are Men, But Some of Us Are Brave' is the title given to an anthology edited by Gloria T. Hull, Patricia Bell Scott, and Barbara Smith (1982). It is, indeed, somehow devious to think that WOMAN also encompasses the Chinese with bound feet, the genitally mutilated Africans, and the one thousand Indians who committed *suttee* for one royal male. Sister Cinderella's foot is also enviably tiny but never crooked! And, European witches were also burnt to purify the body of Christ, but they do not pretend to 'self-immolation.' 'Third World,' therefore, belongs to a category apart, a 'special' one that is meant to be both complimentary and complementary, for First and Second went out of fashion, leaving a serious Lack behind to be filled.

Third World?

To survive, 'Third World' must necessarily have negative *and* positive connotations: negative when viewed in a vertical ranking system – 'underdeveloped' compared to over-industralized, 'underprivileged' within the already second sex – and positive when understood sociopolitically as a subversive, 'non-aligned' force. Whether 'Third World' sounds negative or positive also depends on *who* uses it. Coming from you Westerners, the word can hardly mean the same as when it comes from Us members of the Third World. Quite predictably, you/we who condemn it most are both we who buy in and they who deny any participation in the bourgeois mentality of the West. For it was in the context of such a mentality that 'Third World' stood out as a new semantic finding to designate what was known as 'the savages' before the Independences. Today, hegemony is much more subtle, much more pernicious than the form of blatant racism once exercised by the colonial West. I/i always find myself asking, in this one-dimensional society, where I/i should draw the line between tracking down the oppressive mechanisms of the system and aiding their spread. 'Third World' commonly refers to those states in Africa, Asia and Latin America which called themselves 'non-aligned,' that is to say, affiliated with neither the Western (capitalist) nor the Eastern (communist) power blocs. Thus, if 'Third World' is often rejected for its judged-to-be-derogative connotations, it is not so much because of the hierarchical, first-second-third order implied, as some invariably repeat, but because of the growing threat 'Third World' consistently presents to the Western bloc the last few decades. The emergence of repressed voices into the worldwide political arena has already prompted her (Julia Kristeva) to ask: 'How will the West greet the awakening of the 'third world' as the Chinese call it? Can we [Westerners] participate, actively and lucidly, in this awakening when the center of the planet is in the process of moving toward the East?' Exploited, looked down upon, and lumped together in a convenient term that denies their individualities, a group of 'poor' (nations), having once sided with neither of the dominating forces, has slowly learned to turn this denial to the best account. 'The Third World to Third World peoples' thus becomes an empowering tool, and one which politically includes all non-whites in their solidarist struggle against all forms of Western dominance. And since 'Third World' now refers to more than the geographically and economically determined nations of the 'South' (versus 'North'), since the term comprises such 'developed' countries as Japan and those which have opted for socialist reconstruction of their system (China, Cuba, Ethiopia, Angola, Mozambique) as well as those which have favored a capitalist mode of development (Nigeria, India, Brazil), there no longer exists such a thing as a unified unaligned Third World bloc. Moreover, Third World has moved West (or North, depending on where the dividing line falls) and has expanded so as to include even the remote parts of the First World. What is at stake is not only the hegemony of Western cultures, but also their identities as unified cultures. Third World dwells on diversity; so does First World. This is our strength and our misery. The West is painfully made to realize the existence of a Third World in the First World, and vice versa. The Master is bound to recognize that his Culture is not as homogeneous, as monolithic as He believed it to be. He discovers, with much reluctance, He is just an other among others.

Thus, whenever it is a question of 'Third World women' or, more disquietingly, of 'Third World Women in the US,' the reaction provoked among many whites almost never fails to be that of annoyance, irritation, or vexation. 'Why Third World in the US?' they say angrily; 'You mean those who still have relatives in South East Asia?' 'Third World! I don't understand how one can use such a term, it doesn't mean anything.' Or even better, 'Why use such a term to defeat yourself?' Alternatives like 'Western' and 'non-Western' or 'Euro-American' and 'non-Euro-American' may sound a bit less charged, but they are certainly neither neutral nor satisfactory, for they still take the dominant group as point of reference, and they reflect well the West's ideology of dominance (it is as if we were to use the term 'non-Afro-Asian,' for example, to designate all white peoples). More recently, we

have been hearing of the Fourth World which, we are told, 'is a world popu-
lated by indigenous people who still continue to bear a spiritual relationship
to their traditional lands.' The colonialist creed 'Divide and Conquer' is here
again, alive and well. Often ill at ease with the outspoken educated natives
who represent the Third World in debates and paternalistically scornful of
those who remain reserved, the dominant thus decides to weaken this term
of solidarity, both by invalidating it as empowering tool and by inciting divi-
siveness within the Third World – A Third World within the Third World.
Aggressive Third World (educated 'savages') with its awareness and resistance to domination must therefore be classified apart from gentle Fourth
World (uneducated 'savages'). Every unaligned voice should necessarily/
consequently be either a personal or a minority voice. The (impersonal)
majority, as logic dictates, has to be the (aligned) dominant.

> It is, apparently, inconvenient, if not downright mind stretching
> [notes Alice Walker (1980: 133–4)], for white women scholars to
> think of black women as women, perhaps because 'woman' (like 'man'
> among white males) is a name they are claiming for themselves, and
> themselves alone. Racism decrees that if they are now women (years
> ago they were ladies, but fashions change) then black women must,
> perforce, be something else. (While they were 'ladies' black women
> could be 'women' and so on.)

Another revealing example of this separatist majority mentality is the story
Walker relates of an exhibit of women painters at the Brooklyn Museum:
when asked 'Are there no black women painters represented here?' (none
of them is, apparently), a white woman feminist simply replies 'It's a *women's*
exhibit!' (Walker 1980: 136) Different historical contexts, different semantic
contents. . . .

'Woman' and the subtle power of linguistic exclusion

What is *woman*? Long ago, during one of the forceful speeches she delivered
in defense of her people, Sojourner Truth was asked by a threatened white
doctor in the audience to prove to all those present that she was truly a woman:

> 'There are those among us,' he began in a tone characteristic of insti-
> tutional training, 'who question whether or not you are a woman. Some
> feel that maybe you are a man in a woman's disguise. To satisfy our
> curiosity, why don't you show your breasts to the women [sic] in this
> audience?' (Quoted Bell *et al.* 1979: xxv)

It seemed, indeed, profoundly puzzling for this man-child doctor's mind
to see the Woman (or Breasts) in someone who had 'never been helped

into carriages, lifted over ditches, nor given the best places everywhere,' who had 'plowed, and planted, and gathered into barns,' and who, beyond measure, triumphantly affirmed elsewhere: 'Look at me! Look at my arm! . . . and no man could head me – and *ar'nt I a woman!*' (Blicksilver 1978: 335) Definitions of '*woman,*' 'womanhood,' 'femininity,' 'femaleness,' and, more recently, of 'female identity' have brought about the arrogance of such a sham anatomical curiosity – whose needs must be 'satisfied' – and the legitimation of a shamelessly dehumanizing form of Indiscretion. Difference reduced to sexual identity is thus posited to justify and conceal exploitation. The Body, the most visible difference between men and women, the only one to offer a secure ground for those who seek the permanent, the feminine 'nature' and 'essence,' remains thereby the safest basis for racist and sexist ideologies. The two merging themes of Otherness and the Identity-Body are precisely what Simone de Beauvoir discussed at length in *The Second Sex*, and continued until the time of her death to argue in the French Journal she edited, *Questions Féministes*. The lead article written by the Editorial Collective under the title of 'Variations on Common Themes' explains the purpose of the journal – to destroy the notion of differences between the sexes, 'which gives a shape and a base to the concept of 'woman' '':

> Now, after centuries of men constantly repeating that *we* are different, here are women screaming, as if they were afraid of not being heard and as if it were an exciting discovery: 'We are different!' Are you going fishing? No, I am going fishing.
>
> The very theme of difference, whatever the differences are represented to be, is useful to the oppressing group. . . . any allegedly natural feature attributed to an oppressed group is used to imprison this group within the boundaries of a Nature which, since the group is oppressed, ideological confusion labels 'nature of oppressed person' . . . to demand the right to Difference without analyzing its social character is to give back the enemy an effective weapon. (1981: 80–219)

Difference as the Editorial Collective of *Questions Féministes* understands and condemns it is bound to remain an integral part of naturalist ideology. It is the very kind of colonized-anthropo-logized difference the master has always happily granted his subordinates. The search and the claim for an essential female/ethnic identity-difference today can never be anything more than a move within the male-is-norm-divide-and-conquer trap. The malady lingers on. As long as words of difference serve to legitimate a discourse instead of delaying its authority to infinity, they are, to borrow an image from Audre Lorde, 'noteworthy only as *decorations.*'

Reprinted from Trinh T. Minh-ha, *Woman, Native, Other,* (Bloomington: Indiana University Press, 1989).

Gender, language and literature

Chapter 3

Virginia Woolf

WOMEN AND FICTION

T HE TITLE OF THIS ARTICLE can be read in two ways; it may allude to women and the fiction that they write, or to women and the fiction that is written about them. The ambiguity is intentional, for in dealing with women as writers, as much elasticity as possible is desirable; it is necessary to leave oneself room to deal with other things besides their work, so much has that work been influenced by conditions that have nothing whatever to do with art.

The most superficial enquiry into women's writing instantly raises a host of questions. Why, we ask at once, was there no continuous writing done by women before the eighteenth century? Why did they then write almost as habitually as men, and in the course of that writing produce, one after another, some of the classics of English fiction? And why did their art then, and why to some extent does their art still, take the form of fiction?

A little thought will show us that we are asking questions to which we shall get, as answer, only further fiction. The answer lies at present locked in old diaries, stuffed away in old drawers, half obliterated in the memories of the aged. It is to be found in the lives of the obscure – in those almost unlit corridors of history where the figures of generations of women are so dimly, so fitfully perceived. For very little is known about women. The history of England is the history of the male line, not of the female. Of our fathers we know always some fact, some distinction. They were soldiers or they were sailors; they filled that office or they made that law. But of our mothers, our grandmothers, our great-grandmothers, what remains? Nothing but a tradition. One was beautiful; one was red-haired; one was kissed by a

Queen. We know nothing of them except their names and the dates of their marriages and the number of children they bore.

Thus, if we wish to know why at any particular time women did this or that, why they wrote nothing, why on the other hand they wrote master-pieces, it is extremely difficult to tell. Anyone who should seek among those old papers, who should turn history wrong side out and so construct a faithful picture of the daily life of the ordinary woman in Shakespeare's time, in Milton's time, in Johnson's time, would not only write a book of astonishing interest, but would furnish the critic with a weapon which he now lacks. The extraordinary woman depends on the ordinary woman. It is only when we know what were the conditions of the average woman's life – the number of her children, whether she had money of her own, if she had a room to herself, whether part of the housework was her task – it is only when we can measure the way of life and the experience of life made possible to the ordinary woman that we can account for the success or failure of the extra-ordinary woman as a writer.

Strange spaces of silence seem to separate one period of activity from another. There was Sappho and a little group of women all writing poetry on a Greek island 600 years before the birth of Christ. They fall silent. Then about the year 1000 we find a certain court lady, the Lady Murasaki, writing a very long and beautiful novel in Japan. But in England in the sixteenth century, when the dramatists and poets were most active, the women were dumb. Elizabethan literature is exclusively masculine. Then, at the end of the eighteenth century and in the beginning of the nineteenth, we find women again writing – this time in England – with extraordinary frequency and success.

Law and custom were of course largely responsible for these strange intermissions of silence and speech. When a woman was liable, as she was in the fifteenth century, to be beaten and flung about the room if she did not marry the man of her parents' choice, the spiritual atmosphere was not favourable to the production of works of art. When she was married without her own consent to a man who thereupon became her lord and master, 'so far at least as law and custom could make him', as she was in the time of the Stuarts, it is likely she had little time for writing, and less encourage-ment. The immense effort of environment and suggestion upon the mind, we in our psychoanalytical age are beginning to realize. Again, with memoirs and letters to help us, we are beginning to understand how abnormal is the effort needed to produce a work of art, and what shelter and what support the mind of the artist requires. Of those facts the lives and letters of men like Keats and Carlyle and Flaubert assure us.

Thus it is clear that the extraordinary outburst of fiction in the begin-ning of the nineteenth century of England was heralded by innumerable slight changes in law and customs and manners. And women of the nineteenth century had some leisure; they had some education. It was no longer the exception for women of the middle and upper classes to choose their own husbands. And it is significant that of the four great women novelists – Jane Austen, Emily Brontë, Charlotte Brontë, and George Eliot – not one had a child, and two were unmarried.

Yet though it is clear that the ban upon writing had been removed, there was still, it would seem, considerable pressure upon women to write novels. No four women can have been more unlike in genius and character than these four. Jane Austen can have had nothing in common with George Eliot; George Eliot was the direct opposite of Emily Brontë. Yet all were trained for the same profession; all, when they wrote, wrote novels.

Fiction was, as fiction still is, the easiest thing for a woman to write. Nor is it difficult to find the reason. A novel is the least concentrated form of art. A novel can be taken up or put down more easily than a play or a poem. George Eliot left her work to nurse her father. Charlotte Brontë put down her pen to pick the eyes out of the potatoes. And living as she did in the common sitting-room, surrounded by people, a woman was trained to use her mind in observation and upon the analysis of character. She was trained to be a novelist and not to be a poet.

Even in the nineteenth century, a woman lived almost solely in her home and her emotions. And those nineteenth-century novels, remarkable as they were, were profoundly influenced by the fact that the women who wrote them were excluded by their sex from certain kinds of experience. That experience has a great influence upon fiction is indisputable. The best part of Conrad's novels, for instance, would be destroyed if it had been impossible for him to be a sailor. Take away all that Tolstoy knew of war as a soldier, of life and society as a rich young man whose education admitted him to all sorts of experience, and *War and Peace* would be incredibly impoverished.

Yet *Pride and Prejudice, Wuthering Heights, Villette,* and *Middlemarch* were written by women from whom was forcibly withheld all experience save that which could be met with in a middle-class drawing-room. No first-hand experience of war, or seafaring, or politics, or business was possible for them. Even their emotional life was strictly regulated by law and custom. When George Eliot ventured to live with Mr Lewes without being his wife, public opinion was scandalized. Under its pressure she withdrew into a suburban seclusion which, inevitably, had the worst possible effects upon her work. She wrote that unless people asked of their own accord to come and see her, she never invited them. At the same time, on the other side of Europe, Tolstoy was living a free life as a soldier, with men and women of all classes, for which nobody censured him and from which his novels drew much of their astonishing breadth and vigour.

But the novels of women were not affected only by the necessarily narrow range of the writer's experience. They showed, at least in the nineteenth century, another characteristic which may be traced to the writer's sex. In *Middlemarch* and in *Jane Eyre* we are conscious not merely of the writer's character, as we are conscious of the character of Charles Dickens, but we are conscious of a woman's presence – of someone resenting the treatment of her sex and pleading for its rights. This brings into women's writing an element which is entirely absent from a man's, unless, indeed, he happens to be a working man, a negro, or one who for some other reason is conscious of disability. It introduces a distortion and is frequently the cause of weakness. The desire to plead some personal cause or to make a character the mouthpiece of some personal discontent or grievance always had a distressing effect, as if the spot at which the reader's attention is directed were suddenly twofold instead of single.

The genius of Jane Austen and Emily Brontë is never more convicing than in their power to ignore such claims and solicitations and to hold on their way unperturbed by scorn or censure. But it needed a very serene or a very powerful mind to resist the temptation to anger. The ridicule, the censure, the assurance of inferiority in one form or another which were lavished upon women who practised an art, provoked such reactions naturally enough. One sees the effect in Charlotte Brontë's indignation, in George Eliot's resignation. Again and again one finds it in the work of the lesser women writers – in their choice of a subject, in their unnatural self-assertiveness, in their unnatural docility. Moreover, insincerity leaks in almost unconsciously. They adopt a view in deference to authority. The vision becomes too masculine or it becomes too feminine; it loses its perfect integrity and, with that, its most essential quality as a work of art.

The great change that has crept into women's writing is, it would seem, a change of attitude. The woman writer is no longer bitter. She is no longer angry. She is no longer pleading and protesting as she writes. We are approaching, if we have not yet reached, the time when her writing will have little or no foreign influence to disturb it. She will be able to concentrate upon her vision without distraction from outside. The aloofness that was once within the reach of genius and originality is only now coming within the reach of ordinary women. Therefore the average novel by a woman is far more genuine and far more interesting today than it was a hundred or even fifty years ago.

But it is still true that before a woman can write exactly as she wishes to write, she has many difficulties to face. To begin with, there is the technical difficulty – so simple, apparently; in reality, so baffling – that the very form of the sentence does not fit her. It is a sentence made by men; it is too loose, too heavy, too pompous for a woman's use. Yet in a novel, which covers so wide a stretch of ground, an ordinary and usual type of sentence has to be found to carry the reader on easily and naturally from one end of the book to the other. And this a woman must make for herself, altering and adapting the current sentence until she writes one that takes the natural shape of her thought without crushing or distorting it.

But that, after all, is only a means to an end, and the end is still to be reached only when a woman has the courage to surmount opposition and the determination to be true to herself. For a novel, after all, is a statement about a thousand different objects – human, natural, divine; it is an attempt to relate them to each other. In every novel of merit these different elements are held in place by the force of the writer's vision. But they have another order also, which is the order imposed upon them by convention. And as men are the arbiters of that convention, as they have established an order of values in life, so too, since fiction is largely based on life, these values prevail there also to a very great extent.

It is probable, however, that both in life and in art the values of a woman are not the values of a man. Thus, when a woman comes to write a novel, she will find that she is perpetually wishing to alter the established values – to make serious what appears insignificant to a man, and trivial what is to him important. And for that, of course, she will be criticized; for the critic of the opposite sex will be genuinely puzzled and surprised by an attempt to alter the current scale of values, and will see in it not merely a difference of view, but a view that is weak, or trivial, or sentimental, because it differs from his own.

But here, too, women are coming to be more independent of opinion. They are beginning to respect their own sense of values. And for this reason the subject-matter of their novels begins to show certain changes. They are less interested, it would seem, in themselves; on the other hand, they are more interested in other women. In the early nineteenth century, women's novels were largely autobiographical. One of the motives that led them to write was the desire to expose their own suffering, to plead their own cause. Now that this desire is no longer so urgent, women are beginning to explore their own sex, to write of women as women have never been written of before; for of course, until very lately, women in literature were the creation of men.

Here again there are difficulties to overcome, for, if one may generalize, not only do women submit less readily to observation than men, but their lives are far less tested and examined by the ordinary processes of life. Often nothing tangible remains of a woman's day. The food that has been cooked is eaten; the children that have been nursed have gone out into the world. Where does the accent fall? What is the salient point for the novelist to seize upon? It is difficult to say. Her life has an anonymous character which is baffling and puzzling in the extreme. For the first time, this dark country is beginning to be explored in fiction; and at the same moment a woman has also to record the changes in women's minds and habits which the opening of the professions has introduced. She has to observe how their lives are ceasing to run underground; she has to discover what new colours and shadows are showing in them now that they are exposed to the outer world.

If, then, one should try to sum up the character of women's fiction at the present moment, one would say that it is courageous; it is sincere; it keeps closely to what women feel. It is not bitter. It does not insist upon its femininity. But at the same time, a woman's book is not written as a man would write it. These qualities are much commoner than they were, and they give even to second- and third-rate work the value of truth and the interest of sincerity.

But in addition to these good qualities, there are two that call for a word more of discussion. The change which has turned the English woman from a nondescript influence, fluctuating and vague, to a voter, a wage-earner, a responsible citizen, has given her both in her life and in her art a turn towards the impersonal. Her relations now are not only emotional; they are intellectual, they are political. The old system which condemned her to squint askance at things through the eyes or through the interests of husband or brother, has given place to the direct and practical interests of one who must act for herself, and not merely influence the acts of others. Hence her attention is being directed away from the personal centre which engaged it exclusively in the past to the impersonal, and her novels become more critical of society, and less analytical of individual lives.

We may expect that the office of gadfly to the state, which has been so far a male prerogative, will now be discharged by women also. Their novels will deal with social evils and remedies. Their men and women will not be observed wholly in relation to each other emotionally, but as they cohere and clash in groups and classes and races. That is one change of some importance. But there is another more interesting to those who prefer the butterfly to the gadfly – that is to say, the artist to the reformer. The greater impersonality of women's lives will encourage the poetic spirit, and it is in poetry that women's fiction is still weakest. It will lead them to be less absorbed in facts and no longer content to record with astonishing acuteness the minute details which fall under their own observation. They will look beyond the personal and political relationships to the wider questions which the poet tries to solve – of our destiny and the meaning of life.

The basis of the poetic attitude is of course largely founded upon material things. It depends upon leisure, and a little money, and the chance which money and leisure give to observe impersonally and dispassionately. With money and leisure at their service, women will naturally occupy themselves more than has hitherto been possible with the craft of letters. They will make a fuller and a more subtle use of the instrument of writing. Their technique will become bolder and richer.

In the past, the virtue of women's writing often lay in its divine spontaneity, like that of the blackbird's song or the thrush's. It was untaught; it was from the heart. But it was also, and much more often, chattering and garrulous – mere talk spilt over paper and left to dry in pools and blots. In future, granted time, and books, and a little space in the house for herself, literature will become for women, as for men, an art to be studied. Women's gift will be trained and strengthened. The novel will cease to be the dumping-ground for the personal emotions. It will become, more than at present, a work of art like any other, and its resources and its limitations will be explored.

From this it is a short step to the practice of the sophisticated arts, hitherto so little practised by women – to the writing of essays and criticism, of history and biography. And that, too, if we are considering the novel, will be advantage; for besides improving the quality of the novel itself, it will draw off the aliens who have been attracted to fiction by its accessibility while their hearts lay elsewhere. Thus will the novel be rid of those excrescences of history and fact which, in our time, have made it so shapeless.

So, if we may prophesy, women in time to come will write fewer novels, but better novels; and not novels only, but poetry and criticism and history. But in this, to be sure, one is looking ahead to that golden, that perhaps fabulous, age when women will have what has so long been denied them – leisure, and money, and a room to themselves.

Reprinted from Virginia Woolf, *Collected Essays*, Vol. II, (London: Hogarth Press, 1966).

Chapter 4

Cora Kaplan

LANGUAGE AND GENDER

Poetry is a privileged metalanguage in western patriarchal culture. Although other written forms of high culture – theology, philosophy, political theory, drama, prose fiction – are also, in part, language about language, in poetry this introverted or doubled relation is thrust at us as the very reason-for-being of the genre. Perhaps because poetry seems, more than any other sort of imaginative writing, to imitate a closed linguistic system it is presented to us as invitingly accessible to our understanding once we have pushed past its formal difficulties. Oddly we still seem to expect poetry to produce universal meanings. The bourgeois novel is comfortably established as a genre produced by and about a particular class, but there is an uneasy feel about the bourgeois poem. Poetry is increasingly written by members of oppressed groups, but its popular appeal is so small in western society today that its shrinking audience may make its elitism or lack of it a non-issue. Its appeal may have diminished in relation to other literary forms but its status and function in high culture continues to be important. This paper examines women's poetry as part of an investigation of women's use of high language, that is, the language, public, political and literary, of patriarchal societies.

A study of women's writing will not get us any closer to an enclosed critical practice, a 'feminist literary criticism'. There can in one sense be no feminist literary criticism, for any new theoretical approach to literature that uses gender difference as an important category involves a profoundly altered view of the relation of both sexes to language, speech, writing and culture. For this reason I have called my paper 'Language and gender' rather than

'Women and poetry' although it grew out of work on a critical anthology of English and American women's poetry that I introduced and edited a few years ago (Kaplan 1975). Some of the problems raised there still seem central to me – the insertion of female-centred subject-matter into a male literary tradition, the attendant problems of expressing this matter in a formal symbolic language, the contradictions between the romantic notion of the poet as the transcendent speaker of a unified culture and the dependent and oppressed place of women within that culture. New problems have occurred to me as equally important. The difficulty women have in writing seems to me to be linked very closely to the rupture between childhood and adolescence, when, in western societies (and in other cultures as well) public speech is a male privilege and women's speech restricted by custom in mixed sex gatherings, or, if permitted, still characterized by its private nature, an extension of the trivial domestic discourse of women. For male speakers after puberty, the distinction between public and private speech is not made in nearly such a strong way, if at all. Obviously, in the twentieth century and earlier, such distinctions have been challenged and in some cases seem to be broken down, but the distinction is still made. The prejudice seems persistent and irrational unless we acknowledge that control of high language is a crucial part of the power of dominant groups, and understand that the refusal of access to public language is one of the major forms of the oppression of women within a social class as well as in trans-class situations.

A very high proportion of women's poems are about the right to speak and write. The desire to write imaginative poetry and prose was and is a demand for access to and parity within the law and myth-making groups in society. The decision to storm the walls and occupy the forbidden place is a recognition of the value and importance of high language, and often contradicts and undercuts a more radical critique in women's poetry of the values embedded in formal symbolic language itself. To be a woman and a poet presents many women poets with such a profound split between their social, sexual identity (their 'human' identity) and their artistic practice that the split becomes the insistent subject, sometimes overt, often hidden or displaced, of much women's poetry.

The first part of my paper will try out a theoretical account of the process by which women come to internalize the suppression and restriction of their speech. The second part[*] demonstrates how the struggle to overcome the taboo is presented as the hidden subject in poems that seem deliberately difficult and opaque.

Do men and women in patriarchal societies have different relationships to the language they speak and write? Statements of such a difference, questions about its source, persistence and meaning run through western writing since Greek times. Often buried in that larger subject, the exploration and definition of gender difference in culture, it becomes a distinct issue when

*[The second part of this essay has been omitted from this collection.]

women speak or write, and men protest, not only or primarily at what they say, but at the act itself. Recently left feminists have used work on ideology by the French political philosopher, Louis Althusser, together with the psychoanalytic theories of Freud and his modern French interpreter, Jacques Lacan, to clarify their understanding of the construction of femininity (Althusser 1971; Lacan 1977a, 1977b; Mitchell and Rose 1982). Contemporary work on ideology in France accepts Freud's theory of the unconscious and is concerned, among other things, with the construction of the subject in culture. Language is the most important of all the forms of human communication. Through the acquisition of language we become human and social beings: the words we speak situate us in our gender and our class. Through language we come to 'know' who we are. In elaborating and extending Freud's work, Lacan emphasizes the crucial importance of language as the signifying practice in and through which the subject is made into a social being. Social entry into patriarchal culture is made in language, through speech. Our individual speech does not, therefore, free us in any simple way from the ideological constraints of our culture since it is through the forms that articulate those constraints that we speak in the first place.

The account that follows here is necessarily very schematized, designed simply to show the crucial nexus between the acquisition of subjectivity through language and the recognition of the social nature of female identity.

Every human child, according to Lacan, goes through an encounter with his own image in the mirror, somewhere between 6 and 18 months, which is particularly significant and a precondition of the acquisition of subjectivity. For in that encounter the image is misrecognized as an ideal whole – a counterpart, an Other, of the fragmented, feeling being. During this period the child is angrily conscious of the capricious comings and goings, which he is helpless to control, of persons on whom he relies for physical care and emotional comfort. The perception of the image in the mirror as both self and other, as the same and different, the projection of an ideal form of the self through a spatial relation acts as the basis for the acquisition of subjectivity, and is, as well, the crude form, self and other for all intersubjective relations. Although the child may learn words quite early, during the first year and a half of life, the mastery of language succeeds the mirror stage and is the true point at which subjectivity is attained. Nevertheless even the early use of very simple abstractions shows how the child gains some small form of control over the absence and presence of his caretaker. The classic example, taken from Freud, is the *fort/da* game, in which the child in the mother's absence, throws away an object 'fort' and retrieves it 'da' to symbolize and, in part, control, her absence and presence. As the child acquires more linguistic competence, for example the correct use of names and pronouns to differentiate self from others, he moves from the omnipotence implicit in the prelinguistic fantasy when he and the mirror image are one, to the necessary limitation of his own desires and powers when he acceded to language, to subjectivity and the world of social relations. In language the child acquires the necessary abstractions to situate himself in relation to others and to speak the particular meanings of his own experience in a public, socially understood discourse (Lacan 1977a: 1–7).

For Lacan, language, adult or competent speech, is the Symbolic order. It embodies the abstracted relations of the laws of a particular culture. Language only exists through individual speech, so in each speech act the self and the culture speak simultaneously or, to put it another way, each time we speak we are also spoken: this formulation is abstract, but is not meant to be understood as a mechanical operation in which a ventriloquist culture moves our lips. Lacan uses and transforms the linguistic theories of Ferdinand de Saussure who makes the basic distinction between language and speech. Saussure also suggests that meanings, words, can only be understood as differences from other meanings. Meanings – signifiers – are part of chains – think of a sentence as a chain – and refer not to some fixed phenomenological object but to the meanings, either present or implied in the chain, which therefore make up the sense of the chain. To the extent that the words we choose have meanings other than the particular ones that an individual speech act intends, these absent but still invoked relations of meaning are responsible for a 'veering off of meaning' or 'the sliding of the signified under the signifier', of sense under meaning in any given signifying chain (Lacan 1977c: 146–78). It will become clear quite soon how the distinction between language and speech, the definition of meanings as relations of difference and the crucial role of language in the development of the child's consciousness of self, relates to women's use of language.

Symbolic language, which includes everyday speech as well as written or imaginative forms, uses two basic tropes, metaphor and metonymy. These tropes 'present the most condensed expression of two basic modes of relation; the internal relation of similarity (and contrast) underlies the metaphor; the external relation of contiguity (and remoteness) determines the metonymy' (Jakobson 1971). While metaphor and metonymy are the stuff of poetry (Roman Jakobson, who I have quoted here, sees metaphor as the principal mode in romantic and symbolic poetry, and metonymy as the mode of the epic), these linguistic tropes are the modes through which we come to perceive all relations of difference, such as gender difference and the separation of the self from others. Lacan has identified these figures of speech with Freud's concept of the modes that occur in dreams. Metaphor equals condensation; metonymy equals displacement. Language like the unconscious resists interpretation even as, through dreams and in ordinary discourse it invites us to interpret it. We ought not to think of the use of metaphor and metonymy in imaginative genres as uniquely isolated or sophisticated. How men and women come to speak at all, how they see each other through speech, the social taboos on speech for children and women, all these relations bear upon the way in which individual poets are seen to 'create' new symbolic identifications and relations.

Having gone so deep into language we must now go back to the construction of the subject in culture, and pick up our child at what Freud and Lacan designate the Oedipal stage which is also the point at which the child's competence in speaking means that he has virtually entered the Symbolic order. Entry into the Symbolic order is necessary, says Lacan, for mental stability. If the subject cannot be located in linguistic abstraction, then in extreme cases, as observed in the broad disorder termed schizophrenia, words cannot be constructed in an individual discourse. The dislocated subject treats them as things, sounds, associations, and does not use them in a logical pattern to situate herself in her intersubjective (social) situation. The difference between male and female entry into the Symbolic has to do with the stage of development which overlaps the full acquisition of language, and through which the child accepts his or her gender identity – the Oedipal phase. In Lacan, the phallus (not to be confused with the actual penis) is the 'missing' signifier to which both sexes must reconcile their relationship. Full entry into the Symbolic does not depend on having or not having a penis, but on the symbolic interpretation a child places on its absence or presence in him/herself and in the two powerful figures of the mother and father. In order for women to identify finally with their mothers and take their place as female in culture they must accept the missing phallus as a permanent loss in themselves. According to Freud's account of the Oedipal resolution, the lack of a phallus in the mother is a nasty shock for both boys and girls. Boys repress their incestuous feelings for their mothers and their anger with their fathers as a result of the implied threat of castration – seen as already accomplished in the mother. At this point they accede to an identification with the father, which seals their gender identity and holds out the promise of a future alignment with authority, the Symbolic order, or law of the Father in place of the lost identification with the mother. Little girls, who must position themselves very differently in relation to the missing phallus, accept, sometimes reluctantly and with ongoing hostility, their likeness to the mother. The introduction of the father/phallus as the third term in the child's social world, breaks the early mother–child relationship for both sexes and brings on all the ensuing crises of identity through gender differentiation, so that all children lose the dyadic relation to the mother as they enter a wider society. Girls, as Freudian theory would have it, have a particular relation to loss or lack in that they must substitute for it, not the possession of the phallus but babies and/or an intersubjective relation with men (who are necessary for the production of babies).

The phallus as a signifier has a central, crucial position in language, for if language embodies the patriarchal law of the culture, its basic meanings refer to the recurring process by which sexual difference and subjectivity are acquired. All human desire is, in Lacan's view, mediated through language, through the 'defiles of the signifier', and is expressed through the desire of the other – the projected ideal form of the imago (remember the model of the mirror phase) which becomes dispersed through our entry into the

Symbolic in our real relation to others. Only if we accept the phallus as a privileged signification (a meaning which *does* relate to something outside itself) do we see that the little girl's access to the Symbolic, that is to language as the embodiment of cultural law, is always negative, or more neutrally, eccentric.

Even if we do accept the phallus as a privileged meaning, the concept of negative entry, as it has been posed so far seems at once too easy and too difficult to grasp. It is a convenient way of describing a phenomenon not yet fully understood or articulated in psychoanalytic theory. I would prefer, cautiously, to call the entry into the Symbolic 'different' rather than 'negative' for girls, since lack, in Lacanian theory, is as much an experience for men as for women. Also the production of subject as the place and origin of meanings (the entry into language) is necessary for both men and women. The formation of the unconscious in the first instance occurs when the child substitutes language for drives, demand for need, duplicating in the unconscious the prelinguistic arrangement of drives. A second stage of formation can be noted when abstractions, even those as simple but central as the fort/da game, allow the child to produce itself as the subject who controls absence. All of language can then be seen as an extended system of mastery over primary need which can never entirely succeed, since the repressed material 'escapes' through dreams, through slips of the tongue, and so on. Why should women whatever the relation of difference through which they enter the Symbolic be less adept at this system than men? Empirical studies that I have seen don't suggest that there is that much significant variation between male and female speech until puberty, if ever, although it is a subject only recently taken up in linguistics. I will return to this problem briefly in the next section, but I want to suggest tentatively here that it is at puberty, the second determining stage of gender identity in culture, that a distinction between male and female speakers is confirmed.

At puberty female social identity is sealed by the onset of menstruation and fertility, and here, in western culture, is where the bar against the public speech of females is made. Puberty and adolescence fulfil the promises of the Oedipal resolution. The male is gradually released from the restrictions of childhood, which include the restriction of his speech among adults. The girl's different relation to the phallus as signifier is made clear by a continued taboo against her speech among men. Male privilege and freedom can now be seen by the adult female to be allied with male use of public and symbolic language. In many cultures there is a strong taboo against women telling jokes. If we think of jokes as the derepressed symbolic discourse of common speech, we can see why jokes, particularly obscene ones, are rarely spoken from the perspective of femininity. Adult femininity thus requires (at least in western culture) an extension of the injunction: 'Children should be seen but not heard'. A sexual division of labour in the reproduction of ideology thus appears. Men reproduce it directly through the control of public speech, and women indirectly through the reproduction of children in the institution of the family. Since women have spoken and learned speech up to and through adolescence they continue to speak among themselves, and to their men in the domestic situation. It is a taboo which seems, in modern society, made to be broken by the demands of women themselves. When women are freed from constant reproduction, when they are educated equally with men in childhood, when they join the labour force at his side, when wealth gives them leisure, when they are necessary and instrumental in effecting profound social change through revolution – at these points women will protest and break down the taboo.

It should be clear to the reader that what I have produced so far is an account of a process by which women become segregated speakers, not an explanation of why this process should take place. Nor have I claimed for it a universal application, but limited myself to western societies. If we assume for the sake of the rest of my argument that the segregation of male and female speech, although apparent to little girls as they observe the social relations of adults and interact with them, is crucially and traumatically confirmed in adolescence, then we may say that the predominance of expressed male perspectives in common and high speech stems from the taboo after childhood. There are therefore two very important and distinct stages at which women's apparently weaker position in language is set. The first is at the Oedipal stage where the child, constructed as a speaking subject, must acknowledge social sex difference and align herself with women and restricted speech – a distinction blurred by the restrictions on children's speech. The second stage, puberty, further distinguishes girls from boys by the appearance of adult sex difference and access to public discourse for men.

This account makes some sense in psychic terms of the significant but statistically small presence of women as makers of high culture, of their anxiety about their precarious position, about their difficulties (which are often made into strengths) when using what is clearly in many ways a 'common' language. It is not an alternative to other sorts of social and political analysis of the oppression of women in patriarchal culture through more brutal means, and in other ideological forms.

The seventeenth century in England produced a number of important women poets whose first task seemed to be to challenge the bar against women as speakers and writers. Anne Bradstreet (1612–72) says

> I am obnoxious to each carping tongue
> Who sayes, my hand a needle better fits

and looks back towards a golden age when there was no bias:

> But sure the antique Greeks were far more mild
> Else of our sex, why feigned they those nine
> And poesy made Calliope's own child.

Anne Finch, Countess of Winchelsea (1661–1720) attacks with more vigour and subtlety symbolic associations as spoken from the masculine position. For example, a rose, a cupped flower has no gender in English but to male poets it often represents the female. Its metaphorical associations are with the female sexual organs, its metonymic associations are with muteness, frailty. In asserting her right to an original poetic gift Anne French rejects both the rose/woman image and woman's approved leisure occupation, embroidery.

> My hand delights to trace unusual things,
> And deviates from the known and common way;
> Nor will in fading silks compose
> Faintly the inimitable rose. . . .

The use of 'deviates' and 'inimitable' in this passage seems especially suggestive. She uses deviate when she might use wander or swerve or some softer verb. For women to write at all was to be deviant. The poet refuses to be positioned in mute nature. The rose is therefore 'inimitable'. 'Trace' and 'compose' are reversed and ironized; 'trace' used for creative writing and 'compose' for embroidery. It is a brave and largely successful attempt to challenging metaphor through the subtle inversion of a traditional poetic image, but it strikes me as damned hard work. And the sliding of meaning, the effect of metonymy, is obvious. In defying traditional male-centred associations she reminds us of them; they assert themselves as meanings in spite of her skill and care. The ghosts of the meanings she wishes to resist shadow her words.

There is a haunting painting by Odilon Redon of a woman's face in ivory cameo, further enclosed in a green oval mist. A wraithlike madonna, still, and at the same time full of intense activity, she holds two fingers to her lips, and, perhaps, a cupped paw to her ear. The picture is titled *Silence*. Enjoining silence, she is its material image. A speaking silence – image and injunction joined – she is herself spoken, twice spoken we might say – once by the artist who has located *his* silence in a female figure, and once again by the viewer who accepts as natural this abstract identification of woman = silence and the complementary imaging of women's speech as whispered, subvocal, the mere escape of trapped air . . . shhhhhhhh.

More, her speech seems limited by some function in which she is wrapped as deeply as in the embryonic mist. Mother or nurse, the silence she enjoins and enacts is on behalf of some sleeping other. In enforcing our silence and her own she seems to protect someone else's speech. Her silence and muted speech, as I interpret it, is both chosen and imposed by her acceptance of her femininity. It has none of the illusory freedom of choice that we associate with a taciturn male. It is not the silence of chosen isolation either, for even in a painting significantly without other figures it is an inextricably social silence.

Redon's Madonna trails meanings behind it like the milky way. *Silence* makes a point central to my argument that it is perhaps difficult to make with any literary epigraph. Social silence as part of the constitution of female identity – i.e., subjectivity – is a crucial factor in her handling of written language. In an as yet almost unresearched area there is very little evidence to suggest that women's common, everyday speech is in any way less complex than men's, and some evidence to suggest that girls not only speak earlier than boys but develop linguistic complexity earlier too. It has been tentatively suggested that although girls are more 'verbal' (whatever that may mean) by the age of eleven or twelve, there is less meaning in their speech, though the phonemic complexity is greater. Robin Lakoff, in *Language and Woman's Place* (1975), does not adduce any particular evidence for her ideas or locate her women speakers in any class, race or locale, but suggests that women do speak a sort of second-class English which is more interrogatory, more full of 'empty' qualifiers ('lovely', 'kind of'), and, because vulgarity is censored, is super-genteel and grammatically more correct than men's speech. It is by no means clear that these observations would be true (if at all) of any group of women except perhaps upwardly mobile middle-class white American women, and if true of this group it seems much more likely to be related to a class plus gender instability than to be a particular quality of women's speech. In any case, recent debate over the language of class and of Black English has produced persuasive evidence that a restricted or alternative code does not necessarily produce restricted meanings. The variations that Lakoff lists as being special to women's speech seem very slight when compared to the variations of grammatical structure in Black English compared to standard English. Obviously the subject has barely been opened much less closed, but one might hazard that women speak the language of their class, caste, or race and that any common variants, which are in any case never fully observed, do not in themselves limit the meanings their speech can have. The sanction against female obscenity can have a particular application in the sanction against the telling of jokes and the use of wit by women, since dirty jokes are forms of common speech in which the repressed meanings of early sexual feelings are expressed in tight symbolic narratives.

It is the intra- and trans-class prejudice against women as speakers at all which seems most likely to erode women's use of 'high' language. This preference is connected with the patriarchal definition of ideal femininity. 'Silence gives the proper grace to women', Sophocles writes in *Ajax*. Its contradictions are expressed succinctly in the play, *The Man who Married a Dumb Wife*. A famous physician is called in to cure the beautiful mute. He succeeds, she speaks, and immediately begins to prattle compulsively, until the husband bitterly regrets his humane gesture. His only wish is to have her dumb again so that he might love her as before. Women speak on sufferance in the patriarchal order. Yet although the culture may prefer them to be silent, they must have the faculty of speech in order that they may be recognized as human. One reading of the Dumb Wife, whose speech is her only flaw, is that the physician's alchemy was necessary to reassure the husband that he had married a human woman, although her unrestrained, trivial speech destroys his ability to see her as the ideal love object.

Elizabeth Barrett Browning comments bitterly on the prohibition against women as speakers of public language in her long feminist poem *Aurora Leigh*. Aurora, who defies society to become a major poet, recounts her education at the hands of her aunt who was a model of all that was 'womanly':

> I read a score of books on womanhood
> . . . books that boldly assert
> Their right of comprehending husband's talk
> When not too deep, and even of answering
> With pretty 'may it please you', or 'so it is', –
> Their rapid insight and fine aptitude,
> Particular worth and general missionariness,
> As long as they keep quiet by the fire
> And never say 'no' when the world says 'ay',
> . . . their, in brief,
> Potential faculty in everything
> Of abdicating power in it.

Aurora calls 'those years of education' a kind of water torture, 'flood succeeding flood/To drench the incapable throat . . .'. The imposed silence is described as intersubjective, a silence whose effort is bent towards 'comprehending husband's talk'. Women writers from the seventeenth century onwards (when women first entered the literary ranks in any numbers) comment in moods which range from abnegation to outright anger on the culture's prohibition against women's writing, often generalizing it to women's speech. They compare their situation to that of 'state prisoners, pen and ink denied' and their suppressed or faulty speech to the child's or the 'lisping boy's.' Emily Dickinson's 'They shut me up in Prose/As when a little Girl/They put me in the Closet – / Because they liked me "still" – ' condenses all these metaphors by connecting verbal imprisonment to the real restrictions of female childhood, and adds the point that the language most emphatically denied to women is the most concentrated form of symbolic language – poetry.

The consciousness of the taboo and its weight seemed to press heavily on the women who disobeyed it, and some form of apology, though tinged with irony, occurs in almost all of the women poets, as well as in many prose writers, whether avowed feminists or not, as an urgent perhaps propitiating preface to their speech. In the introduction to the anthology I ascribed this compulsion to an anticipatory response to male prejudice against women writers, and so it was. But it now seems to me that it goes much deeper, and is intimately connected as I have said with the way in which women become social beings in the first place, so that the very condition of their accession to their own subjectivity, to the consciousness of a self which is both personal and public is their unwitting acceptance of the law which limits their speech. This condition places them in a special relation to language which becomes theirs as a consequence of becoming human, and at the same time not theirs as a consequence of becoming female.

Reprinted from Cora Kaplan, *Sea Changes,* (London: Verso, 1986).

Chapter 5

Sara Mills

THE GENDERED SENTENCE

ONE OF THE DEBATES WHICH IS of long standing within feminist literary analysis is concerned with whether women writers produce texts which are significantly different in terms of language from those of males. This debate began with the work of Virginia Woolf when she asserted that there was a sentence which women writers had developed which she termed the 'female sentence' or the 'sentence of the feminine gender'. For Woolf, certain women writers crafted a new type of sentence which is looser and more accretive than the male sentence. This view that women's writing is fundamentally different from men's seems to be echoed in the more recent statements by French feminists such as Luce Irigaray and Hélène Cixous (Irigaray 1985; Cixous 1976). Both Woolf and some French feminists assert that there is a difference between men's and women's writing, but their discussions frequently remain at a rather abstract level, since they rarely give concrete examples. [. . .]

It is rare that Virginia Woolf and French feminists are discussed together, but I would argue that their assumptions about language, writing and gender are surprisingly similar, and the elisions which they make, although in different terms, result in a similar confusion about sexual/gender difference and writing. A great deal of theoretical work has been predicated on defining the female/feminine in terms of lack in relation to the male/masculine. This is certainly true when the female sentence is discussed. Most theorists have focused on descriptions of the female sentence alone, as if the male sentence were an implicit norm. This practice of describing things associated with women as if they were deviant from a male norm can be termed phallocentric (see Ellman 1968 for a full discussion). Phallocentrism is the practice of placing the male at the centre of theoretical models, and assuming that 'male' is in fact coterminous with 'human'. As Monique Wittig says: 'There are not two genders. There is only one: the feminine; the masculine not being a gender. For the masculine is not the masculine but the general' (Wittig 1983: 2). [. . .]

Female sentence/Écriture féminine

To turn now to the male and female sentence in literature, I will first discuss the views of Virginia Woolf, as she has perhaps defined the terms within which the debate has been argued, and she is also one of the first to describe the female sentence in positive terms. She states that

> it is still true that before a woman can write exactly as she wishes to write, she has many difficulties to face. To begin with, there is the technical difficulty – so simple apparently; in reality, so baffling – that the very form of the sentence does not fit her. It is a sentence made by men; it is too loose, too heavy, too pompous for a woman's use. Yet in a novel, it covers so wide a stretch of ground, an ordinary and usual type of sentence has to be found to carry the reader on easily and naturally from one end of the book to the other. And this a woman must make for herself, altering and adapting the current sentence until she writes one that takes the natural shape of her thought without crushing or distorting it. (Woolf, this volume)

Here, Woolf seems to be prefiguring Dale Spender's statement that language is literally 'man-made', that somehow women cannot fit their ideas and expressions into a language which has been constructed according to the needs of males (Spender 1980). Therefore, for Woolf it is necessary that women craft their own type of language. When writing about Dorothy Richardson, Woolf claims that Richardson invented 'the psychological sentence of the feminine gender'. She defines this female sentence as 'of a more elastic fibre than the old, capable of stretching to the extreme, of suspending the frailest particles, of enveloping the vaguest shapes' (Woolf 1965: 204–5).

Woolf also suggests that the male sentence was insufficient for women writers: the example of the male sentence which Woolf gives is 'The grandeur of their works was an argument with them not to stop short but to proceed.' Here Woolf seems to be arguing that males write in a more formal mode than women, using nominalizations (grandeur, argument) rather than verbs or adjectives; the parallel phrasing of 'not to'/'but to' also has a very formal feel to it. It is also a very impersonal statement partly because of the use of nominalizations which lead to the omission of agency. However, Woolf's analysis of this sentence as male seems to be confusing the public/formal sphere with maleness, and although the two are often elided, it is important to recognize that it is formality that she is locating and not a gender difference.

However, Woolf's position on the gendered sentence is ambiguous, for whilst stating that there is such a thing as the 'female sentence', and praising Emily Brontë and Jane Austen for using it, she also condemns Charlotte Brontë for writing as a woman. She says: 'It is fatal for anyone who writes to think of their sex' (Woolf 1977: 99). She suggests that writing about one's sex in anger at inequality leads to poor writing: Shakespeare was great, as he 'had no desire to protest, to preach, to proclaim an injury, to pay off a score' (Woolf 1977: 99). It is a fairly widely held view that writing should be androgynous or sexless; for example, as Joyce Carol Oates states: 'If there is a distinctly "female voice" – if there is a distinctly "male" voice – surely this is symptomatic of inferior art? Of course the serious artistic voice is one of individual *style* and it is sexless' (Oates 1986: 208). Here, both Woolf and Oates seem to propose an androgyny or a sexlessness for the good writer which is in essence male. In considering Woolf's view of the differences between the male sentence and the female sentence, it is interesting to consider what she says about how women *should* write. The standard which Woolf suggests women should be aiming for could be interpreted as that of the stereotypical male sentence: 'She will write in a rage where she should write calmly. She will write foolishly where she should write wisely. She will write of herself where she should write of her characters. She is at war with her lot' (Woolf 1977: 99). That is, the supposedly neutral but in fact male sentence is implicitly described as calm, wise and apparently objective and impersonal.

The difference in type between these sentences is due in part to sentence structure but it must be noted that Dorothy Richardson's style is very much a product of her time and of avant-garde writing in general. When Woolf describes the female sentence it seems to be less a matter of style or language and more a question of content and subject-matter. A further ambiguity, which she shares with some of the French feminists, is that she states that men can in fact use this type of sentence too. At other points in her writing she suggests that the best type of writing is androgynous, not sexless but bisexual writing, which, as we will see, is very close to the position of Hélène Cixous.

Turning now to the French feminists, it is interesting to note how, even though they are working within an entirely different theoretical framework, they have still reached a position similar to Woolf's. Many French feminists work in the tradition of, and in reaction to, Jacques Lacan's theoretical work. As Ann Rosalind Jones remarks: 'Lacanian theory reserves the "I" position for men. Women because they lack the phallus, the positive symbol of gender, self-possession and worldly authority around which language is organised, occupy a negative position in language' (Jones 1985: 83). Feminists such as Hélène Cixous consider that this negative position in language can be celebrated; they term this position *écriture féminine*. Hélène Cixous reacted against the Lacanian idea of women as lack, and asserted women as pleni-tude, turning qualities assigned to women by society, such as hesitation and irrationality, into virtues. She stresses the multiple physical capacities of women: gestation, birth, lactation, etc.; and she has also elaborated the notion of a specifically female writing which reflects this multiplicity. Her defini-tion of *écriture féminine* is essentially reactive, as she is recuperating an earlier derogatory definition of it which encompassed women writers who wrote about women's experience in a way which did not challenge French male stereotypes. It is these qualities of writing, the subjective and the formless, which are often the ones which men desire in women's writing and in women, but would not want for themselves. (See for a discussion of some of Cixous' ideas Helen Wilcox *et al.* 1990).

In some ways, by transforming this male definition of *écriture féminine* we are still trapped within the notion of women's language being deviant, power-less and submissive, and male language being normal, no matter how much we assert the contrary. However, this type of language is seen by Cixous in an entirely positive light, as being revolutionary. As she says: 'we are living through [the] very period when the conceptual foundation of a millennial culture is in the process of being undermined by millions of species of mole as yet not recognised' (Cixous 1981b: 93). These moles referred to here can be taken to be the women who are slowly eroding the fixed ideas and even sentence structures of patriarchy through subversive writing. She goes on to say 'The [political] economy of the masculine and the feminine is organised by different requirements and constraints, which, when socialised and metaphorised, produce signs, relations of power, relationships of production and of reproduction, an entire immense system of cultural inscription read-able as masculine or feminine' (Cixous 1981b: 93). She states that if there were changes in these structures of political economy, there would also be changes in what we consider masculine and feminine, so she is not, as she at first appears, attributing unchanging categories of behaviour and character to females.

Cixous, like Luce Irigaray, has achieved a fusion of the critical and the creative in her own writing, putting *écriture féminine* into practice: in this *mélange*, she uses the dreams of her students, the journals of patients in psychoanalysis and liturgical passages. However, she says: 'It is impossible to *define* a feminine practice of writing, for this practice can never be theorised, enclosed, encoded – which doesn't mean that it doesn't exist. But it will always surpass the discourse that regulates the phallocentric system (Cixous 1981a: 253). In her later writing Cixous shifts her position slightly so that, like Woolf, she states that men and women can both write this type of femi-nine sentence, but that women are more likely to use it. She says that writing must be bisexual which recalls Woolf's notion of androgyny: 'There is no invention of other I's, no poetry, no fiction without a certain homosexuality' (Cixous 1981b: 97).

Luce Irigaray employs many elements of Lacanian psychoanalysis in her work. She describes women's writing as *parler femme*: 'her language in which "she" goes off in all directions and in which "he" is unable to discern the coherence of any meaning. Contradictory words seem a little crazy to the logic of reason, and inaudible for him who listens with ready-made grids, a code prepared in advance' (Irigaray 1985: 103). Again, we can see a recuperation of qualities which are attributed to women by men. She believes that women are able to use this type of language because, as she says, our sexual morphology is multiple and based on contiguity, in contrast to male sexuality which is unitary; thus she locates the difference in writing. She states: 'One must listen to her differently in order to hear an "other meaning" which is constantly in the process of weaving itself, at the same time ceaselessly embracing words and yet casting them off to avoid becoming fixed, immobilized. . . . Her statements are never identical to anything. Their distinguishing feature is contiguity. They touch *upon*' (ibid.: 84).

Irigaray herself has turned from writing on philosophy and psychoanalysis to writing short experimental prose passages; she is opposed to the authoritarian subject/object division of conventional syntax; she leaves out verbs, making her style almost telegraphic in structure; her writing is full of puns: for example, the title of one article is 'Ce Sexe qui n'en est pas un'('This sex which is not *one* sex', i.e. which is multiple, but also 'This sex which is not a sex at all'). The structure of her texts is repetitive, cumulative rather than linear, using double or multiple voices, often ending without full closure.

Julia Kristeva, like Cixous and Irigaray, works from within an essentially Lacanian framework, but she is strongly opposed to the notion of *écriture féminine*. Nevertheless, she uses the term 'the semiotic' to refer to the pre-linguistic stage of development of the child; the semiotic is an area of rhythmic pulsions in active opposition to the symbolic, the stable system of language. The semiotic is described as anarchic and as an area of rhythm, colour and play in language. The semiotic breaks through into the symbolic from time to time; for example, in poetic writing. The semiotic is associated with the pre-Oedipal stage of unity with the mother, and is repressed into the unconscious on entering the symbolic order of the Father, the Law. Kristeva thinks that women, because they do not have a proper place within the symbolic, have a special relationship with the semiotic. Thus, although she rejects *écriture féminine*, women, for her, still have a privileged access to the semiotic, and are more likely to exploit this in writing. It is, therefore, rather paradoxical that when studying the rupture of the semiotic in literature, she studies male writers such as Céline, Mallarmé and Lautréamont. Perhaps we can understand this when she suggests that this type of writing is available to all speaking subjects prepared to take on bisexuality: 'All speaking subjects have within themselves a certain bisexuality which is precisely the possibility to explore all the sources of signification, that which posits a meaning as well as that which multiplies, pulverises and finally revives it' (Kristeva 1981: 165). This seems very similar to statements by Woolf, Cixous and Irigaray which attempt to state that women's writing is different from men's, whilst being unable to ignore the fact that men have written in this experimental fashion, and have perhaps been more renowned for this type of writing than women. This is not to suggest that women have not written in an experimental way, and in fact this type of analysis can be used when analysing their writing (see Hanscombe and Smyers 1987).

Kristeva believes that the use of the semiotic in literature is potentially revolutionary for she says: 'To the extent that any activity resists the symbolic (or in the case of semiotic signifying, occupies it in a hit and run fashion), it is revolutionary' (Kristeva 1981: 166). Thus, in the same way as Irigaray and Cixous, she holds that significant political action can be undertaken in language itself. And she goes on to say: 'In a culture where the speaking subjects are conceived of as masters of their speech, they have what is called a "phallic" position. The fragmentation of language in a text calls into question the very posture of this mastery' (ibid.: 166). Thus, for Kristeva, the invoking of the semiotic in literature will shake the foundations of this phallic position.

To sum up what I have said about Woolf and the French feminists, it is possible to see that all of them begin with a position of stating that female writing is radically different from male writing in terms of linguistic structure and content. None of them, however, with the exception of Woolf, really goes on to define the male sentence as such. Woolf gives one example of the male sentence but does not describe its linguistic components in general. The French feminists give no examples, and do not define the male sentence, assuming perhaps that it is a commonsense 'naturalized' category to which we all have access. They all also state that male writers can use the female sentence when they have achieved a form of bisexuality or androgyny. They give no guidelines on situations when or if women can use the male sentence. Finally, they do not make clear whether this use of a 'feminine' sentence is part of unconscious processing to which all women have access or whether its use is a conscious artistic decision.

Linguistic analyses of difference

There have been a number of linguistic analyses which have tried to test empirically claims that women and men have different styles of writing. Mary Hiatt chose to focus on a range of elements which it is claimed differentiate women's writing from men's (Hiatt 1977). However, throughout her analysis of one hundred passages from popular fiction and non-fictional writing, Hiatt consistently confuses content analysis and linguistic analysis, and bases her analysis largely on stereotypes of what women are supposed to be like. For example, she states that 'The aim of . . . women apparently is to please, to be charming, witty and amusing. This aim can fairly be said to be a manifestation of approval-seeking behaviour of which women in general are accused. They "win" by cajoling, a subtle sort of seductiveness, by pretending that they aren't serious' (ibid.: 24). This interpretation of her results is clearly informed by phallocentrism. She asserts that in her set of passages from books by males and females, she found that there were significant differences between the writing styles. For example, she states that women writers in general use shorter sentences, which she assumes are structurally less complex than longer sentences – a value-judgement in itself. She goes on to claim that, because of a perceived lack of variety in sentence length, 'fewer of the female writers possess a noteworthy style than do their male counterparts' (ibid.: 32) and, although she claims that the female fiction writer's style is in fact complex and varied, 'their stylistic complexity is far less individualized than is that of the men. Perhaps it is just that they do not "dare" as does a Mailer' (ibid.: 34). Here, Hiatt is confusing an analysis of the feminine with an analysis of the female, in that what she seems to be describing is a style of writing which *could* be categorized as feminine and which only a limited number of women writers actually employ.

In addition to sentence length, she analyses the frequency of use of exclamation marks and parenthetical statements, both of which she assumes would be stereotypically more characteristic of female writing. Finding that the women writers in her sample use parenthesis more frequently than the men, she interprets this in the following way: 'if parentheses indicate non-essential material, then the women non-fiction writers certainly seem to feel that more of what they have to say is in a sense disposable' (ibid.: 45). She also considers logical connectives such as 'however', 'because', 'so', etc. On the basis of this evidence, she argues that women use a less authoritative style than men. In her discussion on the type of adverbs used by men and women she states: 'There is an apparent active quality to the men's fiction as opposed to the emotive quality of the women's' (Hiatt 1977: 99). She claims that women use 'really' more often than men, and this she states is indicative of a lack of assertiveness; however, one might be led to ask whether an overuse of 'really' might not indicate an excess of assertiveness (especially if it had occurred within men's writing). She concludes by asking:

> One might ask *why* is the way women write more moderate, consistent and evenhanded than the way men write? The chief reason is doubtless that women are a minority group, more likely to conform than to dare. . . . Under the circumstances, it is to be expected that they seem at times unsure that anyone will believe them, reluctant to arrive at conclusions, a bit over-determined to present a cheerful face. (Ibid.: 136)

She goes on to say: 'The women's style is also more perceptive than that of the men [since] they are denied access to a world of actions' (ibid.: 137). However, before accepting Hiatt's arguments that on linguistic grounds there are clear distinctions to be made between male and female writing, it must be noted that Hiatt frequently overinterprets on the basis of minimal differences in style, and frequently labels elements which she feels occur within women's writing as negative. Similarly, she does not consider that her categorization of texts into male and female might be at all problematic. Feminist theory has been concerned in the last twenty years with the differences within the term 'woman', far more than it has been concerned with making global statements about 'woman'.

Susan Leonardi is another critic who has analysed the gendered sentence in terms of its language components, this time in relation to Woolf's fictional writing; she shows that the gendered sentence can be analysed in terms of sentence structure/syntax, subject-matter, completion and logic or reference. In terms of sentence structure, Leonardi says that Woolf wanted to reject the man's sentence which she defines as 'the hierarchical sentence of the literary tradition she inherited, a sentence which, with its high degree of subordination, makes so clear the judgement about what is more important and what is less' (Leonardi 1986: 151). David Tallentire (1986) has carried out a statistical analysis of Woolf's writing and found that she does not use subordinate clauses frequently. Her writing can be characterized by the use of co-ordination, primarily 'and'. This is quite interesting, since co-ordination is considered to be a less sophisticated way of organizing text. Woolf defines the male sentence as a hierarchical sentence in terms of its structure, and as Leonardi says: 'The hierarchical sentence is a kind of metaphor for an ordered world, for ordered relationships in general' (Leonardi 1986: 151). Thus, the male sentence is seen as a sentence which contains subordinate clauses, but the explanation given for the effect of these clauses is one of hierarchizing and ordering. We might be able to find examples of the female sentence, full of subordination, where the subordination could be interpreted as refusing closure, endlessly deferring an authoritative statement, and therefore it is clearly not sentence structure which is really at issue here, but interpretative schemata.

Leonardi also asserts that in Woolf's prose there is a lack of completion which she takes to be a feature of the female sentence. Yet when we even discuss the notion of the sentence we are talking in terms of completion, which creates an immediate contradiction. There are perhaps other ways of classifying language which are not concerned with the notion of units being complete in this way. Leonardi also alludes to a common assumption about women's writing: that there is a lack of rationality and authority. The female sentence is often seen to be one where the writer simply pours out her feelings into the text; women's writing is often characterized as the outpouring of the soul, without the mediation of a structure or plan. Control is an important element in defining the male sentence, as one of its primary characteristics is that the writer chose to include a certain element and could have chosen to express himself in a different way. Thus, male modernist writers could also write critical 'masculine' essays about their 'feminine' writing, showing that their 'feminine' writing was a matter of conscious choice. Yet, this assumes that women do not write in a rational, controlled way and that their writing is not a matter of choice. Mary Ellman even criticizes Simone de Beauvoir for 'the authority of her prose' (Ellman 1968: 212). However much we attempt to 'deconstruct' the rational, and logic, it seems rather counterproductive to suggest that the rational is allied to maleness and hence out of bounds for females. The male sentence is therefore seen to be one which is clear and rational, where the author appears to have control. This type of sentence is typically seen as an assertion, appealing to authority. Yet, are these in fact characteristics of sentences, or are they rather elements of the ideological stereotype of males in our society?

A further point which Leonardi points to is subject-matter; many critics have been led slightly astray into defining the female sentence as that which describes female experience, and thus the male sentence would, in this perspective, be one which described male experience. Since a great deal of western literature is concerned with a description of women's experience, by men, this cannot be the case. Furthermore, from a poststructuralist point of view, we might also question the notion that writing is about experience in the real world. Any man who has learned the conventions of *écriture féminine* or of women's writing, can write a 'woman's' book. Similarly, any woman can write a male sentence.

When I asked a group of students to give typical male and female sentences they came up with sentences which were different in terms of content on stereotypical grounds. For example, they produced the following opposing pairs:

> 1 I came I saw I conquered. *Male*
> Shelia felt as if her whole being was conquered by this man whom she hardly knew. *Female*
>
> 2 I'm hungry and I want something to eat. *Male*
> I wonder if there's something to eat. *Female*

These sentences can be categorized as male and female according to their stereotypical subject-matter, but also interestingly in terms of some of their linguistic features. In example 1, the aggression of the first statement is characterized as male together with its brevity – context might also have some bearing here. The female sentence is far more grammatically complex than the male sentence which is linked only by parataxis, that is, by that fact that the clauses are placed side by side; but it is classified as female because it is concerned with emotion and dominance. The second set of sentences is largely to be distinguished, not by subject-matter, but by indirectness of expression. Thus subject-matter can be seen to be a factor which may lead people to assume that sentences are gendered in some way, but it cannot be considered in isolation from other factors.

A number of feminist theorists have suggested that the use of metaphor is crucial to describing the distinction between women's and men's writing. For example, Ellen Moers suggests that women tend to use bird metaphors when they describe women characters; she cites lines from Christina Rossetti's poetry; for example, 'My heart is like a singing bird / Whose nest is in a watered shoot' (Moers in M. Eagleton 1986: 209) and also 'Me, poor dove that must not coo – eagle that must not soar' (ibid.). Moers says: 'Is the bird merely a species of the littleness metaphor? Or are birds chosen because they are tortured, as little girls are tortured by boys . . . or because bird-victims can be ministered to by girl victims . . . or is it because birds are beautiful and exotic creatures, symbols of half-promised, half-forbidden sensual delights . . . because birds are soft and round and sensuous, because they palpitate and flutter when held in the hands and especially because they sing?' (ibid.: 209). This analysis of the use of bird metaphors in women's writing has a number of problematic assumptions about women themselves: that women are always weak, are victims and are sensual. Moers goes on to say: 'From Mary Wollstonecraft's *Maria* – to Brontë's *Jane Eyre* – to Anne Frank's *Diary of a Young Girl* – I find that the caged bird makes a metaphor that truly deserves the adjective female' (ibid.: 210). Horner and Zlosnick argue in a similar way that women's writing is characterized by a preponderance of certain types of metaphor. They suggest that 'many novels by women writers of the late nineteenth and early twentieth centuries have certain configurations of metaphor in common. What are these configurations? We noticed repeated use of a dynamic relationship between room, house, land and sea and we begin to realise that this relationship carried a significance which went beyond plot' (Horner and Zlosnick 1990: 6). For them, women writers in this period tend to concentrate on descriptions of enclosed and open spaces and this entails a metaphorical pattern throughout their work. However, whilst it may be the case that certain women writers within a very specific period and style of writing may be characterized as drawing on certain metaphorical tendencies, it is clearly not the case for other women writers. [. . .]

Finally, in addition to these elements, the gendered sentence is also defined as one where it is assumed that meaning is different for male- and female-authored texts. For the male sentence, meaning is a simple matter, where language is a transparent medium, not drawing attention to itself, a medium which simply carries thought. The thought which is carried is rational, assertive, clear. These adjectives which we are using to describe the male sentence bear a striking resemblance to the ideologically formulated notion of the male character. The female sentence, in contrast, is presented as opaque and difficult to understand.

In order to challenge some of these assumptions, we should analyse some sentences which would, according to these theorists, normally be classed as male or female. The following two passages might well be considered as being made up of 'male' sentences:

1 This incident, which might be said to have added to his undoing, did not arise out of Mr Stone's passion for gardens. Gardening as he practised it was no more than a means, well suited to his age, which was 62, of exhausting the spare time and energy with which his undemanding duties in one of the departments of the Excal company, his status as a bachelor and his still excellent physique amply provided him.

2 I went to the cloakroom and put on my overcoat and cap. I could never bring myself to sport a trilby or a bowler; the cap provided some protection, even though it signally failed to cover the ears. I could not descend to the Arthur woolly beret level. I set off down the stairs. I always used the lift to come up, the stairs to come down. The lift carried the hazards of social life. It was a concession to old age that I no longer walked up.

According to the criteria outlined above, we could classify these two texts as containing examples of the male sentence: both texts are made up of sentences which have subordinate clauses; the sentences used are complete; they are rational and straightforward (neither text has any foregrounded language items); both texts are about male characters. Because of these facts, we should be led to assume that the authors are male; however, whilst text 1 is indeed by a male, V. S. Naipaul, text 2 was written by Iris Murdoch.

Let us then consider the following examples of the 'female' sentence:

O
tell me about
Anna Livia! I want to hear all

About Anna Livia. Well, you know Anna Livia? Yes, of course, we all know Anna Livia. Tell me all. Tell me now. You'll die when you hear. Well, you know when the old cheb went futt and did what you know. Yes I know go on. Wash quit and don't be dabbling. Tuck up your sleeves and loosen your talktapes. And don't butt me – hike! – when you bend. Or whatever it was they threed to make out when he thried in the Fiendish park.

4 She is giving birth. With the strength of a lioness. Of a plant. Of a cosmogony. Of a woman. . . . A desire for text! Confusion! What

possesses her? A child! Paper! Intoxications! I'm overflowing! My breasts overflow! Milk. Ink. The moment of suckling. And I? I too am hungry. The taste of milk, of ink.

Both texts could be classified as being made up of 'female' sentences, since they do not use subordinate clauses (most of the clauses are non-co-ordinated); some of the clauses are incomplete; neither of these texts could be defined as particularly rational or authoritarian (there does not appear to be in either text one 'voice' which is dominant); both are about women's experience, both draw attention to themselves in terms of their language use and they are quite difficult to read. Yet, although text 4 is by a woman, Hélène Cixous, text 3 is by James Joyce. It would seem that these definitions of sentences according to gender are clearly inadequate, and perhaps they are eliding avant-garde or experimental writing with feminine/female writing.

Challenges to the gendered sentence

To attempt to escape from this critical impasse, let us look briefly at the work of Monique Wittig whose position is in contrast to the work of other French feminists. One noticeable point of divergence is in her aim to 'deconstruct' the difference between male and female sentences.

> That there is no feminine writing must be said at the outset, and one makes a mistake in using and giving currency to this expression. What is this 'feminine' in feminine writing? It stands for Woman, thus merging a practice with a myth, the myth of Woman. 'Woman' cannot be associated with writing because 'Woman' is an imaginary formation and not a concrete reality; it is that old branding by the enemy now flourished like a tattered flag refound and won in battle. (Wittig 1983: 2)

Thus, for Wittig, it is important to dispense with a monolithic notion of 'woman'. She goes on to say: ' "Feminine writing" is the naturalising metaphor of the brutal political fact of the domination of women, and as such it enlarges the apparatus under which "femininity" presents itself' (ibid.: 2). She shows how this metaphor of the feminine is used to undermine the fact that women's writing is work, a production process, like men's writing. She notes that *écriture féminine* seems to refer to an almost biological process, what she terms a 'secretion' (ibid.: 2).

Thus, as with everything which is labelled masculine/male or feminine/female, these terms have very little to do with biological sex difference, but a great deal to do with assertions of power. In defining the female sentence we are not in fact defining a sentence at all, but defining females; this is just part of an ideological enterprise; we do not define males to anything like the same extent. As Cameron says: 'Stereotypes, however false, tend to persist for as long as they reinforce important social inequalities' (Cameron 1985: 33). Defining the feminine sentence as lacking rationality, coherence, assertiveness and so on, is an attempt to set up a particular subject-position for females in the real world.

Reprinted from Sara Mills, *Feminist Stylistics,* (London: Routledge, 1995).

Further reading for part one

(full publication details are given in the bibliography)

MANY OF THE ISSUES RAISED in this part are explored with subtlety and depth in fictional and autobiographical writings. The complex interconnections of identity, self, voice and language (in the literal sense of *which* language(s) you speak) for women who migrate from one culture to another are well explored, for instance, in Eva Hoffman's memoir *Lost in Translation: A Life in a New Language* (1989); they are also a theme of Maxine Hong Kingston's *The Woman Warrior* (1977). Both these authors have interesting things to say on how learning a new language affects identity, and how femininity is done differently in different language communities (English versus Polish for Hoffman, and versus Chinese for Hong Kingston).

The question of women acquiring a 'public' language, one with currency and/or prestige outside the immediate family and community, is taken up in A.J. Verdelle's novel *This Rain Coming* (1996), which is written in an African–American vernacular. For US readers, probably the best-known discussion of the public/private question is Richard Rodriguez's *Hunger of Memory* (1981). This memoir by a Mexican–American writer does not take up issues of gender, and its argument is controversial; but a good deal of what Rodriguez says about the negotiation of identity and the potential for empowerment through language has application to gender as well as ethnicity.

On women and writing, Virginia Woolf's classic *A Room of One's Own* (1977 [1929]) remains a text every feminist should read; as I suggested in the introduction, an interesting text to place alongside it is Gcina Mhlophe's story 'The Toilet' (1987). Cherrie Moraga and Gloria Anzaldua have edited an influential collection, *This Bridge Called My Back* (1981), in which US women of colour discuss their relation to writing (Anzaldua has also explored questions of bilingualism, writing in both Spanish and English). Adrienne Rich (see especially *On Lies, Secrets and Silence* (1980)) and Alice Walker (*In Search of Our Mothers' Gardens* (1984)) are among the feminist writers who have reflected in essays on their relation to language, to writing and to other women writers.

I noted in the preface that there are several textbooks, anthologies and readers on the subject of women's writing and feminist literary theory; accessible and relatively recent ones include Mary Eagleton's *Feminist Literary Theory: A Reader* (revised edn. 1996) and Pam Morris's *Feminism and Literature* (1993). Elaine Marks and Isabelle de Courtivron's *New French Feminisms* (1981) is much less recent, and the picture it presents of 'French feminism' has been much criticized; nevertheless it has been very influential, containing selections from the work of theorists like Hélène Cixous, Luce Irigaray, Julia Kristeva and the journal Simone de Beauvoir was associated with, *Questions Féministes*.

Some collections of work more specifically by feminist *linguists* include contributions focusing on writing, style and literary production. An early collection which contains several useful essays is *Women and Language in Literature and Society* (McConnell-Ginet, Borker and Furman 1980); being 'old' it is no longer easy to get hold of, especially outside the USA, but copies may be found in academic libraries. Sara Mills's more recent edited collection *Language and Gender: Interdisciplinary Perspectives* (1995b) contains material about women, language and literature; her *Feminist Stylistics* (1995a) from which an extract is reprinted above, also deals with questions of gender in texts (broadly defined, not only literary).

PART TWO

Representations: Sexist language and sexist discourse

Introduction to part two

THE PIECES REPRINTED IN THIS section take up a range of questions about the representation of gender in language. I have grouped them under three subheadings: 'Theoretical Questions', 'The Debate on Nonsexist Language' and 'Approaches to Discourse'.

Theoretical Questions

The 'Theoretical Questions' taken up in the first set of chapters concern the origins and the significance of sexism in language: where does sexist language come from and what are the arguments for thinking it matters? The first piece, consisting of extracts from Dale Spender's *Man Made Language* (1980) advances an argument that language is sexist because men have had power to determine the meanings it encodes, and these meanings embody men's perceptions of reality rather than women's. Since Spender also supports a strong version of the 'Sapir–Whorf hypothesis' according to which languages *impose* a certain classification of reality on their speakers, this sexism is self-perpetuating.

The next chapter, Maria Black and Rosalind Coward's 'Linguistic, social and sexual relations' (1981) is a critical review of *Man Made Language* that takes issue with Spender's line of argument. Black and Coward have a complicated agenda which it may be helpful to comment on here. On the one hand they use linguistic theory to criticize Spender's notion of 'language', devoting a lot of space to explaining why this does not make sense from the point of view of linguistics (for instance, Spender does not properly distinguish between what linguists would regard as the 'real' rules of grammar and the kinds of arbitrary pronouncements made by prescriptive grammarians – on the latter see Bodine, this volume). On the other hand they think linguistics, even in its socially-oriented variants, has serious limitations when it comes to understanding the *ideological* nature of language. The political position from which Black and Coward approach this issue is a socialist-feminist one, and they are intervening in a debate about ideology that was going on, in 1981, within Marxist and poststructuralist theory – though it is not necessary to appreciate the fine nuances of that debate in order to understand what they are saying about Dale Spender, and more generally about the ideological effects of language in relation to gender.

Black and Coward locate sexism not in fixed meanings encoded by the linguistic system ('language') but in the way meaning is constructed in particular contexts ('discourse[s]'). They observe for instance that it is common to read newspaper reports that say things like 'ten survivors, two of them women', but you never read a report saying 'ten survivors, two of them men'. This is a regular pattern, but it is not to do with the *structure* of the English language. 'Ten survivors, two of them men' is not ungrammatical in English: in principle there is no reason why it should not occur just as often as the 'two of them women' alternative. The fact that it does *not* occur as often is part of what Black and Coward view as a key form of asymmetry between men and women: women are always defined by their gender, whereas men are permitted to pass themselves off as generic human beings with no gender. In some cases (for example, the generic use of *he*) one could argue this asymmetry is institutionalized in (prescriptive) grammatical rules, but it shows up just as often in cases where no rule compels language-users to reproduce it. Black and Coward suggest that the way to tackle the asymmetry is not to de-gender women but to *engender* men.

There are some interesting parallels with this line of argument, though also some divergences from it, in the work of the French philosopher and psychoanalyst Luce Irigaray, whose 1987 essay 'Linguistic sexes and genders' is reprinted here. Irigaray, like Black and Coward, points to an asymmetry between men and women, but while she would agree that men are represented as the universal human subjects, her argument is not that men have no gender whereas women are defined by it, it is rather that men are the *only* gender that is recognized in language or culture. The structure of language and the conventions of discourse obliterate sexual difference, working as if there were only one sex, namely men.

This might seem an odd claim to make in relation to French, the language Irigaray discusses. French is a 'grammatical gender' language, in which nouns are categorized as either masculine or feminine, whether or not they refer to sexed beings. It could be (and has been) argued that languages of this type are far more attentive to sexual difference than English. Conversely it could be (and has been) argued that since grammatical gender languages obey *formal* principles (that is, it is the form and not the meaning of a word that dictates its gender), gender distinctions in them have nothing to do with sexual difference, and so cannot give rise to the kinds of sexism English-speaking feminists complain of. Irigaray, however, wants to show that neither of these arguments holds water. In French, she suggests, the masculine gender tends to denote something more valuable than the feminine. She gives the example of masculine/feminine pairs like *moissoneur* (masculine, meaning 'harvester', 'person who harvests' and *moissoneuse* (feminine, but not meaning 'female person who harvests'; instead it refers to the machine a harvester uses). The difference that underpins gender distinctions of this kind is not 'man/woman' but 'man/not-man'. It is one sex, men, around whom everything revolves.

Ann Bodine is also concerned with the historical processes that give rise to sexism in our linguistic practices, but her 'Androcentrism in prescriptive grammar' (1975) deals less in theoretical abstraction than in historical facts about the development of particular prescriptive rules governing the generic use of the masculine gender in English. This classic discussion is a useful reminder that specific pieces of linguistic sexism do have a history, which it is possible to uncover by looking at historical records (in this case, prescriptive grammar texts): as Black and Coward also underline when they note that prescriptive grammar is an excellent example of an 'ideological discourse', it is a mistake to imagine sexist discourse practices have all been with us since the dawn of time, and are inextricably built into the core structure of language.

This point brings us back to the 'language or discourse' issue: the documents Bodine quotes show that the *reasons* grammarians originally gave for enforcing prescriptions about the generic masculine were invariably to do with beliefs about the proper relationship between men and women (that the former should take precedence over the latter), and *not* beliefs about grammar, etymology or any other primarily linguistic phenomenon. Over time, interestingly, the reverse has come to be true: today, defenders of traditional androcentrism usually protest that it is 'just a fact about grammar' which is not intended to mark women's inferiority in the real world, and is not interpreted by reasonable people as doing so. This change in the commonest arguments for using masculine terms generically goes along with a change in social attitudes: the idea that women are inferior to men is no longer unquestioned common sense − indeed, it is repugnant to most contemporary sensibilities. Thus a rule that was originally made on overtly ideological grounds (language should express the natural law of male superiority) can now only be justified by portraying it as intrinsic to the structure of English and devoid of any ideological significance.

The debate on nonsexist language

The chapters grouped together under the heading of 'The debate on nonsexist language' deal with feminist arguments and strategies for tackling the problem of sexism in English. The first piece, Douglas Hofstadter's 'A person paper on purity in language' (presented under the pseudonym 'William Satire', a pun on the name of the *New York Times*'s conservative language columnist William Safire), sets out to show the hollowness of many familiar arguments against reforming sexist language. It asks us to imagine a kind of English where race is treated as gender is in the English we actually speak: for instance, *white* is the generic term equivalent to our *man*, and there are different pronouns and titles denoting white and black people. Hofstadter does not pose the question whether such a way of talking would cause or reinforce racist thinking; clearly, there is plenty of racism among English-speakers even without racial differences being encoded in English grammar. But whether or not it affects thought, language is a potent cultural symbol. Hofstadter's point is that if we find his imaginary racist version of English shocking and offensive it is somewhat illogical to find the real-life sexist version any more tolerable.

The next two chapters debate the value of (and the values embodied in) guidelines on nonsexist language. The first is the introduction to a recent handbook, Margaret Doyle's *A–Z of Non-Sexist Language* (1995), which represents the most common or 'orthodox' view among people with feminist sympathies on what sexist language is and what should be done about it. My own piece, 'Lost in translation', takes issue with Margaret Doyle directly and rather polemically: originally published in the radical feminist journal *Trouble & Strife*, it is a critical review of her *A–Z* and another publication in the same genre, Miller and Swift's *A Handbook of Non-Sexist Language* (revised UK edition 1995). Criticism focuses on the liberal, 'equal opportunities' ideology underlying most nonsexist language guidelines, and their liberal ambivalence about being seen as either 'prescriptive' or 'politically correct'.

Susan Ehrlich and Ruth King also suggest that the guideline-writing approach has its limitations: their piece, 'Gender-based language reform and the social construction of meaning' (1992) takes us back to the 'sexist language or sexist discourse' argument. Ehrlich and King show how feminist linguistic reforms can be neutralized or turned against their original feminist spirit as they are widely used with other meanings in discourse. This suggests that the kind of language change embodied in guidelines and handbooks can only ever be provisional: it does not 'work' uniformly and forever because meaning is not fixed by authorities, it is ongoingly constructed in real social contexts; and the latter continue to be pervaded by sexist and antifeminist assumptions. Language reform is most successful, Ehrlich and King assert, when it is part of some wider antisexist initiative and enjoys strong institutional support.

Approaches to discourse

The last two chapters have been placed under the heading 'Approaches to discourse', underlining their authors' commitment to the view that both the origins and the effects of sexism are best analysed at the level of discourse – where language is being used to communicate in particular contexts. Kate Clark's 'The linguistics of blame' (1992) belongs to the current of work (not exclusively a feminist current, though feminists are well represented in it) known as 'critical discourse analysis'. It is a study of the reporting of male violence against women in the *Sun* newspaper, and it shows that texts can be extremely sexist, indeed misogynist, even though they may make little use of the kinds of expressions that are discussed disapprovingly in nonsexist language handbooks. Instead of looking for such expressions, Clark looks for recurring patterns in the choices *Sun* writers make about vocabulary and grammar. These work, she argues, to create an overall message that women are often to blame for men's violence.

Sally McConnell-Ginet's 'The sexual (re)production of meaning: a discourse-based approach' (1989) is a much more theoretical piece, which I could have put in the first, 'theoretical' section (in some ways it is an extension of the argument between Dale Spender and her critics Black and Coward; it also has points of contact with Ann Bodine's historical discussion). I have chosen to put it here, however, because McConnell-Ginet's argument constructs a bridge to the topic of Part Three, the speech behaviour of women and men. (Indeed, her argument might suggest – I would not disagree – that the structural division I have imposed between 'representation' (the topic of this part) and gendered behaviour (Part Three) is to some extent artificial.) This is a densely-argued piece (though it rewards the effort needed to appreciate it), and I will therefore devote some space to putting its argument in context.

McConnell-Ginet argues that the asymmetries researchers have uncovered between women and men in actual communicational situations are likely to affect what utterances are conventionally taken to mean. Drawing on insights from 'pragmatics' (the study of how utterances are interpreted in real-life contexts) McConnell-Ginet notes that to understand someone we have to make inferences about their intentions. The words they utter are just the tip of the communicative iceberg: understanding also depends on a lot of background knowledge. And in a sexist culture, that knowledge includes numerous sexist assumptions, which we have to make use of to make sense of utterances, even if we do not agree with them. As McConnell-Ginet points out, a person who says to me 'you think like a woman' almost certainly intends to insult me, and can succeed in insulting me *even though I don't agree there's anything wrong with the way women think*, because I recognize the intention and am aware of the widely-held belief that women think illogically. Conversely, I can reply 'and you think like a man', intending this to be an insult, and not be understood by a man as insulting him because the proposition 'men think illogically' is only my private opinion, not a piece of societal common knowledge. (A less flippant example cited by McConnell-Ginet is that women still can't say 'no' to men's sexual advances and be sure they will be understood as 'really meaning no'. As Ehrlich and King also remark, common knowledge still holds that when women say no in this context it really means 'yes' or 'maybe' or 'keep trying'.)

Conversation is a co-operative, joint endeavour where all participants are predisposed to work at seeing the world through the eyes of another, in the interests of understanding what the other is trying to convey. Communication will not happen unless you make some kind of imaginative identification with your interlocutor. But you are probably even more predisposed to do this – more able to do it or less able *not* to do it – when you occupy a subordinate position, not merely in the abstract 'society' but in the actual, concrete situation where conversation is taking place. Sexist meanings circulate and are viewed as legitimate or normal, not (as Dale Spender might argue) because men have in some mysterious abstract way fixed the semantics of every word in the language, but because they are dominant in many of the situations where language is actually put to use.

On a more optimistic note, McConnell-Ginet adds that women working together in a feminist context can use the same principle – that meanings are legitimated when they are constantly invoked as 'common knowledge' – to generate and then reinforce new, shared understandings in opposition to sexism. For instance, she says (and she is surely correct) that it is getting progressively harder to use masculine terms generically *and be understood in the generic sense*. You may genuinely intend the terms to be generic, but after twenty-five years of the feminist critique you can no longer rely on this intention being attributed to you automatically by other people; so the old meaning doesn't work any more. This realization impels many speakers who do not feel strongly about nonsexist language to start using it anyway – it is the price they pay for understanding, for communication, and most language-users will put those things first.

Changing the language?

Overall, the aim of this section of the book is to show that the most familiar ideas about sexism in language may well be oversimplified, and that the issues involved provoke disagreement among feminist linguistic researchers. As a matter of both theory and practical experience, many feminists now want to emphasize the degree to which meaning is context-bound and variable; it is more difficult than has commonly been assumed (whether by liberal guideline writers or by those who rant against the Orwellian 'excesses' of 'political correctness') for organized interest groups of any ideological persuasion to exert control over it. The difficulty is, however, more acute for feminists than it is for sexists, since sexism is so much more ingrained than feminism in most contexts where language is used. Though it certainly serves the interests of a particular group (men), sexism is not so much the ideology of an organized interest group as it is our default way of thinking and talking.

As many contributors to this section say explicitly, however, that does not mean either that feminists should do nothing, or that their interventions to date have achieved nothing. Rather it means that the feminist critique of language is an ongoing project, and will doubtless remain ongoing for the foreseeable future. 'Changing the language' is a well-worn expression, but it is also a misleading one: really it is shorthand for 'changing the behaviour of those who use the language'. That is not something you can accomplish once and for all in the space of twenty-five years. The prescriptive grammarians discussed by Ann Bodine did not succeed in eradicating singular *they* from ordinary speech in 250 years – though they did succeed in stigmatizing it. Today a stigma attaches, somewhat similarly, to the use of some kinds of sexist language in certain contexts (that is precisely what the anti-'political correctness' lobby complains of: not that they are *forbidden* to use generic *he*, say, for that is almost never true,[1] but that *if* they use it, they are liable to be stigmatized with the pejorative label 'sexist'); so it might well be argued that, all things considered, feminist reformers are not doing badly.

Note

1   In Britain, the one context in which generic masculine terms may not used by law is job advertisements. Otherwise, my own research suggests that the status of nonsexist language rules is variable, and usually equivocal. Some academic journals, publishing houses and professional/educational institutions do enforce their nonsexist language guidelines quite strictly (especially for official documents which do not have a named individual author), but most use guidelines

to assist and encourage *voluntary* compliance – adherence to the recommendations is rarely enforced and quite often it is not even monitored. So while guidelines are very common, there continues to be individual choice about using or not using nonsexist language in the majority of contexts. What you don't have a choice about, as noted above, is how your choices are interpreted; but being liable to accusations of prejudice if you ignore the guidelines is not the same thing as being censored or punished for ignoring them. Many 'anti-PC' arguments rest on not making this distinction.

Theoretical questions

Chapter 6

Dale Spender

EXTRACTS FROM *MAN MADE LANGUAGE*

'THE OBJECTS AND EVENTS OF the world do not present themselves to us ready classified', states James Britton (1975). 'The categories into which they are divided are the categories into which *we divide them*' (p. 23). My question which arises from this statement is not whether it is an accurate assessment, for I readily accept that language is a powerful determinant of reality, but who is the **WE** to whom James Britton refers? Who are these people who 'make the world' and what are the principles behind their division, organization, and classification?

Although not explicitly stated, Britton is referring to males. It is men who have made the world which women must inhabit, and if women are to begin to make their own world, it is necessary that they understand some of the ways in which such *creation* is accomplished. This means exploring the relationship of language and reality.

Susanne Langer (1976) has pointed out that human beings are symbolizing creatures (it is, perhaps, our capacity to symbolize that differentiates us from other species), and we are constantly engaged in the process of producing symbols as a means of categorizing and organizing our world. But it would be foolish to have complete faith in the system of order we have constructed because it is, from the outset, imperfect, only ever serving as an approximation. Yet it seems that we are foolish: we do 'trust' the world order we have created with our symbols and we frequently allow these representations to beguile us into accepting some of the most bizarre rules for making sense of the world. It is our capacity to symbolize and the use (or misuse) we make of the symbols we construct that constitutes the area of language, thought, and reality.

It is because we can be seduced by language that a debate has been waged for many years on the relationship of language, thought, and reality. On the one hand, there is considerable evidence that not all human beings are led to the same view of the world by the same physical evidence and on the other hand, is the explanation – namely the Sapir–Whorf hypothesis – that this is because of language. It is language which determines the limits of our world, which constructs our reality.

One of the tantalizing questions which has confronted everyone from philosophers to politicians is the extent to which human beings can 'grasp things as they really are'; yet in many ways this is an absurd question that could arise only in a mono-dimensional reality which subscribed to the concept of there being only *one* way that 'things' can be. Even if there were only one way, it is unlikely that as human beings we would be able to grasp that 'pure', 'objective' form, for all we have available is symbols, which have their own inherent limitations, and these symbols and representations are already circumscribed by the limitations of our own language.

Language is *not* neutral. It is not merely a vehicle which carries ideas. It is itself a shaper of ideas, it is the programme for mental activity (Whorf 1976). In this context it is nothing short of ludicrous to conceive of human beings as capable of grasping things as they really are, of being impartial recorders of their world. For they themselves, or some of them, at least, have created or constructed that world and they have reflected themselves within it.

Human beings cannot impartially describe the universe because in order to describe it they must first have a classification system. But, paradoxically, once they have that classification system, once they have a language, *they can see only certain arbitrary things*.

Such an understanding is not confined to linguistics. The sciences of physiology and biology have also helped to substantiate – sometimes inadvertently – the false nature of impartiality or objectivity. Evidence gathered from these disciplines demonstrates that we ourselves come into the process of organizing and describing the universe. Unfortunately for those advocates of the human capacity to 'grasp things as they really are' there is one basic flaw in their argument – they have failed to take into account that the brain can neither see nor hear:

> To speak metaphorically, the brain is quite blind and deaf, it has no direct contact with light or sound, but instead has to acquire all its information about the state of the outside world in the form of pulses of bio-electrical activity pumped along bundles of nerve fibres from the external surface of the body, its interface with the environment.
>
> (Smith 1971: 82)

The brain too, has to interpret: it too can only deal in symbols and never know the 'real' thing. And the programme for encoding and decoding those symbols, for translating and calculating, is set up by the language which we possess. What *we see* in the world around us depends in a large part on the principles we have encoded in our language:

> each of us has *to learn to see*. The growth of every human being is a slow process of learning 'the rules of seeing', without which we could not in any ordinary sense see the world around us. There is no reality of familiar shapes, colours and sounds to which we merely open our eyes. The information that we receive through our senses from the material world around us has to be interpreted according to certain human rules, before what we ordinarily call 'reality' forms.
>
> (Williams 1975: 33)

When one principle that has been encoded in our language (and thought) is that of sexism, the implications for 'reality' can readily be seen. So too can the implications for 'objectivity', because 'scientific method' has been frequently accepted as being 'above' fallible human processes and, because its truths have been paraded as incontestable, many individuals have had little confidence in their own experience when this has clashed with prevailing scientific 'truths'.

It is not just feminists who have come to challenge some of the accepted notions about the impartiality of science and who have focused on the relationship of language, thought, and reality – although there are distinctive and additional features of the feminist approach which I will discuss later. There is new interest in such areas as the philosophy or sociology of science in which the question of 'objectivity' is being taken up, and where old answers are being viewed as inadequate and false (Chalmers 1978: Kuhn 1972). That science is a dogma, just as were the feudal, clerical and market dogmas which preceded it, that is open to query and to challenge (Young 1975: 3), is not a traditional evaluation of scientific method, but it is an evaluation that is becoming increasingly more popular. That reason, objectivity and empiricism have been used to justify 'science' in a way that revelation, divine inspiration, and mythology have been used to justify 'religion', is a factor which has not been explored: yet the parallels exist. It has been just as heretical or crazy to challenge one dogma as it was in the past to challenge the other.

But this is changing. Alan Chalmers (1978), for example, tackles some of the misapprehensions that are held about science and scientific method, whereby the meaning of somethings as 'science' has implied 'some kind of merit, or special kind of reliability' (p. xiii). He, too, takes up some of the issues of language, thought, and reality when he readily demonstrates (partly by use of a diagram, p. 22) that not all human beings – scientists included – are led to the same view of the world by the same physical evidence, for what observers see when they view an object or event 'is not determined solely by the images on their retinas but depends also on the experience,

95

knowledge, expectations and general inner state of the observer' (p. 24), which, as Chalmers illustrates, may very often be culturally specific and which I would argue is largely determined by language, which is the means of ordering and structuring experiences, knowledge, expectations, and inner states.

Chalmers is intent on discrediting the premise that science *begins* with observation and he convincingly points out that this is a fallacy: contrary to the belief of the 'purity' of empiricism, he indicates that 'theory precedes observation' (p. 27) and the types of theories which are culturally available play a substantial role in determining what the observers – empirical scientists among them – can *see*.

When there are a sexist language and sexist theories culturally available, the observation of reality is also likely to be sexist. It is by this means that sexism can be perpetuated and reinforced as new objects and events, new data, have sexist interpretations projected upon them. Science is no more free of this bias than any other explanatory activity.

It is this recognition that human beings are part of the process of constructing reality and knowledge which has led Dwight Bolinger (1975) to 'reinterpret' our past and to assert that our history can validly be viewed *not* as the progressive intuiting of nature but as exteriorizing a way of looking at things as they are circumscribed by our language. Once certain categories are constructed within the language, we proceed to organize the world according to those categories. We even fail to see evidence which is not consistent with those categories.

This makes language a paradox for human beings: it is both a creative and an inhibiting vehicle. On the one hand, it offers immense freedom for it allows us to 'create' the world we live in; that so many different cultures have created so many different 'worlds' is testimony to this enormous and varied capacity (Berger and Luckmann 1972, have categorized this aspect of language as 'world openness', p. 69). But, on the other hand, we are restricted by that creation, limited to its confines, and, it appears, we resist, fear and dread any modifications to the structures we have initially created, even though they are 'arbitrary', approximate ones. It is this which constitutes a language *trap*.

It could be said that out of nowhere we invented sexism, we created the arbitrary and approximate categories of male-as-norm and female as deviant. A most original, imaginative creation. But, having constructed these categories in our language and thought patterns, we have now been trapped for we are most reluctant to organize the world any other – less arbitrary or imperfect – way. Indeed, it could even be argued that the trap which we have made is so pervasive that we cannot envisage a world constructed on any other lines.

It is, however, at this point that feminist insights into language, thought and reality are differentiated. While it could be said that we invented sexism from out of nowhere and utilized the principle in encoding reality, I doubt that feminists would make such a statement. While it could be argued that it was mere accident that 'objectivity' and the 'scientific method' came to acquire their meritorious[1] status and while such a discussion could occur without reference to gender, I also doubt whether feminists would completely accept such an explanation. The distinctive and additional feature of feminist analysis of language, thought, and reality is that feminists assert that we did *not* create these categories or the means of legitimating them. To return to James Britton's statement at the beginning of this chapter, I would reiterate that it has been the dominant group – in this case, males – who have created the world, invented the categories, constructed sexism and its justification, and developed a language trap which is in their interest.

Given that language is such an influential force in shaping our world, it is obvious that those who have the power to make the symbols and their meanings are in a privileged and highly advantageous position. They have, at least, the potential to order the world to suit their own ends, the potential to construct a language, a reality, a body of knowledge in which they are the central figures, the potential to legitimate their own primacy, and to create a system of beliefs which is beyond challenge (so that their superiority is 'natural' and 'objectively' tested). The group which has the power to ordain the structure of language, thought, and reality has the potential to create a world in which they are the central figures, while those who are not of their group are peripheral and therefore may be exploited.

In the patriarchal order this potential has been realized.

Males, as the dominant group, have produced language, thought, and reality. Historically it has been the structures, the categories, and the meanings which have been invented by males – though not of course by *all* males – and they have then been validated by reference to other males. In this process women have played little or no part.

[. . .] In order to live in the world, we must *name* it. Names are essential for the construction of reality for without a name it is difficult to accept the existence of an object, an event, a feeling. Naming is the means whereby we attempt to order and structure the chaos and flux of existence which would otherwise be an undifferentiated mass. By assigning names we impose a pattern and a meaning which allows us to manipulate the world.

But names are human products, the outcome of partial human vision and there is not a one-to-one correspondence between the names we possess and the material world they are designed to represent. We are dependent on names, but we are mistaken if we do not appreciate that they are imperfect and often misleading: one of the reasons that people are not led to the same view of the universe by the same physical evidence is that their vision is shaped by the different names they employ to classify that physical evidence.

Naming, however, is not a neutral or random process. It is an application of principles already in use, an extension of existing 'rules' (Sapir 1970) and of the act of naming. Benjamin Whorf has stated that it is no act of unfettered imagination, even in the wildest flights of nonsense, but a strict use of already patterned materials. If asked to invent forms not already prefigured in the patternment of his [*sic*] language, the speaker is negative in the same manner as if asked to make fried eggs without eggs.

(Whorf 1976: 256)

Names which cannot draw on past meanings are meaningless. New names, then, have their origins in the perspective of those doing the naming rather than in the object or event that is being named, and that perspective is the product of the prefigured patterns of language and thought. New names systematically subscribe to old beliefs, they are locked into principles that already exist, and there seems no way out of this even if those principles are inadequate or false.

All naming is of necessity biased and the process of naming is one of encoding that bias, of making a selection of what to emphasize and what to overlook on the basis of a 'strict use of already patterned materials'. Theoretically, if *all* members of a society were to provide names and these were to be legitimated, then a variety of biases could be available; the speakers of a language could 'choose', within the circumscribed limits of their own culture. Practically, however, difficulty arises when one group holds a monopoly on naming and is able to enforce its own particular bias on everyone, including those who do not share its view of the world. When one group holds a monopoly on naming, its bias is embedded in the names it supplies and these 'new' names help to maintain and strengthen its initial bias.

It is relatively easy to see how this is done. John Archer (1978) has documented this process at work in the construction of knowledge about sex roles, and he quotes one example of the work of Witkin *et al.* (1962). Witkin and his colleagues wanted to find out whether there were sex differences in the perception of a stimulus in a surrounding field and they designed an experiment where the subjects could either *separate* the stimulus (an embedded figure) from the surrounding field or else they could see the *whole*, they could see the stimulus as part of the surrounding field.

In many of these experiments Witkin and his colleagues found that females were more likely to see the stimulus and surrounding field as a whole while males were more likely to separate the stimulus from its context.

Witkin of course was obliged to name this phenomenon and he did so in accordance with the principles already encoded in the language. He took the existing patterns of male as positive and female as negative, and objectively devised his labels. He named the behaviour of males as *field independence*, thereby perpetuating and strengthening the image of male supremacy; he named the female behaviour as *field dependence* and thereby perpetuated and strengthened the image of female inferiority.

It is important to note that these names do not have their origins in the events: they are the product of Witkin's subjective view. There is nothing inherently dependent or independent in seeing something as a whole, or dividing it into parts. Witkin has coined names which are consistent with the patriarchal order and in the process he has extended and reinforced that order.

There are alternatives. With my particular bias I could well have named this same behaviour as positive for females and negative for males. I could have described the female response as *context awareness* and the male response as *context blindness*, and though these names would be just as valid as those which Witkin provided they would no doubt have been seen as *political* precisely because they do not adhere to the strict (sexist) rules by which the names of our language have traditionally been coined.

From this it can be seen that those who have the power to name the world are in a position to influence reality. Again, if more than one set of names were available, users of the language could elect to use those names which best reflected their interests; they could choose whether to call males field independent or context blind, and the existence of such a choice would minimize the falseness which is inherent in but one or other of the terms. But because it has been males who have named the world, no such choice exists and the falseness of the partial names they have supplied goes unchecked.

Note

1   At this point I consulted *The Concise Oxford English Dictionary* to find out if the word I wanted was meritorious or meretricious. Obviously it is meritorious: meretricious (the closest entry to my feeling for meritricious) is defined as 'of, befitting a harlot'. Now where does that one come from!

Reprinted from Dale Spender, *Man Made Language* (London: Routledge & Kegan Paul, 1980).

Chapter 7

Maria Black and Rosalind Coward

LINGUISTIC, SOCIAL AND SEXUAL RELATIONS: A REVIEW OF DALE SPENDER'S *MAN MADE LANGUAGE*

DALE SPENDER'S BOOK, *Man Made Language*, is the latest, and probably the most widely read, in a long series of books and papers about the categorization and positioning of women in language. The debates around language are, and have been, crucial to feminist theoretical and political practices. At the theoretical level, they have focused attention on ideology, gender identification, and sexual difference not as 'ideas' or 'attitudes' but as material practices with their own mode of organization and specific effects on other social practices. At the political level, objections to linguistic expressions that demean and exclude women have been an important means of introducing and sustaining feminist positions and concerns in political groups. We do not, therefore, dispute the importance of Dale Spender's work, and we welcome the data she has made available. Some aspects of her analysis, however, and some of the conclusions she reaches raise several questions, particularly since Dale Spender's approach seems to reproduce many of the problems inherent in previous discussions of language and class. The purpose of this paper is a reconsideration of some of these issues. The paper is divided into three main sections. In the first, we examine the assumptions that underlie her notion of 'man-made', and the problems that these assumptions give rise to. In the second, we discuss her notion of language, and try to show that a distinction between language as a system and discourse is necessary to the development of feminist theory. Finally, we attempt to provide the beginnings of an alternative analysis, and discuss some of the implications of this shift.

Man-made

Women's subordination in language, Dale Spender argues, lies in women's negative relation to language. The effect of subordination attached to women's relation to language cannot be overruled by the construction of new and positive terms, for 'the problem lies not in the words but in the semantic rule which governs their positive or negative connotations' (p. 29). Intentionally or otherwise, men 'have formulated a semantic rule which posits them as central and positive as the norm, and they have classified the world from that standpoint, constructing a symbolic system which represents patriarchal order' (p. 58).

Dale Spender's notion of women's negative relation to language is drawn from discussions of ideology and language which have taken place within socialist feminism. This tendency attempted to look at the specificity of women's oppression as it occurred in systems of representation as well as in social practices. It remained within an account of the social structure which did not neglect class antagonisms. Language was recognized as having an active role in the construction of social definitions and the possibility of subject positions. Dale Spender, however, has disregarded the context in which these ideas emerged and the function which they fulfilled. In attempting to foreground 'sexism' in language she disregards the developments which had taken place around issues of language and ideology within socialism.

At certain moments, Dale Spender also argues for the importance of language in constructing notions of sexuality and playing an active role in the construction of reality. At the next moment, language is reduced to being an instrument of expression, simply reflecting the 'interests' of given social groups, i.e., men and women. Language constructs the positions of men and women, but men pre-exist language and use it to perpetuate their interests. Dale Spender's arguments to some extent reproduce those made within a version of Marxism indifferent to any questions of ideology and its effectivity within the social formation. Society is seen as structured around two dominant classes with antagonistic interests. These dominant classes are sometimes argued to have different relations to language. In Dale Spender's account, class division is replaced by sex division. Although in the first half of her book Dale Spender discusses the suspect nature of research designed to prove that women speak differently from men, she then goes on to hegemonize all instances of sexism in language under the idea of women's negative relation to language. Thus, grammatical presumptions, sexist idioms, the effect of the sex of the speaker are all encompassed as essentially the same phenomena, produced by the different relation which men and women have to language. Dale Spender explains the dominance of the 'male semantic rule' as an effect of the dominance of male definitions or meanings. Men, like the ruling class in some Marxist arguments, have the power to define reality, and the rules of language reflect men's meanings. Women, like the working class, are deprived of power; they are always defined by male language and unable to promote their own. Dale Spender does not suggest that women speak a different language, and in this respect her ideas are not unlike Harold Rosen's (1972). Rosen took Bernstein to task for setting up a model of two dominant modes of speech, to the denigration of 'non-standard English'. But he also assumed a separate 'reality' for the two classes: the one defines reality, the other produces its own meanings in its own dialect.

In a similar way, Dale Spender suggests that male meanings are now dominant; women's definitions can hardly be heard. Childbirth, for example, is defined by men as the ultimately satisfying experience for a woman. All references to pain and fear are obliterated. Women's accounts, she argues, would not conceal the pain and the difficulties. This understanding of language is problematic, assuming as it does that 'meanings' derive from clear-cut groups, generated by their different social experiences. The division between these groups is simply assumed; all empirical data of speech acts and utterances is then forced to fit these divisions. This position assumes that 'meanings' are derived from experience. Meaning reflect the individual's experience of reality and are simply expressed in language. The communality of 'meanings', i.e., group meanings, is seen as an effect of groupings of individuals with structurally similar experiences. Serious reservations can be raised to this position. One is that it reduces language to being an instrument through which reality is expressed. This contradicts assertions that language has a material existence and effectivity. To stress that language is not an instrument expressing the meanings of pre-existent groups is to argue, on the contrary, that meaning derives from the relationships between linguistic entities. This relationship is socially constrained but is not an expression of a social order that pre-exists language. Language participates in the social and has an active role in the construction of subject positions.

This leads on to our second reservation, which is that notions of class or group meanings have proved very blunt instruments for the investigation of the production and circulation of attitudes. To assume pre-given groups gives us no real purchase on how ideologies participate in the production of groups and secure identification with the subject positions produced there. We can see the limitations of this approach by taking Dale Spender's own example of childbirth. There are women prepared to testify to the simultaneous pain and pleasure of childbirth. Indeed feminists have themselves been at the forefront of attempts to restore dignity to the ways in which childbirth has been seen. It has been feminists recently who have insisted on the significance of motherhood and the need to fight against belittling treatment of pregnant women and mothers. Debates around the introduction of anaesthetics in childbirth in the nineteenth century clearly show that suffering and pain in childbirth were seen by men as necessary states in the moral life of women. It is easy to produce evidence from men about the horror of childbirth, and the disgust and fear at exposure to such pain. What this indicates is that 'meanings' do not accrue exclusively to pre-existing groups, but are produced in definite ideologies. The problem is not male definitions of childbirth but systematic representations about childbirth where women are deprived of control of the forms in which childbirth can occur. Here what needs to be challenged is professional male hierarchies, alienating medical practices, and the policies around, and the ideological treatment of, child-birth and childcare. Another reservation derives from this. It relates to the notion of power at play. This assumes that one group literally has power over the other. This is a simplistic analysis of the workings of power. In a society structured along a series of unequal divisions, there are clearly a number of groups who have power in relation to other groups: whites, men, managers. The forms of domination and subordination are by no means always identical. A woman can be subordinated as a woman and be actively racist. It is rarely a case of direct, literal coercion with one clearly identifiable ruling group responsible for all the forms of domination found in the society. Marxist discussions around the term ideology emerged precisely to investigate the fact that social practices and systems of representation appeared to work without any direct coercion. Moreover, ideologies did not seem to corre-spond in any direct sense with given interest groups.

These discussions within Marxism, to which we will return, themselves had implications for the conceptualization of the relationship between systems of representation and interest groups. Systems of representation are seen as producing the possibilities and positions for the subject rather than being the product of any individual or group meaning. All meaning is recognized to be social and could not properly be understood as the instrument of expres-sion. From such a perspective, experience and identity cannot be seen as the origin of meaning but its outcome. The discussion of ideology within Marxism was at first envisaged as refining ways of understanding how equilibrium was maintained between two unequal classes. However, the more it has been considered the more it has been a challenge to the whole way in which Marxism has conceived of society as structured by the antagonistic interests of two monolithic classes. Dale Spender, however, in ignoring any of these considerations, has returned to an unreclaimed version of Marxism, as a matter of intersubjective domination; different groups have different expe-riences; language is expressive of the meanings available to these two radically different groups. She thereby contradicts her claim that language has an active role to play in the construction of social reality, and reduces it to being the expression of something pre-existent and independent of language.

Which language?

If we are to develop an adequate analysis of sexism in language, it is impor-tant to specify what we mean by 'language'. We can't simply assume that we are dealing with a transparent and homogeneous phenomenon: some explicit theoretical distinctions are necessary. Dale Spender rejects many of the theoretical distinctions of linguistics, but does not provide an alternative specification of her theoretical object. She employs the term 'language' to cover a variety of different phenomena – anything and everything that has to do with words. We are left, therefore, either with a theoretically useless, common-sense notion of 'language', or with the undifferentiated empiricist notions that underlie much of the sex-language research.

Language, as the object of linguistic theory, is a system of rules and representations (Saussure's *langue*, Chomsky's *grammar*), considered independently of its users and uses in context. The distinction was not drawn because of some implicit sexism, racism or classism as Dale Spender appears to suggest. Linguistic theory had to construct its own theoretical object to move away from the notion of language of prescriptive grammar, and those forms of empiricist investigation where everything observable or given in 'verbal behaviour' was considered as theoretically relevant. Dale Spender claims that any general distinction of this kind is bound to produce 'inadequacies and inaccuracies' without making explicit what these are, nor detailing how 'the definitions of what constitutes "proper linguistic study" have (conveniently?) acted as obstacles in pursuing feminist based questions' (p. 29). She seems to favour and adopt a sociolinguistic framework for her analysis. But sociolinguistics has not really 'collapsed the traditional dichotomy'. Sociolinguistic analysis is often carried out at such a level of generality that the specific properties of linguistic systems are not an issue: theoretical distinctions can thus be obscured. At best, sociolinguistics presupposes, or explicitly makes use of, theoretical concepts which could not have been developed without such a dichotomy. Dale Spender gives the impression that sociolinguistics is somehow more progressive than linguistics. This partly reflects the kneejerk approach of some sections of the Left to theoretical and semi-theoretical disciplines. Any discipline that mentions class, sex, or race has to be better than one that does not. Contrary to Dale Spender's suggestion, the 'widespread belief that there was something *wrong* with the language of Blacks and the working class' does not originate in linguistic theory. It has far more to do with prescriptive grammar and related educational and cultural practices. Theoretical linguists would openly deride any claim that, for example, the existence of glottal stops in Cockney is an indication of slovenliness, cultural deprivation, or 'restricted code'. Linguistically speaking, glottalization is such a complex process that its theoretical description has required major changes in phonological theory. The theoretical notion of 'grammatical' does not correspond to the prescriptive notion of 'correct English'. A grammatical structure is simply one that is generated by the rules of the grammar. For instance, the sentence – The man the feminist Dale inspired challenged became aphasic – is perfectly grammatical in so far as the syntactic rules of English predict it as a possible structure of the language. But it hardly corresponds to the common-sense notion of 'good English'. Most of the sex-language research that Dale Spender rightly criticizes is far more rooted in sociolinguistics and social psychology than in linguistic theory. [. . .] Some general notion of language as a 'social product', or a reflection of society, usually serves as a starting point for soci-olinguistic analysis. If groups of speakers have particular positions in society, their language then ought to correspond to, or reflect, their social situation. Hence the search for evidence of linguistic sex differences and/or the 'infe-riority' of women's language.

One of the fundamental claims of linguistic theory is that linguistic systems are not homogeneous. They consist of quite distinct sets of rules and representations. Three main levels of linguistic representation are usually identified: phonology, syntax and semantics – roughly, sounds, structures and meaning. The theoretical concepts used to specify phonological, syntactic and semantic representations are different, and there is no necessary one-to-one correspondence between the categories involved on each level. For instance, the domain of application of phonological rules can be a string defined in terms of phonological symbols and boundaries, while the domain of syntactic rules is a structure defined in terms of syntactic categories and relations. If we accept that language, in this sense, is not homogeneous, then it is more appropriate to evaluate the effects of the distinction between a system and its users or uses in context in relation to each of these 'subsys-tems'. Similarly, claims about the 'man-made' nature of language can be usefully broken down into claims about the nature and effects of phonolog-ical, syntactic, and semantic representations. The concepts and distinctions of theoretical linguistics are not sacrosanct. But, unless we direct our criti-cisms to specific concepts, analyse their effects, and show explicitly how they 'have acted as obstacles' to feminist analysis, we will not be able to identify our theoretical enemies and develop alternatives. Generalized accusations of sexism do not amount to an argument.

Sexist syntax

Although Dale Spender makes no claims about phonology, she argues that syntax, as well as semantics, is 'man-made'. However, the 'evidence' she produces in support of her claim is at best irrelevant, and at worst misleading. Her evidence falls into two categories: the statements of various prescriptive grammarians and the use of *man/he*. The pronouncements of prescriptive grammarians are interesting material for the analysis of ideolog-ical discourses which undoubtedly have effects on educational policies and practices. But they do *not* constitute evidence of the structural and system-atic properties of syntactic structure. Dale Spender appears to have no conception of syntax as distinct from prescriptive grammar, as it is evident from her astonishing statement that 'the structure of the language is more concrete and readily traced' than its 'semantic base'. Syntax is hardly that, though grammarians' statements may well be, as they are couched in the apparently obvious, common-sense terms that are so typical of ideological discourses. For instance, one of the prescriptive 'rules' Dale Spender mentions requires that the male term be placed before the female term in conjoined phrases like *men and women, husband and wife*. This is not a syntactic rule, but merely an ideological pronouncement, since it does not express any general *syntactic* property of co-ordinate structures. While all co-ordinate structures in English are constrained in other ways (for example, only syntactic categories of the same type can be conjoined), there is no *ordering* restriction. Thus, *women and men*, or *wife and husband* are as syntactically well-formed as a *sandwich and a cake*, or *very tired and depressed* instead of *a cake and a sandwich, depressed and very tired*. We do not need to change the syntax of the language once we distinguish clearly between prescriptive grammar and syntax. It is to our advantage to do so: we can then challenge and expose more effectively the grammarians' prescriptions. It is unfortunate, therefore, that Dale Spender's 'syntactic' evidence has been taken quite so seriously by other feminists, particularly since this sort of 'evidence' often triggers 'consensus' explanations of language: 'As Dale Spender points out, our rules of grammar are not based on any consensus of female and male opinion, but on the dictates of individual men' (Coote 1981). One wonders how, without already having a language, the patriarchs around the linguistic conference table managed to communicate to each other their plans about such a complex and sophisticated system. Did they draw pictures, or did they have syntax-free language? The question is not 'how did men make syntax?'; the issue here is how did certain idioms and stereotypical phrases like *men and women* arise, and why are idioms often a central component of ideological discourses where they function *as if* they were required by the structure of language, the organization of society or 'human nature'.

The only other issue Dale Spender discusses under the heading of syntax is the use of *man/he*. Her discussion makes clear that what she is talking about is the gender of the referent of both noun and pronoun. Reference has little to do with syntax; the relationship between a word and its referent, or possible referents, is not determined or constrained by syntactic factors. Therefore, 'this use of *man* and *he* as terms to denote a male, but on occasion to encompass a female' may well be sexist, but is *not* 'an example of sexist linguistic structure'. Structure does not come into it, and we cannot use 'structure', 'symbol', or 'word interchangeably as Dale Spender does. Structural conditions do affect relations between a pronoun and its antecedent – for example, in (1) *John/Mary* and *he/she* can be co-referential on one interpretation

$$1 \quad \left\{ \begin{array}{c} John \\ Mary \end{array} \right\} \text{ said that } \left\{ \begin{array}{c} he \\ she \end{array} \right\} \text{ was leaving}$$

but not in (2)

$$2 \quad \left\{ \begin{array}{c} He \\ She \end{array} \right\} \text{ said that } \left\{ \begin{array}{c} John \\ Mary \end{array} \right\} \text{ was leaving.}$$

However, structural constraints on pronoun-antecedent relations are quite independent of gender. What probably underlies Dale Spender's treatment of pronoun gender as a syntactic phenomenon is the nebulous notion from school-book grammar that pronouns are 'grammatical words' and thus have something to do with syntax. But, in that case, Dale Spender's unified account of *man/he* would be wrong, as nouns are not 'grammatical words' and should be treated quite differently.

So the whole discussion of sexism and language is really a discussion of sexism and semantics, or sexism and some other level of representation which may not be specifiable within the framework of theoretical linguistics as it stands.

Sexist meaning

The issue of *man/he* could be incorporated into Dale Spender's analysis of 'meaning'. In fact, it is not clear why she does not consider it as an instance of one of her 'semantic rules'. Her data and observations about meaning are essentially the same as those of previous feminist analyses (cf. Miller and Swift 1979), but she attempts to generalize them and give them some theoretical status. That is where the problems start: both her general approach to 'meaning' and the specific 'semantic rules' she puts forward are problematic. Her use of the terms 'meaning' and 'semantic' is as unclear as that of 'language'. As we have already seen, Dale Spender leaves us suspended between two interpretations of meaning, neither of which can advance feminist theory. Either everything is reducible to meaning, or meaning is a sort of experiential or mental entity that exists independently of language. Dale Spender's approach is fraught with problems and contradictions which are not explicitly recognized, and makes use of terms that we do not know how to interpret. As a consequence we do not now how seriously to take some of her claims.

For theoretical linguistics, the meaning of an expression is determined by the relations of paraphrase, synonymy, antonymy, entailment, and contradiction which that expression has with other expressions in the system. 'Meaning' is therefore a purely linguistic phenomenon, a product or effect of systematic relationships between expressions. The theoretical concept of meaning does not include any feelings, images or connotations which may be associated with particular expressions, nor is the semantic status of an expression evaluated in terms of what is plausible, usual or likely to happen 'outside' language.[1] Thus, Dale Spender's claim that 'it is a semantic contradiction to formulate representations of women's autonomy or strength' is patently false on the most common interpretation of 'semantic contradiction', since it would imply that

Sue's friends are all strong and independent women

is as semantically peculiar as

Sue killed Tom and Tom is alive and kicking.

107

But we are not given any other interpretation of 'semantic contradiction' that might lead to different predictions. Dale Spender claims that 'one semantic rule which we can see in operation in the language is that of the male as the norm'. This rule is complemented by, and sometimes subsumed under, a second general semantic rule: '. . . any symbol which is associated with the female must assume negative (and frequently sexual – which is also significant) connotations' (p. 29). Dale Spender stresses that 'it is not just a question of elimination or addition of words . . . for the problem lies not in the words but in the semantic rule which governs their positive or negative connotations . . ., and any strategies which are predicated on the removal of sexist words are unable to deal with this phenomenon' (p. 29). These rules play a central role in Dale Spender's analysis, so both their formulation and their implications have to be taken seriously.

There is clearly a problem with those analyses which focus on the meaning of single words such as *Man* and *he*. Feminists have often argued that *Man* does not mean 'human being' but 'male human being'; such claims are usually backed up by sentences like (1–2).

1 *Man's* vital interests are food, shelter, and access to females.
2 *Man* is the only primate that *commits rape*.

If *Man* is genuinely inclusive, (1–2) ought to be semantically anomalous, or at least have the same status as

3 *Man*, unlike other mammals, has difficulties in *giving birth*.

But utterances like (1–2) are commonly produced and readily accepted by many speakers, while utterances like (3) are not. Hence feminists have concluded that, contrary to the claims of semanticians and lexicographers, *Man* only means 'male'. This argument, however, is problematic because it would force us to conclude that there are no general terms referring to both men and women. That is, many apparently non-gender specific terms that bear no resemblance to the exclusively masculine *man*, occur in utterances where the same pattern of exclusive reference exemplified by (1–2) is also found, for example,

4 *People* will give up *their wives* but not power.
5 *Americans* of higher status have less chance of having a fat *wife*.
6 Young *people* should be out interfering with the local *maidens* (based on *The Times* June 1981).
7 *Drivers* – belt the *wife* and kids. Keep them safe. [*sic*!] (Road Safety sign).

The feminist argument thus has to be extended to a variety of words other than *Man*. Dale Spender's analysis in terms of general 'semantic rules' is presumably an attempt to overcome this problem and go beyond the meaning of individual words. Her first rule expresses the claim that the 'exclusion of women' from the language is a general phenomenon and not restricted to *Man/he*. Similarly, her second rule is an attempt to unify different manifestations of the semantic pejoration of women. But Dale Spender's 'semantic rules' raise a number of other problems. First of all, both rules are much *too general*. There are cases where non-specific terms do include, for example,

8 *People* don't like being ill, but *women* put up with *it* better than men.
9 I met several *Americans* this summer and the most interesting of *them* were a *journalist* and *her daughter*.

or sometimes refer exclusively to women, for example,

10 The consumer will not know that *she* is buying foreign eggs.

11 A $\left\{ \begin{array}{c} \textit{nurse} \\ \textit{speech therapist} \end{array} \right\}$'s first duty is to *her* patients.

Similarly, there are cases where the generalization expressed by the second rule that '*any* symbol associated with the female' has pejorative and/or sexual connotations does not hold at all, for example,

12 My $\left\{ \begin{array}{c} \textit{sister} \\ \textit{daughter} \\ \textit{aunt} \end{array} \right\}$ took (her) *grandmother* out for lunch.

13 The new *headmistress* introduced herself to the pupils' *mothers*.

or cases where one female term has pejorative connotations but another, fairly similar term does not, for example, compare (14) and (15)

14 We have not spoken to the female who lives upstairs.

15 We have not spoken to the $\left\{ \begin{array}{c} \textit{woman} \\ \textit{girl} \end{array} \right\}$ who lives upstairs.

Dale Spender's rules do not always apply and, therefore, cannot be formulated as general 'semantic rules'. Linguistic rules are either totally general (i.e., apply in all contexts), or have specifiable conditions of application. These conditions usually are expressed in purely linguistic terms: they make reference only to phonological, syntactic or logical structures and relations; furthermore, the set of conditions cannot be an ad hoc list of cases where a rule just happens not to apply. There must be some theoretically principled way of grouping together sets of conditions on the basis of shared properties. None of these requirements are met by Dale Spender's analysis; she does not say anything about the nature of the conditions that constrain the application of her rules, and whether the many cases where they do not apply anything in common. If Dale Spender's rules cannot be reformulated and their conditions of application stated explicitly, the generalizations embodied in them have to brought into question. We cannot assume that a generalization is valid simply because there are examples to back it up: we have to deal with the counter-examples as well. Though there clearly are general patterns to be understood and explained, and this lends intuitive plausibility to Dale Spender's account, it is far from clear that all the relevant phenomena can be unified and adequately described in terms of two semantic rules of this kind.

There are other reasons to doubt the validity of Dale Spender's analysis. The statement of her second rule involves terms like 'pejorative' which have no general, systematic interpretation. Linguistic rules simply specify the structural properties of sentences, and the concepts used in their formulation have stable and identifiable interpretations across and within linguistic systems. But Dale Spender's second rule is quite different. First of all, we are not dealing with sentences, since the same phonological, syntactic, and logical structure – the same *sentence* – can be used to produce, or be interpreted as, different *utterances* with distinct connotations. For instance, both (16) and (17) may or may not have pejorative connotations depending on the speaker-hearers involved and on the context:

16 John is talking to that *woman* again.
17 He really behaved like a *man*.

Dale Spender's rules are not 'semantic rules' in the standard theoretical sense, but, if anything, principles of utterance-production and interpretation. If so, we have to ask whether these principles apply in all contexts, and whether terms like 'pejorative' are to be understood from the point of view of whoever produces the utterance, or those who interpret it, or both. Many examples like (16) and (17), for instance, may be produced but not interpreted as having pejorative connotations, and vice-versa. Precisely where the relationship between what is said and who says it becomes crucial, Dale Spender is strangely quiet about it. This is not surprising as she does not have the concepts to grasp such a relationship. She either relies on a hopelessly vague notion of language so that every speaker–hearer in each context has to be assigned a different 'language' – with a resulting theoretical Babel. Or she falls back on the concepts of linguistic theory which are relevant only to linguistic systems and sentences, without making explicit how they are to be reinterpreted for the purposes of utterance production and interpretation in context. We plainly need different concepts: the phenomena feminists are concerned with have to little to do with linguistic systems. As we have seen, language, as a system of phonological, syntactic, and logical structures and rules, is not inherently sexist or 'man-made' in Dale Spender's sense. Linguistic systems, however, serve as the basis for the production and inter-pretation of sets of related utterances – discourses – which effect and sustain the different categorizations and positions of women and men. It is on these *discourses*, and not on language in general or linguistic systems, that feminist analyses have to focus.

Unfortunately, there is no ready-made theoretical framework that femi-nists can simply take over and apply to the analysis of the relevant phenomena. The theories of discourse or 'pragmatics' developed within modern linguis-tics have little to offer to feminist analysis. On these approaches, examples such as (1) to (11) would probably be handled by reference to social condi-tions and assumptions, which are simply 'reflected' in language. Words like *people, Americans*, or *nurse* are assumed to function semantically as non-gender-specific terms; their varying gender references are explained in terms of 'extra-linguistic' assumptions about who has power, higher status, or is most likely to be a nurse in our society. There are several problems with this kind of approach. It lumps together a whole variety of factors under the common heading of 'social assumptions', 'encyclopedic knowledge', or whatever other term is used. Everything is displaced outside discourse which is then reduced to a mere reflection of reality or society. Both what discourse 'reflects', and the subjects of discourse, as rational, intentional and gendered individuals, are constituted independently of discourse. We are then faced with the same paradox we have already discussed in relation to Dale Spender's analysis: what discourses are supposed to construct and organize turns out to be the cause and origin of these discourses.

In spite of these problems, some approaches within pragmatic theory might be able to handle utterances involving terms that presuppose partic-ular social and sexual relations (cf. Examples 4–7, 11–12); it is not clear, however, that a similar account can be given of the fact that women are often not treated as 'human' on a par with men. Why is it often possible to use general categories such as *Man, human*, or *people* to refer exclusively to males, sometimes to both females and males, but rarely to females alone? The difference in acceptability between utterances like (1 and 2), on the one hand, and (3), on the other, has to be explained, as well as the existence of utterances like

18 This thieving gang consists of three *people* from Latin America, and *a woman* (BBC Radio 4 News).[2]
19 Normal *people* do not go around raping and murdering women.
20 Well, it is only *human* nature (heard at the time of the Yorkshire Ripper's killings).

In contra-position with these utterances, the following would sound distinctly odd:

21 This thieving gang consists of three *people* from Latin America and a *man*.

22 The committee was appointed to review . . . the problems of special groups . . . the handicapped, ethnic groups, Aboriginals and *men* (adapted from Naked Ape,[3] *Guardian* June 1981).

23 You can't argue with Jane's typically *human* $\left\{ \begin{array}{c} logic \\ notions \end{array} \right\}$

What we have here appears to be some systematic patterning of masculine and feminine referents in relation to general categories of humanity. This is what Dale Spender took to be a general rule of language. We have argued that language cannot be understood in general in this way. In other words, we have to make a distinction between what Pecheux and his colleagues call the *linguistic base* (the object of linguistic theory), and *discursive processes* (see Pecheux 1983; Woods 1977). The phenomena in question have to be understood by reference to discursive regularities. We have to ask how gendered meaning is produced in particular utterances, how these utterances are produced and sustained in relation to other utterances.

Discursive formations

In what precedes we have seen how it is impossible to consider meaning outside its production through a particular organization of words into utterances. The meaning of a given utterance is fixed through the arrangement of words, and through the relationship of this utterance to other utterances that have already been made. This implies that it is the discursive organization which speaks the subject, rather than static meanings originating from a group experience. This, however, does not solve the problem of understanding the denigration of women in language, and what relation this has to the social order and the relations between the sexes. We need to understand how the cultural codes of the already-said are understood, put into circulation, and are effective within society. It is for this reason that we see a need to continue discussions around ideology and language already initiated within Marxism. Many socialist feminists adhered to the term as a way of exploring sexual construction and its effects as 'relatively autonomous', but not completely separate from economic structures. But there were two main reasons why socialist feminist theory ran aground before consolidating this exploration. On one hand, the way in which Marxism was taken up as an intellectual discipline as well as political theory was as an explanation of the causal links between various aspects of the social formation. As we know, this all too frequently suggested the ultimate determination by economic class antagonisms. Frequently this was accompanied by a political subordination of so-called 'ideological struggles'. As taken up by socialist feminists Marxism often appeared as the promise of 'the explanation' of the articulation between sex and class. Yet the explanation has never been delivered because there is no *causal* determination. If sexual subordination is relatively autonomous from the economic mode of production, where does it arise if not in some earlier and fundamental division between men and women? If that is the case, then how does this earlier form articulate with class divisions? As their model or cause? If so, what happens to the challenge to the 'naturalness' of class division which Marxism is supposed to deliver? On the other hand, some of the impetus to explore the concept of ideology was almost instantly undermined by a theoretical critique of its generalizing and universalizing claims. It has been argued that the concept of ideology presupposes a model of society and human consciousness where social reality is transmitted directly into ideological representations; it has equally been suggested that what this delivers is a dogmatic description of 'reality' which ultimately denies effectivity to the 'discursive level'. For this reason, attention has been concentrated on 'discursive formations', a strategic attention designed to suspend generalizations about the relationship between social formation and activities of the human mind. Foucault (1972: 29) summarizes this attention as one designed to grasp the forms of regularities in utterances and statements. The aim is to explore

> Relations between statements (even if the author is unaware of them; even if the statements do not have the same author; even if the authors were unaware of each other's existence); relations between groups of statements thus established (even if these groups do not concern the same, or even adjacent fields; even if they do not possess the same formal level; even if they are not the locus of assignable exchanges); relations between statements and groups of statements and events of a quite different kind (technical, economic, social, political). To reveal in all its purity the space in which discursive events are deployed is not to undertake to re-establish it in an isolation that nothing could overcome; it is not to close it upon itself; it is to leave oneself free to describe the interplay of relations within it and outside it.

Some would perhaps like to argue that the dismissal of the term ideology has been somewhat premature. It is possible, for example, to imagine that ideologies might be examined as systems of representation without assuming that they necessarily reflect a principle governing the social structure.

Whatever term becomes the focus of discussion, the point of the argument is the same. Language and the meanings produced therein are not expressive of any simple social division be it class, sex or whatever. If we do not want to reduce language to a simple instrument or effect of a class or sex position but to see it as something productive of the positions we can occupy, then we have to develop these insights of recent discussions of ideology. These see discourses as determinate forms of social practice with

113

their own conditions of existence in other social practices (for example political/economic or scientific) and in social relations, and as having definite effects with regard to those practices and relations. It still seems necessary, in the face of numerous misreadings, to insist that this is not about absenting language from the social formation; on the contrary, it is to insist that language has a material existence. It defines our possibilities and limitations, it constitutes our subjectivities. The insistence on starting where Marxist feminist debates left off comes from no sentimental or unexamined commitment to Marxism or socialism. Far from it, it comes from the fact that discussions of ideology and language arose from precisely the desire not to offer reductive explanations of the social formation. These reductive explanations always ended by denying the subordination of women through sexual and ideological as well as economic and political practices. Indeed, it was exactly this work which emphasized that there were organizations of meaning in language and representational practices which actively participated in the subordination of women. These could in no way be 'explained' by the existence of class divisions. In other words, we are suggesting that we cannot solve the problem of the ways in which representation and language participate in the construction of denigratory attitudes and activities towards women by returning to forms of analysis which reduce language to the expression of pre-existent group positions.

The statement, that we should pay attention to discursive unities, their conditions of existence, and their effects with regard to other practices, is thought by some to avoid analysis. Always insisting on complexity and non-reductionism, it appears not to offer any immediately graspable explanation. We have already outlined why there are pressing reasons to persevere rather than look for easy solutions. To some extent discussions within Marxism have demonstrated anyway that the search for causal explanations understood as 'generative' principles is an unrewarding task which always reduces explanations to dogmatic assertions. In addition, we have argued that the idea of generative principles always reduces accounts of ideology and language to expressions of pre-existent groups.

Ungendered man, endangered species

We argue that there are very distinct advantages in insisting that society is not reducible to generating principles reflected in all social practices. We can see this by re-examining the case on which *Man Made Language* rests, that is, that there is a male 'semantic rule' expressed in man being the norm for humanity, and women being defined negatively or pejoratively. First, there is the problem of how this rule is supposed to have arisen. On the one hand, it is suggested that until now, patriarchy has been in dominance. Male definitions have always dominated because men have always dominated. On the other hand, there is the curious effect of Dale Spender's examination of etymological changes. She suggests that certain words have been devalued through the acquisition of sexual connotations to the female term. Thus, *mistress, hostess, dame* are all presented as words which were somehow, once upon a time, more equal than they are now. This leads us again to express very real reservations about how linguistic data is being interpreted. Etymological data is clearly vital (witness the suggestive use made of it by Miller and Swift in *Words and Women*), but taken in isolation from other changes and uses in the language it can produce a very distorted picture. For example, *mistress* had been in use quite early as a specifically sexual term meaning 'sweetheart'. In addition, the disappearance of *mistress* as head of the household surely could not be separated from the appearance of another term, that of *housewife*, bearing witness to very definite transformations of households and conceptions of women's place in them. Language does not simply reflect its past history nor its current function. Linguistic value has to be understood in relation to other aspects of the overall structure of language. We have to understand not just histories of words, but the relationship of terms to other terms, the relationship between terms in statements, the relationship between statements. This is at the crux of our disagreement with Dale Spender. We do not accept a theory of social organization which posits a 'reality' – patriarchy, capitalism, or whatever – which is simply reflected in language, either as history or function. Instead we see definite discursive constructions with definite conditions of existence which are *effective with regard to other practices*. This suggests a different approach to linguistic phenomena which refuses to start either from a purely historical or a purely functional approach. We can see the difference by re-examining Dale Spender's 'semantic rules'. The two rules are often conflated into a single generalization: language defines women as 'negative'; the term 'negative' means that women are excluded from the meaning or reference of general terms as well as being defined pejoratively. We would like to suggest that this conflation is misleading, and that we are dealing with quite different phenomena which have to be analysed separately. We have already argued that women's exclusion as representatives of generalized humanity is not the product of any 'semantic rule'; there is nothing impossible or even improbable about a sentence like *She was so wretched she looked hardly human*. Women, in other words, can represent humanity and share in the general attributes which the human is said to possess as distinct from the animals. Frequently, however, a term which refers to the human species, i.e., *mankind*, excludes women. It is clear that the attributes of exclusion in the term *mankind* do not come from its relation to the term *man*, a point we have made in connection with terms like *people, Americans*, etc. (cf. Examples (4) to (7)). Perhaps this phenomenon could be understood not in terms of the hidden male gender of general terms, but the fact that the attributes of the male can in fact disappear into a 'non-gendered' subject. Women, on the other hand, never appear as non-gendered subjects. Women are precisely *defined*, never as general representatives of human or all people, but as specifically feminine, and

115

frequently sexual, categories: whore, slag, mother, virgin, housewife. The term 'negative' cannot be understood as synonymous with 'pejorative'. Women are not the norm, but this does not mean that they are *not defined*. The curious feature is exactly the excess of (sexual) definitions and categories for women. A similar profusion is not found for men, whose differentiation from one another comes not through sexual attributes and status, but primarily through occupation, or attributes of general humanity, for example, decent, kind, honest, strong. Men remain men and women become specific categories in relation to men and to other categories. Prince Charles and Lady Diana Spencer disappeared into the church and emerged as *man and wife*. Being a man is an entitlement not to *masculine* attributes but to *non-gendered* subjectivity. We suggest that it is this which gives a certain discursive regularity to the appearance of gender in language. The conditions of existence of this discursive regularity might be looked for in the development of discourses on citizenship, law, anthropology and sexuality.

The development of the state in western capitalism has been understood as producing a political discursive which suppresses reference to different groups and conflicts of interest. Here the classic Marxist understanding of the state may be helpful. The emergence of the state is seen as the point of regulation of class interests at a supra-individual level. Thus, the particularity of the interests of individuals (or in Marx/Engels's case, individuals and their families (!)) is guaranteed by the abstraction of generalized interests, that is, the abstraction characteristic of the political level. Leaving aside critiques of Marxism for the way in which the political level is often reduced to being the expression of the interests of a given group, this outline of the state is a useful starting point. It indicates the necessary emergence of a distinct representation of a generalized political subject who represents all people and in whose representation all conflict is suppressed. The modern state emerged in the disintegration of the relatively diffused hierarchy of the feudal state. Previously, political responsibilities and rights were derived from particular status given in a very definite hierarchy. The capitalist state, however, increasingly addressed its political representations to a generalized 'citizen' – sexless, classless, a citizen of the world. As is well known, the development of these political representations was to some extent accompanied by the emergence of distinctive legal forms whereby feudal status gave way to conceptions of the rights of the free individual. This modern state and its political representations emerged not just in a rigidly divided class society, but in a literally patriarchal society. The representation of the general citizen and the rights of the free individual did not obscure class divisions, but obscured the fact that political representation was the right of certain groups of property-owning men to represent their families.

In the nineteenth century, feminists began to challenge women's political exclusion, and simultaneously to seek employment in certain professions which themselves were coming under the increasing intervention of the state – the law, medicine, education, etc. The challenge of the feminists caused the ideology of citizenship to become explicit; women were not included as *persons*. Numerous legal judgements were produced during the second half of the nineteenth century excluding women from certain employment and from political and legal representations. Citizenship, based on the notion of the rights of the person, did not include women. It is no coincidence either that this period saw a consolidation of definitions of women around their sexuality. The judgements made were frequently supported by statements on women's appropriate 'sphere of influence'. Men had public responsibilities, women had private ones. Men were masters of the realm of the state. Women ruled supreme in the home. This was the period when, according to Foucault (1978) there was increasing development of state activity. In England, the period around 1880–1900 saw unprecedented state activity, intervening in housing, health, education, etc. It has been suggested that this period was especially witness to an intensification of intervention around sexuality concerned with the production of a new conception of the family, loosely policed by the state but able to solve wider social crises. It is clearly the case that the same period saw an unparalleled 'scientific' investigation of sexuality, whose outcome was the appearance of definite categories like 'homosexual'. Finally, this was also the period where the popular definitions of 'mankind among the other animals' were consolidated. Discussions around the specific attributes of 'humanity' themselves emerged in the disintegration of the political theory based on ideas of the male as sovereign power within his home, a microcosm of the sovereign power of the king. While this theoretical approach was overthrown in the nineteenth century, it left its mark on theories of the nature of society. Investigations were profoundly 'androcentric', assuming that the political subject of any given society was the male. These comments are merely a number of hints at the conditions which have contributed to the possibility of men assuming a non-gendered subjectivity while women are always defined and categorized. Perhaps, it might be suggested that this tentative interpretation does not greatly alter the conclusions of Dale Spender. However, our different interpretation and approach has very different political implications.

Dale Spender ultimately sees feminism as a politics of 'making new meaning':

> From providing an alternative individual meaning for motherhood, to constructing a collective understanding of the domestic labour debate, women must take every opportunity to encode their own meanings and to validate the meanings encoded by other women.

We do not see the problem as one of the suppression of female meanings, nor do we see the solution as simply validating everything produced by women, as the expression of pre-existent feminine values. We see one of the major political problems confronting feminism to be the need to force men to recognize themselves as *men*. The discursive formation which allows men to represent themselves as non-gendered and to define women constantly according to their sexual status is a discursive formation with very definite effects. It allows men to deny the effect of their gendered subjectivity on women. It is not a question of men secretly believing that masculine is the norm. What is available to them is a discourse where gender and sexual identity appears to be absent. Thus, Paul Hirst can make the following comment: 'I dispute that there is anything so definite as there being a category of man. I don't recognise myself as a man.'[4] It is precisely this refusal to recognize the effects of masculinity which constitutes the problem for women. The women's movement takes its existence from the fact that however differently we are constituted in different practices and discourses, women are constantly and inescapably constructed *as women*. There is a discourse available to men which allows them to represent themselves as people, humanity, mankind. This discourse, by its very existence, excludes and marginalizes women by making women the sex. Our aim is not just to validate the new meanings of women but to confront men with their maleness. This is not just about masculine behaviour, but about discursive practices. It is about making men take responsibility for being men. Men are sustained at the centre of the stage precisely because they can be 'people' and do not have to represent their masculinity to themselves. They need never see themselves or their maleness as a problem. Our understanding of the effects of discursive practices leads us to suggest that men can never be displaced from the centre until they can be forced to recognize themselves as men and to take responsibility for this.

Notes

1   The term 'semantics' also covers the study of the logical form of sentences, and the properties of 'logical operators' such as negation, disjunction, conjunction, etc. In the rest of the paper, we have used the term 'logical' to indicate this aspect of linguistic structure.
2   The context made clear that the woman was also from Latin America.
3   Naked Ape was a long-running column feature in the *Guardian* which reprinted examples of outrageous sexism sent in by readers.
4   *Leveller* (30 May–12 June 1981).

Reprinted from *Screen Education* 39 (Summer, 1981).

Chapter 8

Luce Irigaray

LINGUISTIC SEXES AND GENDERS

WOMEN'S ENTRY INTO THE public world, the social relations they have among themselves and with men, have made cultural transformations, and especially linguistic ones, a necessity. If the male President of the Republic meets the Queen, to say *Ils se sont rencontrés* (they met) borders on a grammatical anomaly.[1] Instead of dealing with this difficult question, most people wonder whether it wouldn't be better if we were governed by just men or just women, that is, by one gender alone. The rules of language have so strong a bearing on things that they can lead to such impasses. Unfortunately, there's still little appreciation of what's at stake here. Faced with the need to transform the rules of grammar, some women, even feminists – though fortunately not all – readily object that provided they have the right to use it, the masculine gender will do for them. But neutralizing grammatical gender amounts to an abolition of the difference between sexed subjectivities and to an increasing exclusion of a culture's sexuality. We would be taking a huge step backwards if we abolished grammatical gender, a step our civilization can ill afford; what we do need, on the other hand, and it's essential, is for men and women to have equal subjective rights – equal obviously meaning different but of equal value, subjective implying equivalent rights in exchange systems. From a linguistic perspective, therefore, the cultural injustices of language and its generalized sexism have to be analysed. These are to be found in grammar, in vocabulary, in the connotations of a word's gender.

More or less masculine

For centuries, whatever has been valorized has been masculine in gender, whatever devalorized, feminine. So the sun is masculine, and the moon feminine. Yet in our cultures, *le soleil* (the sun) is thought of as the source of life, *la lune* (the moon) as ambiguous, almost harmful, except perhaps by some peasants. The attribution of masculine gender to the sun can be traced in History, and so can the attribution of the sun to the men-gods. These aren't all immutable truths but rather facts that evolve over long periods of time and at different rates of speed depending upon the culture, country, and language. The positive connotation of the masculine as word gender derives from the time of the establishment of patriarchal and phallocratic power, notably by men's appropriation of the divine. This is not a secondary matter. It is very important. Without divine power, men could not have supplanted mother–daughter relations and their attributions concerning nature and society. But man becomes God by giving himself an invisible father, a father language. Man becomes God as the Word, then as the Word made flesh. Because the power of semen isn't immediately obvious in procreation, it's relayed by the linguistic code, the *logos*. Which wants to become the all-embracing truth.

Men's appropriation of the linguistic code attempts to do at least three things:

1 prove they are fathers;
2 prove they are more powerful than mother–women;
3 prove they are capable of engendering the cultural domain as they have been engendered in the natural domain of the ovum, the womb, the body of a woman.

To guarantee loyalty to its authority, the male people consciously or unconsciously represents whatever has value as corresponding to its image and its grammatical gender. Most linguists state that grammatical gender is arbitrary, independent of sexual denotations and connotations. In fact, this is untrue. They haven't really thought about the issue. It doesn't strike them as being important. Their personal subjectivity, their theory is content to be valorized like the masculine, passing for an arbitrary universal. A patient study of the gender of words almost always reveals their hidden sex. Rarely is this immediately apparent. And a linguist will be quick to retort that *un fauteuil* (a sofa) or *un chateau* (a castle) are not more 'masculine' than *une chaise* (a chair) or *une maison* (a house). Apparently not. A degree of thought will show that the former connote greater value than the latter. While the latter are simply useful in our cultures, the others are more luxurious, ornamental, noted for their distinction as higher-class goods. A thorough analysis of all the terms of the lexicon would in this way make their secret sex apparent, signifying their adherence to an as yet uninterpreted syntax.

Another example: *un ordinateur* (a computer) is of course a masculine noun and *la machine à écrire* (the typewriter) a feminine one. Value is what matters . . . Whatever has it must be masculine. Again, *un avion* (an airplane) is superior to *une voiture* (a car), *le Boeing* to *la Caravelle*, not to mention *le Concorde* . . . With each counterexample we find a more complex explanation: the gender could be due to the prefix or the suffix and not to the root of the word; it could depend upon the time when the term entered the lexicon and the relative value of the masculine and feminine genders then (in this respect, Italian is a less coherently sexist language than French); sometimes its determination is consequent upon the language it's borrowed from (English, for example, gives us a number of terms that become masculine in French).

Gender as identity or as possession

How is gender attributed to words? It's done on different levels and in different ways. At the most archaic level, I think there is an identification of the denominated reality with the sex of the speaking subject. *La terre* (the earth) *is* woman, *le ciel* (the sky) *is* her brother. *Le soleil* (the sun) *is* man, the god-man. *La lune* (the moon) is woman, sister of the man-god. And so on. Something of this first identification always remains in the gender of words. The degree to which it is explicit or hidden varies. But there is another mechanism at work apart from the identification of designated reality and gender. Living beings, the animate and cultured, become masculine; objects that are lifeless, the inanimate and uncultured, become feminine. Which means that men have attributed subjectivity to themselves and have reduced women to the status of objects, or to nothing. This is as true for actual women as it is for the gender of words. *Le moissonneur* (a harvester) is a man. But if, in line with current debate on the names of occupations, a linguist or legislator wishes to name a woman who harvests *la moissonneuse*,[2] the word is not available for a female subject: *la moissonneuse* (harvesting machine) is the tool the male harvester makes use of, or else it doesn't exist in the feminine. This state of affairs is even more ridiculous at a higher professional level where sometimes one is presented with hierarchies in the attribution of grammatical gender: *le secrétaire d'Etat/parti* (the secretary of state or a party) is masculine and *la secrétaire steno-dactylo* (the shorthand secretary) is feminine.

There is no sexed couple to create and structure the world. Men are surrounded by tools of feminine gender and by women-objects. Men don't manage the world with women as sexed subjects having equivalent rights. Only through a transformation of language will that become possible. But this transformation can only take place if we valorize the feminine gender once more. Indeed, the feminine, which was originally just different, is now practically assimilated to the non-masculine. Being a woman is equated with not being a man. Which is what psychoanalysis calmly informs us in its theory and its practice of penis or phallus envy. Its reality only corresponds to one cultural period and one state of language. In that case, the way for women to be liberated is not by 'becoming a man' or by envying what men have and their objects, but by female subjects once again valorizing the expression of their own sex and gender. That's completely different.

This confusion between liberation as equal ownership of goods and liberation as access to a subjectivity of the same value is currently upheld by several social theories and practices: psychoanalysis is one of them, but another is Marxism, to a certain extent. These discourses have been elaborated by men. They used Germanic languages. At the present time they have a relative degree of success among women in countries that speak these languages, because gender is expressed in subject–object relations. In these languages a woman can therefore have *her* (*sa*) phallus if not *her* (*sa*) penis.[3] Thus some German, English, or American women are able, for example, to demand equality in relation to the possession of goods and mark them with their gender. Having achieved this, they may abandon their right to denote gender in relation to the subject and criticize the conscious relationship made between the sexuate body and language as 'materialist,' 'ontological,' 'idealist,' etc. This shows a lack of comprehension of the relations between individual bodies, social bodies, and the linguistic economy. A great deal of misunderstanding in the so-called world of women's liberation is perpetuated by this lack of comprehension. For many an Anglo-Saxon – and in general Germanic language – feminist, all she needs is her university post or to have written her book to be liberated. For them it's a question of *her* (*sa*) post and *her* (*sa*) book[4] and this appropriation of ownership seems to satisfy them. In my view, we have to be free female *subjects*. Language represents an essential tool of production for this liberation. I have to make it progress in order to have subjective rights equivalent to men, to be able to exchange language and objects with them. For one women's liberation movement, the emphasis is on equal rights in relation to the possession of goods: difference between men and women is located in the nature, the quantity, and sometimes the quality of goods acquired and possessed. For the other movement, sexual liberation means to demand access to a status of individual and collective *subjectivity* that is valid for them as women. The emphasis is on the difference of rights between male and female subjects.

The sex of occupations

Owning a few goods equivalent to those men have doesn't solve the problem of gender for women who speak Romance languages because these goods don't bear the mark of their owner's subject. We say *mon enfant* (my child) or *mon phallus* (?) (my phallus) whether we are men or women. For valuable 'objects,' then, the mark of ownership is the same. As for other 'objects,' they are generally devalorized when they are likely to be used or appropriated by women alone. The problem of the object and its conquest cannot therefore solve the problem of inequality of sexed rights in all languages. Furthermore, I don't think it can solve it in any language. But it can just about satisfy demands, more or less immediately.

If the issue of names for occupations has been taken up so extensively, it's because such names represent an intermediary space between subject and object, object and subject. Of course, it is a matter of possessing professional status, having a job, but this cannot be possessed just like any object can. It represents a necessary, though not sufficient, part of subjective identity. In addition, this demand fits in well with the social demands already being made in the male world. Therefore, the issue is relatively easy to raise. People generally go along with it. Often its only opposition is reality as it has already been coded linguistically (so *moissonneuse* and *médecine* have become the names of objects or designate a professional discipline and are no longer names for people, and sometimes the female name for an occupation doesn't exist or designates a different job) and social resistance depending upon the level of access available for women. But in this debate about the names of occupations the issue of language's sexism has hardly been broached, and proposed solutions often tend to try to skirt around the problems it raises.

October 1987

Notes

1 Irigaray is referring to the rule of using the masculine plural in French whenever masculine and feminine are combined, according primacy to the masculine, which in this case might be seen to contradict the social custom of according primacy to the one having majesty over the 'ordinary' subject or citizen (even elected presidents). (Tr.)

2 The suffix *euse* designates a feminine term. (Tr.)

3 In French the possessive adjective agrees in gender (and number) with the object possessed rather than with the possessor, as in English. To illustrate the point of her comparison Irigaray uses the possessive adjective for feminine singular nouns, *sa*, instead of the masculine *son*, for the masculine nouns *phallus* and *penis*. (Tr.)

4 University post (*poste universitaire*) and book (*livre*) are masculine, hence Irigaray here again replaces the masculine possessive adjective with the feminine one. (Tr.)

Reprinted from Luce Irigaray, *Je, tu, nous,* trans. Alison Martin (London: Routledge, 1993).

Chapter 9

Ann Bodine

ANDROCENTRISM IN PRESCRIPTIVE GRAMMAR: SINGULAR 'THEY', SEX-INDEFINITE 'HE', AND 'HE OR SHE'

Introduction

THERE HAS ALWAYS BEEN A tension between the descriptive and prescriptive functions of grammar. Currently, descriptive grammar is dominant among theorists, but prescriptive grammar is taught in the schools and exercises a range of social effects. The relations between the beginning of prescriptive grammar in English and a variety of social issues were extensively explored in the early decades of the twentieth century, culminating in the work of McKnight (1928) and Leonard (1929).

Since 1930, interest has shifted elsewhere and new treatment of the subject has usually been restricted to summaries of earlier research, in textbooks for students of linguistics or English. A notable exception is Visser's monumental work (1963), which includes much new material on prescriptive grammar. More typical is Bloomfield and Newmark's comprehensive summary (1967: 288–325). Bloomfield and Newmark discuss prescriptive grammar as the linguistic manifestation of rationalism, of neo-classicism, and of status anxiety accompanying changes in class structure. They also trace the indirect contributions (through the rise of the vernacular) to the origins of prescriptive grammar by such diverse forces as nationalism and the anti-Latinism of the protestant revolution. These writers all see the inception of the prescriptive grammar movement as a whole as having significant social and psychological causes and consequences, but the specific choices of the prescriptive grammarians are rarely explored and are therefore treated as unmotivated and arbitrary.

This paper focuses on one small segment of the content of prescriptive grammar and explores the social factors behind the particular prescriptions and proscriptions that have been offered. Such an approach is suggested by Labov (1972: 64–5 n. 10), who has called for detailed investigation of a single prescribed form in order to better understand the mechanisms of change in prestige forms. The present investigation differs from the work of the 1920s not only because of its focus on the motivation behind *specific* prescriptions, but also because it deals with the issue of androcentrism, which in the 1920s was apparently not discussed with regard to language, despite the attention to sex roles which was generated by the suffragists.

Because of the social significance of personal reference, personal pronouns are particularly susceptible to modification in response to social and ideological change. Two phases of attention to English third-person singular sex-indefinite pronouns are explored here: first, the prescriptive grammarians' attack on singular 'they' and 'he or she', which began at the end of the eighteenth century and continues today; second, the current feminist attack on sex-indefinite 'he' which began in force about 1970. Changes and possible changes in English third person singular pronouns are then compared with changes in second person singular pronouns in a variety of European languages. Finally, implications of change in English third person singular pronouns for several important linguistic issues are considered.

Singular 'they', sex-indefinite 'he', and 'he or she'

There is a tradition among some grammarians to lament the fact that English has no sex-indefinite pronoun for third person singular and to state categorically that the only course is to use 'he' in sex-indefinite contexts. Other grammarians omit the lamentations but state just as categorically that 'he' is the English sex-indefinite pronoun. This matter has taken a new turn recently with the insistence of many feminists that 'he' should not be used when the referent includes women, and that speakers of English should find some substitute. The reaction to this demand has ranged from agreement, to disagreement, to ridicule, to horror, but invariably the feminists' demand is viewed as an attempt to alter the English language.

In fact, the converse is true. Intentionally or not, the movement against sex-indefinite 'he' is actually a counter-reaction to an attempt by prescriptive grammarians to alter the language. English has always had other linguistic devices for referring to sex-indefinite referents, notably, the use of the singular 'they' (their, them) as in sentences 1 to 3.

1 Anyone can do it if they try hard enough. (mixed-sex, distributive)
2 Who dropped their ticket? (sex unknown)
3 Either Mary or John should bring a schedule with them. (mixed-sex, disjunctive)

This usage came under attack by prescriptive grammarians. However, despite almost two centuries of vigorous attempts to analyse and regulate it out of existence, singular 'they' is alive and well. Its survival is all the more remarkable considering that the weight of virtually the entire educational and publishing establishment has been behind the attempt to eradicate it.

Figures 9.1 and 9.2 show two different analyses of the English pronominal system; only nominative case is given, since the accusative and possessive pronouns have the same semantic ranges. Figure 9.1 represents the reality of the language – the pronominal system as developed and used by speakers of English, who have been striving for communicative effectiveness under a variety of social and cognitive pressures. Figure 9.2 represents the construct of early English grammarians, who were striving for tidy analysis under social and cognitive pressures peculiar to that small and unrepresentative subset of the English-speaking population. (One striking feature of Figure 9.1, the extension of the pronoun 'you' to first and third persons, falls outside the scope of this paper and is presented only so as not to falsify what, according to my best understanding, is the correct picture.

Surprising as it may seem in the light of the attention later devoted to the issue, prior to the nineteenth century singular 'they' was widely used in written, therefore presumably also in spoken, English. This usage met with no opposition. Dozens of examples from several centuries of English literature are listed by Poutsma (1916: 310–12), McKnight (1925: 12–13; 1928: 197, 528–30), and Visser (1963: vol. I, 75–8). In formal analyses of the English pronominal system, however, 'they' was incorrectly analysed as only plural in meaning as in Figure 9.2, and nineteenth-century prescriptive grammarians tried to change the language to their conception of it. Of course, they attempted the same thing with vast numbers of English usages, but what is socially significant about this particular 'correction' is the direction in which the change was attempted.

If the definition of 'they' as exclusively plural is accepted, then 'they' fails to agree with a singular, sex-indefinite antecedent by one feature – that of number. Similarly, 'he' fails to agree with a singular, sex-indefinite antecedent by one feature – that of gender. A non-sexist 'correction' would have been to advocate 'he or she', but rather than encourage this usage the grammarians actually tried to eradicate it also, claiming 'he or she' is 'clumsy', 'pedantic', or 'unnecessary'. Significantly, they never attacked terms such as 'one or more' or 'person or persons', although the plural logically includes the singular more than the masculine includes the feminine. These two situations are linguistically analogous. In both cases the language user is confronted with an obligatory category, either number or sex, which is irrelevant to the message being transmitted. However, the two are not socially analogous, since number lacks social significance. Consequently, number and gender have received very different treatment by past and present prescriptive and descriptive grammarians of English. Of the three forms which existed in English for a sex-indefinite referent ('he or she', 'they', and 'he'), only

Number
Person
Singular
Plural
1st
I
WE
2nd
YOU
3rd
IT
SHE
HE
THEY

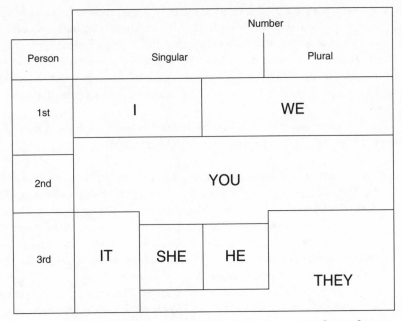

Figure 9.1 English pronouns according to usage (Two significant features of Figure 9.1 are the extension of 'you', which will not be discussed here, and the extension of 'they', which is the subject of this paper. Personal pronominal usages not included in Figure 9.1 are 'it' when used of a baby, second person plural 'ya'll or 'you all', and impersonal 'one'.)

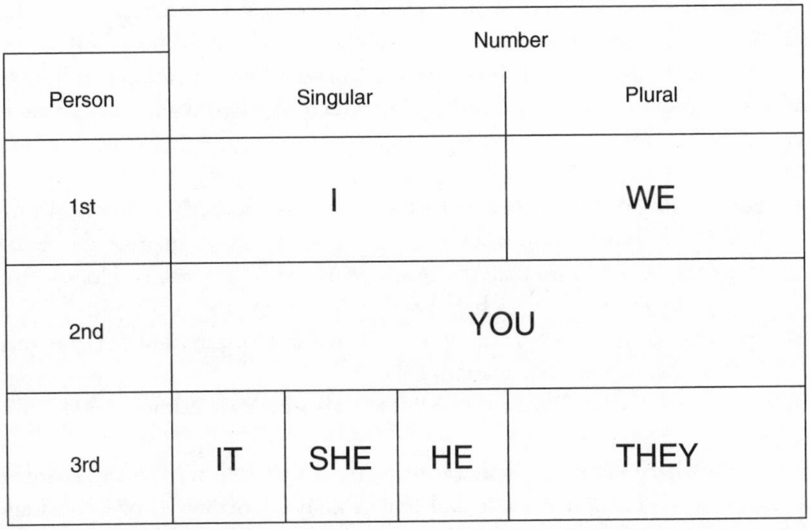

Number
Person
Singular
Plural
1st
I
WE
2nd
YOU
3rd
IT
SHE
HE
THEY

Figure 9.2 English pronouns according to traditional grammatical analysis

one was selected as 'correct' while the other two were proscribed. Although the grammarians felt they were motivated by an interest in logic, accuracy, and elegance, the above analysis reveals that there is no rational, objective basis for their choice, and therefore the explanation must lie elsewhere. It would appear that their choice was dictated by an androcentric world-view; linguistically, human beings were to be considered male unless proven otherwise.

This principle has been resisted by speakers, and to a lesser extent by writers, of English. According to Leonard (1929: 225),

> [T]he minute attention to agreement, particularly of pronouns, had little effect on the writers of the period following; probably quite as many cases of reference of 'they' and 'their' to words like 'person' and 'one' and 'everybody' could be discovered in an equal number of pages of Jane Austen or Walter Scott and of Addison or Swift. And though the matter was brought to sharp focus and fully attended to by the critics of the succeeding period, there is good evidence that British usage is still about equally unfettered in the matter. The greater conservatism of American writers, as usual, has led them to follow this rule more carefully.

By 'conservatism' here Leonard does not mean avoidance of change and adherence to established pattern, since established pattern included singular 'they'. 'Conservatism' here means reliance on the authority of grammarians, which has been more characteristic of American writers and editors than of British writers and editors (McKnight 1925).

The advocacy by grammarians of English of the linguistic embodiment of an androcentric worldview was evident over two centuries before the invention of the proscription against singular 'they'. Wilson (1553) is one of the earliest to berate English language users who neglect to express linguistically the androcentric social order, for which Wilson claims the status of the 'natural' order.

> Some will set the Carte before the horse, as thus. My mother and my father are both at home, even as thoughe the good man of the house ware no breaches or that the graye Mare were the better Horse. And what thoughe it often so happeneth (God wotte the more pitte) yet in speaking at the leaste, let us kepe a natural order, and set the man before the woman for maners Sake.
> (Wilson 1560: 189; also in Mair edition 1909: 167)

Wilson elsewhere states the general principle to be followed with regard to the linguistic ordering of female and male as, 'the worthier is preferred and set before: As a man is sette before a woman' (1560: 234; also in Mair edition 1909: 208).

The same principle was repeated in the seventeenth century with reference to agreement of relative pronoun and antecedent.

> The Relative agrees with the Antecedent in gender, number, and person. . . . The Relative shall agree in gender with the Antecedent of the more worthy gender: as, the King and the Queen whom I honor. The Masculine gender is more worthy than the Feminine.
>
> (Poole 1646: 21)

Throughout the seventeenth and early eighteenth centuries English grammarians were sufficiently influenced by Latin grammar that the discussion of English syntax scarcely went beyond the Latin-derived Three Concords (subject and verb, substantive and adjective, relative pronoun and antecedent), with the above quotation from Poole being a restatement and discussion of the Third Concord. S. Saxon (1737) was among the first to enlarge upon the Three Concords, giving several distinct rules under each, as well as three additional Concords, each with their several rules, ending with a total of thirty-three distinct rules. But neither Poole nor S. Saxon, nor any grammarian of the intervening period whose work I have examined, specifically discusses agreement between personal pronouns and sex-indefinite antecedents. This is true despite the facts that, first, most of these grammarians include a version of the Third Concord among their syntactic rules and, second, until Ward (1765: 127) 'she, her, he, him' were often classed as relative pronouns. Thus, although androcentrism was present, it had not yet resulted in the proscription of singular 'they', which was still freely used along with 'he or she' and sex-indefinite 'he'.

Kirby (1746) continues the increase of syntactic rules, presenting eighty-eight rules, among which appears the earliest example I have found of the explicit advocacy of sex-indefinite 'he'. Rule 21: 'The masculine Person answers to the general Name, which comprehends both Male and Female; as Any Person, who knows what he says' (Kirby 1746: 117). Kirby has stopped referring to the masculine gender as the 'worthier' gender, but he substitutes the 'comprehensive' masculine for the 'worthy' masculine. One eighteenth-century grammarian explicitly denied the need for having an unmarked gender ('he'):

> *he* must represent a male; *she* a female; and *it*, an object of no sex. . . . But the plural *they* equally represents objects of all the three genders; for a plural object may consist of singular objects, some of which are masculine, others feminine, and others neuter; as, *a man and a woman and some iron were in the wagon, and they were all overturned*. . . .
>
> This frees the English, in a great measure, from the perplexity of such rules, as, 'The masculine gender is more worthy than the feminine. . . .' These rules arise in the Latin and Greek, because the adjectives and possessive pronouns must agree, in grammatic gender,

with the gender of the substantives to which they are applied; and when several substantives of different genders happen to denote a complex object, no one gender of an adjective or possessive pronoun, will suit those of such a series of substantives. And therefore neither the English adjectives, nor the plural personal, nor the plural possessive pronouns, have a distinction of gender.

(Ward 1765: 459–60)

The comprehensiveness and huge size (554 pages) of Ward's work make it unlikely that he overlooked prohibitions which were considered important by his contemporaries. Rather it would appear that Kirby's and Ward's contemporaries had not yet applied the concept of the preferential masculine to personal pronouns and that Kirkby's Rule 21 is best viewed as an unusually early and very incipient form of the attack on singular 'they'.

Murray (1765) sets the tone for this attack, presenting the first 'false syntax' examples I have found for singular 'they':

RULE V. Pronouns must always agree with their antecedents, and the nouns for which they stand, in gender, number, and person, . . . Of this rule there are many violations. '*Each* of the sexes should keep within *its* particular bounds, and content *themselves* with the advantages of *their* particular districts.' 'Can any one, on their entrance into the world, be fully secure that they shall not be deceived?' 'on *his* entrance,' and 'that *he* shall.' 'Let each esteem others better than themselves;' 'than *himself*.

(Murray 1795: 95–6)

Later authors expanded their sections on the 'false syntax' of singular 'they' up to several pages.

This virtual explosion of condemnation of singular 'they' culminated in an Act of Parliament in 1850, which legally replaced 'he or she' with 'he'. The act clearly reveals a recognition that specification of both gender (for pronouns) and number (for pronouns and concrete nouns) is obligatory in English, even when such information is irrelevant to the communication. However, when the precision is unneeded it is disposed of quite differently for number, which has no social significance, than for gender. Whereas necessary number is to be dispensed with by the arbitrary choice with by the use of the masculine *only*.

An Act for shortening the language used in acts of Parliament . . . in all acts words importing the masculine gender shall be deemed and taken to include females, and the singular to include the plural, and the plural the singular, unless the contrary as to gender and number is expressly provided.

(Cited in Evans and Evans 1957: 221).

Similarly, Kirby's Rule 21, cited above (p. 129), that the masculine comprehends both male and female, is immediately followed (Rule 22) by the *equation* of singular and plural, under certain circumstances, so that either may represent the other. Thus, in Rule 22 Kirby equates 'The Life of Men' and 'The Lives of Men' (1746: 117).

Thus, the 1850 Act of Parliament and Kirby's Rules 21–2 manifest their underlying androcentric values and worldview in two ways. First, linguistically analogous phenomena (number and gender) are handled very differently (singular *or* plural as generic vs masculine *only* as generic). Second, the precept just being established is itself violated in not allowing singular 'they', since if the plural shall be deemed and taken' to include the singular, then surely 'they' includes 'she' and 'he', and 'she or he'.

This special pleading for sex-indefinite 'he' was no less strong in America than in Britain, as may be seen in the following quotation from an American prescriptive grammarian.

> *Their* is very commonly misused with reference to a singular noun. Even John Ruskin has written such a sentence as this: 'But if a *customer* wishes you to injure *their* foot or to disfigure it, you are to refuse *their* pleasure.' How Mr Ruskin could have written such a sentence as that (for plainly there is no slip of the pen or result of imperfect interlinear correction in it), or how, it having been written, it could be passed by an intelligent proof-reader, I cannot surmise. It is, perhaps, an exemplification of the straits to which we are driven by the lack of a pronoun of common gender meaning both he and she, his and her. But, admitting this lack, the fact remains that *his* is the representative pronoun, as *mankind* includes both men and women. Mr Ruskin might better have said, 'If a customer wishes you to injure his foot you are to refuse his pleasure.' To use 'his or her' in cases of this kind seems to me very finical and pedantic.
>
> (White 1880: 416)

Another quotation from White shows his clear recognition of the social implications of grammar:

> MARRY. – There has been not a little discussion as to the use of this word, chiefly in regard to public announcements of marriage. The usual mode of making the announcement is – Married, John Smith to Mary Jones; Some people having been dissatisfied with this form, we have seen, of late years, in certain quarters – Married, John Smith with Mary Jones; and in others – John Smith and Mary Jones. I have no hesitation in saying that all of these forms are incorrect. We know, indeed, what is meant by any one of them; but the same is true of hundreds and thousands of erroneous uses of language. Properly speaking, a man is not married to a woman, or married with her; nor are a man and a

woman married with each other. The woman is married to the man. It is her name that is lost in his, not his in hers; she becomes a member of his family, not he of hers; it is her life that is merged, or supposed to be merged, in his, not his in hers; she follows his fortunes, and takes his station, not he hers. And thus, manifestly, she has been attached to him by a legal bond, not he to her; except, indeed, as all attachment is necessarily mutual. But, nevertheless, we do not speak of tying a ship to a boat, but a boat to a ship. And so long, at least, as man is the larger, the stronger, the more individually important, as long as woman generally lives in her husband's house and bears his name, – still more should she not bear his name, – it is the woman who is married to the man.

(White 1886: 139–40)

[. . .]

Although in the nineteenth and twentieth centuries the masculine gender was generally no longer championed as the 'worthier' gender, there has remained an underlying realization of the social implications of sex-indefinite 'he'. Fowler (1926) refers to the views of the scholar Whately, archbishop of Dublin in the early nineteenth century, concerning the use of singular (distributive) 'they': 'Archbishop Whately used to say that women were more liable than men to fall into this error, as they objected to identifying 'everybody' with "him" ' (p. 635). Fowler himself mentions, but dismisses with a joke, the possibility that the grammarians' invention and perpetuation of the proscription against singular 'they' constitutes a social injustice.

> [The use of sex-indefinite 'he'] involves the convention (statutory in the interpretation of documents) that where the matter of sex is not conspicuous or important the masculine form shall be allowed to represent a person instead of a man, or say a man (homo) instead of a man (vir). Whether that convention, with *himself or herself* in the background for especial exactitudes, and paraphrase always possible in dubious cases, is an arrogant demand on the part of male England, everyone must decide for himself (or for himself or herself, or for themselves).
>
> (Fowler 1926: 404)

Curme (1931: 552) considers the possibility that sex-indefinite 'he' is 'one-sided', but then invokes 'the idea of the oneness of man and woman [which] is present to our feeling' as the basis for the generic use of the masculine. A linguist in Sterling A. Leonard's jury-based study[1] of current English usage rejects 'Each person should of course bear *his or her* share of the expense', on the basis that 'I prefer simply *his*. This seems to be a matter of pleasing the women'(cited in Leonard 1932: 103). Unlike these earlier commentators McCawley (1974: 103) sees no need to defend the equation of 'he' with 'person'. So unquestioningly does McCawley accept this equation that he claims that sex-indefinite 'he' carries no overtones of its primary, masculine meaning if it is used consistently in sex-indefinite contexts. On this basis McCawley further implies that the phrase 'he or she' is sexist in that it 'makes women a special category of beings' by mentioning them in addition to 'people' (i.e., 'he').

The changed social climate and the dispassionate tone in which textbooks are written today make it virtually impossible that any textbook writer in the second half of the twentieth century could make as explicitly androcentric a statement as, for instance, the tirade by White, the nineteenth-century American prescriptive grammarian quoted at length above (pp. 131–2).

To determine how the issue is taught today I surveyed thirty-three of the school grammars now being used in American junior and senior high schools. Twenty-eight of these books condemn both 'he or she' and singular 'they', the former because it is clumsy and the latter because it is inaccurate. And then the pupils are taught to achieve both elegance of expression and accuracy by referring to women as 'he'. One of the modern textbook writers does show his awareness and approval of the hierarchy implied by the use of sex-indefinite 'he', when he tells children not to use 'he or she', which is 'awkward', but instead to follow the convention that 'grammatically, men are more important than women' (Roberts 1967: 355).

Most of the modern textbook writers, like most of the early prescriptive grammarians, give no such explicitly androcentric justification for prescribing sex-indefinite 'he', but instead argue that sex-indefinite 'he' is 'correct', whereas singular 'they' is 'inaccurate' and 'he or she' is 'awkward.' However, the line of argument developed in connection with the prescriptive grammarians is equally applicable here. That is, disagreement of number, as in the proscribed singular 'they', is no more 'inaccurate' than disagreement of gender, as in the unproscribed sex-indefinite 'he'. Similarly, the proscribed 'he or she' is no more 'clumsy' than the unproscribed 'one or more' and 'person or persons'. Thus, these writers appear to be the docile heirs to the androcentric tradition of the prescriptive grammarians, failing to confront, if not implicitly subscribing to, the androcentric motive.

The fact that the controversy over singular 'they' has anything to do with sex seems to have escaped the notice of today's textbook writers, or if they have noticed, they are not letting the kids in on it. Twenty-five of the above twenty-eight textbooks tell students that the reason 'they' is 'mistakenly' used for a singular antecedent is that the antecedent has a plural meaning. This is obviously an inadequate explanation, since 'they' is used for antecedents with both plural and singular meaning, as may be seen in the following sentences, collected by the author from the ordinary conversation of native speakers of American English holding bachelors, masters, and doctoral degrees.

4 Did everyone say they missed you like mad yesterday?
5 Somebody left their sweater.

6 Not one single child raised their hand.

7 When you call on a student, it's better if you can remember their name.

In 4, the antecedent of 'they' has a plural meaning, but the antecedents of 'they' in 5, 6, and 7 are clearly singular. Notice particularly 6 and 7. If the subjects were perceived as plural, surely the speakers would have said 'their hands' and 'their names' rather than 'their hand' and 'their name'.

Of all twenty-eight school grammars reviewed, only three gave children an adequate explanation of the use of 'they'. Although still condemning the use of 'they' in this manner, these three textbooks did give a socially and psychologically realistic assessment of why it is done. One of these realistic textbooks says, 'the pronoun *his* would apply equally to a man or to a woman. Nevertheless some people feel awkward about using *his* to refer to a woman and instead use *their*' (Blumenthal and Warriner 1964: 139). Blumenthal and Warriner then say this is unacceptable, at least in writing, and they also advise against the use of 'he or she' because it is 'clumsy'. The second of the realistic textbooks has more to say.

> English has a problem in that it has no common gender [in the third person singular]. . . . The most awkward solution is to use both the masculine and the feminine pronoun: 'Everyone should raise his (or her) hand when he (or she) is ready.' We usually try to avoid this by following the convention that, grammatically, men are more important than women. For reference to mixed groups, we use just the pronoun *he*. 'Everyone should raise *his* hand when *he* is ready.'
>
> (Roberts 1967: 354–5)

Robert's next suggestion has been offered by numerous grammarians from the nineteenth century right up to writers of textbooks now being used in the schools. They say, in effect, that if you cannot bring yourself to use 'he' for women then do not use a singular subject at all, but go back and start the sentence over again with a plural subject. 'Sometimes we avoid the issue by pluralizing the noun phrase to which the pronoun refers. "All boys and girls should raise their hands when they are ready" ' (1967: 355).

Actually, this advice to start the sentence over again with a clearly plural subject is a necessary escape, because some of the grammarians unable to see the frequent singular semantic content of the word 'they' are apparently equally unable to see the frequent plural semantic content of words like 'everyone' and 'everybody', for example, sentence 4. Sentence 8 was written by a 12-year-old boy in a school composition describing a dunking by a group of classmates; it is cited as an example of hypercorrection by Leonard (1929: 224 n. 57).

8 When I came up, everybody was laughing at me, but I was glad to see him just the same.

None of the modern textbook writers reviewed went quite so far as to recommend sentences like 8, but they did go so far as to condemn the use of 'them' even in a sentence like 8. Sentence 9 was given as an example of bad grammar in one textbook.

9 Everyone in the class worried about the midyear history examination, but they all passed (Tressler, Christ and Starkey 1960; book 4: 343).

Tressler *et al.* could not quite bring themselves to recommend 'Everyone in the class worried about the midyear history examination, but *he* all passed', so they told the pupils to rewrite the sentence, 'The class members worried about the midyear history examination, but they all passed.'

The effect on actual written and spoken usage of the movement to eradicate 'he or she' and singular 'they' is complex. The continuing attack of textbook writers and teachers indicates that both forms are still very much a part of American English. On the other hand, the counter-attack on sex-indefinite 'he' by feminists indicates that sex-indefinite 'he' is also widely used.

The most clear-cut success of the movement to eradicate singular 'they' has been the near-universality of agreement in *discussions about* English, as opposed to its actual usage, that 'they' can not have singular meaning. A notable exception to the acceptance of the traditional analysis of English third person pronouns is Key (1972: 27–8). Key lists eight instances of lack of agreement of usage with the traditional analysis and implies that more may be found. Key's examples differ from those being discussed in this paper in that all are in some way special – non-native speakers, homosexuals, small children, humour – whereas this discussion concerns ordinary usage.

The persistence for almost two centuries of the original movement to eradicate 'he or she' and singular 'they' suggests that the counter–movement against sex-indefinite 'he' is unlikely to disappear. Furthermore, since the countermovement has more explicit social and ideological buttresses as well as a larger number of supporters than the original movement had at its inception, it is reasonable to predict that the countermovement against sex-indefinite 'he' will affect English pronominal usage. Therefore, during the next few years students of language development may have the opportunity to follow the progress of a particularly visible type of language change.

Of course it is possible that the pronominal changes foreseen by this writer will not come to pass, and contrary predictions have indeed been made. For instance, Lakoff has suggested that the current feminist attack on sex-indefinite 'he' is misguided, since 'an attempt to change pronominal usage will be futile' (Lakoff 1975: 45). Conklin (1973) has also expressed doubt as to whether 'so stable a portion of language as the pronominal system will yield to change'. These writers do not recognize how widespread the use of singular 'they' is at present and they also tend to see the pronominal system as a categorical given. However, looking at the wider context of language change in general, it can be seen that pronominal systems are particularly susceptible to alteration in response to social change.

Comparison with changes in second person pronouns

The spread of the ideology of feudalism caused most European languages to develop two sets of second person singular pronouns, for the representation of hierarchy (Brown and Gilman 1960: 254–5; Jespersen 1938: 223–4). In both English and Russian this change came about by a process analogous to the inclusion of singularity in the pronoun 'they', i.e., the plural pronouns (English 'ye–you', Russian 'vy') were extended to include singularity. This resulted in two sets of second-person singular pronouns: English 'thou–thee' (nominative and accusative) and Russian 'ty' for an inferior or an intimate vs English 'ye–you' (nominative and accusative) and Russian 'vy' for a superior or a non-intimate. Later, under the pressure of social structural changes and the beginnings of egalitarian ideology, English's second person singular pronouns contracted to a single word. More recently, second person pronouns have been undergoing change in a number of other European languages – French, German, Italian, Serbo-Croatian and Swedish.

These analyses of change in second-person pronoun usage rank among the most convincing demonstrations ever given of the social motivation of linguistic change. Their importance for linguistics is that they show the futility of attempting to explain language change as taking place on an autonomous linguistic level. Their importance for sociology is indicated by Grimshaw: 'I don't see how any sociologist could read the piece by Friedrich on Russian pronominal usage . . . without being persuaded of the imperative necessity of incorporating a sociolinguistic dimension into sociological research and theory.

(Grimshaw 1974: 5)

Implications

Careful observation of change in English pronominal usage could contribute to our understanding of a number of issues of general importance within linguistics including (*a*) continuing linguistic enculturation, (*b*) conscious vs unconscious change, and (*c*) compensatory adjustment within the linguistic system.

(*a*) The only aspect of post-childhood linguistic enculturation which has received much attention is vocabulary learning. Grimshaw is foremost among scholar calling for a broad investigation of all kinds of later language learning. He states,

studies of language acquisition – like their companion studies of socialization done by sociologists – frequently tend . . . to ignore continuing
linguistic and other socialization. I have recently had occasion to try
and find out what is known about continuing language and other socialization of older adolescents and young adults. The answer thus far seems
to be 'very little'.

(Grimshaw 1973: 584)

Because the particular language forms under discussion here have ties with
age-related concerns and awareness they are a likely source of information
on continuing language acquisition. No stable age differentiation is predicted,
however, since as feminists grow older they are unlikely to return to the
pronominal usage, sex-indefinite 'he', which they have rejected.

(b) Much of the writing on language change prior to 1960 pictures
language change as slow, inexorable, unconscious, largely unmotivated
drifting within free variation. Although sound change is still far from understood, work by Labov and his followers has clearly demonstrated that free
variation is not so free and sound change is not so unmotivated nor always
so unconscious. The same has been documented for morphology and syntax
by Rubin, who concludes,

> On the basis of the already reported cases, it seems reasonable to
> presume that any aspect of the language code or language usage is
> susceptible to conscious change provided that the necessary motivation
> and proper field for implementation exists.

(Rubin 1972: 8)

And, 'From the above examples, we can see that language structure has been
molded deliberately to serve a number of different motivations, ranging from
purely communicative to purely socio-political' (ibid.: 10).

Although the extent to which a speech community's members talk about
talking varies from culture to culture, and between individuals within any
single culture (Hymes 1961), most communities promote sufficient leisure,
introspection, and argumentation to assure that differential acceptance and
promotion of linguistic forms will play some role in lexical and grammatical
change. As English pronominal usage is increasingly affected by the feminist
countermovement discussed in this paper, it will provide an ideal opportunity to study differences in language change among those who make a
conscious decision and deliberate effort to change, among those who are
aware that the change is taking place but have no particular interest in the
issue, among those who are oblivious to the change, and among those who
are consciously resisting the change.

(c) It is rare that linguists have the opportunity to analyse changes and
adjustments in the relatively tightly structured pronominal system of a
language at the very time when the systematic change is taking place. Such

an opportunity is now being continuously exploited for Swedish second person pronouns by Paulston (1971: Paulston and Featheringham 1974) who is consequently able to provide an unusually complete record and analysis of the change. Baseline description of present day English third person pronominal usage coupled with continual monitoring of usage trends offers another such opportunity for the detailed investigation of systematic change in progress.

In most instances of multiple, related language changes it is impossible to extricate from the near-simultaneous changes what is cause and what is effect, especially when the changes are studied after the fact. However, if change (for example, the pronominal change discussed here) is anticipated, or detected at its inception, it should be possible to hypothesize about areas of language in which compensatory adjustments might take place (for example, a general weakening of number concord, for which there is no particular social pressure) and to subject those areas of potential instability to continuing observation.

Conclusion

Personal reference, including personal pronouns, is one of the most socially significant aspects of language. As such, it is particularly likely to become the target of deliberate efforts to bring symbolic representation of interpersonal relations into line with the way those relationships are structured in either the ideal or behavioural patterning of the members of a speech community. With the increase of opposition to sex-based hierarchy, the structure of English third person pronouns may be expected to change to reflect the new ideology and social practices, as second person pronouns did before them. Analysis of the processes and results of this change can further elucidate the contributions of social forces to language development.

Note

1   A panel of linguists, editors, writers, etc. was asked to vote on the acceptability of disputed English usages.

Reprinted from *Language in Society* 4, 1975.

The debate on nonsexist language

Chapter 10

William Satire (alias Douglas Hofstadter)

A PERSON PAPER ON PURITY
IN LANGUAGE

September 1983

IT'S HIGH TIME SOMEONE blew the whistle on all the silly prattle about revamping our language to suit the purposes of certain political fanatics. You know what I'm talking about – those who would radically change our language in order to 'liberate' us poor dupes from its supposed racist bias?

Most of the clamour, as you certainly know by now, revolves around the age-old usage of the noun 'white' and words built from it, such as *chairwhite, mailwhite, repairwhite, clergywhite, middlewhite, Frenchwhite, forewhite, whitepower, whiteslaughter, oneupswhiteship, straw white, whitehandle*, and so on. The Negrists claim that using the word 'white', either on its own or as a component, to talk about *all* the members of the human species is somehow degrading to blacks and reinforces racism. Therefore the libbers propose that we substitute 'person' everywhere where 'white' now occurs. Sensitive speakers of our secretary tongue of course find this preposterous. There is great beauty to a phrase such as 'All whites are created equal.' Our fore-bosses who framed the Declaration of Independence well understood the poetry of our language. Think how ugly it would be to say 'All persons are created equal', or 'All whites and blacks are created equal.' Besides, as any schoolwhitey can tell you, such phrases are redundant. In most contexts, it is self-evident when 'white' is being used in an inclusive sense, in which case it subsumes members of the darker race just as much as fairskins.

There is nothing denigrating to black people in being subsumed under the rubric 'white' – no more than under the rubric 'person'. After all, white is a mixture of all the colours of the rainbow, including black. Used inclusively, the word 'white' has no connotations whatsoever of race. Yet many people are hung up on this point. A prime example is Abraham Moses, one of the more vocal spokeswhites for making such a shift. For years, Niss Moses, authoroon of the well-known Negrist tracts *A Handbook of Nonracist Writing* and *Words and Blacks*, has had nothing better to do than go around the country making speeches advocating the downfall of 'racist language' that ble objects to. But when you analyse bler objections, you find they fall apart at the seams. Niss Moses says that words like 'chairwhite' suggest to people – most especially impressionable young whiteys and blackeys – that all chairwhites belong to the white race. How absurd! It is quite obvious, for instance, that the chairwhite of the League of Black Voters is going to be a black, not a white. Nobody need think twice about it. As a matter of fact, the suffix 'white' is usually not pronounced with a long 'I' as in the noun 'white', but like 'wit', as in the terms, *saleswhite, freshwhite, penwhiteship, first basewhite*, and so on. It's just a simple and useful component in building race-neutral words.

But Niss Moses would have you sit up and start hollering 'Racism!' In fact, Niss Moses sees evidence of racism under every stone. Ble has written a famous article, in which ble vehemently objects to the immortal and poetic words of the first white on the moon, Captain Nellie Strongarm. If you will recall, whis words were: 'One small step for a white, a giant step for whitekind.' This noble sentiment is anything but racist; it is simply a celebration of a glorious moment in the history of White.

Another of Niss Moses's shrill objections is to the age-old differentiation of whites from blacks by the third-person pronouns 'whe' and 'ble'. Ble promotes an absurd notion: that what we really need in English is a single pronoun covering *both* races. Numerous suggestions have been made, such as 'pe', 'tey', and others. These are all repugnant to the nature of the English language, as the average white in the street will testify, even if whe has no linguistic training whatsoever. Then there are advocates of usages such as 'whe or ble', 'whis or bler', and so forth. This makes for monstrosities such as the sentence 'When the next President takes office, whe or ble will have to choose whis or bler cabinet with great care, for whe or ble would not want to offend any minorities.' Contrast this with the spare elegance of the normal way of putting it, and there is no question which way we ought to speak. There are, of course, some yapping black libbers who advocate writing 'bl/whe' everywhere, which, aside from looking terrible, has no reasonable pronunciation. She we say 'blooey' all the time when we simply mean 'whe'? Who wants to sound like a white with a chronic sneeze?

One of the more hilarious suggestions made by the squawkers for this point of view is to abandon the nature distinction along racial lines, and to replace it with a highly unnatural one along sexual lines. One such suggestion – emanating, no doubt, from the mind of a madwhite – would have us say 'he' for male whites (and blacks) and 'she' for female whites (and blacks). Can you imagine the outrage with which sensible folk of either sex would greet this 'modest proposal'?

Another suggestion is that the plural pronoun 'they' be used in place of the inclusive 'whe'. This would turn the charming proverb 'Whe who laughs last, laughs best' into the bizarre concoction 'They who laughs last, laughs best'. As if anyone in whis right mind could have thought that the original proverb applied only to the white race! No, we don't need a new pronoun to 'liberate' our minds. That's the lazy white's way of solving the pseudo-problem of racism. In any case, it's ungrammatical. The pronoun 'they' is a plural pronoun, and it grates on the civilized ear to hear it used to denote only one person. Such a usage, if adopted, would merely promote illiteracy and accelerate the already scandalously rapid nosedive of the average intelligence level of our society.

Niss Moses would have us totally revamp the English language to suit bler purposes. If, for instance, we are to substitute 'person' for 'white', where are we to stop? If we were to follow Niss Moses's ideas to their logical conclusion, we would have to conclude that ble would like to see small blackeys and whiteys playing the game of 'Hangperson' and reading the story of 'Snow Person and the Seven Dwarfs'. And would ble have us rewrite history to say. 'Don't shoot until you see the *persons* of their eyes!'? Will pundits and politicians henceforth issue *person* papers? Will we now have egg yolks and egg *persons*? And pledge allegiance to the good old Red, *Person*, and Blue? Will we sing, 'I'm dreaming of a *person* Christmas'? Say of a frightened white, 'Whe's *person* as a sheet!'? Lament the increase of *person*-collar crime? Thrill to the chirping of bob*persons* in our gardens? Ask a friend to *person* the table while we go visit the *persons'* room? Come off it, Niss Moses – don't personwash our language!

What conceivable harm is there in such beloved phrases as 'No white is an island', 'Dog is white's best friend', or 'White's inhumanity to white'? Who would revise such classic book titles as Bronob Jacowski's *The Ascent of White* or Eric Steeple Bell's *Whites of Mathematics*? Did the poet who wrote 'The best-laid plans of mice and whites gang aft agley' believe that blacks' plans gang *ne'er* agley? Surely not! Such phrases are simply metaphors; everyone can see beyond that. Whe who interprets them as reinforcing racism must have a perverse desire to feel oppressed.

'Personhandling' the language is a habit that not only Niss Moses but quite a few others have taken up recently. For instance, Nrs Delilah Buford has urged that we drop the useful distinction between 'Niss' and 'Nrs' (which, as everybody knows, is pronounced 'Nissiz', the reason for which nobody knows!) Bler argument is that there is no need for the public to know whether a black is employed or not. *Need* is, of course, not the point. Ble conveniently sidesteps the fact that there is a *tradition* in our society of calling unemployed blacks 'Niss' and employed blacks 'Nrs'. Most blacks – in fact, the vast majority – prefer it that way. They *want* the world to know what their employment status is, and for good reason. Unemployed blacks want prospective employers to know they are available, without having to ask embarrassing questions. Likewise, employed blacks are proud of having found a job, and wish to let the world know they are employed. This distinction provides a sense of security to all involved, in that everyone knows where ble fits into the scheme of things.

But Nrs Buford refuses to recognize this simple truth. Instead, ble shiftily turns the argument into one about whites, asking why it is that whites are universally addressed as 'Master', without any differentiation between employed and unemployed ones. The answer, of course, is that in America and other northern societies, we set little store by the employment status of whites. Nrs Buford can do little to change that reality, for it seems to be tied to innate biological differences between whites and blacks. Many white-years of research, in fact, have gone into trying to understand why it is that employment status matters so much to blacks, yet relatively little to whites. It is true that both races have a longer life expectancy if employed, but of course people often do not act so as to maximize their life expectancy. So far, it remains a mystery. In any case, whites and blacks clearly have different constitutional inclinations, and different goals in life. And so I say, *Vive na différence!*

As for Nrs Buford's suggestion that both 'Niss' and 'Nrs' be unified into the single form of address 'Ns' (supposed to rhyme with 'fizz'), all I have to say is, it is arbitrary and clearly a thousand years ahead of its time. Mind you, this 'Ns' is an abbreviation concocted out of thin air: it stands for absolutely nothing. Who ever heard of such toying with language? And while we're on this subject, have you yet run across the recently founded *Ns* magazine, dedicated to the concerns of the 'liberated black'? It's sure to attract the attention of a trendy band of black airheads for a little while, but serious blacks surely will see through its thin veneer of slick, glossy Madison Avenue approaches to life.

Nrs Buford also finds it insultingly asymmetric that when a black is employed by a white, ble changes bler firmly name to whis firmly name. But what's so bad about that? Every firm's core consists of a boss (whis job is to make sure long-term policies are well charted out) and a secretary (bler job is to keep corporate affairs running smoothly on a day-to-day basis). They are both equally important and vital to the firm's success. No one disputes this. Beyond them there may of course be other firmly members. Now it's quite obvious that all members of a given firm should bear the same firmly name – otherwise, what are you going to call the firm's products? And since it would be nonsense for the boss to change whis name, it falls to the secretary to change bler name. Logic, not racism, dictates this simple convention.

What puzzles me the most is when people cut off their noses to spite their faces. Such is the case with the time-honoured coloured suffixes 'oon' and 'roon', found in familiar words such as *ambassadroon, stewardoon*, and *sculptroon*. Most blacks find it natural and sensible to add those suffixes on to nouns such as 'aviator' or 'waiter.' A black who flies an airplane may proudly proclaim, 'I'm an aviatroon!' But it would sound silly, if not ridiculous, for a black to say of blerself, 'I work as a waiter.' On the other hand, who could object to my saying that the lively Ticely Cyson is a great actroon, or that the hilarious Quill Bosby is a great comedioon? You guessed it – authoroons such as Niss Mildred Hempsley and Nrs Charles White, both of whom angrily reject the appellation 'authoroon', deep though its roots are in our language. Nrs White, perhaps one of the finest poetoons of our day, for some reason insists on being known as a 'poet'. It leads one to wonder, is Nrs White *ashamed* of being black, perhaps? I should hope not. White needs Black, and Black needs White, and neither race should feel ashamed.

Some extreme Negrists object to being treated with politeness and courtesy by whites. For example, they reject the traditional notion of 'Negroes first', preferring to open doors for themselves, claiming that having doors opened for them suggests implicitly that society considers them inferior. Well, would they have it the other way? Would these incorrigible grousers prefer to open doors for whites? What do blacks want?

Another unlikely word has recently become a subject of controversy: 'blackey'. This is, of course, the ordinary term for black children (including teenagers), and by affectionate extension it is often applied to older blacks. Yet, incredible though it seems, many blacks – even teenage blackeys – now claim to have had their 'consciousness raised', and are voguishly skittish about being called 'blackeys'. Yet it's as old as the hills for blacks employed in the same office to refer to themselves as the 'the office blackeys'. And for their superior to call them 'my blackeys' helps make the ambiance more relaxed and comfy for all. It's hardly the mortal insult that libbers claim it to be. Fortunately, most blacks are sensible people and realize that mere words do not demean; they know it's how they are *used* that counts. Most of the time, calling a black – especially on older black – a 'blackey' is a thoughtful way of complimenting bler, making bler feel young, fresh, and hirable again. Lord knows, I certainly wouldn't object if someone told me that I looked whiteyish these days!

Many young blackeys go through a stage of wishing they had been born white. Perhaps this is due to popular television shows like *Superwhite* and *Batwhite*, but it doesn't really matter. It is perfectly normal and healthy. Many of our most successful blacks were once tomwhiteys and feel no shame about it. Why should they? Frankly, I think tomwhiteys are often the cutest little blackeys – but that's just my opinion. In any case, Niss Moses (once again) raises a ruckus on this score, asking why we don't have a corresponding word for young whiteys who play blackeys' games and generally manifest a desire to be blacks. Well, Niss Moses, if this were a common phenomenon, we most assuredly *would* have such a word, but it just happens not to be. Who can say why? But given that tomwhiteys are a dime a dozen, it's nice to have a word for them. The lesson is that White must learn to fit language to reality; White cannot manipulate the world by manipulating mere words. An elementary lesson, to be sure, but for some reason Niss Moses and others of bler ilk resist learning it.

Shifting from the ridiculous to the sublime, let us consider the Holy Bible. The good book is, of course, the source of some of the most beautiful language and profound imagery to be found anywhere. And who is the central character of the Bible? I am sure I need hardly remind you; it is God. As everyone knows, Whe is male and white, and that is an indisputable fact. But have you heard the latest joke promulgated by tasteless Negrists? It is said that one of them died and went to Heaven and then returned. What did ble report? 'I have seen God, and guess what? Ble's female!' Can anyone say that this is not blasphemy of the highest order? It just goes to show that some people will stoop to any depths in order to shock. I have shared this 'joke' with a number of friends of mine (including several blacks, by the way), and, to a white, they have agreed that it sickens them to the core to see Our Lord so shabbily mocked. Some things are just in bad taste, and there are no two ways about it. It is scum like this who are responsible for some of the great problems in our society today, I am sorry to say.

Well, all of this is just another skirmish in the age-old Battle of the Races, I guess, and we shouldn't take it too seriously. I am reminded of words spoken by the great British philosopher Alfred West Malehead in whis commencement address to my *alma secretaria*, the University of North Virginia: 'To enrich the language of whites is, certainly, to enlarge the range of their ideas.' I agree with this admirable sentiment wholeheartedly. I would merely point out to the over-zealous that there are some extravagant notions about language that should be recognized for what they are: cheap attempts to let dogmatic, narrow minds enforce their views on the speakers lucky enough to have inherited the richest, most beautiful, and flexible language on earth, a language whose traditions run back through the centuries to such deathless poets as Milton, Shakespeare, Wordsworth, Keats, Walt Whitwhite, and so many others. . . . Our language owes an incalculable debt to these whites for their clarity of vision and expression, and if the shallow minds of bandwagon-jumping Negrists succeed in destroying this precious heritage for all whites of good will, that will be, without any doubt, a truly female day in the history of Northern White.

Post scriptum

Perhaps this piece shocks you. It is meant to. The entire point of it is to use something that we find shocking as leverage to illustrate the fact that something that we usually close our eyes to is also very shocking. The most effective way I know to do so is to develop an extended analogy with something known as shocking and reprehensible. Racism is that thing, in this case. I am happy with this piece, despite – but also because of – its shock value. I think it makes its point better than any factual article could. As a friend of mine said, 'It makes you so uncomfortable that you can't ignore it.' I admit that rereading it makes even me, the author, uncomfortable!

Numerous friends have warned me that in publishing this piece I am taking a serious risk of earning myself a reputation as a terrible racist. I guess I cannot truly believe that anyone would see this piece that way. To misperceive it this way would be like calling someone a vicious racist for telling other people 'The word "nigger" is extremely offensive.' If *allusions* to racism, especially for the purpose of satirizing racism and its cousins, are confused with racism itself, then I think it is time to stop writing.

Some people have asked me if to write this piece, I simply took a genuine William Safire column (appearing weekly in the *New York Times Magazine* under the title 'On language') and 'fiddled' with it. That is far from the truth. For years I have collected examples of sexist language, and in order to produce this piece, I dipped into this collection, selected some of the choicest, and ordered them very carefully. 'Translating' them into this alternate world was sometimes extremely difficult, and some words took weeks. The hardest terms of all, surprisingly enough, were 'Niss', 'Nrs' and 'Ns', even though 'Master' came immediately. The piece itself is not based on any particular article by William Safire, but Safire has without doubt been one of the most vocal opponents of non-sexist language reforms, and therefore merits being safired upon.

Interestingly, Master Safire has recently spoken out on sexism in whis column (5 August 1984). Lamenting the inaccuracy of writing either 'Mrs Ferraro' or 'Miss Ferraro' to designate the Democratic vice-presidential candidate whose husband's name is 'Zaccaro', whe writes:

> It breaks my heart to suggest this, but the time has come for *Ms*. We are no longer faced with a theory, but a condition. It is unacceptable for journalists to dictate to a candidate that she call herself *Miss* or else use her married name; it is equally unacceptable for a candidate to demand that newspapers print a blatant inaccuracy by applying a married honorific to a maiden name.

How disappointing it is when someone finally winds up doing the right thing but for the wrong reasons! In Safire's case, this shift was entirely for journalistic rather than humanistic reasons! It's as if Safire wished that women had never entered the political ring, so that the Grand Old Conventions of English – good enough for our grandfathers – would never have had to be challenged. How heartless of women! How heartbreaking the toll on our beautiful language!

A couple of weeks after I finished this piece, I ran into the book *The Nonsexist Communicator*, by Bobbye Sorrels. In it, there is a satire called 'A Tale of

Two Sexes', which is very interesting to compare with my 'Person paper'. Whereas in mine, I slice the world orthogonally to the way it is actually sliced and then perform a mapping of worlds to establish a disorienting yet powerful new vision of our world, in hers, Ms Sorrels simply reverses the two halves of our world as it is actually sliced. Her satire is therefore in some ways very much like mine, and in other ways extremely different. It should be read.

I do not know too many publications that discuss sexist language in depth. The finest I have come across are the aforementioned *Handbook of Nonsexist Writing* by Casey Miller and Kate Swift; *Words and Women* by the same authors; *Sexist Language: A Modern Philosophical Analysis* edited by Mary Vetterling-Braggin; *The Nonsexist Communicator* by Bobbye Sorrels; and a very good journal titled *Women and Language News*.

My feeling about non-sexist English is that it is like a foreign language that I am learning. I find that even after years of practice, I still have to translate sometimes from my native language, which is sexist English. I know of no human being who speaks non-sexist as their native tongue. It will be very interesting to see if such people come to exist. If so, it will have taken a lot of work by a lot of people to reach that point.

One final footnote: my book *Gödel, Escher, Bach*, whose dialogues were the source of my very first trepidations about my own sexism, is now being translated into various languages, and to my delight, the Tortoise, a green-blooded male if ever there was one in English, is becoming *Madame Tortue* in French, *Signorina Tartaruga* in Italian, and so on. Full circle ahead!

Reprinted from Douglas Hofstadter, *Magical Metathemas* (Harmondsworth: Penguin, 1988).

Chapter 11

Margaret Doyle

INTRODUCTION TO *THE A–Z OF NON-SEXIST LANGUAGE*

The English language has far more lives than a cat. People have been murdering it for years.

Farmers' Almanac

ENGLISH CAN CREDIT ITS SURVIVAL TO its marvellous adaptability. New words make their way quite easily into common usage, while words that fall out of favour are gently shed, giving the language a fluidity that allows it to respond to changes in society. On the other hand, we can be stubborn language users, clinging to archaic rules and usages as if they were inscribed in stone. Yet there are problems with English usage when it does not reflect the way we live. It becomes awkward, ambiguous, inaccurate, and insensitive. If our language leads to misunderstandings or offends people we are trying to reach, it fails to do what we want it to do; it ceases to be an effective tool for communication. Language that is sexist has this effect.

What is sexist language?

'Sexist language' in this book refers to terms and usages that exclude or discriminate against women. This includes presuming that maleness is standard, the norm, and that femaleness is non-standard, or the exception. One way this most often manifests itself is in the use of 'he/his/him' pronouns and terms like 'man' and 'mankind' to represent women as well as men. Another way is in the use of job titles ending in '-man'. These are often considered to be 'generic' terms, when people using them believe they are genderless, representing neither male nor female subjects, or that they are inclusive, representing both male and female subjects. 'Businessman' (especially in its plural form), 'salesman' and 'chairman' are commonly used in this way.

Another term for sexist language is 'exclusive' language: using *he* as a generic pronoun, and using *mankind* and '-man' compounds as generic terms, excludes women. We associate these with maleness; they bring male images to mind. The opposite, non-sexist language, is thus also known as 'inclusive' language. There are many other types of inclusive language; truly inclusive language would attempt to include all groups that are marginalised by the presumption of a norm that is white, male, heterosexual, middle class. This book, however, deals only with non-sexist inclusive language.

Language is sexist, and exclusive, in many other ways. It can be used to promote sexist stereotypes of, for example, men's and women's roles in society or male and female characteristics. Referring to 'mother and toddler playgroups' or 'mother' helpers', for example, suggests that men take a secondary role in looking after children and household chores. While it might be true that many do, some do not; and by perpetuating this stereotype, this language may give support to the idea that this division of roles is acceptable. It may also make it easier for some men to justify not taking on this role and harder for others to feel comfortable doing so. Referring to a fussy person (usually a man) as 'an old woman' suggests that older women are, as a rule, fussy and complaining. Though some certainly might be, so are some older men, and younger men, and younger women. Older women are no more likely to be fussy or complaining than are members of any of these other groups – yet the inaccurate stereotype persists in this phrase.

Using inclusive language does not have to be clumsy. Nor does it necessarily remove the 'colour' from our language. Most sexist terms have many alternatives, and replacing them can be easy. The result will be clearer, more accurate, and more widely received language.

Why be concerned?

The reason for avoiding sexist language is that it can be used to discriminate against women not only by reinforcing harmful stereotypes but also by rendering women's presence and achievements invisible. Many people believe that discrimination in society will not change simply by ridding our language of sexism. In this view, using non-sexist language is only paying lip-service to reform rather than addressing the very real problems of sexism in society, including discrimination, harassment, violence against women, and economic inequality. Furthermore, in this view, efforts to adopt non-sexist language can be harmful because they can provide a superficially progressive veneer for an organisation while masking its systemic sexism. Others believe that using non-sexist language is an essential part of tackling societal sexism. In this view, language influences our attitudes and behaviour; watching our language goes hand in hand with being careful how we treat others.

Ultimately, the question many people ask is 'why change?' There are as many reasons as there are ways: because sexist language is unclear and inaccurate, because it excludes more than half the population, because it encourages destructive stereotypes, because it hurts. It is also bad for business, and it makes clear communication difficult. We do ourselves a disservice when we use sexist language when writing or speaking because it is often ambiguous. When a pollster goes out to investigate what 'the man on the street' thinks of the prime minister, is she or he also investigating the views of 'the woman' on the street'? This is an important distinction; the two will most likely have quite different opinions. Effective communication also requires reaching out to your target audience. Because many people are offended by sexist language, by using it you run the risk of losing the attention of those you intend to reach.

The aims of this book are to put a spotlight on the sexism in our language and bring it to people's attention, and to make it easier to use non-sexist language wherever possible. It is also intended to encourage the creation of organisational guidelines specifically addressing sexist language and making practical recommendations for change. Many professional bodies have established such guidelines for their members and/or employees, and these are described here as examples of the positive changes taking place in Britain today. In highlighting these individual efforts, I am not suggesting that this is all that needs to be done. Clearly, using inclusive or gender-specific terms (rather than male-based terms used as generics) for job titles, for example, will not obliterate job or pay discrimination against women. But using inclusive terms and, where appropriate, using both male and female terms (*spokesman* and *spokeswoman*, for example) helps to make women more visible, both to the public and within organisations; it sends a signal that women's presence (or lack of it) must be addressed. For an organisation to be effective in recruiting female staff, attracting female customers, and serving the needs of a public that is at least half female, it must make positive efforts to reach out to women and to reflect their concerns and accomplishments. Using language that puts women on an equal basis with men is one (albeit not the only, but often the most visible) method of doing this.

Political correctness

Language is often identified as a key issue in the debate about political correctness, or PC as it is known. The origins of the term continue to be debated — some claim it started out as a label created by the right wing for a movement on American campuses to expand the traditional curriculum; others that it is a term coined by the left as a self-deprecating description of some of its own party-line attitudes. Today, the label has become a broad brush applied to any effort to reflect our changing society that goes against the status quo. That is why it is most often characterised as a tool employed by the left and, in the 'backlash' against feminism, by women in particular, who, conservatives feel, mutilate language in the name of ideology.

The struggle for control of language has always been a political and highly charged one, however. (Consider, for example, the Conservative Government's appropriation of the language of the liberal left, where 'care in the community' and 'empowerment' now mean cuts in welfare and service provision.) For generations our use of language has adapted to reflect changes in society and sensibilities, most recently as the hard-won result of social struggle against discrimination. Replacing 'crippled' with 'disabled' or 'Negro' with 'black' are not new efforts, nor are they resisted – these days – by most members of society. They had to be fought for, however, and are part of broader movements (in themselves much older than the term 'PC'), one aim of which has been to give members of marginalised groups the opportunity to define how they would like to be described by others. (One aspect of this move is the 'reclaiming' of negative terms. Some terms that are considered offensive as 'labels' are being adopted among members of the labelled group as positive, self-defining terms. 'Nigger' and 'queer' are two examples.) Like efforts to combat sexism in language, these fights for self-identity have long, distinguished histories tied to struggles for self-determination and equality. They are some of the many constant shifts we make in our use of language.

'Political correctness' has attracted a great deal of media and press attention and has become a useful (though wildly misapplied) label for ridiculing an opposing viewpoint. The most common examples cited of the absurdity of PC language – 'vertically challenged' for 'short', and other such '-challenged' compounds – are products of imagination. No one uses or proposes to use such terms. They are, however, one aspect of the way that inclusive language is confused with euphemism. But the effect of such caricatures is to attempt to discredit the legitimate aspirations of different communities and their desire for a language that includes rather than excludes them, and to undermine the important gains that have been made in achieving general acceptance of non-sexist language and effecting positive change. Inclusive language is not narrow and prescriptive; it does not aim to create a canon of 'politically correct' words. It aims instead to clarify and distinguish, to move away from labelling and name-calling. In so doing, it reflects the positive changes taking place in our society; it enables, and genuinely empowers.

Which words or usages are sexist?

Everyone has her or his own definition of what constitutes sexist language. What is sexist to one person may be acceptable usage to another. Many people, for instance, look to the origins of a word – its etymology – to investigate its original meaning and determine if it is sexist. Words like *patron* and *patronising* derive from the Latin for 'father'; *dominate* derives from the Latin for 'lord'. Because of this, some people may object to their use as generic terms applied to women and men. Analysing a word's derivation is not always helpful, however, as its original meaning may be far removed from its current use – *patron* and *patronising* are used equally for women and men today. Other words, like *fellow*, are not sexist in their origin but through the years have acquired masculine meaning ('that fellow over there' can only be a man; '(she's/he's) a jolly good fellow', however, can be either). *Master* is used sometimes as a generic (*taskmaster*, *masterpiece*) and sometimes as a sex-specific term (*schoolmaster*). Most people rely on the context and the way the word is used when deciding whether the word is objectionable; referring to all who manage local post offices as 'postmasters' may be sexist, whereas calling an original a 'master copy' may not be. Some people, however, prefer to replace words incorporating 'fellow' and 'master', so alternatives are provided in the A–Z listing of the book.

Another aspect of sexist language that is referred to in this book is non-parallel treatment of female and male subjects. The terms 'Essex man' and 'Essex girl' are an example of this – calling women 'girls' and men 'men'. This demeans women and gives the impression that women are taken less seriously (unless it is a term women use for themselves: *Riot grrrls* and *out with the girls* are two examples). Another type of non-parallel usage involves the connotations of the terms: the feminine term is often negative or derogatory, whereas the masculine term is often positive or at least non-judgemental (contrast, for example, *ladies' man* and *man-eater*). Similarly, many negative terms for women have no masculine counterpart, and even when counterparts exist they are often little used. *Nymphomania*, for example, is widely used to describe the condition of a woman who is considered sexually active and eager. The masculine 'equivalent', *satyriasis*, is rarely, if ever, heard.

Non-parallel usage also appears in the common construction of adding 'and women' after a compound word incorporating '-men' (as in 'craftsmen and women'), a mistake made in the attempt to avoid using '-man' as a generic term, where a subject is or might be female. The correct construction is parallel – 'craftsmen and craftswomen' or 'craftswomen and craftsmen.' Using terms ending in '-woman' and '-man' (*saleswoman, salesman*) is one way to incorporate parallel usage, but it is not necessarily the best way. It can be long-winded and awkward, and in most cases it is unnecessary to specify the sex of the subject. In the above example, *craftworkers* or *artisans* would be appropriate gender-neutral alternatives. On the other hand, in some instances it might be desirable to flag the fact that some subjects are female – especially, for instance, in male-dominated professions – to combat the assumption of maleness that is usually made.

Using the book as a guide

The intention of this book is not to obliterate words or usages from the language. Some readers will feel that not all of the words listed in the book as such are objectionable. This is to be expected; we each have a different threshold of what offends us and what does not. If a term or usage is not objectionable to you, and if you feel that it will not appear sexist to others, and especially if you feel that no suitable alternative can be found, you will probably want to use that term. Its inclusion in the book is not meant to indicate that it should be 'banned' from use. Many people, however, may feel that they want to use non-sexist language but are unsure what terms and usages might be interpreted as sexist. That is why the A–Z listing is so comprehensive.

Finding your way around

This is meant to be a practical, hands-on guide that will make it easy for writers, speakers and everyone who cares about the language they use to find a non-sexist alternative that enhances their language instead of restricting it, that clarifies rather than muddies. [. . .]

Using non-sexist language should be as simple and straightforward as using correct spelling, punctuation, and grammar. It should also be tailored to particular needs, as are all good employee handbooks and how-to manuals.

Adding to it

The adaptability of English means that new words make their way into the common vocabulary with remarkable frequency and speed. Because of this, sexist terms and usages that do not appear in this volume may spring to readers' minds. It is hoped that readers will add these – by actually writing them into their copies and also by suggesting them to the author, care of the publisher, to consider in future editions.

Reprinted from Margaret Doyle, *The A–Z of Non-Sexist Language* (London: Women's Press, 1995).

Chapter 12

Deborah Cameron

LOST IN TRANSLATION: NON-SEXIST LANGUAGE

NON-SEXIST LANGUAGE IS ONE OF those feminist ideas that has somehow managed to achieve the status of orthodoxy, not just among feminists, but for a great mass of well meaning people and vaguely liberal institutions. Of course it has its enemies, and very vocal they are too, but it also meets with pious approval in the most unexpected quarters. I work at a university that was among the first to have a policy on what it was pleased to call 'gender-free language', and when I arrived there I quickly lost count of the number of times men drew my attention to it, almost bursting with pride, while I was still reeling from the shock of being one of only two-and-a-half women in my department. Non-sexist language: the symbolic concession you can make to feminism without ruining your dominant status.

This might seem like a cynical attitude; in reality I'm not quite that cynical. Though it annoys me when non-sexist language policies are touted for PR purposes to make an institution look more progressive than it really is, I take it for granted that institutions ought to have them (as well as other policies, not instead). I would never take the line that language is 'trivial' or a 'distraction' from more important issues. There probably are more important issues, but political struggle invariably takes place on many fronts at once. No feminist fairy with a magic wand ever comes up and says: 'OK, you can have non-sexist language or equal pay; now which is it to be?'

So my cynicism is not directed towards the idea that something needs to be done about sexism in language. What I'm cynical about – indeed, increasingly appalled by – is the genre of handbooks and guidelines that define the problem and tell people what to do about it. It is now more than

20 years since the first non-sexist language guidelines for English appeared, and they have not improved with time – in fact I would argue they are actually getting worse. They haven't kept pace with developments in feminist politics since the 1970s, and in certain respects they have regressed from anything that was radical about them originally.

I don't want to imply that non-sexist language policies were ever particularly radical. Even at their best they could never do enough to satisfy a radical feminist, because 'non-sexist' is inherently a minimalist concept (the absence of overt sexism as opposed to anything more positive). Non-sexist language policies and guidelines are part of a moderate, reformist feminist agenda. But I don't want to dismiss this out of hand, or criticise women who work within the constraints of mainstream institutions for not going beyond reformism. You have to start from where you are. Nor do I underestimate the opposition which even moderate interventions attract in the average organisation. My starting point in this discussion is that reformist initiatives do have their uses, and it matters, therefore, how they are approached.

What worries me is that current approaches to sexism in language are failing on their own (minimalist and moderate) terms. Over time, they seem to have gone from having modest political ambitions to having virtually none, unless you count inoffensiveness as a political goal. In theory I suppose this could be because guideline writers have felt obliged to make more and more concessions in order to win mainstream acceptance; but actually I don't think that's the case. I would say the climate now is more receptive than it was 20 years ago, and where people remain hostile, their hostility is to the whole idea, and is not mitigated by watering down the arguments. Anyway, whatever the causes, I think it's time for some plain speaking about the awfulness of most guidelines: the blandness of their arguments, their failure to get to grips with even their own definition of the problem, and the increasing idiocy of the solutions they propose.

For those who wish to adopt non-sexist language in their own practice, or who are preparing guidelines tailored to the needs of a particular institution, the obvious place to turn for comprehensive guidance is to one of a number of published handbooks. Handbooks stand to the guidelines used in individual institutions much as something like the *Oxford Dictionary for Writers and Editors* stands to a particular publisher's or newspaper's 'house style sheet' – that is, as an 'authoritative' general work of reference – and as such they are the most influential texts of their type. The established ones are revised periodically, and new ones also appear at regular intervals, commissioned by publishers who rightly believe there is a market. The Women's Press for instance has just reissued Casey Miller and Kate Swift's *A Handbook of Non-Sexist Writing* (first published in 1980), and has also brought out a new book, *The A–Z of Non-Sexist Language*, by Margaret Doyle. [. . .]

If I can just get one complaint out of the way, it's notable that both books are written by women from the USA. The Women's Press have put editors to work taking out the more glaringly American bits and adding a few British touches, but no-one involved seems to have enough grasp on the (extensive) dialect differences to do a decent job of this; we are still stuck with entries that will puzzle or annoy the average British reader.

For instance, Doyle mentions the playful feminist coinage *himmicane* for *hurricane*. If you know that in most US accents *hurricane* sounds like 'hericane' you will get the joke: but in British English varieties the two vowels are distinct and it doesn't make sense. In addition there are dozens of examples in both books which are more or less intelligible to British readers, but which no-one here would ever actually say or write, either because our idiom is different or our social reality is. Who in Britain needs a non-sexist equivalent for *busboy* ('waiter's assistant')? Who could contemplate *state trooper* as an alternative to *policeman*?

The Women's Press preface to Miller and Swift's book comments that the American bias is 'of secondary importance' so long as 'the message comes across loud and clear'. But the argument that it's what you say that matters and not how you say it seems singularly inappropriate in a book about *language*. Isn't there a rather obvious analogy between expecting British readers to treat American English as the generic norm of English usage and expecting women to take men as the generic norm of English grammar?

The message that comes across loud and clear to me is that America calls the shots in the English-language publishing industry. Otherwise why, after all these years, can a British publisher not commission a native speaker of British English to write a handbook for the British market? This isn't intended to be a chauvinist point: I have nothing against US usage *per se*, but even leaving questions of cultural imperialism aside, you can't produce a useful linguistic reference text if the examples don't relate concretely to the usage of the target audience.

The first sentence of Doyle's introduction reads: 'English can credit its survival to its marvellous adaptability'. A more accurate if less catchy rendition might be: 'English owes its current privileged position in the world to the historical power and current political dominance of some of the nation-states in which it is the majority language.'

The implication of Doyle's remark is that languages which have not survived, like Cornish, or whose survival is precarious, like Irish and Cherokee, are in this position because of a lack of 'adaptability'. Really, what these languages lacked were speakers with institutional power, and what killed or maimed them was imperialism. Even if English really were more 'adaptable' than, say, Spanish, Arabic or Chinese, the qualities of the language itself would not insulate it from the effects of wider social and historical forces. Look what happened to Latin.

All this may seem irrelevant in a discussion of sexism in language (though linguistic imperialism certainly isn't irrelevant to all women, a point I will come back to later on). However, if someone cannot understand the relationship between language and power in its starkest and most obvious form – which languages survive and which do not – then it is unlikely their analysis of sexism will be any more incisive. One of the most serious problems with most current handbooks is that they do not have anything like an adequate concept of power. They are liberal to a fault, determinedly inoffensive, and as a result totally lacking in clarity or conviction.

The shortcomings of the liberal approach are revealed in what is said in the two handbooks about 'political correctness'. It's obvious why they feel the need to refer to the issue: since the early 1990s the smear-term 'political correctness' has provided a new pretext for attacking the whole idea of politically-motivated linguistic reform. The subject was bound to come up, but I was hoping the authors would take the opportunity to launch a spirited feminist attack on the new clothes in which anti-feminists have taken to dressing up their ancient and fatuous arguments.

No such luck. What's startling is the defensiveness of the authors' responses. While they do suggest that the PC furore is basically reactionary, the line they take is to argue that fears of censorship and brainwashing are simply mistaken, and particularly unjustified in the case of non-sexist language. They don't engage with the politics, but focus instead on the sweet reasonableness of feminist reforms: Miller and Swift for instance dwell on how wrong-headed the anti-PC brigade are being when they suggest that 'advocates of equality are attempting to restrict freedom of speech and enforce language rules' (p. x). Later I will explain why I think this is a completely incoherent argument even on its own terms; but first I want to point out another serious political problem with using it in this context.

To put the point briefly, stressing that (liberal) feminists are not authoritarian extremists in matters of language gives rise to the implication (not directly stated, but not denied either) that some of those attacked under the heading of 'political correctness' *are* authoritarian extremists, and their arguments about language can therefore be dismissed. This is problematic for several reasons. For a start, who on earth do Miller, Swift and Doyle think will be reading their soothing remarks in search of reassurance? The main market for these particular books is women who identify as feminists, and it's insulting that feminist authors should make such concessions to an anti-feminist agenda. It also implicitly means they are privileging one kind of discriminatory language (sexist language) over others (e.g. racist or ableist language). Yet in fact the same principles underlie all the politically-motivated changes in linguistic practice that radicals have tried to make, and feminists cannot just draw a line around sexist language while ignoring parallels with, say, the representation of minority ethnic groups or people with disabilities.

Far from worrying about excessive 'political correctness'. I find it both astonishing and disturbing that allegedly feminist handbooks are still, in 1995, so completely *inattentive* to the need for guidance on usage in areas where sexism interacts with other oppressions, or where differences exist among women. Among many entries which surprisingly do *not* appear in *The A–Z of Non-Sexist Language* are 'black', 'disability', and 'lesbian' (Doyle skips from *leprechaun* to *liftman* without a mention of the word, though *dyke* is marked 'use with care' and *homosexual* is identified as problematic because it can exclude women – no mention of any other objections to it).

Partly these omissions are because the *A–Z* is most concerned with telling readers what words to avoid rather than discussing shades or meaning within current feminist usage (a negative emphasis which I find problematic in itself). But the consequence is that if you constructed a picture of British society from the examples that appear in the *A–Z*, it would be as dominated by white Anglo-Saxon middle-class professionals as a 1950s propaganda film, the only difference being that the cast is now all-female. Miller and Swift are slightly better on race, but you won't find any specific guidance in either of the handbooks about, for instance, the forms of naming and polite address used by women in any British or US community, where English is not the only language in use – though this is an area where many majority-group members lack the most basic information needed to address/write about other women in a respectful manner (if only by getting their names in the right order).

If 'political correctness' means paying attention to the implications of *all* the words you use in an effort to avoid recycling disrespectful and oppressive propositions, I would say that non-sexist language guidelines need more of it rather than less. But in any case, as I said before, the argument about why feminist linguistic reform should not be confused with extreme and nasty 'political correctness' is completely incoherent.

This argument turns on the idea that non-sexist language is not *prescriptive*, not about telling people what they can and can't say or write. Or as Margaret Doyle puts it: 'Inclusive language is not narrow and prescriptive; it does not aim to create a canon of "politically correct" words. It aims instead to clarify and distinguish, to move away from labelling and name-calling' (p. 5).

Sorry, have I missed something here? Of course language guidelines are 'prescriptive'; what else could they be, and what would be the good of them otherwise? When Margaret Doyle says, in her entry for the phrase *old maid*, 'DO NOT USE', the reader may have a choice about whether to adopt this prescription or reject it, but that doesn't mean the actual guideline is not prescriptive: 'do not use' is clearly a prescription – and quite right too.

Non-sexist language may seem less 'narrow' than the masculist norm, but the effect of taking it seriously is inevitably to 'narrow' writers' choices (for instance, they can no longer refer to someone as an 'old maid'). Of course, it is also true of the masculist norm that it restricts writers' choices, though people are less likely to notice restrictions which have been in force for centuries.

The point is, it is true by definition of all linguistic norms (feminist or otherwise) that they 'create a canon' of acceptable (and unacceptable) usage. There is no point denying this; denying that your guidelines have any particular agenda only means that you will not be able to make a convincing argument for preferring them to the alternatives.

The idea that non-sexist language aims to 'clarify and distinguish' is so thoroughly confusing that I honestly don't know what it means: do we really have to 'clarify' the fact that women exist? Of course not: the problem is not that some people remain unaware of our existence, it is that they choose not to acknowledge it, or (just as often) to disparage it. As for 'distinguish', frequently non-sexist language is based on the principle of *not* making traditional gender distinctions (like *poet/poetess*) – antifeminists have harped for years on the loss of fine distinctions that non-sexist language entails, a red herring to which Doyle here gives credence. And 'mov[ing] away from labelling' is an odd way to describe an enterprise whose real aim is to *change* the labels we hang on the world, not get rid of them (which would be equivalent to getting rid of language itself).

The reference to 'name-calling' is also obscure, but I think what Doyle has in mind is an idea which is rapidly becoming language-guideline orthodoxy, and which I find infuriating: the idea that avoiding terms which are racist, sexist, ableist, homophobic, etc. is just a matter of 'civility' or 'sensitivity' (the word the BBC chose in its recent guidelines for broadcast language). In other words, you wouldn't want to hurt the tender feelings of Black/female/disabled/gay and lesbian people, who sometimes listen to the radio or read a book, and as we all know are very sensitive about their unfortunate disadvantages.

Apart from being patronising enough to pulverise your brain, this view logically implies that if the groups in question were not represented in a particular audience, there would be no reason at all to bother about linguistic bigotry. It's always a wonder to behold how our ruling elites can reduce political challenges to a gentleman's code prescribing courtesy to those less fortunate than yourself; but when the same argument turns up in feminist writing it's time to get seriously worried. The new commandment non-sexist language gurus urge upon us – 'Thou shalt not offend' – is an impossible one to observe while retaining any coherent political outlook at all. When you politicise language, or more exactly draw attention to the fact that it always was political, you are bound to give offence to someone. The only question is who; and this too is a political choice.

Overall, what we get from the remarks I've just dissected is a totally mixed message: 'we want you to use non-sexist language, but we don't want you to think that this will restrict your freedom of expression in any way, or make you sound offensive to anyone'. Of course, this is totally spurious. One might have thought the entire point of non-sexist guidelines was to restrict the freedom of sexists to air their prejudices in the public sphere of language, or hide behind 'the rules of grammar' as a convenient excuse for prejudice. The sexists understand this, even if the guideline-writers don't: that's why they do in fact take offence, greeting even the mildest non-sexist language proposals with such weeping and wailing and gnashing of teeth.

The proposals themselves, and the accompanying arguments, appear to be getting milder all the time. Doyle's use of the term 'inclusive language' as if it were interchangeable with 'non-sexist language' tells us much about what she considers sexism to be: a lack of inclusiveness. The creed of 'inclusiveness' is that language should include everybody, women and men alike; that careless use of words can make either sex feel bad; that expressions like 'women and children first' (do men's lives not matter?) are deplorably sexist, and that noninclusive language distorts a reality in which women and men are marching side by side towards an ever-more-equal future.

There are two shortcomings here. One is the liberal failure to see sexism as a systemic relation of power, as opposed to a set of misguided beliefs and stereotypes about men and women. 'Women and children first' is a sexist expression, but not because it discriminates against men: it belongs to a patriarchal discourse in which men are there to 'protect' women and children – the women and children being by implication men's property, men's to control.

The other shortcoming is the naive concept of language as a purely representational medium whose purpose is to reflect reality accurately. If that were true, then conventional sexist language would do the job well enough, since we (still) live in a sexist world. But in fact language is ideological. The same reality can be represented in any number of ways, and the power of linguistic conventions lies precisely in the selectiveness with which they represent the world, making one way of perceiving reality seem like the only natural way.

Feminists are of course right to object when it comes to seem 'natural' that the world represented in writing and speech should be peopled exclusively by men, or that women should be confined to minor roles as appendages, victims, nurturers, sex-objects and idiots. But mechanically replacing this picture with an 'inclusive' version of the world has some peculiar implications of its own – notably the curious idea that if only some word or concept can be made 'inclusive', we need ask no further questions about what it actually means.

This reminds me of the assumption behind bad foreign-language phrase books: that communication in a new language can be achieved by making a word-by-word literal translation from the old one. The problem is conceived as purely technical, a question of not knowing the Finnish for 'where are the toilets', or the non-sexist for 'I can't wear man-made fibres'. So a typical entry in a non-sexist language handbook is a 'troublesome' expression like 'man-made' followed by a series of non-sexist equivalents ('constructed', 'artificial', 'human caused').

A Portuguese friend once showed me an old phrasebook called *English as she is spoke*, which makes crystal clear that you do not get an acceptable translation by just substituting one word for another. The crucial aspect of language is meaning: the point of non-sexist language is not to change the forms of words for the sake of it but to change the repertoire of meanings a language conveys. It's about redefining rather than merely renaming the world—a point which many current guideline-writers seem to grasp imperfectly if at all.

The phrasebook approach might work for terms like 'man-made [artificial] fibre', but in many cases literal translation is not only hard to do, it is not worth attempting in the first place. Another well-known source of humour in old phrasebooks is their inclusion of bizarre remarks like 'lo, the position has been struck by lightning', where the question is not so much how you would express this in another language as why you would ever want to say it at all. The same question might well be asked about some of the entries in non-sexist language guidelines.

I find it extraordinary, for instance, that *The A–Z of Non-sexist Language* should include an entry telling me what to substitute for the sexist expression 'maternal instinct' (the suggested 'inclusive' alternatives are 'parental instinct' and 'nurturing instinct'). The reason why the first of these options in particular sounds ludicrous is exactly the reason why we do not need a non-sexist expression for this concept: the idea of an 'instinct' to nurture children acquires 100 per cent of its meaning and force from a sexist frame of reference which attributes this 'instinct' to women. Detached from that frame, the whole concept becomes meaningless – why would we use it except to assert that female biology is destiny? The correct thing to do with 'maternal instinct' is file it under 'history of sexist ideas' along with 'wandering womb'. (Or would the handbook compilers want to revive this term in a new 'inclusive' form like 'wandering gonad'?)

Automatically translating sexist into non-sexist language will be superficial, ineffectual, and on occasion actually counterproductive, unless the process is at some point mediated by the exercise of a writer's critical faculties. Unfortunately, the handbooks and guidelines being churned out nowadays seem designed almost to prevent this critical intervention from happening. They are, in fact, the feminist equivalent of Roget's Thesaurus: lists of allegedly interchangeable words which have been so decontextualised and so detached from any coherent political analysis of language, we might as well use them as many people use Roget, to do crossword puzzles with.

I've always been ambivalent about language guidelines because of the risk that they will be applied in a totally mechanical way, without the thought and reflection which I would define as the key point in any truly progressive linguistic practice. In an ideal world I would rather people thought about language and took responsibility for their own use of it (if they're sexists, by all means let them express that clearly and take any flak that results).

But this is not an ideal world, and I concede there is a place in it for guidelines (for instance, in composing texts which represent an institution rather than being attributed to an individual author). It is also true in my experience that many people, while they are not necessarily inflexible bigots, do need clarification of the arguments and assistance with the details if they are to abandon their sexist habits. And these people are very poorly served by most of the guidelines in common use today.

I have already criticised the liberalism underpinning most efforts in this field. That isn't just because I am politically opposed to liberalism, it's also because liberal arguments about language, placed in the context of a set of guidelines about how to use it, are inherently contradictory and consequently self-defeating. Once you have made the decision to have language guidelines, it is no good abdicating the authority which comes with the territory, or trying to minimise it with arguments that wouldn't convince even a basically sympathetic audience, let alone the sceptical one many guidelines will actually encounter.

Anyone who has ever been responsible for producing an institutional policy within the 'orthodox' framework I have described will recognise the problems that result. If you confront people with the patently ridiculous claim that nonsexist language rules are not restrictive in any way, you will provoke bitter and pointless arguments which would be better directed to the actual substance of the restrictions ('No, you can't call the students "girls" and this is why'). If you do not explain to people what the *political* rationale is for identifying certain ways of using language as 'sexist', they may stick to the letter of your prescriptions, but they will disregard the spirit. They will think, or pretend to think, that the problem is not to do with meaning or content, but simply consists of a few isolated forms like 'man', and the solution is to mechanically change every occurrence of these forms irrespective of the context (this is the source of all those side-splitting examples like 'personagement'). If you do not provide realistic examples consisting of more than single words, you will get non-sexist prose which reads like the minutes of a particularly dull committee meeting translated from the Hungarian by a computer. In sum, if you cannot get people to understand what they are supposed to be doing and why, there is no chance they will do it with any commitment or skill.

For all kinds of reasons, I regard guidelines on non-sexist language in the abstract as a necessary evil. Most concretely existing examples, however, are an unnecessary evil – a dire combination of liberalism, self-righteousness and downright muddled thinking, in whose alphabet A is for Apologetic, B is for Banal and C is for Confused. Guideline-writers should grasp the nettle and do their job, which is both to prescribe and to persuade: not by stroking ('this won't hurt at all') or indeed by guilt-tripping ('better do what I say or you'll *hurt my feelings*') but by presenting arguments about language and power that will actually bear scrutiny.

Reprinted from *Trouble & Strife* 32 (Winter 1995/6).

Chapter 13

Susan Ehrlich and Ruth King

GENDER-BASED LANGUAGE REFORM AND THE SOCIAL CONSTRUCTION OF MEANING

Introduction

IN NOVEMBER 1989, Queen's University in Kingston, Ontario, Canada, sponsored its annual 'NO MEANS NO' rape awareness campaign. In reaction to the campaign, obscene and violent messages appeared in the windows of men's dormitories: 'NO MEANS HARDER', 'NO MEANS DYKE', 'NO MEANS MORE BEER', 'NO MEANS "TIE ME UP" '. In March 1991, during a nationally televised Ontario university hockey game, two University of Waterloo students held signs saying 'NO MEANS HARDER' and 'STOP MEANS PLEASE'. While these signs are extremely disturbing in terms of their normalizing and justifying of violence against women, they are also a strong illustration of the way in which meanings are socially constructed and constituted: the meaning of the word 'no' in this particular context has been appropriated by the dominant culture. Another example of this phenomenon came in April 1991 when British Columbia Supreme Court Judge Sherman Hood announced in his judgment of an alleged rape case that 'at times "no" may mean "maybe" or "wait a while" '.[1]

This appropriation of meaning has profound consequences for gender-based language reform. As McConnell-Ginet [Chapter 15, this volume] points out (in connection with women saying 'no' to men's sexual advances), 'meaning is a matter not only of individual will but of social relations embedded in political structures'. Because linguistic meanings are, to a large extent, determined by the dominant culture's social values and attitudes, terms initially introduced to be non-sexist and neutral may lose their neutrality in the 'mouths' of a sexist speech community and/or culture.

In arguing for the necessity of language reform, feminist theorists have generally assumed that language is not a neutral and transparent means of representing reality. Rather, language is assumed to codify an androcentric world-view. For example, the 'names' that a language attaches to events and activities, especially those related to sex and sexuality, often encode a male perspective. Cameron (1985) discusses terms such as *penetration, fuck, screw, lay,* all of which turn heterosexual sex into something men do to women. (*Penetration*, from a female perspective, could be given more appropriate names such as *enclosure, surrounding, engulfing*.) In a similar way, the absence of 'names' representing women's perceptions and experiences also reveals a male bias. Steinem (1983: 149) sees terms such as *sexual harassment* and *sexism* as significant in this respect: 'A few years ago, they were just called life.' At the level of grammar, the 'so-called' generics, *he* and *man*, render women invisible, thereby encoding a sexist world-view.

While sexist language clearly reflects sexist social structures, the continuing existence of such social structures throws into question the possibility of successful language reform. Graddol and Swann (1989: 110) comment:

> Sexist language is not simply a linguistic problem. The existence of unmarked expressions 'in the language' does not mean that these will be used and interpreted in a neutral way. This may lead one to question the value of the linguistic reforms advocated in writers' and publishers' guidelines.

Cameron (1985: 90) makes a similar point:

> Therefore, in the interests of accuracy we should strive to include the female half of the human race by replacing male terms with neutral ones. But the 'reality' to which language relates is a sexist one, and in it there are no neutral terms. . . . In the mouths of sexists, language can always be sexist.

Given that language is not a neutral vehicle in the representation of reality and that it is necessarily laden with social values, the introduction of neutral and/or non-sexist terms does not guarantee neutral and/or non-sexist usage. In this article, we argue that the relative success of attempts at gender-based language reform is dependent on the social context in which the language reform occurs. When language reform occurs within the context of a larger sociopolitical initiative whose primary goal is the eradication of sexist practices (e.g. employment equity programmes), it is more likely to succeed. By contrast, when language reform occurs within the context of a speech community that embraces sexist values and attitudes, it is less likely to succeed.

The appropriation of meaning

The appropriation of meaning by the dominant culture is by no means a phenomenon restricted to innovative forms in a language. Schulz (1975) traces the semantic derogation of terms, designating women in English, showing that words, such as *hussy* and *spinster*, originally neutral or positive in interpretation took on negative connotations in a way that was unparalleled for words designating men. That is, sexist values also influence the meanings of terms that already exist in a language.

In Britain and North America today, the New Right has quite deliberately used the strategy of redefining and/or appropriating terms originally used by the Left in an attempt to delegitimize issues such as anti-sexism and anti-racism. Seidel (1988) cites examples from the *Salisbury Review* in Britain, 'a quarterly journal of conservative thought' (p. 131), in which racism is dismissed as a 'vulgar and banal catchphrase' (p. 134) and anti-racism is defined as racism in disguise:

> [. . .] through a combination of facile agreement, political opportunism and moral intimidation, the Left, under the specious banner of 'anti-racism', has succeeded in forcing 'institutional racism' onto the legitimate political agenda of politics and, in the process, is fostering the very racial *dis*harmony it purports to condemn.
>
> (p. 135)

In a *Time* magazine article (Henry 1991) on the controversial topic of 'Political Correctness' on North American campuses, it is reported with dismay that 'professors teach that white males can never be victims of racism, because racism is a form of repressive political power – and white males already hold the power in Western society'. The implication here is both that racism is *not* a form of repressive political power and that white males *can* suffer from racism. We see here that the term racism is being redefined by this writer as non-institutional and, in the process, its effects are trivialized, given that all individuals – in particular, even white males – can now be victims of racism.

This kind of redefinition is taken to an extreme in an example from Seidel where the (white) editor of the *Salisbury Review* concludes that he is 'black' because he belongs to a minority of educated people who are excluded from the power structures of the Inner London Education Authority. This type of discursive strategy where WHITE = BLACK, NO = YES, ANTIRACISM = RACISM illustrates the extent to which redefinition and even reversal of meanings operates quite independently of the intended meanings/uses of words. It should be clear from these kinds of examples why the introduction of non-sexist terms into a language will not necessarily lead to non-sexist usage.

(Mis)Interpretation and (mis)use of non-sexist terms

In attempting to characterize the type of social conditions that are conducive to successful language reform, Labov's (1972) findings concerning the effect of social factors on linguistic change are relevant. Labov claims that the spread of a particular linguistic innovation is determined by the status of the social subgroup leading the change.[2]

> If the group in which the change originated was not the highest-status group in the speech community, members of the highest-status group eventually stigmatized the changed form through their control of various institutions of the communication network.
>
> (p. 179)

Extrapolating from Labov's observations, we can say that the success of gender-based language reform will be determined by the extent to which high-status subgroups within a speech community adopt non-sexist values. Assuming that non-sexist language reform originates in a social subgroup that is not of the highest status within a given speech community (i.e. it originates among socially conscious women), then Labov's findings predict that, all else being equal, these linguistic innovations will be stigmatized unless the highest-status social group also displays non-sexist values. Indeed, there is much evidence to suggest that innovative, non-sexist linguistic forms do undergo a kind of depreciation. While this does not always manifest itself in overt stigmatization of the innovative forms, it does lead to the misuse and misinterpretation of non-sexist terms.[3] Examples of this misuse and misinterpretation follow.

The title Ms was originally popularized by feminists in the 1970s to replace Miss and Mrs and provide a parallel term to Mr, in that both Ms and Mr designate gender without indicating marital status. Miller and Swift (1976) see the elimination of Mrs and Miss in favor of Ms as a way of allowing women to be seen as people in their own right, rather than in relation to someone else. Unfortunately, while Ms was intended to parallel Mr, considerable evidence suggests that its use is often resisted, or it is not used and/or interpreted in the intended way. Fasold (1988: 190), in a survey of news organizations' style guides, reports that the *Washington Post's* manual disallows Ms 'except in direct quotations, in discussing the term itself, or "for special effect" '. The Associated Press 1987 style guide (French 1987) recommends Ms *only* if known to be the preference of the individual woman.

Examples of 'misuses' of the term Ms abound. Frank and Treichler (1989: 218) cite the following directive, sent to public information officers in the state of Pennsylvania: 'If you use Ms for a female, please indicate in parentheses after the Ms whether it's Miss or Mrs.' In a similar way, Graddol and Swann (1989: 97) explain that Ms is not a neutral title for women in

167

Britain: 'in some contexts it seems to have coalesced with Miss (official forms sometimes distinguish only Mrs and Ms)'. Atkinson (1987), in a Canadian study of attitudes towards the use of Ms and birthname retention among women, found that many of her respondents had a three-way distinction: they used Mrs for married women, Miss for women who had never been married and Ms for divorced women. All three usages described here demonstrate the high premium placed on identifying women by their relationship (current or otherwise) to men, in spite of the intended neutrality associated with Ms.[4]

In a similar way, neutral terms such as *chairperson* and *spokesperson*, introduced to replace masculine generics such as *chairman* and *spokesman*, seem to have lost their neutrality in that they are often only used for women. The following example containing announcements of academics' changing jobs, cited by Dubois and Crouch (1987) (from the *Chronicle of Higher Education*, 1977), demonstrates that a woman is a *chairperson*, but a man is a *chairman*.

> Margarette P. Eby, *Chairperson* of Humanities at U. of Michigan at Dearborn, to Dean of the College of Humanities and Fine Arts and Professor of Music at U. of Northern Iowa.
>
> David W. Hamilton, Assoc. Professor of Anatomy at Harvard, to *chairman* of Anatomy at U. of Minnesota.
>
> Eileen T. Handelman, *Chairperson* of Science at Simon's Rock Early College, to Dean of Academic Affairs.
>
> Elaine B. Harvey, Acting *Chairperson* of Graduate Pediatrics at Indiana U. to Dean of the School of Nursing at Fort Hays Kansas State U.
>
> Philip E. Hicks, Professor of Industrial Engineering at New Mexico State U., to *Chairman* of Industrial Engineering at North Carolina A & T State U.

From this example, we can see that the attempt to replace a masculine generic with a neutral one has been somewhat unsuccessful in that neutral terms like *chairperson, spokesperson*, etc., are functioning to designate only female referents. Rather than ridding the language of a masculine generic, the introduction of neutral generic *person* forms has (in some situations, at least) led to a sex-based distinction between forms such as *chairperson* vs *chairman*.

Much research has demonstrated that *he/man* generics do not function generically (even though they may be intended generically) to the extent that they readily evoke images of males rather than of males and females. Other studies have shown that the use of *he/man* language has detrimental effects on individuals' beliefs in females' ability to perform a job, and on females' own feelings of pride, importance and power. The use of neutral generic pronouns such as *he or she, she or he* or singular *they* is thus advocated by supporters of language reform, given the negative effects, both symbolic and practical, of *he/man* language.

A recent study by Khrosroshahi (1989) attempts to investigate the effects of neutral generics vs masculine generics in terms of the mental imagery evoked. Her subjects included both males and females with both reformed and traditional language usage (i.e. four groups of subjects). Khrosroshahi summarizes her results:

> All groups were androcentric except the women who had reformed their language; androcentric in the sense that when they read a paragraph that was ambiguous with respect to gender, they were more likely to interpret it as referring to a male than to a female character. Even if the paragraph used *he or she* or *they*, feminine referents did not become more salient than masculine ones.
>
> (p. 517)

Thus, these results demonstrate that for most of the subjects in this experiment the use of masculine vs neutral generics had no significant effect on the image evoked: male referents were always more salient than female ones. Khrosroshahi explains her results:

> Given the repeatedly documented fact that women are significantly underrepresented in a variety of literatures, the finding that the masculine tends to be read as representative is not very surprising. [. . .] In a literature dominated by male characters, initially sex-indefinite words must quickly develop masculine connotations.
>
> (p. 518)

Thus, like the misuse of Ms described above, this research shows that neutral generic terms are not readily interpreted as neutral. Again, we see that it is the prevailing values and attitudes of a culture that determine, to a large extent, how these innovative, non-sexist terms get used and interpreted, in spite of their intended neutrality. It is interesting to note here that the exceptional group in Khrosroshahi's study, the reformed language women, not only interpreted neutral generics in terms of female referents but also interpreted the masculine generic mostly in terms of female referents. In other words, they displayed the opposite pattern to the three other groups: female (as opposed to male) referents were evoked regardless of the type of generic pronoun used. Again, we see that the interpretation of terms (neutral or not) seems to be heavily influenced by the ideologies of an individual or speech community rather than by the particular pronoun used in a given context.

As stated previously, feminist attempts at language reform have also involved the introduction of terms to express women's perceptions and experiences, phenomena previously unnamed. Penelope (1990) cites an example of the way that one such term, consciousness-raising, is 'perverted' when used in the film *The Billionaire Boys' Club*.

> In the made-for-television movie, *The Billionaire Boys' Club* (1989), one of the rich, white men used the phrase 'consciousness-raising' to describe his changed perception of what the club was doing when he saw the body of one of the men his friends had murdered. For all the women who participated in consciousness-raising groups in the 1960s and 1970s, the word referred very specifically (and exclusively) to the resulting process of change in how we perceived ourselves, our situation in the world, and our relationship to men. For us, consciousness-raising was a profound, mind-altering experience that impelled us to change our lives. We couldn't have imagined that that word would be so perverted as to end up describing a yuppie's shocked repulsion when he saw his first dead body.
>
> (p. xxx)

Again we see that terms originally with very specific feminist-influenced meanings are subject to redefinition and, not accidentally, are redefined in terms of the perspective of a white male's experience.

While the evidence presented above is meant to demonstrate the way in which non-sexist meanings and usages can be socially constituted by a sexist speech community, we are not suggesting that language reform is always or ever futile. First, it should be noted that even in gender-based language reform is not immediately and/or completely successful, it does sensitize individuals to ways in which language is discriminatory towards women: language has become one of the many arenas in which social inequalities are elucidated. Penelope (1990: 213) maintains that becoming aware of linguistic choices forces us to monitor our thought processes and 'will gradually enable us to unlearn patriarchal ways of thinking'. Second, language reform can be a source of empowerment for members of disadvantaged groups. Finally, by considering 'unsuccessful' cases of language reform, we can better understand the social mechanisms at work in cases of successful language reform.

McConnell-Ginet [see Chapter 15, this volume] takes a positive moral from the observation that non-sexist meanings and usages are very often appropriated by a sexist speech community. If meanings are socially constructed and constituted, then the existence of a speech community dedicated to the elimination of sexist practices can provide the necessary support for successful language reform. In what follows, we show that the relative success of attempts at gender-based language reform is dependent on the social context in which the language reform occurs. When language reform occurs within the context of a larger sociopolitical initiative whose primary goal is the eradication of sexist practices, it is more likely to succeed. By contrast, when language reform occurs within the context of a speech community that embraces sexist values and attitudes, it is less likely to succeed.

Successful and unsuccessful language reform

That the introduction of non-sexist terms does not guarantee non-sexist usage is clear. Along with cases of the appropriation of intended non-sexist terms such as those just discussed, there are also cases of non-sexist innovations, documented in the language and gender literature, which have not entered into (mainstream) usage; indeed, the average person has probably never heard of them. Consider in this regard the long history of attempts to reform the English pronominal system through the introduction of a third-person singular indefinite pronoun. Baron (1986) cites numerous innovations dating from 1850 to the present (e.g. *thon* (1884), *hes* (1935), *hse* (1945), *tey* (1972), *hir* (1975), *E* (1977), *hiser* (1984). These neologisms were suggested in newspaper articles and letters to the editor and in scholarly journals and books, but, as Baron (p. 241) notes, 'most coiners of new pronouns have no specific plan in mind to ensure the adoption of their creations, other than the basic attraction of the new words themselves'. Likewise, the spelling of *woman* as 'womyn' is occasionally used for political effect, but few individuals use it consistently. Many regard *womyn* as being too reminiscent of attempts to trivialize on the part of opponents of language reform. A similar case is *herstory*, which very clearly makes the point that mainstream *history* is essentially a history of men. Again, *herstory* is used in special contexts to highlight the contributions of women, but it is not in general usage.

A first step in achieving language reform is thus some consensus in the innovating speech community, in our case, socially conscious women, that a particular innovation is an appropriate non-sexist solution. The next step is the development of non-sexist language guidelines incorporating these solutions. In the past two decades a number of non-sexist style guides and pamphlets have appears, some aimed at a general audience, some at specialized audiences. And, finally, the support of a speech community is essential for the successful implementation of non-sexist language guidelines.

Below we consider a number of attempts at institutional change, i.e. at the implementation of language reform in agencies, companies and organizations in the form of policy statements and/or guidelines *and* the ensurance of compliance with those guidelines. We consider individual change i.e. change in a person's personal usage, only in the context of an institution which adopts a non-sexist language policy but which leaves language reform to the discretion of the individual. We show that the extent to which language reform is couched within larger, shared sociopolitical goals is a determining factor in its degree of success.

Language reform and employment and educational equity

Consider the relationship between language reform and general employment equity initiatives. In Canada, non-sexist language has come to be widely regarded as an essential component in achieving employment equity in the workplace. Given that in this case language reform is connected to a larger sociopolitical goal, we predict that it will have a certain amount of success.

The term 'employment equity' was defined by Judge Rosalie Abella in 1984 as 'a strategy designed to obliterate the present and residual effects of discrimination and to open equitably the competition for employment opportunities to those arbitrarily excluded' (Government of Canada 1984: 254). Both the 1986 Employment Equity Act and the Federal Contractors' Program, implemented the same year, identify four social groups with a history of disadvantage: women, visible minorities, native peoples and people with disabilities. The Employment Equity Act covers regulated federal employers such as crown corporations like Canada Post while the Federal Contractors' Program is binding on employers bidding for government contracts of over $200,000.00. If large federal contractors, including universities as well as private-sector businesses, were not already working (altruistically) to fight discrimination in the workplace, the results of lack of compliance with the FCP – loss of the possibility of bidding for government contracts – has provided added incentive. To comply, institutions must sign a certificate of commitment to implement employment equity and must establish an employment equity office to develop an employment equity policy and plan for implementation. Compliance is under regular review.

Strategies for achieving employment equity include: active recruitment and fair consideration for promotion; accessible, quality childcare; paid parental leave for both parents; pay equity (i.e. the elimination of the gap between the average wages of women and men which results from the undervaluing of women's work), equal pensions and benefits; and the introduction of supportive initiatives *such as the use of non-sexist language* (emphasis added; Ontario Women's Directorate 1988: 2–3). The emphasis on language issues comes largely from the concerns (over at least a decade) of Canadian women's advocates. For example, *Employment Equity for Women: A University Handbook*, published in 1988 by the Committee on the Status of Women of the Council of Ontario Universities, devotes a large section of its discussion of 'The University Environment' to language and visual imagery.

The current emphasis on employment equity in the workplace has led many institutions to adopt non-sexist language policies and guidelines, if they had not already done so. The anti-feminist backlash on university campuses over the past few years, especially the December 1989 Montreal Massacre, has also led many institutions to attempt to deal with the negative university climate for women. Climate issues and concern over university accessibility for the four designated groups has come to be seen as part of 'educational equity'. As in the case of employment equity, non-sexist language is an issue for the task forces and committees set up over the past couple of years to deal with educational equity. For instance, a 1990 University of Alberta plan, intended to reduce discrimination against women on campus, calls for professors to eliminate sexist language from their educational materials. Some universities have addressed the issue of spoken as well as written language by including questions on language usage in teaching evaluations.[5] A number of professional organizations, including the Canadian Association of University Teachers, no longer publish job advertisements using *he/man* language. In our own institution, York University, efforts to ensure that people abide by our non-sexist language policy began with the Status of Women office and only recently has the central administration taken responsibility for compliance. Requests received by the Status of Women office from other universities for help with the development of non-sexist language policies and guidelines have tended to come from academic departments and concerned faculty.

In the university setting, an important area for language reform has been the naming of courses. Compliance with institutional change is not always uniform, particularly when it may be seen as conflicting with other principles and policies. For example, while sexist course titles such as '*Man* and *his* Environment' have virtually disappeared, some individuals and departments may still appeal to their academic freedom to name courses as they wish. Likewise, in an institution with formally adopted non-sexist guidelines, individuals may still contend that they are free to write as they choose. However, non-sexist language policies sanction the initiatives of proponents of reform. They can also be persuasive to individuals who might not agree with, or even feel strongly about, language reform but who see themselves as team players or company people.

In our own case, York University now has a supportive climate for language reform: it was the first university in Ontario to have a Status of Women office and has had active women's studies programmes since the early 1970s. It has also been a pioneer in the development of sexual harassment policy and education.

One case of successful language reform at York took place in the early 1980s. The university's division of humanities removed, over a two-year period, all course titles with *man*, such as 'Modern *Man* in Search of Understanding'. Two faculty members involved remember that the general university atmosphere of the time (including support for women's studies in the humanities and social sciences, the completion of a major report on sexual harassment) was an important factor. Language reform was also facilitated by the fact that the division had already embarked on a more general curriculum reform so that, while there was some in-committee debate, change was seen in a wider context.

In other sectors of the university, course titles have been the subject of heated debate and language reform has been somewhat less successful. Where change is not seen as part of a larger initiative, or where change is left to the discretion of individual instructors (as opposed to curriculum committees), reform has been less easily effected. The university's Status of Women Communications Committee, of which we are both members, works to promote the implementation of York's non-sexist language policy. When the committee was set up in 1989, we found that the York non-sexist language policy, dating from 1985, had clearly had a positive effect. Most university documents now use non-sexist alternatives to the so-called generic *he*, and *chair* rather than *chairman* is the norm. However, it was clear to us that there was still room for improvement. For instance, a number of course titles still used *man* to refer to the species as a whole. The committee wrote to each department which listed such a course title and explained the rationale for change. Responses varied widely. In some cases, we were thanked for bringing such 'anachronistic' usage to a unit's attention and the title was changed. In other cases, we received no reply but noticed the title was changed.

The one remaining area of resistance at York is within the Faculty of Science, some of whose members oppose non-sexist language reform because it challenges what they deem to be 'natural'. Like much anti-feminist discourse, the opponents to language reform within our university context base their arguments on the notion that social practices (i.e. language) are grounded in nature. Biological determinism is the most prevalent example of this kind of thinking: women's biology, particularly women's reproductive biology, is used to justify women being relegated to the home. In other words, the invocation of 'nature' has been one way of rationalizing a whole range of social practices that oppress women. In a similar way, the representation of language as having a 'natural order' exemplifies the way in which 'nature' is invoked to maintain language practices that demean and diminish women.

An analysis of the university discourse surrounding non-sexist language reform in Toronto reveals at least three manifestations of the 'sexist language is natural' argument.[6] First, it is argued that the purity of the English language must be maintained:

> English is a rich language, and it seems to me that one ought to be able to overcome gender-biased problems by working within the language as such.

> As an editor I am as concerned with racism and sexism as I am with the purity and elegance of the English language.

In these two examples, we see that English is inherently pure and rich and elegant and that it will lose its intrinsic purity, richness and elegance if it falls victim to language reform. Like the natural environment, English is uncontaminated, but runs the risk of losing its 'natural' beauty through the infusion of atrocities: 'The guidelines [non-sexist language guidelines] . . . include some linguistic atrocities that as an editor I abhor: "s/he", "her/his".'

Second, language is represented in this corpus as frozen and immutable. On the use of the 'generic' *man*, the following comments appear:

> I also personally believe that the use of 'Man' in a scientific context is correct and without any connotation of gender. The word comes

directly from the dead language of Anglo Saxon in which it means person. The gender specific terms require prefixes to man, viz. weardenman, a male person, and wifman, a female person. Only the latter has come down to us in the vernacular (as woman). The word is also used in the gender free sense in other modern Germanic dialects. One of the advantages of using dead languages (such as ancient Greek and Latin) to specify scientific terms is that the meaning is more likely to remain frozen, since there is not a parallel constantly changing vernacular.

Here we see that 'man' is believed to have 'no connotation of gender' just as it had no such connotation in Anglo-Saxon. In a similar example, the dictionary is invoked to justify the use of the so-called generic *man*: 'My unabridged dictionary has 25 definitions of man, 6 are gender (male) specific, 19 non-specific. I'd like to stick with the majority.'

In these examples, sexist language is justified by appealing, in one case, to a dead language and, in the other case, to the dictionary. (We know that dictionaries not only reflect usages of a particular period in time but also reflect particular world-views.) Thus, language, rather than being viewed as a system that is specific to a social and historical context, is seen as unchanging just as the social roles of men and women are often represented as unchanging and inevitable, i.e. natural.

Finally, we see from this corpus that language is not only unaffected by social and political forces but, like other natural entities, seems to have a life of its own. The following comments are illustrative:

I trust, however, that in your committee's efforts to foster a greater respect for women, respect for the English language will also be demonstrated. I am appalled by some of the 'gender-neutral solutions' adopted by other institutions which reveal an almost complete disregard for the etymology of many words.

What *would* bother me, and very deeply, would be the slightest possibility that they [the members of the University of Toronto's Ad Hoc Committee on the Status of Women] were chosen for other than their knowledge of and respect for the nuance and absurdities, richnesses and traditions of the language itself.

The suggestion here is that the language 'itself' should be respected and protected, often, it appears, at the expense of respect for half of its speakers, i.e. women.

Interestingly, this is largely from a faculty with very few women professors, few women graduate students and a reputation for vocal resistance to the university's affirmative action hiring policy. The particular division we dealt with has an unofficial policy of leaving catalogue copy, including course titles, up to the discretion of the individual who usually teaches the course. This is the opposite of the division of humanities example given above, where the climate within the faculty was more positive, course title reform was part of more general curriculum reform and decisions were taken in committee.

Language reform and mainstream media

The second example of attempted language reform we look at concerns mainstream media. In a longitudinal study of a number of US newspapers, Fasold (1988) found that a newspaper's non-sexist language policy correlated positively with (non-)sexist language use in the newspaper. For example, he reports that 'change in language use policy over the years has succeeded in eliminating the discriminatory practice of referring to married women by their husbands' names only' (p. 202). However, while the new editions of the style books studied by Fasold and his students 'invariably decry sexism and the use of language in a discriminatory fashion' (p. 189), they are also fairly conservative. For example, while they concede that compounds with *man* may not always be appropriate, there is considerable resistance to compounds with *person*.

In March and April of 1991, the students in our language and gender course at York studied the extent to which Toronto's two major newspapers, the *Globe and Mail* and the *Star* abided by their non-sexist language policy. Both newspapers had published new style guides in 1990 with fairly good coverage of non-sexist usage. Of course, like their US counterparts, there is a certain sensitivity to perceived public opinion in the Toronto papers: the *Toronto Star* guide proscribes *chair* on the grounds that '[it] irritates many readers'.

The 168 essays submitted on the topic all found that the newspapers' adherence to their own guidelines was sporadic: e.g. usage of the so-called generic *he* and *man* abound. For instance, while the guidelines for both newspapers tell writers not to use *he* as a generic, usages such as the following are common:

> Give your local horticulturist the dimensions of your balcony and tell him that you want to plant in a container that will limit growth to the size that complements, rather than overwhelms, your space. (Jeffrey Freedman, 'Tenant Gardening Trend Is to Be Beautiful and Tasty', Toronto Star, 17 March 1991)

> What seller would want (could afford) to lose a serious buyer who had already sold his existing home? (Alan Silverstein, 'Return of "Conditional on Sale" Offers a Good Sign', *Toronto Star*, 16 March 1991)

Similarly, the *Star* tells its writers not to use *man* as a generic[7] and its guidelines give a number of examples of gender-neutral usage. However, a survey of one week's issues of the paper found that this guideline was not often followed. The great majority of individuals referred to that week were male and, in more than 80 percent of cases, they were referred to as *chairman, spokesman, businessman*, etc. When women were referred to, compounds with *person* or *woman* were used, never compounds with *man*. One article that week was highly reminiscent of the examples cited above from the *Chronicle of Higher Education*. In 'PM Showing CBC Contempt Watson Charges', two sources are quoted: Canadian Broadcasting Corporation *Chairman* designate Patrick Watson and the *Chairperson* of the Council of Canadians, Maude Barlow. So we have found the opposite results from those reported by Fasold since we have widespread sexist usage in the face of non-sexist guidelines.

Some insight into the lack of enforcement of these guidelines was gained by one student on the course who interviewed a number of *Toronto Star* writers (Chelin 1991). When asked why they used sexist language, a variety of responses were given. A gossip columnist announced that she 'wasn't performing brain surgery' but was just reporting the news and that she 'gives the audience what they want to read'. A business writer quoted from his copy of the *Star* style guide: 'it specifically says to use chairman or chairwoman but not chairperson', not realizing that his 1983 edition was out of date. A second business writer said he 'didn't realize there was a rule'. Attempts to justify usage included an appeal to the relative length of *man* vs *person* (this from a music writer): 'The nature of the newspaper game is to shorten; *person* has six letters and *man* has three'. There was also an argument based on the representation of women in the professions (this from another business writer): 'We are talking about men. We are talking about big companies who are all dominated by men and therefore we reflect that attitude. If we were talking about smaller companies it would be a whole different thing.' We see, then, that the (sexist) attitudes and values of individual writers have their influence. This can also be the case when a newspaper actually tries to enforce its policy. Fasold gives a revealing example from the *Washington Post*:

> 'The reporter had just referred to a woman by last name alone in a second reference, when he added parenthetically: ' "This newspaper's rules require that I call her merely that, though I would prefer Mrs.——" '.'

Clearly, then, having non-sexist language guidelines is not enough; an organization's commitment to enforcing them is crucial. As we see in the *Washington Post* case above, this enforcement may be subverted. The *Toronto Star* examples parallel the Faculty of Science course title example: language reform is less successful when it is left to the discretion of the individual to abide by the policy or not and when the speech community in question displays sexist values.[8]

Conclusion

In the first part of this article we demonstrate the extent to which linguistic meanings are determined by the social values and attitudes of the dominant culture. We argue that simply introducing non-sexist terms and phrases into a language will not necessarily lead to non-sexist usage. Just as words such as 'no' (in the context of a woman refusing a man's sexual advances), 'anti-racism' and 'racism' (among others) undergo a kind of 'semantic reversal' (Seidel's, 1988, term) in the mouths and hands of a sexist, racist culture, so innovative non-sexist terms may lose their non-sexist meanings or interpretations as they are appropriated by a sexist speech community. The conclusion that we draw from this, however, is *not* that non-sexist language reform should be abandoned. Rather, we demonstrate that language reform is most successful when it takes place within the context of a non-sexist speech community, i.e. when the social values and attitudes of a speech community support non-sexist meanings rather than undermine them. More specifically, we show that the association of non-sexist language with high-status groups is necessary for the adoption of a non-sexist language policy. The implementation of such a policy and/or guidelines, however, does not guarantee immediate and total compliance. Successful implementation depends on a number of factors, including visible institutional support, support by subgroups (e.g. women faculty) and the perception that language reform is part of social reform.

Notes

1. 'Judge Rules "No" May Mean "Maybe" in Sex Assault Case', *Toronto Star*, 25 April 1991.
2. This is not to say that linguistic innovations will always begin with the highest-status subgroup; the relative prestige associated with a particular subgroup and its linguistic innovations may be based on factors other than the socioeconomic ones typically associated with high prestige, e.g. ethnic identity, class loyalty, etc. may play a role. See Labov (1972) for discussion.
3. Henley (1987) makes a similar point regarding the possibility of successful language reform. However, Henley focuses on the way in which non-sexist forms are stigmatized and stereotyped because women, a lower prestige group, are the innovators.
4. There is also some evidence to suggest that Ms has been overtly stigmatized, as Labov predicts of linguistic innovations that are not introduced by the highest-status group within a speech community. Pierre Berton in a column in the *Toronto Star*, 15 June 1991, reports that a *Star* copyeditor would not allow him to use Ms before a woman's name because it was 'demeaning'.
5. This has been implemented at the University of Toronto Law School and is under consideration for Osgoode Hall Law School (York University).

6. Our corpus consists of letters to members of the Status of Women Communications Committee (York University) regarding course titles, letters to members of the committee regarding language reform at York more generally and articles on the subject of language reform appearing in campus newspapers.

7. The *Globe*'s guidelines are less straightforward: while it advocates a number of non-sexist alternatives to *man*, it states that no satisfactory gender-neutral term exists for titles such as *chairman* or *spokesman* and that the writer should in such cases use sex-specific terms, e.g. *chairman/chairwoman*.

8. One year previously a major report by a task force on women's opportunities was commissioned by owners of the *Toronto Star*, the Southam Newspaper Group. It reported that less than 5 per cent of senior management was female and that sexist attitudes in newsrooms impeded women's chances for shattering the traditional glass ceiling. On a positive note, senior management were, in print at least, supporting reform. (Michele Landsberg, 'Some Editors Fight Sexism in Newsrooms', *Toronto Star*, 8 June 1990.)

Reprinted from *Discourse and Society* 3, 1992.

Approaches to discourse

Chapter 14

Kate Clark

THE LINGUISTICS OF BLAME
Representations of women in The *Sun*'s reporting of crimes of sexual violence

IN OUR SOCIETY MEN COMMIT acts of violence on women every day. All women's lives are affected by this: by actual violence or by the fear of it. For this reason, the messages that a popular newspaper engenders in its reporting of such crimes are critical. In this study of reports by The *Sun* newspaper (a tabloid daily with the largest circulation of all the British dailies) of male violence against women and girls, I am interested in who is blamed for an attack and how language is used to convey that blame.

Language forms a useful method of examining ideology. Sometimes The *Sun*'s point of view is manifested very blatantly (consider, for example, a report entitled 'VICTIM MUST TAKE THE BLAME', of January 1982). Often, however, language is used to convey blame subtly, with the motivating value system only subliminally present, so that an analysis of that language is not just an end in itself, but a way of decodifying and laying bare the patterns of blame.

These patterns found in The *Sun* will be familiar to anyone who has looked at how sexual violence is usually treated in contemporary British society. The attacker is not always held responsible for his actions, even though the attacks reported tend to be of the most brutal kind; the victim or another person (always a woman, incidentally) may be blamed. Of interest is the way in which language is used to manipulate this blame. [. . .]

In this study, copies of The *Sun* from 10 November 1986 to 3 January 1987 were examined (copies of other newspapers were consulted for comparative purposes). This yielded fifty-three reports from The *Sun*, dealing with thirty-six cases, of male/female violence. All types of violence were included, as it was found that The *Sun*'s treatment was the same for all attacks, whether sexual (e.g. indecent assault, rape) or not (e.g. murder, assault, hit-and-run). The gender of the participants was the overriding factor in the nature of the reporting, and one to which I shall return later.

Two frameworks were used, naming analysis and transitivity analysis. Both work by showing the range of forms through which something can be expressed. The actual forms used in a report are chosen from this range. By comparing the selected form with the available options, the probable effects and the possible motivations can be deduced. Before showing how The *Sun* uses transitivity and naming to construct blame, I shall give the outline of these two frameworks.

Naming analysis

Naming is a powerful ideological tool. It is also an accurate pointer to the ideology of the namer. Different names for an object represent different ways of perceiving it. An example from another area of violence illustrates this: how do you refer to a person who seeks political aims using aggression? Is s/he a terrorist, guerrilla, freedom-fighter, rebel, or resistance fighter? Different connotations of legitimacy and approval are carried by these labels. The naming of the participants in a case of assault works in a similar way.

The attacker

The *Sun* has two naming choices for an attacker: whether to regard him as sub-human or not. It may name him as a *fiend, beast, monster, maniac,* or *ripper,* using verbs which further suggest his non-humanness:

MONSTER CAGED

(29/11/86, p. 22)

DOUBLE MURDER MANIAC PROWLS CITY OF TERROR
(26/12/86, p. 1)

or it may keep solely to terms which treat him in terms of social normality, i.e., name, address, age, or occupation. Apart from those men who are arrested, on trial, or have been found 'not guilty', where the laws of libel or contempt of court prevent the use of 'fiend' naming, The *Sun* has a free choice. The emotive hyperbole of a term like 'fiend' indicates how utterly alien, terrible, and scandalous the newspaper finds the attacker and his actions. An absence of these names implies that The *Sun* does not find an attacker or his actions particularly shocking. A last naming option, occasionally used, is to name an attacker sympathetically. This is done, as will be seen later, by building apparent excuses into an attacker's name.

The victim

The naming of the victim (and this applies to any other woman involved) takes the form of a selection of personal details. She is identified by such information as her name, address, age, appearance, occupation, marital status, and whether she is a mother or not. Few victims have all details given. There are some legal restrictions: for example, it is illegal in Britain to publish the names and addresses of rape victims. Otherwise, The *Sun* again has a free choice on how to name, and its selection of details varies from report to report.

Almost always details are given not so as to individualize the victim but to label her. Such labels include *wife, unmarried mum, mother of two,* and *vice-girl.* It should be stressed that these role-assignments are somewhat at the newspaper's discretion. Thus a woman who has blonde hair, four children and is divorced could be labelled as either 'mother of four' or 'blonde divorcee'. What is not arbitrary is the correlation between the naming of attackers and victims: only certain victim roles are linked to 'fiend' attackers.

Of the thirty-one reports where it was possible to name the attacker as 'fiend' (i.e. his identity was unknown or he had been found guilty in court), The *Sun* chose to refer to the attackers as *fiend, monster, beast,* or similar in thirteen reports. In these reports the victims were given the following names:

> wife (2)
> bride
> housewife
> mother (3)
> young woman
> girl, schoolgirl, girl guide (3)
> daughter
> blonde
> prostitute
> woman/victim (no role)
> individualized (no role)

There were also a few reports which, although not using the hyperbolic fiend terms, did convey blame of the attacker with such terms as *thug, gang,* and *kidnapper.* Victims in these reports were named in the following way:

> mother and children
> girl (in fact, a young woman)
> old woman

The labels for victims in those reports where the attacker was named sympathetically or in terms of normality are noticeably different. Apart from those attackers who were related to their victims (where completely different rules apply) and one short report where sexual murders were treated jokingly because they took place in Australia (too far away from the parochial *Sun* for it to get worried), victims of 'non-fiend' attackers were given the following names:

> blonde
> unmarried mum
> Lolita (in *Sun* language, a sexually active under-aged girl)
> blonde divorcee/mum
> woman/victim (no role)

Similar labels are given to those women other than the victim who are sometimes held responsible for an attack, e.g. 'blonde' and 'blonde divorcee'. These names seem to relate to a supposed sexual availability: 'fiends' attack 'unavailable' females (wives, mothers, and girls) while 'non-fiends' attack 'available' females (unmarried mothers, blondes, and sexually active girls). (The 'blonde' (16/12/86) and the 'prostitute' (11/11/86, p. 1) who were attacked by 'fiends' and the 'girl' who was attacked by a 'non-fiend' are anomalies to this general rule and will be looked at in more detail in due course.)

Transitivity

Blame or lack of responsibility, absence, emphasis or prominence of a partic- ipant can all be encoded into a report by The *Sun* through its choice of transitivity (on this model of transitivity analysis see Halliday 1985). Transitivity is concerned with language at the level of clauses. These are potentially made up of three components:

> 1 The Process – material, mental, verbal, or relational.
> 2 The Participants in the process.
> 3 The Circumstances of the process.

The elements in this theory most relevant to the reports studied are material processes and participants. Material processes involve 'doing'. There are two possible roles for participants: the Agent who 'does' the process and the Goal who is affected by the process. The Agent role is obligatory (i.e. always inherent in the process), but the Goal is only optional:

> HUBBY (Agent) KICKED (process) NO-SEX WIFE (Goal) OUT
> (4/12/86, p. 3)

> RAPED GIRL (Agent) WEEPS (process) (no Goal)
> (13/12/86, p. 1)

In clauses where both Agent and Goal are inherent, the Agent may be emphasized by the choice of active voice or the Goal may be put into focus as the grammatical subject by choice of passive voice, with optional agent-deletion:

> Hubby kicked No-sex wife out of bed. (active voice)
> No-sex wife kicked out of bed by Hubby. (passive, with agent)
> No-sex wife kicked out of bed. (passive, agent deleted)

In the violent acts reported by The *Sun*, the attacker affects the victim. In transitivity terms, he acts as Agent in a material process on the victim as Goal. If an attack is reported in this way, the attacker is shown acting intentionally upon the victim and the responsibility for the attack is (usually) seen to be his. There are several linguistic strategies used by The *Sun* to ensure that the attacker is not shown in his role as Agent affecting the victim as Goal. In these ways, blame for the attack can be withheld from the attacker and transferred to the victim or to someone else. This will be seen in the following analyses of the reports.

The reports

By itself, one clause or sentence is not very significant because a piece of writing is usually varied. Where a pattern emerges or one form is used insistently, the selection becomes more meaningful. Headlines are an exception. They can stand investigation by themselves because newspapers use them to encapsulate the view of the whole report. The headline below demonstrates how language can be used to focus blame upon an attacker. Not only is he shown as Agent acting upon the victim as Goal, but his naming as 'fiend' (and later also as 'sex-fiend', 'beast', and 'rapist'), and the naming of his victim in the report as a married woman, clearly point to his culpability:

FIEND RAPES WOMAN IN A BIG MAC BAR
(27/11/86, p. 23)

The *Sun* has several strategies for not blaming an attacker. One of the most common is to lessen the awareness of a man's guilt by making him invisible. Sometimes, this non-blaming will be masked by blaming someone else. Both these devices are used in this report (headline and opening sentence reproduced here) of 20/12/86, p. 7:

GIRL 7 MURDERED WHILE MUM DRANK AT THE PUB
Little Nicola Spencer was strangled in her bedsit home – while her Mum was out drinking and playing pool in local pubs.

Both these sentences have two clauses, one details the murder, the other describes what the victim's mother, Christine Spencer, was doing at the time of the murder. The 'murder' clauses are passive and the murderer is made invisible by deletion. This minimizes the reader's awareness of his guilt: compare 'Girl 7 murdered' with 'Man Murdered Girl, 7'. This structure – a 'drinking mother' clause linked to 'a murder-less murder' clause – is used in four out of the five sentences. The insistent repetition joins the child's death and the mother's absence so directly and so forcibly that a causal relationship is formed. The implication is that Nicola Spencer died because Christine Spencer was out. The naming of Nicola and her mother underscores the mother's supposed responsibility. Nicola's names all refer to her small size and age, which is usual for child victims. However, whereas in all other similar reports the connotations of innocence and vulnerability given by this naming emphasize the cruelty of a 'fiend' attacker, here, with the murderer invisible, the naming of the child implies that the mother is heartless. Christine Spencer is put further beyond the pale by her own naming, as 'blonde divorcee' (in The *Sun*'s coding she is an 'unrespectable woman').

Blaming the mother of the victim is a judgement passed by the newspaper. A radically different perception of the crime could have been given by choosing other structures, within the newspaper's normal range. In the example below, blame and attention are focused on the now visible murderer, who is seen to act intentionally, on the victim. Christine Spencer is no longer callous but suffering.

FIEND STRANGLES ONLY CHILD, 7 [headline]

Divorced Mum Grieves Alone [sub-heading]

In a report of 11/11/86, pp. 1, 4, and 5, the interpretation of a case where the attacker is again not held responsible is even more clearly a consciously chosen one. The *Sun* diverges in its judgement of the case, not only from other newspapers but from its source – a legal ruling. In court, the attacker, John Steed, was sentenced to four life-sentences for raping three women and killing a fourth. The killing was accepted as manslaughter, on the grounds of diminished responsibility (Steed was taking drugs at the time). Otherwise, the court saw him as responsible and blameworthy. Throughout its interpretation of the case, The *Sun* casts Steed in a passive role. Rather than affecting his victims, he is himself shown being acted upon, at times a victim himself. Simultaneously, the women involved in his life are shown as the real criminals. In this seventy-eight sentence report, The *Sun* chose to devote 63 per cent of the space to the defence lawyer's summing-up while only 4 per cent is used actually detailing the attacks. The paper's views are apparent in its encoding of events in the Page One headline:

SHARON'S DEADLY SILENCE [headline]

Lover Shielded M4 Sex Fiend [subheading]

The crimes are not mentioned here. Neither are the victims. Both are implicated in the term, 'sex fiend', but this is not an emphatic or conspicuous
reference. They are certainly not the focus of the headline. Instead, the theme
(Halliday 1970: 160–2) and the person shown acting refer not to Steed but
to his girlfriend, Sharon Bovil. The attacker is relegated to the sub-heading,
to an inactive role and furthermore to a role where Bovil acts upon him, as
Goal. This makes it seem as though *the* central event of the case was one in
which Bovil was active, Steed was acted upon and the victims were not
involved. Bovil is blamed for Steed's crimes, by the newspaper, because she
failed to inform the police about them. Whether this is a fair assessment
of her actions, let alone a fair assessment of Steed's attacks will be looked
at later. For now, it suffices to notice that, already a shift of blame has
taken place. Just as the word 'deadly' has been taken away from the actual
killer, so, in a wider sense, Steed's deadliness has been transferred, by The
Sun, to Bovil.

At the same time, Bovil is presented as an 'unrespectable' woman: she
is 'blonde', 'beautiful', and 'petite' (cf. non-sexual synonym – 'small'). Steed
is named with some fiend references, but rather than indicate his guilt, these
are used to point to Bovil's responsibility. He is named as evil only in relation to her. Some possessives are used, indicating their relationship and her
supposed control over him:

> Blonde, Sharon Bovil . . . M4 rapist John Steed (sentence 1)
>
> Bovil, 21 . . . her psychopath boyfriend (sentence 2)

Elsewhere, his naming ameliorates markedly to non-fiend references, for
example, when the attacks are being described. These take up only three
sentences, which in a seventy-eight sentence report is unusually short. They
are not in a prominent position, but are a continuation of the Page One
report which has Bovil as its theme (the numbers in parentheses refer to the
sentence number of the original text):

> Two of Steed's rape victims – aged 20 and 19 – had a screwdriver
> held at their throats as they were forced to submit (21)(a). His third
> victim, a 39 year old mother of three was attacked at gunpoint after
> Steed forced her car off the M4 (22). Two days later, he gunned down
> call-girl, Jacqueline Murray, 23, after picking her up in London's Park
> Lane (23).

In both descriptions of the rapes (21 and 22) the perception of Steed as rapist
is reduced by making the sentences passive and deleting him as Agent. This
perception is further reduced by using the euphemism 'attacked' to mask the
terrible details of abduction, repeated rape, and death threats (not mentioned
at all in this newspaper).

The description of the manslaughter makes a startling contrast. This is an exceptional sentence; it is the only one where Steed is shown acting intentionally and therefore blameworthily against a victim. The sentence is active and the nature of the attack is specified and forcibly described. This anomaly may be explained as being due to Jacqueline Murray being named as a 'call-girl' and 'prostitute', killed only after being 'picked up'. In a report where the attacker's guilt is assessed at an absolute minimum, it is only the 'unrespectable' woman who the attacker can be shown as intentionally killing.

After Steed's responsibility for his actions is minimized on page one, the part of the report on pages four and five forms a further exhortation to excuse him. As a defence lawyer, quoted in sentence 27, says with coerciveness: '. . . we must search for the causes.' Again, Steed is put into a passive role. He is seen as a victim, as being created by his past.

PSYCHO SAW MUM RAPED

Boyhood horror 'scared M4 sex fiend for life'

Sex killer John Steed was set on the path to evil by seeing his mother raped when he was a little boy, it was claimed yesterday (24). The M4 monster's lawyer Mr Robert Flack told the Old Bailey that young Steed had walked into his mother's bedroom when she was being raped by his father (25). 'He saw her struggles and heard her screams and suffered the first trauma to his mind' said Mr Flack (26). He added: 'On the face of it, the horror of this case precludes sympathy with the defendant, but we must search for the causes' (27). 'The tragedy that caused four women to cross the path of John Steed has left one of them dead and three with horrendous memories that can never be erased' (28). Mr Flack then outlined 23 year old Steed's grim childhood that led to him becoming a woman-hating, sex-mad, psychopathic killer (29).

The rape of his mother is given as the central cause of Steed's deviance and of his later crimes. Interestingly, it is the rape of the mother and not the father's act of raping which is shown as the cause. In the headline, the father-rapist is unrealized and the rape process passivized. With no explicit agency given, the rape becomes a quality of the woman rather than an act upon her. The mother and her 'raped-ness' are Steed's 'boyhood horror', not the father's attack. Only once is the father actualized, in sentence 25. Even here, the mother is still the focus because the sentence is passive. As in the Page One part of the report, Steed only appears as a 'fiend' in relation to the woman who is being blamed:

Psycho . . . Mum
Boyhood horror . . . M4 sex fiend
sex-killer, John Steed . . . his mother

> young Steed . . . his father
> four women . . . John Steed
> grim childhood . . . woman-hating, sex-mad, psychopathic killer

Sentence 28 in the extract exemplifies the extent to which blaming an attacker can be withheld, using linguistic manipulation. It is a general summing up of the attacks, quoted directly from the defence lawyer. In this interpretation of events, the agent which 'caused' the women's movements and 'left' them dead or raped is not the actual attacker, Steed, but 'tragedy'. The use of this word implies that the attacks were an unavoidable misfortune, something which no-one – and certainly not Steed – was responsible for. Steed actually performs no act in this when they 'cross' his 'path'. In this way, the defence lawyer (and The *Sun*, which chooses to quote him verbatim) suggests that the women were in some measure responsible for the attacks on them.

Girlfriend, mother, victims: at every stage it is the women who are blamed, while the actual attackers, the men – both Steed and his father – are released from the responsibility for their crimes. This is a chosen stance. Within its own ideology of blame The *Sun* could have indicated the 'genuineness' of the victims, by using a different naming strategy. Only the manslaughter victim is cast in the usually given role, which indicates the blame or non-blame of the attacker and, as mentioned before, as a 'vicegirl' this role, if anything, obscures rather than acknowledges the evident guilt of her attacker. Information is so lacking about the first two victims – only their ages are given – that it is difficult even to picture them. Although the third victim is named once as 'mother of three', no mention is made of her being pregnant when she was abducted and repeatedly raped.

Other interpretations are possible. The court saw Steed as guilty enough to receive four life sentences. Other papers followed this line. While all except for the *Daily Mirror* focus not on the victims, but on Bovil and the father's rape of the mother, they do not, for example, find Bovil blameworthy. Other papers interpreted Bovil's actions not as intentional or voluntary, but motivated by fear of Steed, for example:

SECRET TERROR OF M4 RAPIST'S GIRLFRIEND
(Daily Telegraph)

SHARON'S SECRET
Terror of Girlfriend

(Daily Mirror)

Most quote the policeman in charge of the investigation:

> 'She was no different from his other victims. She herself was in stark terror of him.'

The coverage of the rape by Steed's father of his mother points to one last area of male/female violence which I would like to consider, that of husband/wife attacks. So far, all the reports I have examined have been of attacks on women by strangers. In the Steed report the husband-rapist was not blamed. This is not an uncommon way of perceiving such attacks, as the following headline indicates:

HUBBY KICKED NO-SEX WIFE OUT OF BED
(4/12/86, p. 3)

In terms of transitivity, this headline is identical to the 'Big Mac' heading, but the attacker here is not viewed with the same abhorrence as the rapist then was. Here it is the naming which is the conveyor of blame. The attacker in this case was so violent that his wife had to obtain a divorce. Yet, he is named as 'Hubby', a term not of censure, but a diminutive name of affection – an odd choice in this context. The naming of the victim is similarly odd. There is a tension between 'no-sex' and 'wife'. Rather like 'lady doctor' or 'male nurse', the use of 'no-sex' implies a deviation from the norm. The implication is that a 'normal' wife would have sex with her husband. This feeling is reinforced by her second naming: 'his pretty blonde wife' perceives the woman in terms of her sexual attractiveness and her husband's possession of her ('his . . . wife'). Given this naming, it seems understandable that he became 'sex-mad' (sentence 1) and 'kicked her out of bed'. As in the following report, sex is perceived as a wife's duty and a husband's right. Failure to service a husband's sexual needs is seen as a justification for violence, either against his wife or against another woman. In the case below, 'the other woman' was a 16-year-old girl:

SEX-STARVED SQUADDIE STRANGLED BLONDE, 16
Love ban by teenage wife
(29/11/86, p. 11)

The pattern of blame and language is similar: the naming of the victim by her hair colour fails to individualize her in any way which could draw sympathy towards her. Instead, it portrays her in terms of her sexual attractiveness, as something which any man, especially one named as 'sex-starved', could not help responding to. Indeed, this sympathetic naming of the attacker, in combination with the paper making a reference to his wife not wishing to have sex with him, implies that the person to blame for the murder was the murderer's wife.

Women are often held responsible, by the newspaper, for the actions of their husbands or boyfriends, although the link is never explicitly made, just assumed to be true (why should sexual frustration lead to a tendency towards homicide?). For women who are attacked by their own partners, this is especially true. There is a clear division between 'stranger-attackers' and 'husband-attackers' in The *Sun*'s world-view. Although the attacks by husbands can be as serious and as bloody as the fiendish stranger-attackers, they are almost never named as fiends. The divergence between the gravity of the attacks and the non-blaming of the husband-attackers, as judged by their naming in the headlines and first sentences, can be seen below:

VIOLENT HUBBY
Violent husband, Bob Sleightholme
The victim was beaten over a period of twelve years by her husband, before he almost killed her.

(21/11/86, p. 13)

CRAZED WIFE-KILLER
A tormented husband
The husband almost decapitated his wife with a knife.

(28/11/86, p. 13)

DOCTOR DEATH
Wife-killer
An evil doctor
The man murdered his first wife and attempted to murder his second.

(19/12/86, p. 16)

DEBT-RIDDEN DAD
Tormented Kevin Banks
A woman was murdered by her husband, who then killed himself.

(19/12/86, p. 11)

HUSBAND
Spurned husband, Derek Ord
A man shot his wife and her mother dead.

(27/12/86, p. 1)

For all the reports, after the first sentence, the naming of the husband consisted of references to his status as husband or father, and his job, appearance, or age, i.e. in terms of social normality. Only in one of the reports (19/12/86, p. 16) is an attacker ever referred to in fiendish terms. Even then, he is mainly referred to with non-fiendish names (two fiendish and nine non-fiendish). Significantly, all the other men who murdered their wives are seen as themselves suffering: they are 'debt-ridden', 'tormented', 'crazed', or 'spurned'. This is the key note, not the suffering they themselves have caused, but their own plight. These men are named sympathetically, with excuses built into the naming. They are seen as suffering so much they became 'crazed' or 'tormented' and then committed murder. This makes it seem that they were not responsible for their actions – a man who is mad cannot be blamed. It also raises the question of why they were suffering. Kevin Banks was under financial pressure and killed both his wife and himself, but

Derek Ord and the 'crazed wife-killer' of 28/11/86 were both suffering because their wives had left them and, in the latter case, because she had also taken a new lover. In other words, the wives are shown to cause the suffering which supposedly leads to their husbands killing them. This cause is particularly highlighted in the Ord case by the use of the emotive adjective, 'spurned', meaning to 'reject with disdain . . . treat with contempt . . . repel with one's foot' (OED).

This lack of fiends, monsters, and beasts in the ranks of the husbands must be due to husband-attackers being an anomaly in The Sun's ideology. A fiend is outside human society and a man who attacks a stranger can be viewed as abnormal and alien. A husband is always and unarguably within society. It is a position ratified by society in the marriage institution. As such it is difficult for a husband to be seen as a fiend. Therefore, these violent men are normalized and humanized by 'suffering' naming. This keeps the ideology intact, although it does mean that the women victims must take the blame. They bear the burden of reconciling anomaly to ideology. The tension between the theory and actuality is revealed in the Sleightholme headline. On one level the man is seen as 'violent', on another he is affectionately seen as 'hubby'. These two concepts are incompatible and contradictory. The forcing together of them into a single name shows the tension these husband-attackers create in the ideology.

Possible motivations

This chapter has attempted to demonstrate that The Sun does manipulate blame. It has also shown some of the way in which this is linguistically achieved. It has not yet tackled the question of why the newspaper should want to do this. There can only be conjecture as to The Sun's motivations, but clearly, the linguistic analysis points to the world-view through which the events are mediated and encoded. Two possible reasons are implied by the manipulations of language.

The Sun's interest in attacks involving male violence against women and girls may be part of its general concern with sex. This might seem far-fetched because not all the crimes are sexually violent. However, in its encoding of blame, the type of attack (whether sexual or not) had no effect on the blaming pattern. The significant factor was not the type of crime, but the gender of the participants. Murder, assault, even hit-and-run victims were cast in roles of sexual availability or unavailability and their attackers were named as fiends or not. This indicates that the reporting of male/female attacks could well be conditioned by an interest in sex. If this is so, these reports would tie in with other facets of this fascination: with the sexual mores of the 'stars' (and there is a clear crossover here – MOWER HIT ME FOR SAYING NO TO SEX (16/12/86, p. 15), MURDER QUIZ FOR ESTHER'S IN-LAW (10/12/86, pp. 1, 4), WIFE BEATER, SHILTON IN CELLS (4/12/86, p. 1), with offers of sexy lingerie, with advice on 'your love-life', and with The *Sun*'s 'Page Three Girl' – the soft-porn photographs of models which daily appear in this paper). In the last instance, there is a definite merger of interest.

In the Steed report, the photographs clearly show a Page Three influence. Two pictures of Bovil, the attacker's girlfriend, dominate. The second one, covering most of pages four and five, shows Bovil full length with a low-cut black leather dress pushed up her thighs in an eminently 'rapeable', Page Three posture. Like the Page Three Girls she is viewed here and in the text as a sexual 'bad girl'.

The concurrence of interest is no more clearly shown than when the newspaper's favourite 'model' is involved with a rapist, albeit indirectly. The report – SAM FOX AND THE RAPIST (16/12/86, p. 1) – tells how a man, Raymond Genas, was arrested after his victim noticed a photograph of Genas, with Samantha Fox, in the car in which he raped her. (Genas and Fox met only once on a brief and impromptu occasion when Fox let the photograph be taken as a favour to her fan.) Most of the front page is taken up by a huge reproduction of this photo, an image of the brutal rapist with his arms around the soft-porn star. This titillating proximity is the theme of the report, completely eclipsing the victim's suffering. In the headline, it is not the victim or the process of rape which is given priority, but the supposed relationship between Fox and Genas. The real interest in the case also emerges in the naming; Genas is only portrayed as a fiend in sentences relating to Fox. With the victim, apart from one racist reference, he is named simply as 'Genas':

> An evil rapist . . . Sam Fox
> The Beast . . . Beauty
> Hulking, 17 stone, Raymond Genas . . . the Page Three Beauty
>
> Genas . . . the terrified blonde (a reference to the victim)
> Genas, 23 . . . the girl
> The Black Giant . . . his victim

A general interest in sex seems to be a strong motivation for The *Sun*'s way of reporting events of male/female violence. Certainly, the neo-Gothic naming of men as beasts, fiends, and monsters helps to sensationalize the attacks and maybe helps to sell papers. Perhaps, also, labelling victims, as opposed to individualizing them, lends itself to a voyeuristic rather than a sympathetic reading of events.

A possible alternative to fiend naming would be a more neutral style. It could be argued that fiend naming is preferable to this because it, at least, conveys some of the horror of the events and the culpability of the attackers. It is dubious whether this sort of naming does in fact carry much blame towards the attackers (as will be argued below). It also seems doubtful whether it actually conveys much horror. Rather, it seems to trivialize. When

195

victims are portrayed as roles, rather than as individuals, it is difficult fully to imagine and sympathize with their experiences. It is also hard to believe the outrage apparently intended by the hyperbolic fiend naming when it is withheld from 'non-genuine' victims and used in the same routine way with all attackers of 'genuine' victims, no matter how serious the attack was; according to these values a sex-murderer can be and is (22/12/86, p. 23) treated in the same way as a male motorist who accidentally hit female pedestrians with his car (NB they were 'respectable' victims, 'a mother strolling with her baby'). Both attackers are perceived to be fiends.

Perhaps most importantly, it is highly unlikely that fiend naming or The *Sun*'s general choice of language, does anything to change the present conditions which produce men who commit violence against women. But 'Sex as a good sell' can only be a partial reason for The *Sun*'s style of reporting events: it explains the general interest but not the intricate patterns of blame and language. A more detailed examination of the newspaper's conditioning world-view supplies the rest of the probable motivation for The *Sun*'s choice of language. Several pieces of linguistic evidence indicate this world-view, the central one being the naming patterns of the victims and attackers. The *Sun*'s ideology is based on the premise that fiend attackers are distinguishable from non-fiends and 'genuine' victims from 'non genuine' ones. Furthermore, these distinctions are based not on what is done, but on who it is done against, as defined by the paper, of course. Any attack is fiendish when committed against a female who is named as 'respectable', i.e. sexually 'unavailable' and is a stranger to her attacker (and also when another woman is not held responsible for the attack). It is not seen as fiendish when committed against a woman who the attacker is married to or against a woman who is named as 'unrespectable'.

The naming of the victims clearly reflects a patriarchal viewpoint because women are categorized in terms of possible sexual encounters with men, rather than as autonomous individuals. It is also getting close to a 'property' view of male violence. 'Availability' could be rephrased as 'unattachment to a man'. So, for example, attacks on other men's wives are treated with abhorrence, while those on a man's own wife are seen as 'legitimate' or understandable.

The distinction between fiends and non-fiends is also a patriarchal myth. It assumes that violent, anti-female attitudes are abnormally rare and that strangers are the men to be feared. Actually attacks by men known to their victims are extremely common. Just how ordinary the inclination to rape is, for example, can be seen by looking intelligent, (mainly white, and middle-class) men. A survey in America found that of 341 male students, 87 had made at least one attempt at:

> coital access with a rejecting female during the course of which physical coercion is utilized to the degree that offended responses are elicited from the females.
>
> (Kirkpatrick, quoted in Toner 1977: 83)

Russell (1982: 133) also quotes 'several recent studies' of male college students undertaken to find out if there was 'some likelihood they would rape a woman if they could get away with it'. Results ranged from 35 per cent to 51 per cent positive.

Actual acts of violence by men on women are also very common and the men from whom women are most at risk are not strangers but those they know and those they live with. The 'Rape Counselling and Research Project' found that 'over 50% of women have had some prior contact with the man who raped them' (1979: 7). This is undoubtedly an underestimate because their sample included only those reported to the police, which would exclude marital rape, which at the time was legal in Britain. Russell found, in a statistically impeccable study, that one in seven wives are or have been raped by their husbands and that married women are six times more likely to be raped by their husbands than by strangers (1982: 1, 67). She also discovered that 21 per cent of wives had been 'subjected to physical abuse by a husband'. Eighty per cent of sex crimes committed against children are by attackers well known to them and 50 per cent are by the father (Laneless, quoted in Ward 1984: 82). The largest category of murders is of spouses or co-habitees (24 per cent) and of these more than 80 per cent of the victims are female (Home Office figures for 1979, quoted in NCCL 1983: 12). If it is thought that an attack from someone who the victim knows is less devastating, less 'fiendish', this also is false: violence from someone known will probably be endured over a longer period of time, access to the victim is usually unlimited, and the after-effects are harder to recover from because a trust has been violated and the victim is less likely to confide in others and, if she does, is less likely to be believed (Ward 1984: 82–7; Martin 1976: 63).

Given that the idea of a 'fiend' attacker is so false, there must be strong reasons for The *Sun* to use it. It does mean that in every permutation of blame the men always win. This is obvious where the attacker is not held responsible, but is less so if he is apparently blamed. Fiend naming suggests that the attacker is so evil and so alien that he is utterly outside human kind and society. This is in effect an excuse for his crime because a fiend or a monster or a beast cannot be held responsible for its actions. By implying that these men are extra-societal, this naming also excuses our society which produces them. By creating a false dichotomy between fiends and non-fiends, The *Sun* blurs the wider continuum of male violence against females. The intense hyperbole of fiend naming focuses a self-righteous fury on stranger-attacks, which are actually a very small area of male/female violence. By obscuring the whole range of aggressive acts, it becomes impossible even to ask the vitally important question of why, in our society, so many men commit acts of violence against women and girls. Under its veneer of moral indignation against fiends, therefore, The *Sun* helps to maintain the status quo.

Reprinted from Michael Toolan (ed.) *Language, Text and Context* (London: Routledge, 1992).

Chapter 15

Sally McConnell-Ginet

THE SEXUAL (RE)PRODUCTION OF MEANING: A DISCOURSE-BASED THEORY

SCHOLARSHIP ON WOMEN AND language has addressed two main topics: (1) how women (and men) speak (and write); (2) how they (and other gender-marked topics) are spoken of. In each case, feminists have argued, some kind of linguistic sexism is at work. Sexism in how we speak has many aspects. Women's favored styles of language use are often negatively evaluated by the larger community, for example, and women are frequently the victims of male oppression in discourse, suffering interruptions and inattention to their conversational contributions. In more public arenas, similar problems exist on a larger scale: women speaking from pulpits or podiums are still rare, and their writings are viewed as somehow tainted by their sex. Sexism in how women are spoken of manifests itself in a variety of ways, such as 'the semantic derogation of women' in the vocabulary and the so-called generic masculines that contribute to women's relative 'psychological invisibility'.

[. . .]

My major aim in this essay is to give a brief theoretical account of the roots of sexist semantics in sexist discourse.[1] This way of putting it is, of course, somewhat oversimplified. By *sexist semantics* I mean not only such phenomena as the sexualization and homogenization of words denoting women (e.g., *mistress* and *girl*) and the universalization of words originally denoting men (e.g.., *guys*) but also subtler aspects of the relative absence of a 'women's-eye view' in the most readily accessible linguistic resources. What I mean by *sexist discourse* also goes beyond the more blatant kinds of male oppression of women in conversation, though I include some examples of these. More generally, I am interested in how sex differences influence both communication and interpretation in discourse.

Whatever we think of the merits of particular studies, it is relatively easy to see how sexism in a community could have implications for how its members speak and how their speech is evaluated. Because using language is a socially situated action, it is clearly embedded in the same sociocultural matrix that supports sexual bias in the work we do, the wages we receive, the expectations we have of ourselves and others, and so on. What is more difficult to understand is the connections between a sexist society and the semantics of a language; the most familiar theoretical models of linguistic meaning do not illumine the question of how particular meanings become attached to particular forms.

Stated like this, however, the question is misleading, for its suggests that meanings somehow exist independently of their articulation, as though languages merely paste linguistic labels on the semantic furniture of the universe, tagging an independent realm of concepts with sounds (or, in the graphic medium, strings of letters). Not all the possible semantic stock is tagged by a particular language-using community, but no theoretical barrier prohibits its members from adding labels whenever they choose. Or so a common line of thinking goes, a line that I refer to as the *code view* of language. This view finds popular expression in such comments as 'Oh, that's just a question of semantics' (which implies the triviality of the connection between forms and their meanings) or in such familiar adages as 'A rose by any other name would smell as sweet'. What the code view fails to address is the significance of the tagging process itself and the possibility that this process shapes and gives coherence to the sometimes inchoate stuff that we seek to wrap our tags around. To understand the source of sexist semantics, the way sexism in society and culture interacts with the system of linguistic meanings, we really need to ask how meaning is produced and reproduced.

The production of meaning designates the processes through which speakers mean something by what they say (or writers by what they write) and through which hearers (or readers) interpret what is said (or written). The reproduction of meaning refers to our dependence, in producing meanings, on previous meanings or interpretations, to our dependence in particular on one another's experience with the linguistic forms being used. I argue that to understand the ways that meanings are produced and reproduced and the significance of sex and gender in these processes, we must consider the conditions of discourse. The key to explaining so-called sexist semantics and, ultimately, to reclaiming the 'power of naming' (Spender 1980) lies in analyzing the sexual politics of discourse. Macropolitical structures play a significant role, of course, in genderizing discourse. Who writes and who reads? Who preaches sermons to large congregations? Who publishes books? Whose speeches are beamed by satellite around the world? Although these are important questions, I will not consider them here but will focus instead on the micropolitics of daily discourse between ordinary individuals. Because most of what we say about daily discourse is more widely applicable, however, this restriction is not so severe as it might seem.

I am indebted to the work of the philosopher H. P. Grice for my basic framework, though I use his ideas in a somewhat special way. Grice bases his account of meaning on what speakers intend to accomplish by speaking (Grice 1957; 1967). The crucial feature of the Gricean account for my purposes is that meaning depends not just on the speaker but on a kind of relation between the speaker and the hearer. It is this potentially social perspective that gives insight into the (re)production of meaning.

What is involved in this account? Grice's explanation goes something like this: in saying *A*, a speaker means to express the thought *B* if the speaker intends to produce in her hearer a recognition of thought *B* by virtue of his recognizing that she is trying to produce that recognition in him by saying *A*. (Grice does not restrict his account to female speakers and male hearers, as the pronouns I have used may imply that he does. I am following many other authors in using both *she* and *he* as 'generic' singular pronouns; but since I later discuss in more detail the hypothetical case of a woman talking with a man, the choice of pronouns is not entirely arbitrary.) This back-and-forth intending and recognizing and thinking is, of course, not usually a conscious process. In informal speech, coordination adequate for the purpose is generally taken for granted and not reflected on. The more complex (and the more novel) the thoughts one seeks to express, the more conscious the attention given to the meaning process. There is generally greater self-awareness in writing and reading than in speaking and hearing, because the memory and time constraints are less severe.

In linguistic communication, the speaker typically takes as common ground with the hearer certain beliefs about the language system and, in particular, about familiar connections between linguistic forms (signifiers) and thoughts and concepts (signified). It would seem safe to assume this common ground in most conversations. The assumption can certainly not be maintained, however, in linguistic transactions with very young children. How then do children come to manipulate sounds (and ultimately other means of signaling) to express thoughts? The issue of how much the development of this ability depends on the child's experience and how much I reflects the biologically controlled maturation process does not concern us here. What I do want to stress is that parents usually act as if their child intentionally behaves in certain ways to express thoughts, even though they may well know better.

Let us imagine the bizarre case of a child whose exposure to language involved no social interaction. We might suppose that a loudspeaker intoned English sentences into the nursery and that the child's needs were attended to with no accompanying speech. This child might indeed begin to speak, matching the loudspeaker's output, but there would be no reason to assume that the child *meant* by articulating 'I love you, Mommy.' This child would be like the parrot that produces linguistic forms with no appreciation of how the wider speech community uses those forms.

In contrast, most children in English-speaking families have a radically different experience. When the child produces something like 'ma' or 'mama' – whether to imitate the language of others or just to attempt vocal control – the parents attach significance to the sounds: they treat the child as if the utterance meant 'mama'. That is, they begin to make it possible for the child to give this meaning to the sounds by showing that they have attended to those sounds, using the same or somewhat similar sounds themselves in conjunction with such actions as pointing to Mama or having Mama present herself to the child. The crucial thing is that children thus start to participate in a coordinative activity, recognizing their own and others' articulations as somehow the same. The motives they begin to attribute to others' articulations can also serve to guide their own. Let me emphasize that much of this development may well be guided by children's prewired or innate capacities and dispositions, including access to a fairly rich and highly structured conceptual system as well as a natural bent to coordinate their own speech with the articulations of their community. That is, children may have a preexisting stock of concepts waiting to have tags affixed; nonetheless, as tags are placed, some of those concepts are modified or joined with others in various ways that we do not yet clearly understand but that nonetheless result in the production of new conceptual systems. The conceptual systems that children evolve will to a considerable extent reproduce those prevalent in the community.

We cannot, in this essay, follow the child's entire linguistic development. What matters for our purposes is that the child and those around the child manage to *mean* something by what they say because (1) they jointly take the saying to be aimed at triggering a common recognition of thoughts, (2) they jointly take themselves to be relying on shared resources to achieve this coordinated recognition – a common language system plus a certain amount of shared experience. To a considerable extent, the coordination is achieved through the child's adapting to what is customary for the community. Those in the community, however, may also adapt to the child's productions – perhaps accepting novel forms or understanding the child as giving certain standard forms nontraditional meanings. But, by and large, the child and its parents do not endow language forms with meaning by coordinating their uses of them de novo. Rather, the parents (and all the other language users whom the child encounters) exploit the basic consensus achieved in earlier uses, and the meanings the child manages to produce in exchanges basically reproduce those already familiar in the community.

For certain concepts – especially for talking about perceptions of the external world – the reproduction of meaning is probably almost literally that, for the simple reason that children are evidently predisposed to note certain distinctions, to attend to certain sorts of environmental stimuli, and to ignore others. Their innate conceptual systems need only be aligned with the language system in their community. Apparently, for example, children who learn the *up-down* word pair through spatial uses do not need to be taught to apply it to ascending and descending melodies: psychologists have found that even very young prelinguistic infants make this connection between the visual and auditory domains. Nonetheless, most linguistically encoded concepts are not preformed but are produced, in at least their fine detail, as children familiarize themselves with the particular perspectives, beliefs, and practices of the community.

It is by no means clear, for example, that children initially give high priority to sorting people by sex rather than by other characteristics. In languages like Finnish, where *hän* is the only singular third-person pronoun, third-person reference is not differentiated by sex. There is no evidence I know of that Finnish children start by trying to introduce a marking of sex difference here. There is evidence, however, that some English children do not find the *she-he* distinction particularly congenial. Whether or not children find it natural to genderize references to a person – to choose between *he* and *she* even where the sexual information plays no particular role in what is communicated – probably depends on how strongly genderization has figured in their experience. In a household with children of both sexes, for example, the special importance of sex sorting is likely to have established itself fairly well by the time the youngest child is working at pronouns. But some children do resist, perhaps because their rearing has been what Sandra Bem calls *gender-aschematic*. Such children, acculturated into an atypical framework, use the same form for everyone or use the masculine and feminine pronouns in somewhat random fashion, not bothering to attend to the distinction where it does not matter for their purposes. But even they eventually go along with the larger community, and it seems plausible that learning to make the required distinction can serve to heighten the conceptual salience of sex sorting.

The main point here, again, is that endowing linguistic forms with meaning is a socially situated process. The statement applies not just to children learning to communicate but also to more mature speakers struggling to convey increasingly complex thoughts. A major insight of the Gricean perspective is that we can manage to mean much more than what we literally say. How? By relying on what we take to be shared or readily accessible beliefs and attitudes in a particular context.

We can suggest a framework for understanding how cultural biases leave their mark on language systems and, more generally, we can begin to see why and how social inequality results in linguistic inequality. Our focus will be on discourse inequalities created by the sexual division of labor in producing situated meanings. Empirical research on conversational interaction among white middle-class Americans has convincingly demonstrated the influence of sexual stratification on discourse, and I want to extend these results to support an account of how sexual bias can affect the (re)production of meaning.

The major findings on discourse are hardly surprising. Basically, in cross-sex conversation men tend to dominate women in the following ways:

(1) they actually do more of the talking; (2) they interrupt women, in the sense of seizing the floor, more often than women interrupt them; and (3) they more often succeed in focusing the conversation on topics they introduce. In all these respects, the conversational relation between women and men parallels that between children and adults, employees and employers, and other power-differentiated groups. Not surprisingly, matters are more complex than this thumbnail sketch implies; for example, neither interruption (of which there seem to be different kinds) nor amount of talk is always indicative of control over a conversation, and correlation with sex is affected by many contextual factors. Certainly the proposed picture runs counter to some stereotypes – notably, that women are more talkative than men. If there is any truth to this notion, it may lie in situations other than those on which research has focused to date. For example, female groups may spend more of their time in talk than do male groups. Studies of single-sex conversation do suggest that women regard conversation more as a cooperative enterprise than as a competition, enlarging on and acknowledging one another's contributions, responding to coconversationalists' attempts to introduce topics, and signaling active listening by nods and *mmhmms* during a partner's turn. In contrast, men generally view conversation more individualistically and less socially, with each participant's contribution self-contained and the 'right' to one's own turn taking priority over any 'responsibility' to others during their turns.

To some extent, women and men simply operate with different expectations about how linguistic interactions ought to proceed. For example, men are far less likely than women to give signals that say 'I read you loud and clear.' This is true not only when they talk with women but also when they talk with one another. A man may interpret another's *mmhmm* as agreement with what's been said, whereas a woman hears another's *mmhmm* as registering comprehension. One young man in a classroom where these differences were being discussed decided he sometimes might be assuming that his girlfriend agreed with him when indeed she was merely signaling that she was still receiving his communication. He resolved to try to distinguish the genuine signals of assent from those of simple connection. When he thought he had an affirmative response, he would stop and say, 'Oh, so we're agreed about that.' More often than not her reply was 'Of course not.' (I owe this anecdote to Ruth Borker.) Still, what is involved here is more than different expectations; it is also an exercise of power, whether intentional or not.

Daniel Maltz and Ruth Borker (1982) argue that women and men have different models of friendly conversation. Their account draws on such work as Kalčik's study of women's rap groups (1975) and Marjorie Harness Goodwin's analysis of directives issued by girls and boys to each other (1980). From a somewhat different perspective, Carole Edelsky (1981) contends that in addition to the *singly held floor* that is normative in most conversational studies, there is in some conversations a *collectively held floor* (these are my terms for her 'F1' and 'F2'); she observes that women participate on a more nearly equal basis with men under collective floor conditions. Undoubtedly, the full account of sexual differentiation in discourse will be far more complex than our current picture. For example, the more interactive orientation that women and girls have toward conversation does not mean that men and boys have a monopoly on conflict and disagreement – a point the Goodwins make very clear in their interesting study 'Children's Arguing'. (Goodwin and Goodwin 1987). Nonetheless, whatever the explanation, the evidence shows that men generally aim at individual conversational control, whereas women aim at social conversational collaboration.

Male conversational control and female conversational collaboration are, of course, only tendencies: there are women who successfully interrupt men to steer the conversation in their own direction, and there are men who work at helping their female coconversationalists develop a topic by asking questions, elaborating, or simply by actively indicating their continuing engagement in the listening process. Still, a common pattern involves the man's controlling and the woman's supporting cross-sex conversation. Nor is there any reason to believe that this behavior is somehow biologically rather than culturally produced. Early on, children are identified by others as girls or boys and learn to identify themselves in the same way. Tied to this identification is a process that typically leads them to acquire roughly the practices of linguistic communication that prevail among their same-sex peers. And linguistic communication, as one kind of social interaction, is embedded in more general political structures that children are, in some sense, being prepared to reproduce. Whatever the precise mechanisms, the net result is that sex is of considerable significance in the politics of talk among adults.

How does inequality in discourse affect what can be meant and by whom? First, men are more likely than women to have a chance to express their perspective on situations, not only because they have more frequent access to the floor but also because they are more actively attended to. This distinction is especially important, since comprehension goes well beyond simple recognition of the linguistic structures used. In other words, where the sexes have somewhat different perspectives on a situation, the man's view is more likely to be familiar to the woman than hers is to him. This observation leads directly to the second point: men are much more likely than women to be unaware that their own view is not universally shared. As a result, women and men may well be in quite different positions regarding what they believe to be commonly accepted (or accessible) in the speech community. This disparity in turn can have important consequences for what each is able to 'mean' when engaging in linguistic communication. Why? Because what is meant depends not just on the joint beliefs about the language system and its conventional – that is, standard or established – interpretations but also on what interlocutors take to be prevalent beliefs in the speech community about everything else beside language.

'New' or nonconventional meanings involve a speaker's intending the hearer to infer a purpose to the words beyond that of directing attention to the thought 'literally' expressed. Let us take as an example the semantic development of *hussy*, a word that was once merely a synonym for *housewife*. How did it acquire its present meaning? And, once the sexual slur was produced, how was it reproduced and attached to the form so insistently that present generations do not even connect the two words? The example is not in itself important, since *hussy* hardly figures prominently in contemporary discourse, but it is useful for illustrative purposes because its historical development is well documented.

While we cannot, of course, recapture the discourse conditions in which this particular sexual insult was produced, we can sketch what may have happened and reconstruct the course of the word's shift in meaning. It seems plausible that some members of the speech community considered sexual wantonness a salient characteristic of the housewife. Such people could say *huswif* (or, perhaps, the somewhat shortened and familiar form *hussy*) and rely on their hearers to bring that characteristic to bear on interpreting the utterance. Thus they might say something like 'What a hussy!' and try to mean just what such a comment conventionally means today. Of course, if they were wrong in supposing that their hearers would recognize this appeal to the negative stereotype, the attempted communication would fail. But the mere fact that the putative common belief was not universally shared would not in itself spell doom. So long as the negative stereotype of housewives was widely known, even hearers who did not accept it could recognize an appeal to it and understand that the term *hussy* was intended as an insult.

A contemporary example of semantic derogation can be found in what some younger speakers are now doing with the term *gay*. Elementary school children who do not connect the adjective with sexuality simply understand it as a word used to belittle. They will, of course, soon learn that *gay* refers to homosexuality and that the belittlement they rightly recognized in older speakers' use of the word is based on attitudes and emotions about sexuality. Often the early connotations will persist and become associated with homosexuality, tending to reinforce the pervasive heterosexism and homophobia in mainstream social groups.

Or consider a somewhat subtler example. A man who means to insult me by saying 'you think like a woman' can succeed. He succeeds not because I share his belief that women's thinking is somehow inferior but because I understand that he is likely to have such a belief and that his intention is not just to identify my thinking as an objectively characterizable sort but to suggest that it is flawed in a way endemic to women's thought. The crucial point is that I need not know his particular beliefs: I need only refer to what I recognize (and can suppose he intends me to recognize) as a common belief in the community.

In contrast, it is much more difficult for me to mean to insult him by saying 'you think like a man,' because to recognize my intention he would not only have to know that my opinion of men's thinking is low, he would also have to believe that I know he so knows (or that I believe he so believes); though such an understanding is not unimaginable in a conversation between old acquaintances, it is quite unlikely in more general communication. And even where the intended insult works, it is construed as something of a joke or as a special usage, unless the stereotype disparaging women's thought (or at least elevating men's) is not familiar to both interlocutors. Thus it is easy to reproduce notions with widely established currency and difficult to produce unexpected or unfamiliar ones. I need not actually believe some common-place, or even know that my interlocutor does, in order to attribute to him (my choice of pronouns here and throughout this essay is deliberate) the intention to treat it as a view we share. Indeed, even if I explicitly deny that view, I may end up doing so by acknowledging that it is generally believed. Thus, as Finn Tschudi (1979) observes, to say 'women think as well as men do' is already to acknowledge that the standard for comparison is men's thought. No matter how much I might wish to insult someone by saying that *she* or *he* thinks like a man, I could not so intend without relying on more than general linguistic and cultural knowledge.

There are complications, of course. We may each be aware that the general stereotype is under attack. Until it is decisively destroyed, however, the possibility remains that someone will purport to take it as a shared belief – and thereby succeed in relying on it to convey meaning, unless the 'purporting' is exposed. As the stereotype fades, however, the meaning it conveyed may remain but become reattached to the linguistic form as part of its literal meaning. Thus the view of housewives as hussies might not have been robust enough to sustain all the intended uses of *hussy* to insult, but so long as enough of these uses succeeded, subsequent language users could be directed immediately to the insult without a detour through the extralinguistic attitudes. In other words, when enough such insults work in situations that the speakers can take as precedent-setting, where the insult is recognized and associated with the term rather than with the negative view that initiated the term's derogatory connotation, the facilitating stereotype becomes superfluous. One can rely on earlier language experience to reproduce the meaning formerly produced by the stereotype.

This discussion leads to the related issues of what speakers take as background beliefs about the interpretations 'standardly' assigned in the speech community, that is, the literal meanings that can be assumed as 'defaults' in talking with others (operative unless something special in the discourse triggers alternative interpretations). One could, once upon a time, call someone a *hussy* and not intend to insult her. One can no longer do so, however, since a contemporary speaker who is familiar with the form can hardly fail to know how it is now standardly taken—and certainly cannot count on an unfamiliar interlocutor to ignore the negative evaluation. As we probably all realize, for example, it is becoming harder and harder to make *he* mean 'she or he', because only incredibly isolated speakers can have missed the controversy over the so-called generic masculine, the dispute over whether users of *he* in sex-indefinite contexts indeed intend to refer to both sexes and, if they do, how well they succeed in getting their hearers to recognize that intention. Given the doubts raised, one cannot say *he* and mean 'she or he,' because one cannot generally expect hearers to make this identification. Humpty-Dumpty said to Alice, 'When I use a word it means exactly what I choose it to mean,' but that was, to a considerable extent, wishful thinking. Suppose we intend others to recognize a certain thought or concept just by understanding the linguistic forms we have used. This intention will be reasonable only if we can expect our listeners to believe with us that the speech community indeed associates that thought or concept with those linguistic forms. That is, we must get others to cooperate with us in giving our words the meaning we want. At the very least, our listeners must recognize our intention and help us by acknowledging that recognition.

It may well be that women play a major role in reproducing meanings that do not serve their own purposes or express their own perspectives. They are fully aware that female perspectives are not viewed as commonly held (indeed, are often not recognized at all) and, in the interests of facilitating communication, they allow men to continue to believe that a distinctively male view of things is actually not particular but universal. 'This is the oppressor's language,' says Adrienne Rich, 'yet I need it to talk to you.' Indeed, some have argued that language is so little 'woman's language' that women cannot even manage to mean what they say, much less achieve success in meaning more.

This view has been persuasively elaborated by the philosopher Sara Ann Ketchum (1979). How, she asks, can a woman manage to mean no to a man's 'Would you like to go to bed?' She says no with sincerity but he interprets her through a filter of beliefs that transform her direct negative into an indirect affirmative: 'She is playing hard to get, but of course she really means yes.' But of course she does not mean yes; assent is not what she intends to convey. I would contend that indeed she does mean no, even though she faces an extraordinary problem in trying to communicate that meaning to someone ready to hear an affirmative no matter what she says. (I am not, of course, claiming that one never means yes by *no* but only that one often does not; this is the case we are now considering.) Only if she knows that he will never take her *no* to mean no can she not intend the negation. Yet she still would not mean yes; his refusal to cooperate in her attempts to communicate no might reduce her to a desperate silence, but his unreasonableness, his unwillingness to apprehend her as someone who might mean no, can never compel her to mean yes. Even though what my words mean does not depend solely on my intentions, Humpty-Dumpty is right that it does require those intentions.

Nonetheless, Ketchum's main point certainly stands: meaning is a matter not only of individual will but of social relations embedded in political structures. A positive moral can be drawn from this observation as well: it is possible to produce new meanings in the context of a community or culture of supportive and like-thinking people. I can mean no if my intention is supported by a feminist network that recognizes the sexual double standard and articulates male myths regarding female sexual behavior: I am not a single, isolated individual refusing to submit but, rather, part of a collectivity resisting sexism and violence against women. More generally, women are together challenging the view that 'the' culture is what men have told them it is or that 'the' language is what is available and what women must reproduce on pain of being condemned to a solitary silence. Rather, women are uncovering the myth of univocality and discovering new voices, their own and their sisters'.

The philosopher Naomi Scheman has illustrated how a feminist community can produce new meanings. In 'Anger and the Politics of Naming' (Scheman 1980), she looks at how consciousness evolves – is in some sense created – in a women's rap group: using a mass of internal inchoate stuff, women can work together to form something coherent, to build conceptual structures that allow them both to interpret their own experience and to express that interpretation to others. In other words, they do not just tag preexisting concepts but generate new ones. They are able to think new thoughts, to realize, for example, that they may have been angry without recognizing what they felt. This thought is new not just in particular instances but also in its broader implications – enabling women to interpret an earlier emotion as anger when they did not do so at the time, because their language use did not then offer that possibility. This new interpretation matters because it connects past emotions to the option of purposeful current actions. Women cannot 'mean' alone but they can collaborate to produce new meanings and support the reproduction of those meanings in the community.

The research contrasting women's and men's approaches to discourse suggests, in fact, that women may be especially well suited to producing significantly new meanings. Because this possibility depends on the development of a shared new outlook, it might be better promoted in the cooperative mode of discourse than in the competitive, where less attention is paid to the other (and where one extracts meaning by assuming that the speaker reproduces earlier linguistic habits and familiar modes of thinking). It is true, of course, that women will find it harder to express their distinctive perspectives to men than vice versa so long as sexist patterns and practices persist. Nonetheless, women might collectively reshape their conceptual systems, particularly the ways they think about women and men, about individuals and social relationships, and about language and its connection to the individuals and their communities.

Is this possibility what the French feminists mean when they speak of an *écriture féminine*, what English-speaking feminists like Mary Daly mean when they talk of a 'new' gynocentric language? Perhaps, though calls urging women to produce their own meanings are sometimes interpreted as implying that they must leave the old and familiar language to 'him'. But they cannot begin *de novo*. Just as the child must start somewhere – and presumably draws heavily on a conceptual structure that is biologically endowed – so must women. It was because the women in Scheman's rap group could assume they all had access to a common language system that they could evolve together views that differed in important ways from familiar interpretations of that system. No matter what women intend to mean by their new language, they can only convey that meaning if they can expect others to recognize the thoughts to which the language aims to direct attention. And if there are indeed new meanings to be reproduced after they are initially produced in specific contexts, then women must find a community both able and willing to apprehend those new meanings.

It is a matter not just of what women manage to mean but also of what all of us, women and men, interpret others as meaning and, ultimately, of what we help or hinder others to mean. As I pointed out earlier, feminist research has established that *he*, no matter what its user intends, is not unproblematically interpreted as generic, and the consequent shift in the community's beliefs about how *he* is interpreted has influenced what one can intend the pronoun to convey. There are now many contexts in which those who are aware of these developments cannot expect *he* to be understood as 'he or she'. no matter how much they might wish they could. A footnote explaining one's generic intentions does not suffice, since some readers will doubt the sincerity of that announcement and others will forget it. This is not to say that now no one ever means 'he or she' by using *he*: my point is just that it is much harder to convey that meaning than it used to be, in large measure because we now know that many earlier attempts were unsuccessful and that many purported attempts were, in fact, spurious. (Martyna (1980a; 1980b) provides empirical evidence that the actual use and interpretation of so-called generic masculines are quite different from what grammar books prescribe).

Language matters so much precisely because so little matter is attached to it: meanings are not given but must be produced and reproduced, negotiated in situated contexts of communication. Negotiation is always problematic if an inequality of resources enables one negotiator to coerce the other. And because negotiation involves achieving consensus about beliefs and attitudes, it is not surprising that dominant groups have an unfair advantage in working out ways of meaning that are congenial to their beliefs and attitudes. The picture is much more complex than I have indicated here, but the basic point should be clear. Meanings are produced and reproduced within the political structures that condition discourse: though a sexist politics may have helped some men to 'steal the power of naming', that power – a real one – can be reappropriated by feminist women and men building new language communities.

Note

1   'Sexist semantics' corresponds to 'how women are spoken of', i.e. what is popularly glossed as 'sexism in language'; 'sexist discourse' corresponds to 'how women (and men) speak (and write)'. The author argues that the first has its roots in the second [Ed.]

Reprinted from Francine Frank and Paula Treichler (eds), *Language, Gender and Professional Writing* (New York: MLA, 1989).

Further reading for part two

(full publication details are given in the bibliography)

AN UP-TO-DATE, WIDE-RANGING and thoughtful source of information and analysis concerning sexism in language and feminist reform efforts, which also has the virtue of surveying the way sexism has been manifested and tackled in a range of different languages, is Anne Pauwels's *Women Changing Language* (1998). It has an appendix which gives useful and linguistically well-informed advice on how to design effective nonsexist language guidelines.

For a straightforward descriptive treatment of what 'sexist language' means in relation to English, one useful source – designed for learners and teachers of English – is Jane Sunderland's edited volume *Exploring Gender: Questions and Implications for English Language Education* (1994). The best known English-language nonsexist guidelines are probably Miller and Swift's *A Handbook of Nonsexist Writing* (revised UK edition 1995, though in fact this is a US text), along with their book *Words and Women* (1979). A historical treatment of grammaticized gender distinctions in English is Dennis Baron's *Grammar and Gender* (1986). A more radical feminist writer on this topic is Julia Penelope, whose *Speaking Freely* (1990) contains much relevant material. For those wishing to pursue philosophical arguments about sexism in language, *Sexist Language: A Modern Philosophical Analysis* (Vetterling–Braggin 1981) remains worth seeking out in a library.

For readers interested in sexism at the level of discourse/text as well as vocabulary and grammar, an accessible volume that discusses the issues and gives practical guidance on how to analyse texts ranging from novels to

211

sanitary product advertisements is Sara Mills's *Feminist Stylistics* (1995). Some applications of feminist discourse analysis to the understanding of phenomena like anorexia, sexual harassment and attitudes to menstruation can be found in the edited volume *Feminism and Discourse: Psychological Perspectives* (Wilkinson and Kitzinger 1995), which is of particular interest to social psychologists.

'Political correctness' is a topic that has generated more heat than light, and readers should be warned that a lot of books on the subject are, even by the standards of popular or journalistic writing, seriously inaccurate about 'PC' language. The papers collected in Sarah Dunant's *The War of the Words* (1994) are mostly intelligent, though in spite of the title rather few of them focus specifically on the issue of language. That issue is the subject of one chapter in Deborah Cameron, *Verbal Hygiene* (1995), which includes material on feminist linguistic reform and resistance to it. An accessible discussion by Donald MacKinnon of institutional language guidelines dealing with race, sexuality and disability as well as gender takes up part of the last chapter on 'Good and Bad English' in the Open University textbook *English: History, Diversity and Change* (Graddol, Leith and Swann 1996).

Finally, the theory and practice of critical discourse analysis is regularly discussed and illustrated — often in relation to issues of sexism and racism — in the journal *Discourse and Society* (published four times a year by Sage).

PART THREE

Talking gender: Dominance, difference, performance

Introduction to part three

THIS PART OF THE BOOK PRESENTS a number of pieces that bear on the question of how ways of speaking are gendered; how women and men speak, and why. Notice that I haven't defined the subject matter as 'differences between women and men'. This is a common understanding of what feminist linguistics is about, but many feminist researchers have come to believe it is an over-simplification, as likely to obscure as to illuminate the questions that are interesting and important. I have selected contributions to part three to illustrate how feminists have arrived at this newer understanding of what is at stake in the study of gendered linguistic behaviour. The three subsections follow a roughly chronological plan.

Developing a tradition

The first subsection, 'Developing a tradition', contains three 'classic' pieces, the most recent of which dates from the early 1980s, while the earliest, Otto Jespersen's chapter, 'The Woman', from his book *Language: its nature, development and origin*, dates from 1922. As that date suggests, 'The Woman' cannot be regarded as part of the feminist critique proper. Rather it represents the kind of thing which that critique was reacting against. Jespersen was not the only linguist of his time to write about women and language, but because his work was available in English and had been widely read, it was Jespersen who was 'rediscovered' as English-speaking feminists turned their attention to questions of language and gender in the 1970s. 'The Woman' is cited in many early feminist discussions, where it stands for a whole tradition of patronizing and sexist commentary by male linguists before feminism.

The next piece, an excerpt from Robin Lakoff's *Language and Woman's Place* (1975, though published as an article two years earlier), is truly a 'classic'. Often hailed as the first ever work of feminist linguistics, it probably did more than any other text before or since to bring issues of language and gender to wider attention and to place them in the context of the post-1968 Women's Liberation Movement.

It has been said that every radical movement carries traces of the order it is trying to overthrow. Perhaps it is not surprising, then, that Lakoff's work seems to carry over certain assumptions from the tradition of Jespersen, most notably the assumption that 'women's language' is a special or deviant case (Lakoff contrasts 'women's language' not to 'men's language' but to 'neutral language'). This assumption has sometimes been criticized as a kind of unthinking masculist bias, and it has been cited − e.g. by Aki Uchida, whose work is also included in this part − as a reason to place Lakoff within the 'deficit' framework (see Introduction). I am not entirely happy with this: *Language and Woman's Place* does have elements of a 'deficit' approach, but I think it has as much or more affinity with the 'dominance' approach in which subordinate status is understood as the main determinant of women's behaviour. It is clear that Lakoff constructed the 'neutral language/women's language' opposition consciously and deliberately, and that she had a political rationale for doing so. The (alleged) existence of a special, non-neutral 'women's language' mirrors the broader sociocultural fact that women are the *marked* gender (see Black and Coward's argument in Chapter 7) − always 'women', − whereas men are just people. As Simone de Beauvoir had noted in 1949 in *The Second Sex*, women are defined (by men and the cultures men dominate) as Other. Lakoff was saying that 'women's language' is Other in the same way. It is an insight worth attending to even now, and it enabled Lakoff to bring together the scattered observations made by linguists like Jespersen about women's ways of speaking and suggest that they had a common root: the cultural equation of femininity and powerlessness.

A great deal of the subsequent argument about Lakoff's work focused on the question, was she right in her description of the *characteristics* of 'women's language'? *Do* women use more 'empty' vocabulary, more intensifiers and qualifiers, more tag questions, etc., etc.? The least misleading answer to this question, after twenty years of empirical research, would be 'yes and no'. And as my third selection in this part I have chosen a piece that takes issue with Lakoff on other, and to my mind more politically significant, grounds than just the empirical accuracy of her description.

Pamela Fishman's 'Conversational Insecurity' (1983) belongs within the 'dominance' framework, but it rejects Lakoff's tendency towards 'deficit' thinking. Thus Fishman argues against Lakoff's view that 'women's language' is a sign of *insecurity* – a characteristic which according to Lakoff women's socialization forces on them, but which is nevertheless a deficiency and a disadvantage. Looking closely at real interactions between women and men in heterosexual domestic partnerships, Fishman argues that the women are neither insecure nor lacking in linguistic skill, they are simply – and competently – doing the support work of keeping conversation going in a context where men can get away with not contributing equally to this task. 'The underlying issue', Fishman concludes, 'is likely to be hierarchy, not simply gender.' (Here, British readers may care to recall British Telecom's 1990s advertising campaign 'It's good to talk', which specifically praised women for being 'better' than men at doing conversational maintenance work on the phone. What in the 1970s was seen as a sign of 'insecurity' in women has now been redefined as a defect in *men*! Feminists will want to ask, however, if this new enthusiasm for women's allegedly superior 'communication skills' is any more satisfactory or any less sexist than what preceded it.)

What we have in this first section is the outline of a developing feminist tradition; among other things, it is a tradition of argument. As Jespersen's piece shows, the habit of making observations on 'women's language' predates the current wave of feminism; but Lakoff is pursuing an argument with the prefeminist tradition by putting her own observations in the service of an explicit political agenda. Fishman's analysis is political too, but it is explicitly framed *against* Lakoff's. The argument is, by the early 1980s, as much between feminists as between feminism and its opponents. The pieces presented in the second section, 'dominance and difference', underline that this has continued to be the case; as I noted in the introduction, much recent argument among feminists has concerned how far we should follow Fishman in emphasizing hierarchies of *power* between women and men in our accounts of gendered speech behaviour.

Dominance and difference

Deborah Tannen is the best-known scholar associated with the 'difference' framework, and her article 'The relativity of linguistic strategies' (1993) defends her view that the underlying issue when women and men run into conversational trouble may not be hierarchy or inequality at all. Tannen sees male/female differences as comparable to cultural differences, and while she has never denied the existence of gender inequality, she thinks it both inaccurate and unfair to assume that men purposefully and monolithically dominate women in talk. Rather, the sexes have different ways of talking that may give rise to misunderstanding between them. The solution to this problem is greater awareness and greater tolerance, on both sides.

This view gained ground during the 1980s and came to public prominence in 1990 with the massive success of Deborah Tannen's popular book *You Just Don't Understand*. Other feminists, however, responded critically to Tannen's arguments. Aki Uchida's piece 'When "difference" is "dominance"'(1992) is one of the most interesting and wide-ranging critical responses. In fact Uchida has criticisms of both 'dominance' and 'difference' frameworks; she questions whether it makes any sense to *separate* the two concepts in a discussion of gender relations. Even if one can validly talk about women and men forming different subcultures, it still has to be borne in mind that the overall cultural context is one of male dominance.

Uchida also questions the analogy Tannen makes between male–female misunderstanding and communicational breakdown between people from differing cultural backgrounds. She distinguishes between 'cross-cultural' and 'intercultural' communication, arguing that when two groups are in regular contact, as opposed to being totally unacquainted with one another's habits, we are in principle dealing with the 'intercultural' type, which ought to involve the groups *negotiating* meaning and accommodating to one another. If in practice it is women who accommodate to men, that is surely an effect not simply of difference but of power.

The 'dominance/difference' argument is still going on, but at the same time feminist linguistic researchers are moving in new directions, often prompted by developments in other academic disciplines where gender is being theorized in new ways. One way of theorizing it that is currently attracting interest among linguists draws on the notion of 'performance'. The broader context for this notion is feminist postmodernism, one feature of which is a resolute opposition to 'essentialism', the assumption that gender is a fixed and stable characteristic of every individual. Simone de Beauvoir proposed as long ago as 1949 that one is not born a woman, one becomes a woman: the postmodernist take on this is that we never actually finish, or perfectly accomplish, 'be(com)ing a woman' (or a man) but must continually bring our gender identity into being by *performing* various kinds of feminine or masculine behaviour. It is evident that one could treat gendered ways of speaking as part of the performance individuals put on, and in the third section, 'New directions: performing gender', I reprint two pieces which consider linguistic performances of gender.

Performing gender

Jennifer Coates's ' "Thank god I'm a woman": the construction of differing femininities' (1996) comes from her full-length study *Women Talk:*

Conversation Between Women Friends, which is based on a large corpus of data from women's friendship groups. In the chapter reprinted here, Coates uses her data to show how women talking to their friends are 'doing' or 'performing' various different kinds of femininity. Though always constrained to display their gender, these women enact more than one version of it, sometimes switching between several different ideas of what 'women' are, or should be, in a short stretch of conversation. They draw on 'discourses' (Coates explains this term in more detail) which are often contradictory: feminist discourses underlining women's strength and confounding traditional stereotypes (e.g. that all mothers are totally fulfilled by their domestic and childrearing activities), but also discourses in which women are defined by their appearance, at the mercy of their hormones or emotions, and reluctant to value their own talents or skills. These different understandings of what it means to 'be a woman' coexist in present-day western societies, and they show up in the way women talk to their friends.

Coates's observations on women performing varying and contradictory femininities are striking in part because the women she studied seem so 'mainstream'. My second selection on the theme of performance deals with a case many readers will perceive as more 'out of the ordinary' (though of course such judgements always depend on where you stand). It is also a case where the term 'performance' has a literal force. Kira Hall's 'Lip service on the fantasy lines' (1995) is about telephone sex workers, whose job is to perform, using only their verbal skills, a version of femininity which the customer will find sexually arousing. The job description many were hired under is apt: 'fantasy makers'.

The femininity many telephone sex workers choose to perform – and they are quite conscious of it being a performance – turns out to be, in linguistic terms, not a million miles from the powerless 'women's language' discussed by Robin Lakoff. Here Kira Hall explicitly takes up a point which is far more muted in Lakoff's own work, and in most earlier work that centres on the idea of 'women's language' as conditioned by/expressive of powerlessness: that there is something specifically *sexual* about some of the ways of talking that are culturally marked as 'feminine'. To be more exact, these ways of talking are eroticized, invested with a sexual meaning. Part of what makes 'feminine' speech 'sexy' is the fact that it also signals powerlessness: in patriarchal societies, women's weakness or vulnerability is eroticized. (Some men, of course, prefer a fantasy of 'powerful' femininity – the dominatrix or slave mistress. This is a minority taste, but in any case it follows a general rule that *differences* in power are eroticized.)

Hall's piece illustrates how a focus on 'performance' makes the question of power more complicated, less clear-cut. Her discussion takes up the issue of whether women who (knowingly and deliberately) perform the sex workers' particular, stereotypical femininity are empowering themselves individually (since they make money and in some cases derive job satisfaction from doing it 'well', and most feel that the men who use their service are pathetic rather than powerful), or whether they are colluding in the powerlessness of women collectively (since the most 'successful' performance is one of sexual subordination, which the male customer must be persuaded to accept as 'the real thing', not a performance at all).

Interestingly, one of the interviewees who is particularly aware of the contradiction here is a *man* who adopts a female persona for professional purposes. He also adopts a range of racial/ethnic personae, as do many of his female colleagues (in the fantasy phone-line game, we are told, the 'best' black women are white and vice versa). This raises a topic of interest to some current feminist (and 'queer') researchers, namely the way language may be used to perform social identities that do not 'match' the individual's biological characteristics. For some people (those who routinely 'pass'), this kind of performance is consistent across all or most situations; but it becomes easier to experiment with temporary switches when linguistic communication is not face to face – on the phone, or in the new virtual world of the internet. Hall calls this 'cross-expressing', on an analogy with 'cross-dressing'.

For feminists there is a paradox here. If 'crossing' is becoming a more salient social phenomenon, if more people in more contexts see gender identity as something fluid rather than fixed, something you can choose, or play with, this owes much to the social shifts brought about by, among other things, feminism as a political and intellectual movement. People who 'pass' or 'cross' are affirming, as feminism affirms, that anatomy need not be destiny. But while sex workers, transsexuals and transvestites are hardly conventional in the eyes of mainstream society, the gender roles they enact are often startlingly conventional, not to say stereotypical. Hall's informants in their professional personae seem far more faithful to Lakoff's description of 'women's language' than women have been found to be in other contexts (one is tempted to say, than 'real women', as opposed to personae created for male heterosexual consumption). They thus exemplify the postmodernist idea of a 'simulacrum', a copy that has no original.

The same is true of the racial (and racist) stereotypes which are held to be 'better' enacted by someone who does not belong to the group in question. In this case, however, I imagine many readers will feel overt distaste for the performance, which recalls the offensiveness of the 'blacked up' minstrel tradition. A key reason why white women are 'better' at creating fantasies of black women must be that many black women are unwilling to perform someone else's racist script. If there is, as I suspect, a difference in our attitudes to racialized and gendered 'cross-expression' – if we are more ambivalent or more tolerant towards the latter and more clearly repelled by the former – it is interesting to ask why.

More generally, we need to ask: are 'cross-expressing' and similar phenomena a real challenge to current social and sexual relations, or can they be comfortably accommodated within the system? Might they even be helping to maintain that system? Once again, what we have here is an argument between different feminist positions – in this case, between enthusiasts of postmodernism and those who are more sceptical. It may all seem a long way from Jespersen's catalogue of feminine linguistic traits and habits, but the question could be asked: have we in some ways come full circle?

Developing a tradition

Chapter 16

Otto Jespersen

THE WOMAN

Women's languages

THERE ARE TRIBES IN WHICH men and women are said to speak totally different languages, or at any rate distinct dialects. It will be worth our while to look at the classical example of this, which is mentioned in a great many ethnographical and linguistic works, *viz.* the Caribs or Caribbeans of the Small Antilles. The first to mention their distinct sex dialects was the Dominican Breton, who, in his *Dictionnaire Caraïbe-français* (1664), says that the Caribbean chief had exterminated all the natives except the women, who had retained part of their ancient language. This is repeated in many subsequent accounts, the fullest and, as it seems, most reliable of which is that by Rochefort, who spent a long time among the Caribbeans in the middle of the seventeenth century (Rochefort 1665: 449ff.). Here he says that

> the men have a great many expressions peculiar to them, which the women understand but never pronounce themselves. On the other hand, the women have words and phrases which the men never use, or they would be laughed to scorn. Thus it happens that in their conversations it often seems as if the women had another language than the men.. . . The savage natives of Dominica say that the reason for this is that when the Caribs came to occupy the islands these were inhabited by an Arawak tribe which they exterminated completely, with the exception of the women, whom they married in order to populate the country. Now, these women kept their own language and taught

it to their daughters.. . . . But though the boys understand the speech of their mothers and sisters, they nevertheless follow their fathers and brothers and conform to their speech from the age of five or six.. . . It is asserted that there is some similarity between the speech of the continental Arawaks and that of the Carib women. But the Carib men and women on the continent speak the same language, as they have never corrupted their natural speech by marriage with strange women.

This evidently is the account which forms the basis of everything that has since been written on the subject. But it will be noticed that Rochefort does not really speak of the speech of the two sexes as totally distinct languages or dialects, as has often been maintained, but only of certain differences within the same language. If we go through the comparatively full and evidently careful glossary attached to his book, in which he denotes the words peculiar to the men by the letter H and those of the women by F, we shall see that it is only for about one-tenth of the vocabulary that such special words have been indicated to him, though the matter evidently interested him very much, so that he would make all possible efforts to elicit them from the natives. In his lists, words special to one or the other sex are found most frequently in the names of the various degrees of kinship; thus, 'my father' in the speech of the men is *youmáan*, in that of the women *noukóuchili*, though both in addressing him say *bába*, 'my grandfather' is *itámoulou* and *nárgouti* respectively, and thus also for maternal uncle, son (elder son, younger son), brother-in-law, wife, mother, grandmother, daughter, cousin – all of these are different according as a man or a women is speaking. It is the same with the names of some, though far from all, of the different parts of the body, and with some more or less isolated words, as friend, enemy, joy, work, war, house, garden, bed, poison, tree, sun, moon, sea, earth. This list comprises nearly every notion for which Rochefort indicates separate words, and it will be seen that there are innumerable ideas for which men and women use the same word. Further, we see that where there are differences these do not consist in small deviations, such as different prefixes or suffixes added to the same root, but in totally distinct roots. Another point is very important to my mind: judging by the instances in which plural forms are given in the lists, the words of the two sexes are inflected in exactly the same way; thus the grammar is common to both, from which we may infer that we have not really to do with two distinct languages in the proper sense of the word.

Now, some light may probably be thrown on the problem of this women's language from a custom mentioned in some of the old books written by travellers who have visited these islands. Rochefort himself (1665: 497) very briefly says that 'the women do not eat till their husbands have finished their meal', and Lafitau (1724) says that women never eat in the company of their husbands and never mention them by name, but must wait upon them as their slaves; with this Labat agrees.

Taboo

The fact that a wife is not allowed to mention the name of her husband makes one think that we have here simply an instance of a custom found in various forms and in varying degrees throughout the world — what is called verbal taboo: under certain circumstances, at certain times, in certain places, the use of one or more definite words is interdicted, because it is superstitiously believed to entail certain evil consequences, such as exasperate demons and the like. In place of the forbidden words it is therefore necessary to use some kind of figurative paraphrase, to dig up an otherwise obsolete term, or to disguise the real word so as to render it more innocent.

Now as a matter of fact we find that verbal taboo was a common practice with the old Caribs: when they were on the war-path they had a great number of mysterious words which women were never allowed to learn and which even the young men might not pronounce before passing certain tests of bravery and patriotism: these war-words are described as extraordinarily difficult ('un baragoin fort difficile', Rochefort 1665: 450). It is easy to see that when once a tribe has acquired the habit of using a whole set of terms under certain frequently recurring circumstances, while others are at the same time strictly interdicted, this may naturally lead to so many words being reserved exclusively for one of the sexes that an observer may be tempted to speak of separate 'languages' for the two sexes. There is thus no occasion to believe the story of a wholesale extermination of all male inhabitants by another tribe, though on the other hand, it is easy to understand how such a myth may arise as an explanation of the linguistic difference between men and women, when it has become strong enough to attract attention and therefore has to be accounted for.

In some parts of the world the connection between a separate women's language and taboo is indubitable. Thus among the Bantu people of Africa. With the Zulus a wife is not allowed to mention the name of her father-in-law and of his brothers, and if a similar word or even a similar syllable occurs in the ordinary language, she must substitute something else of a similar meaning. In the royal family the difficulty of understanding the women's language is further increased by the woman's being forbidden to mention the names of her husband, his father, and grandfather as well as brothers. If one of these names means something like 'the son of the bull', each of these words has to be avoided, and all kinds of paraphrases have to be used. According to Kranz the interdiction holds good not only for meaning elements of the name, but even for certain sounds entering into them; thus, if the name contains the sound *z*, *amanzi* 'water' has to be altered into *amandabi*. If a woman were to contravene this rule she would be indicted for sorcery and put to death. The substitutes thus introduced tend to be adopted by others and to constitute a real women's language.

With the Chiquitos in Bolivia the difference between the grammars of the two sexes is rather curious (see Henry 1879). Some of Henry's examples may be thus summarized: men indicate by the addition of *-tii* that a male person is spoken about, while the women do not use this suffix and thus make no distinction between 'he' and 'she', 'his' and 'her'. Thus in the men's speech the following distinctions would be made:

He went to his house: *yebotii ti n-ipoostii.*
He went to her house: *yebotii ti n-ipoos.*
She went to his house: *yebo ti n-ipoostii.*

But to express all these different meanings the women would have only one form, *viz.*:

yebo ti n-ipoos,

which in the men's speech would mean only 'She went to her house.'

To many substantives the men prefix a vowel which the women do not employ, thus *o-petas* 'turtle', *u-tamokos* 'dog', *i-pis* 'wood'. For some very important notions the sexes use distinct words; thus, for the names of kinship, 'my father' is *iyai* and *išupu*, 'my mother' *ipaki* and *ipapa*, 'my brother' *tsaruki* and *ičibausi* respectively.

Among the languages of California, Yana, according to Dixon and Kroeber (*The American Anthropologist*, n.s. 5.15) is the only language that shows a difference in the words used by men and women – apart from terms of relationship, where a distinction according to the sex of the speaker is made among many Californian tribes as well as in other parts of the world, evidently 'because the relationship itself is to them different, as the sex is different'. But in Yana the distinction is a linguistic one, and curiously enough, the few specimens given all present a trait found already in the Chiquito forms, namely, that the forms spoken by women are shorter than those of the men, which appear as extensions, generally by suffixed *-(n)a*, of the former.

It is surely needless to multiply instances of these customs, which are found among many wild tribes; the curious reader may be referred to S. Lasch: pp. 7–13, and Ploss and Bartels 1908. The latter says that the Suaheli system is not carried through so as to replace the ordinary language, but the Suaheli have for every object which they do not care to mention by its real name a symbolic word understood by everybody concerned. In especial such symbols are used by women in their mysteries to denote obscene things. The words chosen are either ordinary names for innocent things or else taken from the old language or other Bantu languages, mostly Kiziguha, for among the Waziguha secret rites play an enormous role. Bartels finally says that with us, too, women have separate names of everything connected with sexual life, and he thinks that it is the same feeling of shame that underlies this custom and the interdiction of pronouncing the names of male relatives. This, however, does not explain everything, and, as already indicated, superstition certainly has a large share in this as in other forms of verbal taboo. See on this the very full account in the third volume of Frazer's *The Golden Bough*.

Competing languages

A difference between the language spoken by men and that spoken by women is seen in many countries where two languages are struggling for supremacy in a peaceful way – thus without any question of one nation exterminating the other or the male part of it. Among German and Scandinavian immigrants in America the men mix much more with the English-speaking population, and therefore have better opportunities, and also more occasion, to learn English than their wives, who remain more within doors. It is exactly the same among the Basques, where the school, the military service, and daily business relations contribute to the extinction of Basque in favour of French, and where these factors operate much more strongly on the male than on the female population: there are families in which the wife talks Basque, while the husband does not even understand Basque and does not allow his children to learn it (Bornecque and Mühlen, *Les Provinces françaises*: 53). Vilhelm Thomsen informs me that the old Livonian language, which is now nearly extinct, is kept with the greatest fidelity by the women, while the men are abandoning it for Lettish. Albanian women, too, generally know only Albanian, while the men are more often bilingual.

Sanskrit drama

There are very few traces of real sex dialects in our Aryan languages, though we have the very curious rule in the old Indian drama that women talk Prakrit (*pràkrta*, the natural or vulgar language) while men have the privilege of talking Sanskrit (*samskrta*, the adorned language). The distinction, however, is one of sex really, but of rank, for Sanskrit is the language of gods, kings, princes, brahmans, ministers, chamberlains, dancing-masters, and other men in superior positions, and of a very few women of special religious importance, while Prakrit is spoken by men of an inferior class, like shopkeepers, law officers, aldermen, bathmen, fishermen and policemen, and by nearly all women. The difference between the two 'languages' is one of degree only: they are two strata of the same language, one higher, more solemn, stiff, and archaic, and another lower, more natural, and familiar, and this easy, or perhaps we should say slipshod, style is the only one recognized for ordinary women. The difference may not be greater than that between the language of a judge and that of a costermonger in a modern novel, or between Juliet's and her nurse's expressions in Shakespeare, and if all women, even those we should call the 'heroines' of the plays, use only the lower stratum of speech, the reason certainly is that the social position of women was so inferior that they ranked only with men of the lower orders and had no share in the higher culture which, with the refined language, was the privilege of a small class of selected men.

Conservatism

As prakrit is a 'younger' and 'worn-out' form of Sanskrit, the question here naturally arises: what is the general attitude of the two sexes to those changes that are constantly going on in languages? Can they be ascribed exclusively or predominantly to one of the sexes? Or do both equally participate in them? An answer that is very often given is that as a rule women are more conservative than men, and that they do nothing more than keep to the traditional language which they have learnt from their parents and hand on to their children, while innovations are due to the initiative of men. Thus Cicero in an often-quoted passage says that when he hears his mother-in-law Lælia, it is to him as if he heard Plautus or Nævius, for it is more natural for women to keep the old language uncorrupted, as they do not hear many people's way of speaking and thus retain what they have first learnt (*De oratore*, III. 45). This, however, does not hold good in every respect and in every people. The French engineer, Victor Renault, who lived for a long time among the Botocudos (in South America) and compiled vocabularies for two of their tribes, speaks of the ease with which he could make the savages who accompanied him invent new words for anything.

> One of them called out the word in a loud voice, as if seized by a sudden idea, and the others would repeat it amid laughter and excited shouts, and then it was universally adopted. But the curious thing is that it was nearly always the women who busied themselves in inventing new words as well as in composing songs, dirges and rhetorical essays. The word-formations here alluded to are probably names of objects that the Botocudos had not known previously. . . as for horse, *krainejoune*, 'head-teeth'; for ox, *po-kekri*, 'foot-cloven'; for donkey, *mgo-jonne-orône*, 'beast with long ears.' But well known objects which have already got a name have often similar new denominations invented for them, which are then soon accepted by the family and community and spread more and more.
>
> (Martius, *Beitr. zur Ethnogr. u. Sprachenkunde Amerikas* 1867: I. 330)

I may also quote what E.R. Edwards says in his *Etude phonétique de la langue japonaise* (1903: 79):

> In France and in England it might be said that women avoid neologisms and are careful not to go too far away from the written forms: in Southern England the sound written *wh* [ʍ] is scarcely ever pronounced

except in girls' schools. In Japan, on the contrary, women are less conservative than men, whether in pronunciation or in the selection of words and expressions. One of the chief reasons is that women have not to the same degree as men undergone the influence of the written language. As an example of the liberties which the women take may be mentioned that there is in the actual pronunciation of Tokyo a strong tendency to get rid of the sound (*w*), but the women go further in the word *atashi*, which men pronounce *watashi* or *watakshi*, 'I'. Another tendency noticed in the language of Japanese women is pretty widely spread among French and English women, namely, the excessive use of intensive words and the exaggeration of stress and tone-accent to mark emphasis. Japanese women also make a much more frequent use than men of the prefixes of politeness *o-, go-* and *mi-*.

Phonetics and grammar

In connection with some of the phonetic changes which have profoundly modified the English sound system we have express statements by old grammarians that women had a more advanced pronunciation than men and characteristically enough these statements refer to the raising of the vowels in the direction of [i]; thus in Sir Thomas Smith (1567), who uses expressions like 'mulierculæ quædam delicatiores, et nonnulli qui volunt isto modo videri loqui urbanius', and in another place 'fœminæ quædam delicatiores', further in Mulcaster (1582)[1] and in Milton's teacher, Alexander Gill (1621), who speaks about 'nostræ Mopsæ, quæ quidem ita omnia attenuant'.

In France, about 1700, women were inclined to pronounce *e* instead of *a*; thus Alemand (1688) mentions *Barnabæ* as 'façon de prononcer mâle' and *Bernabé* as the pronunciation of 'les gens polis et délicats. . . les dames surtout'; and Grimarest (1712) speaks of 'ces marchandes du Palais, qui au lieu de *madame, boulevart*, etc., prononcent *medeme, boulevert*' (Thuot I. 12 and 9).

There is one change characteristic of many languages in which it seems as if women have played an important part even if they are not solely responsible for it: I refer to the weakening of the old fully trilled tongue-point *r*. I have elsewhere (*Fonetik*, p. 417 ff.) tried to show that this weakening, which results in various sounds and sometimes in a complete omission of the sound in some positions, is in the main a consequence of, or at any rate favoured by, a change in social life: the old loud trilled point sound is natural and justified when life is chiefly carried on out-of-doors, but indoor life prefers, on the whole, less noisy speech habits, and the more refined this domestic life is, the more all kinds of noises and even speech sounds will be toned down. One of the results is that this original *r* sound, the rubadub in the orchestra of language, is no longer allowed to bombard the ears, but is softened down in various ways, as we see chiefly in the great cities and among the educated classes, while the rustic population in many countries keeps up the old sound with much greater conservatism. Now we find that women are not unfrequently mentioned in connection with this reduction of the trilled *r*; thus in the sixteenth century in France there was a tendency to leave off the trilling and even to go further than to the present English untrilled point *r* by pronouncing [z] instead, but some of the old grammarians mention this pronunciation as characteristic of women and a few men who imitate women (Erasmus: mulierculæ Parisinæ; Sylvius: mulierculæ. . . Parrhisinæ et earum modo quidam parum viri; Pillot: Parisinæ mulierculæ . . . adeo delicatulæ sunt, ut pro *pere* dicant *pese*). In the ordinary language there are a few remnants of this tendency; thus, when by the side of the original *chaire* we now have also the form *chaise*, and it is worthy of note that the latter form is reserved for the everyday signification (English chair, seat) as belonging more naturally to the speech of women, while *chaire* has the more special signification of 'pulpit, professorial chair'. Now the same tendency to substitute [z] – or after a voiceless sound [s] – for *r* is found in our own days among the ladies of Christiania, who will say *gzuelig* for *gruelig* and *fsygtelig* for *frygtelig* (Brekke, *Bidrag til dansknorskens lydlære* 1881: 17; I have often heard the sound myself). And even in far-off Siberia we find that the Chuckchi women will say *nídzak* or *nízak for the male nírak* 'two', *zërka* for *rërka* 'walrus', etc. (Nordqvist; see fuller quotations in my *Fonetik* 431).

In present-day English there are said to be a few differences in pronunciation between the two sexes; thus according to Daniel Jones, *soft* is pronounced with a long vowel [sɔ:·ft] by men and with a short vowel [sɔ:ft] by women; similarly [gɛəl] is said to be a special ladies' pronunciation of *girl*, which men usually pronounce [gɜ:·1]; cf. also on *wh* above, p. 207. So far as I have been able to ascertain, the pronunciation [tʃuldrən] for [tʃildrən *children* is much more frequent in women than in men. It may also be that women are more inclined to give to the word *waistcoat* the full long sound in both syllables, while men, who have occasion to use the word more frequently, tend to give it the historical form [weskət] (for the shortening compare *breakfast*). But even if such observations were multiplied – as probably they might easily be by an attentive observer – they would be only more or less isolated instances, without any deeper significance, and on the whole we must say that from the phonetic point of view there is scarcely any difference between the speech of men and that of women: the two sexes speak for all intents and purposes the same language.

Choice of words

But when from the field of phonetics we come to that of vocabulary and style, we shall find a much greater number of differences, though they have received very little attention in linguistic works. A few have been mentioned by Greenough and Kittredge: 'The use of *common* in the sense of "vulgar" is distinctly a feminine peculiarity. It would sound effeminate in the speech of a man. So, in a less degree, with *person* for "woman", in contrast to "lady." *Nice* for "fine" must have originated in the same way' (1901: 54).

Others have told me that men will generally say 'It's very *good* of you', where women will say 'It's very *kind* of you.' But such small details can hardly be said to be really characteristic of the two sexes. There is no doubt, however, that women in all countries are shy of mentioning certain parts of the human body and certain natural functions by the direct and often rude denominations which men, and especially young men, prefer when among themselves. Women will therefore invent innocent and euphemistic words and paraphrases, which sometimes may in the long run come to be looked upon as the plain or blunt names, and therefore in their turn have to be avoided and replaced by more decent words.

In Pinero's *The Gay Lord Quex* (p. 116) a lady discovers some French novels on the table of another lady, and says: 'This is a little – h'm – isn't it?' – she does not even dare to say the word 'indecent,' and has to express the idea in inarticulate language. The word 'naked' is paraphrased in the following description by a woman of the work of girls in ammunition works: 'They have to take off every stitch from their bodies in one room, and run *in their innocence and nothing else* to another room where the special clothing is' (Bennett *The Pretty Lady*: 176).

On the other hand, the old-fashioned prudery which prevented ladies from using such words as *legs* and *trousers* ('those manly garments which are rarely mentioned by name', says Dickens, *Dombey and Son*: 335) is now rightly looked upon as exaggerated and more or less comical (cf. my GS §247).

There can be no doubt that women exercise a great and universal influence on linguistic development through their instinctive shrinking from coarse and gross expressions and their preference for refined, and (in certain spheres) veiled and indirect expressions. In most cases that influence will be exercised privately and in the bosom of the family; but there is one historical instance in which a group of women worked in that direction publicly and collectively. I refer to those French ladies who in the seventeenth century gathered in the Hôtel de Rambouillet and are generally known under the name of *Précieuses*. They discussed questions of spelling and of purity of pronunciation and diction, and favoured all kinds of elegant paraphrases by which coarse and vulgar words might be avoided. In many ways this movement was the counterpart of the literary wave which about that time was inundating Europe under various names – Gongorism in Spain, Marinism in Italy, Euphuism in England; but the Précieuses went further than their male confrères in desiring to influence everyday language. When, however, they used such expressions as, for 'nose', 'the door of the brain', for 'broom', 'the instrument of cleanness', and for 'shirt' 'the constant companion of the dead and the living' (la compagne perpétuelle des morts et des vivants), and many others, their affectation called down on their heads a ripple of laughter, and their endeavours would now have been forgotten but for the immortal satire of Molière in *Les Précieuses ridicules* and *Les Femmes savantes*. But apart from such exaggerations the feminine point of view is unassailable, and there is reason to congratulate those nations, the English among them, in which the social position of women has been high enough to secure greater purity and freedom from coarseness in language than would have been the case if men had been the sole arbiters of speech.

Among the things women object to in language must be specially mentioned anything that smacks of swearing[2]; where a man will say 'He told an infernal lie', a women will rather say, 'He told a most dreadful fib.' Such euphemistic substitutes for the simple word 'hell' as 'the other place', 'a very hot,' or 'a very uncomfortable place' probably originated with women. They will also use *ever* to add emphasis to an interrogative pronoun, as in 'Whoever told you that?' or 'Whatever do you mean?', and avoid the stronger 'who the devil' or 'what the dickens'. For surprise we have the feminine exclamations 'Good gracious', 'Gracious me', 'Goodness gracious', 'Dear me' by the side of the more masculine 'Good heavens', 'Great Scott'. 'To be sure' is said to be more frequent with women than with men. Such instances might be multiplied, but these may suffice here. It will easily be seen that we have here civilized counterparts of what was above mentioned as sexual taboo; but it is worth noting that the interdiction in these cases is ordained by the women themselves, or perhaps rather by the older among them, while the young do not always willingly comply.

Men will certainly with great justice object that there is a danger of the language becoming languid and insipid if we are always to content ourselves with women's expressions, and that vigour and vividness count for something. Most boys and many men have a dislike to some words merely because they feel that they are used by everybody and on every occasion: they want to avoid what is commonplace and banal and to replace it by new and fresh expressions, whose very newness imparts to them a flavour of their own. Men thus become the chief renovators of language, and to them are due those changes by which we sometimes see one term replace an older one, to give way in turn to a still newer one, and so on. Thus we see in English that the old verb *weorpan*, corresponding to German *werfen*, was felt as too weak and therefore supplanted by *cast*, which was taken from the Scandinavian; after some centuries *cast* was replaced by the stronger *throw*, and this now, in the parlance of boys especially, is giving way to stronger expressions like *chuck* and *fling*. The old verbs, or at any rate *cast*, may be retained in certain applications, more particularly in some fixed combinations and in figurative significations, but it is now hardly possible to say, as Shakespeare does, 'They cast their caps up.' Many such innovations on their first appearance are counted as slang, and some never make their way into received speech: but I am not in this connection concerned with the distinction between slang and recognized language, except in so far as the inclination or disinclination to invent and to use slang is undoubtedly one of the 'human secondary sexual characters'. This is not invalidated by the fact that quite recently, with the rise of the feminist movement, many young ladies have begun to imitate their brothers in that as well as in other respects.

Vocabulary

This trait is indissolubly connected with another: the vocabulary of a woman as a rule is much less extensive than that of a man. Women move preferably in the central field of language, avoiding everything that is out of the way or bizarre, while men will often either coin new words or expressions or take up old-fashioned ones, if by that means they are enabled, or think they are enabled, to find a more adequate or precise expression for their thoughts. Woman as a rule follows the main road of language, where man is often inclined to turn aside into a narrow footpath or even to strike out a new path for himself. Most of those who are in the habit or reading books in foreign languages will have experienced a much greater average difficulty in books written by male than by female authors, because they contain many more rare words, dialect words, technical terms, etc. Those who want to learn a foreign language will therefore always do well at the first stage to read many ladies' novels, because they will there continually meet with just those everyday words and combinations which the foreigner is above all in need of, what may be termed the indispensable small-change of a language.

This may be partly explicable from the education of women, which has up to quite recent times been less comprehensive and technical than that of men. But this does not account for everything, and certain experiments made by the American professor Jastrow would tend to show that we have here a trait that is independent of education. He asked twenty-five university students of each sex, belonging to the same class and thus in possession of the same preliminary training, to write down as rapidly as possible a hundred words, and to record the time. Words in sentences were not allowed. There were thus obtained 5,000 words, and of these many were of course the same. But the community of thought was greater in the women; while the men used 1,375 different words, their female classmates used only 1,123. Of 1,266 unique words used, 29.8 per cent were male, only 20.8 per cent female. The group into which the largest number of the men's words fell was the animal kingdom; the group into which the largest number of women's words fell was wearing apparel and fabrics; while the men used only fifty-three words belonging to the class of foods, the women used 179.

> In general the feminine traits revealed by this study are an attention to the immediate surroundings, to the finished product, to the ornamental, the individual, and the concrete; while the masculine preference is for the more remote, the constructive, the useful, the general and the abstract.
>
> (Havelock Ellis 1904: 189)

235

Another point mentioned by Jastrow is the tendency to select words that rhyme and alliterative words; both these tendencies were decidedly more marked in men than in women. This shows what we may also notice in other ways, that men take greater interest in words as such and in their acoustic properties, while women pay less attention in words as such and in their acoustic properties, while women pay less attention to that side of words and merely take them as they are, as something given once for all. Thus it comes that some men are confirmed punsters, while women are generally slow to see any point in a pun and scarcely ever perpetrate one themselves. Or, to get to something of greater value; the science of language has very few votaries among women, in spite of the fact that foreign languages, long before the reform of female education, belonged to those things which women learnt best in and out of schools, because, like music and embroidery, they were reckoned among the specially feminine 'accomplishments'.

Woman is linguistically quicker than man: quicker to learn, quicker to hear, and quicker to answer. A man is slower: he hesitates, he chews the cud to make sure of the taste of words, and thereby comes to discover similarities with and differences from other words, both in sound and in sense, thus preparing himself for the appropriate use of the fittest noun or adjective.

Adverbs

While there are a few adjectives, such as *pretty* and *nice*, that might be mentioned as used more extensively by women than by men, there are greater differences with regard to adverbs. Lord Chesterfield wrote (*The World*; 5 December 1754):

> Not contented with enriching our language by words absolutely new, my fair countrywomen have gone still farther, and improved it by the application and extension of old ones to various and very different significations. They take a word and change it, like a guinea into shillings for pocket-money, to be employed in the several occasional purposes of the day. For instance, the adjective *vast* and its adverb *vastly* mean anything and are the fashionable words of the most fashionable people. A fine woman. . . is *vastly* obliged, or *vastly* offended, *castly* glad, or *vastly* sorry. Large objects are *vastly* great, small ones are *vastly* little; and I had lately the pleasure to hear a fine woman pronounce, by a happy metonymy, a very small gold snuff-box, that was produced in company, to be *vastly* pretty, because it was so *vastly* little.

Even if that particular adverb to which Lord Chesterfield objected has now to a great extent gone out of fashion, there is no doubt that he has here touched on a distinctive trait: the fondness of women for hyperbole will very often lead the fashion with regard to adverbs of intensity, and these are very often used with disregard of their proper meaning, as in German *riesig klein*, English *awfully pretty, terribly nice*, French *rudement joli, affreusement délicieux*, Danish *roedsom morsom* (horribly amusing), Russian *strast' kakoy lovkiy* (terribly able), etc. *Quite*, also, in the sense of 'very', as in 'she was quite charming; it makes me quite angry', is, according to Fitzedward Hall, due to the ladies. And I suspect that *just sweet* (as in Barrie: 'Grizel thought it was just sweet of him') is equally characteristic of the usage of the fair sex.

There is another intensive which has also something of the eternally feminine about it, namely *so*. I am indebted to Stoffel (Int. 101) for the following quotation from *Punch* (4 January 1896): 'This little adverb is a great favourite with ladies, in conjunction with an adjective. For instance, they are very fond of using such expressions as "He is *so* charming!" "It is *so* lovely!" etc.' Stoffel adds the following instances of strongly intensive *so* as highly characteristic of ladies' usage: 'Thank you *so* much!' 'It was *so* kind of you to think of it!' 'That's *so* like you!' 'I'm *so* glad you've come!' 'The bonnet is *so* lovely!'

The explanation of this characteristic feminine usage is, I think, that women much more often than men break off without finishing their sentences because they start talking without having thought out what they are going to say; the sentence 'I'm so glad you've come' really requires some complement in the shape of a clause with *that*, so glad that I really must kiss you', or, 'so glad that I must treat you to something extra', or whatever the consequence may be. But very often it is difficult in a hurry to hit upon something adequate to say, and 'so glad that I cannot express it' frequently results in the inexpressible remaining unexpressed, and when that experiment has been repeated time after time, the linguistic consequence is that a strongly stressed *so* acquires the force of 'very much indeed'. It is the same with *such*, as in the following two extracts from a modern novel (in both it is a lady who is speaking): 'Poor Kitty! she has been in *such* a state of mind', and 'Do you know that you look *such* a duck this afternoon. . . That hat suits you *so* — you are *such* a *grande dame* in it.' Exactly the same thing has happened with Danish *sà* and *sàdan*, German *so* and *solch*; also with French *tellement*, though there perhaps not to the same extent as in English.

We have the same phenomenon with *to a degree*, which properly requires to be supplemented with something that tells us what the degree is, but is frequently left by itself, as in 'His second marriage was irregular to a degree.'

Periods

The frequency with which women thus leave their exclamatory sentences half finished might be exemplified from many passages in our novelists and dramatists. I select a few quotations. The first is from the beginning of *Vanity Fair*: 'This almost caused Jemima to faint with terror. "Well, I never," said she. "What an audacious" — emotion prevented her from completing either sentence.' Next from one of Hankin's plays. 'Mrs. Eversleigh: I must say! (but words fail her).' And finally from Compton Mackenzie's *Poor Relations*: '"The trouble you must have taken," Hilda exclaimed.' These quotations illustrate types of sentences which are becoming so frequent that they would seem soon to deserve a separate chapter in modern grammars, 'Did you ever!' 'Well, I never!' being perhaps the most important of these 'stop-short' or 'pull-up' sentences, as I think they might be termed.

These sentences are the linguistic symptoms of a peculiarity of feminine psychology which has not escaped observation. Meredith says of one of his heroines: 'She thought in blanks, as girls do, and some women', and Hardy singularizes one of his by calling her 'that novelty among women – one who finished a thought before beginning the sentence which was to convey it'.

The same point is seen in the typical way in which the two sexes build up their sentences and periods; but here, as so often in this paper, we cannot establish absolute differences, but only preferences that may be broken in a great many instances and yet are characteristic of the sexes as such. If we compare long periods as constructed by men and by women, we shall in the former find many more instances of intricate or involute structures with clause within clause, a relative clause in the middle of a conditional clause or vice versa, with subordination and sub-subordination, while the typical form of long feminine periods is that of co-ordination, one sentence or clause being added to another on the same plane and the gradation between the respective ideas being marked not grammatically, but emotionally, by stress and intonation, and in writing by underlining. In learned terminology we may say that men are fond of hypotaxis and women of parataxis. Or we may use the simile that a male period is often like a set of Chinese boxes, one within another, while a feminine period is like a set of pearls joined together on a string of *ands* and similar words. In a Danish comedy a young girl is relating what has happened to her at a ball, when she is suddenly interrupted by her brother, who has slyly taken out his watch and now exclaims: 'I declare! you have said *and then* fifteen times in less than two and a half minutes.'

General characteristics

The greater rapidity of female thought is shown linguistically, among other things, by the frequency with which a woman will use a pronoun like *he* or *she*, not of the person last mentioned, but of somebody else to whom her thoughts have already wandered, while a man with his slower intellect will think that she is still moving on the same path. The difference in rapidity of perception has been tested experimentally by Romanes: the same paragraph was presented to various well-educated persons, who were asked to read it as rapidly as they could, ten seconds being allowed for twenty lines. As soon as the time was up the paragraph was removed, and the reader immediately wrote down all that he or she could remember of it. It was found that women were usually more successful than men in this test. Not only were they able to read more quickly than the men, but they were able to give a better account of the paragraph as a whole. One lady, for instance, could read exactly four times as fast as her husband, and even then give a better account than he of that small portion of the paragraph he had alone been able to read. But it was found that this rapidity was no proof of intellectual power, and some of the slowest readers were highly distinguished men. Ellis (1904: 195) explains this in this way: with the quick reader it is as though every statement were admitted immediately and without inspection to fill the vacant chambers of the mind, while with the slow reader every statement undergoes an instinctive process of cross-examination; every new fact seems to stir up the accumulated stores of facts among which it intrudes, and so impedes rapidity of mental action.

This reminds me of one of Swift's 'Thoughts on Various Subjects':

> The common fluency of speech in many men, and most women, is owing to the scarcity of matter, and scarcity of words; for whoever is a master of language, and hath a mind full of ideas, will be apt in speaking to hesitate upon the choice of both: whereas common speakers have only one set of ideas, and one set of words to clothe them in: and these are always ready at the mouth. So people come faster out of a church when it is almost empty, than when a crowd is at the door.
>
> (1735: I. 305)

The volubility of women has been the subject of innumerable jests: it has given rise to popular proverbs in many countries;[3] as well as to Aurora Leigh's resigned 'A woman's function plainly is – to talk' and Oscar Wilde's sneer, 'Women are a decorative sex. They never have anything to say, but they say it charmingly.' A woman's thought is no sooner formed than uttered. Says Rosalind, 'Do you not know I am a woman! When I think, I must speak' As You Like It, III. 2. 264). And in a modern novel a young girl says: 'I talk so as to find out what I think. Don't you? Some things one can't judge of till one hears them spoken' (Housman John of Jingalo: 346).

The superior readiness of speech of women is a concomitant of the fact that their vocabulary is smaller and more central than that of men. But this again is connected with another indubitable fact, that women do not reach the same extreme points as men, but are nearer the average in most respects. Havelock Ellis, who establishes this in various fields, rightly remarks that the statement that genius is undeniably of more frequent occurrence among men than among women has sometimes been regarded by women as a slur upon their sex, but that it does not appear that women have been equally anxious to find fallacies in the statement that idiocy is more common among men. Yet the two statements must be taken together. Genius is more common among men by virtue of the same general tendency by which idiocy is more

239

common among men. The two facts are but two aspects of a larger zoolog-
ical fact – the greater variability of the male (Ellis 1904: 420).

In language we see this very clearly: the highest linguistic genius and the
lowest degree of linguistic imbecility are very rarely found among women.
The greatest orators, the most famous literary artists, have been men; but
it may serve as a sort of consolation to the other sex that there are a much
greater number of men than of women who cannot put two words together
intelligibly, who stutter and stammer and hesitate, and are unable to find
suitable expressions for the simplest thought. Between these two extremes
the woman moves with a sure and supple tongue which is ever ready to find
words and to pronounce them in a clear and intelligible manner.

Nor are the reasons far to seek why such differences should have developed. They are mainly dependent on the division of labour enjoined in
primitive tribes and to a great extent also among more civilized peoples. For
thousands of years the work that especially fell to men was such as demanded
an intense display of energy for a comparatively short period, mainly in war
and in hunting. Here, however, there was not much occasion to talk, nay,
in many circumstances talk might even be fraught with danger. And when
that rough work was over, the man would either sleep or idle his time away,
inert and torpid, more or less in silence. Woman, on the other hand, had a
number of domestic occupations which did not claim such an enormous
output of spasmodic energy. To her was at first left not only agriculture,
and a great deal of other work which in more peaceful times was taken over
by men; but also much that has been till quite recently her almost exclusive
concern – the care of the children, cooking, brewing, baking, sewing,
washing, etc. – things which for the most part demanded no deep thought,
which were performed in company and could well be accompanied with a
lively chatter. Lingering effects of this state of things are seen still, though
great social changes are going on in our times which may eventually modify
even the linguistic relations of the two sexes.

Notes

1   '*Ai* is the man's diphthong, and soundeth full: *ei*, the woman's, and
     soundeth finish [i.e. fineish] in the same both sense, and vse: a *woman's is
     deintie, and feinteth soon, the man fainteth not bycause he is nothing daintie.*'
     Thus what is now distinctive of refined as opposed to vulgar pronuncia-
     tion was then characteristic of the fair sex.

2   There are great differences with regard to swearing between different
     nations; but I think that in those countries and in those circles in which
     swearing is common it is found much more extensively among men than
     among women: this at any rate is true of Denmark. There is, however, a
     general social movement against swearing, and now there are many men
     who never swear. A friend writes to me: 'The best English men hardly

swear at all.. . . . I imagine some of our fashionable women now swear as much as the men they consort with.'

3   'Où femme y a, silence n'y a.' 'Deux femmes font un plaid, trois un grant caquet, quatre un plein marché.' 'Due donne e un' oca fanno una fiera' (Venice). 'The tongue is the sword of a woman, and she never lets it become rusty' (China). 'The North Sea will sooner be found wanting in water than a woman at a loss for a word' (Jutland).

Reprinted from Otto Jespersen, *Language: Its Nature, Development and Origin* (London: Allen & Unwin, 1992).

Chapter 17

Robin Lakoff

EXTRACT FROM *LANGUAGE AND WOMAN'S PLACE*

IF A LITTLE GIRL 'TALKS ROUGH' like a boy, she will normally be ostracized, scolded, or made fun of. In this way society, in the form of a child's parents and friends, keeps her in line, in her place. This socializing process is, in most of its aspects, harmless and often necessary, but in this particular instance – the teaching of special linguistic uses to little girls – it raises serious problems, though the teachers may well be unaware of this. If the little girl learns her lesson well, she is not rewarded with unquestioned acceptance on the part of society; rather, the acquisition of this special style of speech will later be an excuse others use to keep her in a demeaning position, to refuse to take her seriously as a human being. Because of the way she speaks, the little girl – now grown to womanhood – will be accused of being unable to speak precisely or to express herself forcefully.

I am sure that the preceding paragraph contains an oversimplified description of the language-learning process in American society. Rather than saying that little boys and little girls, from the very start, learn two different ways of speaking, I think, from observation and reports by others, that the process is more complicated. Since the mother and other women are the dominant influences in the lives of most children under the age of 5, probably both boys and girls first learn 'women's language' as their first language. (I am told that in Japanese, children of both sexes use the particles proper for women until the age of 5 or so; then the little boy starts to be ridiculed if he uses them, and so soon learns to desist.) As they grow older, boys especially go through a stage of rough talk, as described by Spock and others; this is probably discouraged in little girls more strongly than in little boys, in whom parents may often find it more amusing than shocking. By the time children are 10 or so, and split up into same-sex peer groups, the two languages are already present, according to my recollections and observations. But it seems that what has happened is that the boys have unlearned their original form of expression and adopted new forms of expression, while the girls retain their old ways of speech. (One wonders whether this is related in any way to the often-noticed fact that little boys innovate, in their play, much more than little girls.) The ultimate result is the same, of course, whatever the interpretation.

So a girl is damned if she does, damned if she doesn't. If she refuses to talk like a lady, she is ridiculed and subjected to criticism as unfeminine; if she does learn, she is ridiculed as unable to think clearly, unable to take part in a serious discussion: in some sense, as less than fully human. These two choices which a woman has — to be less than a woman or less than a person — are highly painful.

An objection may be raised here that I am overstating the case against women's language, since most women who get as far as college learn to switch from women's to neutral language under appropriate situations (in class, talking to professors, at job interviews, and such). But I think this objection overlooks a number of problems. First, if a girl must learn two dialects, she becomes in effect a bilingual. Like many bilinguals, she may never really be master of either language, though her command of both is adequate enough for most purposes, she may never feel really comfortable using either, and never be certain that she is using the right one in the right place to the right person. Shifting from one language to another requires special awareness to the nuances of social situations, special alertness to possible disapproval. It may be that the extra energy that must be (subconsciously or otherwise) expended in this game is energy sapped from more creative work, and hinders women from expressing themselves as well, as fully, or as freely as they might otherwise. Thus, if a girl knows that a professor will be receptive to comments that sound scholarly, objective, unemotional, she will of course be tempted to use neutral language in class or in conference. But if she knows that, as a man, he will respond more approvingly to her at other levels if she uses women's language, and sounds frilly and feminine, won't she be confused as well as sorely tempted in two directions at once? It is often noticed that women participate less in class discussion than men — perhaps this linguistic indecisiveness is one reason why. (Incidentally, I don't find this true in my classes.)

It will be found that the overall effect of 'women's language' — meaning both language restricted in use to women and language descriptive of women alone — is this: it submerges a woman's personal identity, by denying her the means of expressing herself strongly, on the one hand, and encouraging expressions that suggest triviality in subject matter and uncertainty about it; and, when a woman is being discussed, by treating her as an object — sexual or otherwise — but never a serious person with individual views. Of course, other forms of behaviour in this society have the same purpose; but the phenomena seem especially clear linguistically.

The ultimate effect of these discrepancies is that women are systematically denied access to power, on the grounds that they are not capable of holding it as demonstrated by their linguistic behaviour along with other aspects of their behaviour; and the irony here is that women are made to feel that they deserve such treatment, because of inadequacies in their own intelligence and/or education. But in fact it is precisely because women have learned their lessons so well that they later suffer such discrimination. (This situation is of course true to some extent for all disadvantaged groups: white males of Anglo-Saxon descent set the standards and seem to expect other groups to be respectful of them but not to adopt them – they are to 'keep in their place'.)

Talking like a lady

'Women's language' shows up in all levels of the grammar of English. We find differences in the choice and frequency of lexical items; in the situations in which certain syntactic rules are performed; in intonational and other supersegmental patterns. As an example of lexical differences, imagine a man and a woman both looking at the same wall, painted a pinkish shade of purple. The woman may say (1):

1 The wall is mauve,

with no one consequently forming any special impression of her as a result of the words alone; but if the man should say (1), one might well conclude he was imitating a woman sarcastically, or was a homosexual, or an interior decorator. Women, then, make far more precise discriminations in naming colours than do men; words like *beige, ecru, aquamarine, lavender*, and so on are unremarkable in a woman's active vocabulary, but absent from that of most men. I have seen a man helpless with suppressed laughter at a discussion between two other people as to whether a book jacket was to be described as 'lavender' or 'mauve'. Men find such discussion amusing because they consider such a question trivial, irrelevant to the real world.

We might ask why fine discrimination of colour is relevant for women, but not for men. A clue is contained in the way many men in our society view other 'unwordly' topics, such as high culture and the church, as outside the world of men's work, relegated to women and men whose masculinity is not unquestionable. Men tend to relegate to women things that are not of concern to them, or do not involve their egos. Among these are problems of fine colour discrimination. We might rephrase this point by saying that since women are not expected to make decisions on important matters, such as what kind of job to hold, they are relegated the non-crucial decisions as a sop. Deciding whether to name a colour 'lavender' or 'mauve' is one such sop.

If it is agreed that this lexical disparity reflects a social inequity in the position of women, one may ask how to remedy it. Obviously, no one could seriously recommend legislating against the use of the terms 'mauve' and 'lavender' by women, or forcing men to learn to use them. All we can do is give women the opportunity to participate in the real decisions of life.

Aside from specific lexical items like colour names, we find differences between the speech of women and that of men in the use of particles that grammarians often describe as 'meaningless'. There may be no referent for them, but they are far from meaningless: they define the social context of an utterance, indicate the relationship the speaker feels between himself and his addressee, between himself and what he is talking about.

As an experiment, one might present native speakers of standard American English with pairs of sentences, identical syntactically and in terms of referential lexical items, and differing merely in the choice of 'meaningless' particle, and ask them which was spoken by a man, which a woman. Consider:

> 2 *a* Oh dear, you've put the peanut butter in the refrigerator again.
>   *b* Shit, you've put the peanut butter in the refrigerator again.

It is safe to predict that people would classify the first sentence as part of 'women's language', the second as 'men's language'. It is true that many self-respecting women are becoming able to use sentences like (2)*b* publicly without flinching, but this is a relatively recent development, and while perhaps the majority of Middle America might condone the use of *b* for men, they would still disapprove of its use by women. (It is of interest, by the way, to note that men's language is increasingly being used by women, but women's language is not being adopted by men, apart from those who reject the American masculine image (for example, homosexuals). This is analogous to the fact that men's jobs are being sought by women, but few men are rushing to become housewives or secretaries. The language of the favoured group, the group that holds the power, along with its non-linguistic behaviour, is generally adopted by the other group, not vice versa. In any event, it is a truism to state that the 'stronger' expletives are reserved for men, and the 'weaker' ones for women.)

Now we may ask what we mean by 'stronger' and 'weaker' expletives. (If these particles were indeed meaningless, none would be stronger than any other.) The difference between using 'shit' (or 'damn', or one of many others) as opposed to 'oh dear', or 'goodness', or 'oh fudge' lies in how forcefully one says how one feels – perhaps, one might say, choice of particle is a function of how strongly one allows oneself to feel about something, so that the strength of an emotion conveyed in a sentence corresponds to the strength of the particle. Hence in a really serious situation, the use of 'trivializing' (that is, 'women's') particles constitutes a joke, or at any rate is highly inappropriate. (In conformity with current linguistic practice, throughout this work an (*) will be used to mark a sentence that is inappropriate in some sense, either because it is syntactically deviant or used in the wrong social context.)

3   *a* *Oh fudge, my hair is on fire.
    b *Dear me, did he kidnap the baby?

As children, women are encouraged to be 'little ladies'. Little ladies don't scream as vociferously as little boys, and they are chastised more severely for throwing tantrums or showing temper: 'high spirits' are expected and therefore tolerated in little boys; docility and resignation are the corresponding traits expected of little girls. Now, we tend to excuse a show of temper by a man where we would not excuse an identical tirade from a woman: women are allowed to fuss and complain, but only a man can bellow in rage. It is sometimes claimed that there is a biological basis for this behaviour difference, though I don't believe conclusive evidence exists that the early differences in behaviour that have been observed are not the result of very different treatment of babies of the two sexes from the beginning; but surely the use of different particles by men and women is a learned trait, merely mirroring non-linguistic differences again, and again pointing out an inequity that exists between the treatment of men, and society's expectations of them, and the treatment of women. Allowing men stronger means of expression than are open to women further reinforces men's position of strength in the real world: for surely we listen with more attention the more strongly and forcefully someone expresses opinions, and a speaker unable – for whatever reason – to be forceful in stating his views is much less likely to be taken seriously. Ability to use strong particles like 'shit' and 'hell' is, of course, only incidental to the inequity that exists rather than its cause. But once again, apparently accidental linguistic usage suggests that women are denied equality partially for linguistic reasons, and that an examination of language points up precisely an area in which inequity exists. Further, if someone is allowed to show emotions, and consequently does, others may well be able to view him as a real individual in his own right, as they could not if he never showed emotion. Here again, then, the behaviour a woman learns as 'correct' prevents her from being taken seriously as an individual, and further is considered 'correct' and necessary for a woman precisely because society does *not* consider her seriously as an individual.

Similar sorts of disparities exist elsewhere in the vocabulary. There is, for instance, a group of adjectives which have, besides their specific and literal meanings, another use, that of indicating the speaker's approbation or admiration for something. Some of these adjectives are neutral as to sex of speaker: either men or women may use them. But another set seems, in its figurative use, to be largely confined to women's speech. Representative lists of both types are below:

neutral	*women only*
great	adorable
terrific	charming
cool	sweet
neat	lovely
	divine

As with the colour words and swear words already discussed, for a man to stray into the 'women's' column is apt to be damaging to his reputation, though here a woman may freely use the neutral words. But it should not be inferred from this that a woman's use of the 'women's' words is without its risks. Where a woman has a choice between the neutral words and the women's words, as a man has not, she may be suggesting very different things about her own personality and her view of the subject matter by her choice of words of the first set or words of the second.

    4 *a* What a terrific idea!
       b What a divine idea!

It seems to me that *a* might be used under any appropriate conditions by a female speaker. But *b* is more restricted. probably it is used appropriately (even by the sort of speaker for whom it was normal) only in case the speaker feels the idea referred to to be essentially frivolous, trivial, or unimportant to the world at large – only an amusement for the speaker herself. Consider, then, a woman advertising executive at an advertising conference. However feminine an advertising executive she is, she is much more likely to express her approval with (4)*a* than with *b*, which might cause raised eyebrows, and the reaction: 'That's what we get for putting a woman in charge of this company.'

On the other hand, suppose a friend suggests to the same woman that she should dye her French poodles to match her cigarette lighter. In this case, the suggestion really concerns only her, and the impression she will make on people. In this case, she may use *b*, from the 'women's language'. So the choice is not really free: words restricted to 'women's language' suggest that concepts to which they are applied are not relevant to the real world of (male) influence and power.

One may ask whether there really are no analogous terms that are available to men – terms that denote approval of the trivial, the personal; that express approbation in terms of one's own personal emotional reaction, rather than by gauging the likely general reaction. There does in fact seem to be one such word: it is the hippie invention 'groovy', which seems to have most of the connotations that separate 'lovely' and 'divine' from 'great' and 'terrific' excepting only that it does not mark the speaker as feminine or effeminate.

> 5 *a* What a terrific steel mill!
> *b* *What a lovely steel mill! (male speaking)
> *c* What a groovy steel mill!

I think it is significant that this word was introduced by the hippies, and, when used seriously rather than sarcastically, used principally by people who have accepted the hippies' values. Principal among these is the denial of the Protestant work ethic: to a hippie, something can be worth thinking about even if it isn't influential in the power structure, or money-making. Hippies are separated from the activities of the real world just as women are – though in the former case it is due to a decision on their parts, while this is not uncontroversially true in the case of women. For both these groups, it is possible to express approval of things in a personal way – though one does so at the risk of losing one's credibility with members of the power structure. It is also true, according to some speakers, that upper-class British men may use the words listed in the 'women's' column, as well as the specific colour words and others we have categorized as specifically feminine, without raising doubts as to their masculinity among other speakers of the same dialect. (This is not true for lower-class Britons, however.) The reason may be that commitment to the work ethic need not necessarily be displayed: one may be or appear to be a gentleman of leisure, interested in various pursuits, but not involved in mundane (business or political) affairs, in such a culture, without incurring disgrace. This is rather analogous to the position of a woman in American middle-class society, so we should not be surprised if these special lexical items are usable by both groups. This fact points indeed to a more general conclusion. These words aren't, basically, 'feminine'; rather, they signal 'uninvolved', or 'out of power'. Any group in a society to which these labels are applicable may presumably use these words; they are often considered 'feminine', 'unmasculine', because women are the 'uninvolved', 'out of power' group *par excellence*.

Another group that has, ostensibly at least, taken itself out of the search for power and money is that of academic men. They are frequently viewed by other groups as analogous in some ways to women – they don't really work, they are supported in their frivolous pursuits by others, what they do doesn't really count in the real world, and so on. The suburban home finds its counterpart in the ivory tower: one is supposedly shielded from harsh realities in both. Therefore it is not too surprising that many academic men (especially those who emulate British norms) may violate many of these sacrosanct rules I have just laid down: they often use 'women's language'. Among themselves, this does not occasion ridicule. But to a truck driver, a professor saying 'What a lovely hat!' is undoubtedly laughable, all the more so as it reinforces his stereotype of professors as effete snobs.

When we leave the lexicon and venture into syntax, we find that syntactically too women's speech is peculiar. To my knowledge, there is no syntactic rule in English that only women may use. But there is at least one rule that a woman will use in more conversational situations than a man. (This fact indicates, of course, that the applicability of syntactic rules is governed partly by social context – the position in society of the speaker and addressee, with respect to each other, and the impression one seeks to make on the other.) This is the rule of tag-question formation.[1]

A tag, in its usage as well as its syntactic shape (in English) is midway between an outright statement and a yes–no question: it is less assertive than the former, but more confident than the latter. Therefore it is usable under certain contextual situations: not those in which a statement would be appropriate, nor those in which a yes–no question is generally used, but in situations intermediate between these.

One makes a statement when one has confidence in his knowledge and is pretty certain that his statement will be believed; one asks a question when one lacks knowledge on some point and has reason to believe that this gap can and will be remedied by an answer by the addressee. A tag question, being intermediate between these, is used when the speaker is stating a claim, but lacks full confidence in the truth of that claim. So if I say

6 Is John here?

I will probably not be surprised if my respondent answers 'no'; but if I say

7 John is here, isn't he?

instead, chances are I am already biased in favour of a positive answer, wanting only confirmation by the addressee. I still want a response from him, as I do with a yes–no question; but I have enough knowledge (or think I have) to predict that response, much as with a declarative statement. A tag question, then, might be thought of as a declarative statement without the assumption that the statement is to be believed by the addressee: one has an out, as with a question. A tag gives the addressee leeway, not forcing him to go along with the views of the speaker.

There are situations in which a tag is legitimate, in fact the only legitimate sentence form. So, for example, if I have seen something only indistinctly, and have reason to believe my addressee had a better view, I can say:

8 I had my glasses off. He was out at third, wasn't he?

Sometimes we find a tag question used in cases in which the speaker knows as well as the addressee what the answer must be, and doesn't need confirmation. One such situation is when the speaker is making 'small talk', trying to elicit conversation from the addressee:

9   Sure is hot here, isn't it?

In discussing personal feelings or opinions, only the speaker normally has any way of knowing the correct answer. Strictly speaking, questioning one's own opinions is futile. Sentences like (10) are usually ridiculous.

10   *I have a headache, don't I?

But similar cases do, apparently, exist, in which it is the speaker's opinions, rather than perceptions, for which corroboration is sought, as in (11):

11   The way prices are rising is horrendous, isn't it?

While there are of course other possible interpretations of a sentence like this, one possibility is that the speaker has a particular answer in mind – 'yes' or 'no' – but is reluctant to state it baldly. It is my impression, though I do not have precise statistical evidence, that this sort of tag question is much more apt to be used by women than by men. If this is indeed true, why is it true?

These sentence types provide a means whereby a speaker can avoid committing himself, and thereby avoid coming into conflict with the addressee. The problem is that, by so doing, a speaker may also give the impression of not being really sure of himself, of looking to the addressee for confirmation, even of having no views of his own. This last criticism is, of course, one often levelled at women. One wonders how much of it reflects a use of language that has been imposed on women from their earliest years.

Related to this special use of a syntactic rule is a widespread difference perceptible in women's intonational patterns.[2] There is a peculiar sentence intonation pattern, found in English as far as I know only among women, which has the form of a declarative answer to a question, and is used as such, but has the rising inflection typical of a yes–no question, as well as being especially hesitant. The effect is as though one were seeking confirmation, though at the same time the speaker may be the only one who has the requisite information.

12   a When will dinner be ready?
     b Oh. . . around six o'clock. . . ?

It is as though b were saying, 'Six o'clock, if that's OK with you, if agree.' a is put in the position of having to provide confirmation, and b sounds unsure. Here we find unwillingness to assert an opinion carried to an extreme. One likely consequence is that these sorts of speech patterns are taken to reflect something real about character and play a part in not taking a woman seriously or trusting her with any real responsibilities, since 'she can't make up her mind' and 'isn't sure of herself'. And here again we see that people form judgements about other people on the basis of superficial linguistic behaviour that may have nothing to do with inner character, but has been imposed upon the speaker, on pain of worse punishment than not being taken seriously.

Such features are probably part of the general fact that women's speech sounds much more 'polite' than men's. One aspect of politeness is as we have just described: leaving a decision open, not imposing your mind, or views, or claims on anyone else. Thus a tag question is a kind of polite statement, in that it does not force agreement or belief on the addressee. A request may be in the same sense a polite command, in that it does not overtly require obedience, but rather suggests something be done as a favour to the speaker. An overt order (as in an imperative) expresses the (often impolite) assumption of the speaker's superior position to the addressee, carrying with it the right to enforce compliance, whereas with a request the decision on the face of it is left up to the addressee. (The same is true of suggestions: here, the implication is not that the addressee is in danger if he does not comply – merely that he will be glad if he does. Once again, the decision is up to the addressee, and a suggestion therefore is politer than an order.) The more particles in a sentence that reinforce the notion that it is a request, rather than an order, the politer the result. The sentences of 13 illustrate these points: (13)*a* is a direct order, *b* and *c* simple requests, and *d* and *e* compound requests.

13   *a* Close the door.
      b Please close the door.
      c Will you close the door?
      d Will you please close the door?
      e Won't you close the door?

Let me first explain why *e* has been classified as a compound request. (A sentence like *Won't you please close the door* would then count as a doubly compound request.) A sentence like (13)*c* is close in sense to 'Are you willing to close the door?' According to the normal rules of polite conversation, to agree that you are willing is to agree to do the thing asked of you. Hence this apparent enquiry functions as a request, leaving the decision up to the willingness of the addressee. Phrasing it as a positive question makes the (implicit) assumption that a 'yes' answer will be forthcoming. Sentence (13)*d* is more polite than *b* or *c* because it combines them: *please* indicating that to accede will be to do something for the speaker, and *will you*, as noted, suggesting that the addressee has the final decision. If, now, the question is phrased with a negative, as in (13)*e*, the speaker seems to suggest the stronger likelihood of a negative response from the addressee. Since the assumption is then that the addressee is that much freer to refuse, (13)*e* acts as a more polite request than (13)*c* or *d*: *c* and *d* put the burden of refusal on the addressee, as *e* does not.

Given these facts, one can see the connection between tag questions and tag orders and other requests. In all these cases, the speaker is not committed as with a simple declarative or affirmative. And the more one compounds a request, the more characteristic it is of women's speech, the less of men's. A sentence that begins *Won't you please* (without special emphasis on *please*) seems to me at least to have a distinctly unmasculine sound. Little girls are indeed taught to talk like little ladies, in that their speech is in many ways more polite than that of boys or men, and the reason for this is that politeness involves an absence of a strong statement, and women's speech is devised to prevent the expression of strong statements.

Notes

1 Within the lexicon itself, there seems to be a parallel phenomenon to tag-question usage, which I refrain from discussing in the body of the text because the facts are controversial and I do not understand them fully. The intensive *so*, used where purists would insist upon an absolute superlative, heavily stressed, seems more characteristic of women's language than of men's, though it is found in the latter, particularly in the speech of male academics. Consider, for instance, the following sentences:

a I feel *so* unhappy!
b That movie made me *so* sick!

Men seem to have the least difficulty using this construction when the sentence is unemotional, or non-subjective – without reference to the speaker himself:

c That sunset is *so* beautiful!
d Fred is *so* dumb!

Substituting an equative like *so* for absolute superlatives (like *very, really, utterly*) seems to be a way of backing out of committing oneself strongly to an opinion, rather like tag questions (cf. discussion on p. 250). One might hedge in this way with perfect right in making aesthetic judgements, as in *c*, or intellectual judgements, as in *d*. But it is somewhat odd to hedge in describing one's own mental or emotional state: who, after all, is qualified to contradict one on this? To hedge in this situation is to seek to avoid making any strong statement: a characteristic, as we have noted already and shall note further, of women's speech.

2 For analogues outside of English to these uses of tag questions and special intonation patterns, see my discussion of Japanese particles (Lakoff 1972). It is to be expected that similar cases will be found in many other languages as well. See, for example, Haas 1964.

Reprinted from Robin Lakoff, Language and Woman's Place (New York: Harper & Row, 1975).

Chapter 18

Pamela Fishman

CONVERSATIONAL INSECURITY

Introduction

DISCUSSIONS OF THE WAY women act, including the way they talk, often rely on some notion of a female 'personality'. Usually, socialization is used to explain this personality. Women are seen as more insecure, dependent and emotional than men because of the way that they are raised. Socialization is seen as the means by which male–female power differences are internalized and translated into behaviour producing properly dominant men and submissive women (Bardwick and Douvan 1977; Lakoff 1975). Lakoff (1979) has probably been the most explicit in offering this personality–socialization explanation for women's speech patterns:

> Linguistic behavior, like other facets of the personality is heavily influenced by training and education. Women speak as they do – and men speak as *they* do – because they have from childhood been rewarded for doing so, overtly or subtly. Also they speak as they do because their choice of speech style reflects their self-image.
>
> (p. 141)

I want to propose an altogether different analysis. Instead of viewing the behaviour of adult women as indicative of a gender identity acquired through childhood socialization, I will examine the behaviour in terms of the interactional situation in which it is produced. As a methodological strategy, I advocate that *first* we examine the situational context for the forces that explain why people do what they do. If no such forces can be found in the immediate context, only then should we rely on prior socialization to explain present behaviour.

In this paper I will consider two examples of women's conversational style: *question-asking* and the use of *'you know'*. Both are seen as indicative of women's tendency to be more 'insecure' and 'hesitant', and are said to arise from a socialized female personality. Rather than using these as evidence of personality traits, I shall explore the character of conversational interaction in which they occur. By doing so, we will see that these speech patterns are attempted solutions to the problematics of conversation.

The illustrative data in this paper come from fifty-two hours of taped natural conversation, twelve and a half hours of which have been transcribed. Three male–female couples agreed to have tape recorders placed in their apartments for periods ranging from four to fourteen days. Because the couples operated the recorders manually, uninterrupted recording lengths ran from one to four hours. The apartments were all small one-bedroom units, and the recorders picked up all kitchen and living room conversation as well as louder talk from the bedroom and bath. The six participants were between the ages of 25 and 35, white, and professionally oriented. The three men were graduate students, as were two of the women. The third woman was a social worker. Two of the women were feminists. The other woman and all of the men were sympathetic to the women's movement. The participants could erase anything they wished before giving me the tapes, though this was done in only three instances.

Asking questions

Lakoff argues that the asking of questions is a prime example of women's insecurity and hesitancy. She deals with women's extensive use of two interrogatory devices: tag questions ('Isn't it?' 'Couldn't we?') (1975) and questions with declarative functions ('Did you see this in the paper?' 'Should we do a grocery shopping?') (1979):

> [W]omen are more apt than men to use a question when there is a choice for this reason: a woman has traditionally gained reassurance in this culture from presenting herself as concerned about her acceptance as well as unsure of the correctness of what she's saying. . . a woman, believing that a hesitant style will win her acceptance, will adopt it and phrase her opinions. . . deferentially.. . . The single greatest problem women are going to have in achieving parity is surely this pervasive tendency toward hesitancy, linguistic and otherwise.
>
> (1979: 143)

My transcripts support Lakoff's claim that women use tags and declarative questions much more often than men. In fact, women ask more questions of any kind. Out of a total of 370 questions asked in twelve and a half hours of conversation, the women asked 263, two and a half times as many as the men. About a third of the women's questions (87) were tags, or were ones that could have been phrased as declaratives. The women asked three times as many tags or declarative questions as the men (87 to 29) and twice as many requests for information or clarification (152 to 74). (There were 28 questions which I could not categorize, half because of the lack of transcribable words. Twenty-four were asked by the females, four by the males.) A substantial number of women's questions theoretically need not have been questions at all. Why do women speak this way? And why do women ask so many more questions generally?

Instead of interpreting question-asking as the expression of an insecure personality, let us consider the question's interactive attributes. What work does a question do? Question-asking attempts to establish one of the prerequisites of conversation. In order for two or more people to talk to one another, they must agree to do so. They must display that agreement by entering into mutual orientation to one another, and they must speak and respond to one another as one aspect of their mutual orientation. They must take turns speaking, and they must display connectedness between what they say to one another.

Sacks, working within this interactional perspective, has noted that questions are part of a category of conversational sequencing devices; questions from the first part of a pair of utterances, answers being the second part (Sacks 1972). Questions and answers are linked together, conversationally and normatively. Questions are both explicit invitations to the listener to respond and demands that they do so. The questioner has rights to complain if there is no response forthcoming. Questions are stronger forms interactively than declaratives. A declarative can be more easily ignored. The listener can claim they did not know the speaker was finished or that they thought the speaker was musing aloud.

Evidence for the strength of the question–answer sequence can be seen from an analysis of who succeeds in getting their topics adopted in conversation. In earlier work (Fishman 1978) I found that women, using a variety of utterance types to introduce topics, succeeded only 36 per cent of the time in getting their topics to become actual conversations. In contrast, all but one of the men's topic attempts succeeded. However, when we look at the number of topic attempts that women introduced with a question, their success rate jumps considerably. Of eighteen introductory attempts which were questions, thirteen succeeded. This 72 per cent success rate is exactly double the women's overall success rate of 36 per cent. Men used questions to introduce topics six times out of 29, all of which succeeded.

Women ask questions so often because of the conversational power of questions, not because of personality weakness. Women have more trouble starting conversation and keeping it going when they are talking with men. Their greater use of questions is an attempt to solve the *conversational* problem of gaining a response to their utterances.

'You know'

Lakoff discusses hedging as another aspect of women's insecurity. By hedges, she is referring to the frequent use of such phrases as 'sorta', 'like', and 'you know'. I shall deal here with 'you know', since it is a device which I have addressed in my own analyses of conversations (1979). In my transcripts, just as Lakoff would predict, the women used 'you know' five times more often than the men (87 to 17). Why is this?

Let us consider where 'you know' appears in conversation. According to Lakoff, one would expect 'you know' to be randomly scattered throughout women's speech, since its usage is supposed to reflect the general insecurity of the speaker. If, however, 'you know' does some kind of work in conversation, we would expect its occurrence to cluster at points in conversation where the interactional context seems to call for its usage. And this is just what I found. Thirty of the women's 87 'you knows' occur during six short segments of talk. These were all places where the women were unsuccessfully attempting to pursue topics. The six segments of talk total 10 minutes. This means that nearly 35 per cent of the uses occur in less than 2 per cent of the transcribed hours of conversation. (The 'you knows' were not counted for one and a half hours of transcript where four people, rather than the couple, were conversing. Thus, the total transcript time here is eleven hours ($^{10}/_{660}$ = 1.5 per cent). Also during two hours of one couple there were no clustered 'you knows'. Subtracting those two hours, we are left with $^{10}/_{540}$ = 1.9 per cent; a ratio well under the 35 per cent of the total 'you knows' which fall in that time.)

'You know' displays conversational trouble, but it is often an attempt to solve the trouble as well. 'You know' is an attention-getting device, a way to check with one's interactional partner to see if they are listening, following and attending to one's remarks. When we consider 'you know' interactively, it is not surprising to find that its use is concentrated in long turns at talk where the speaker is unsuccessfully attempting to carry on a conversation. If we look briefly at the two longest segments in which 'you know' clusters, we can clarify how it works in actual conversation.

In the two transcripts which follow, the numbers in brackets are the time in seconds of the pauses. The vertical lines in the second transcript indicate overlapping talk. The first segment is five minutes long and only parts of it are reprinted (the full text can be found in Fishman 1979). Here, the woman is attempting to engage the man in conversation about an article she has just read. During the five minutes the man responds only six times, and the woman uses 'you know' sixteen times. Ten of her sixteen uses fall in the two minutes when there is no response from the man at all:

> F   he's talking about the differences, that the women [1.3] uhm [0.8] that the black women represent to the black men, [0.5] white society [0.8] and that uhm [1.5] they stand for all the white values

like they're dressed much neater than the men. They're obviously trying much harder, y'know, and they're more courteous and polite etcetera, etcetera, you know. [1.5] It seems to me that the women because of our [0.7] chauvinism in this society are constantly being put down for things that the same set of the same traits in a man would be put up. [1.5] Like this – he uses different words, you know? [1.5] uhmm [1]. For instance you know they try more they're more conscientious. This sort of thing the goddam blighter used to say about a man, 'n'-, and so on. [1] It's just obvious that – [3] uhh [1], he doesn't know what to do with the fact that the women, the black women [1] uh you know, for a multitude of reasons probably, have come out to be much stronger in many ways than black men. [1] Y'know they hold families together, they're also the bread earners, [1] they just have to go through a lot more shit than the men it seems, and they're stronger for it. [1] and uhm [1.5] he doesn't know what to make of the fact that [0.9] they do all these things, [2] y'know, and so he just puts them down. In a blind and chauvinistic way. [2.5] In other words black women are white. [2] Y'know it's really a simplistic article [0.5] you know he starts off saying – this – [1] y'know, [0.8] sort of this gross, indiscriminate, black versus white [1] vision and .... .

Eight out of ten of the 'you knows' occur immediately prior to or after pauses in the woman's speech. Pauses are places where speaker change might occur, i.e., where the man might have responded. Because the man does not respond and the woman continues talking to keep the conversation going, the pauses become internal to the woman's speech. 'You know' seems to be an explicit invitation to respond. At the same time it displays the man's position as a co-participant when he has not displayed it himself.

'You know' appears to be used somewhat differently in the second segment. In this two-minute piece, the woman uses 'you know' five times. (The 'Richard' referred to in this segment is a mutual friend. He was born in a foreign country which the couple were discussing immediately prior to this piece of conversation.)

> *F*   Many of the men I've met have been incredibly uhh provincial [2] in a sense [1] Umm and it also you know you've got a-, mind you, I know that Richard has had a very good education [2] but he's a very taciturn man and very bitter about the way he's been treated. He's ve-, you know old family in regards
>
> *M*   umphhh
>
> *F*   Well you know some people got caught up in it I mean
>
> *M*   oh of course [1.1]
>
> *F*   You know I mean [0.6] yes I'm sure I mean he's very conserva- tive, right? I mean I'm [1] he hates everything [0.7] and I am I am

sure he didn't before but [1] whenever you talk to his father about it [0.6] he [1.5] he is very confused. I mean apparently he, he was [0.7] very active [0.6] hated Germany [2] and yet turned around afterwards [1] you know which is sort of

M Oh the trouble is that he turned against everything, even the war.

(F then makes another attempt to pursue the topic of Richard's politics, which M responds to with a discussion of cities in the country of Richard's birth.)

Two of the five 'you knows' here follow internal pauses, as in the first transcript we examined. The other three cluster around the man's two minimal responses. Minimal responses display minimal orientation but not full participation. They fill the necessity of turn-taking but add nothing to the substantive progress of the talk, to the content of the conversation.

The use of 'you know' around minimal responses displays and attempts to solve the same problem as its use around pauses. In both cases there is a speaker change problem. The women are either trying to get a response or have gotten an unsatisfactory one. The evidence for women's insecurity is in fact evidence of the work they are doing to try to turn insecure conversations into successful ones.

Concluding remarks

I do not mean to imply that women may not find themselves feeling insecure and hesitant in such conversations. The point is that the feelings are not necessarily something women carry around with them as a result of early socialization. Rather, the feelings arise in situations where the women's attempts at conversation are faltering or failing and they are forced to do considerable work for dubious results.

And why do women have more conversational trouble than men do? Because men often do not do the necessary work to keep conversation going. Either they do not respond, or they respond minimally to conversational attempts by the women. In the few instances where men have trouble in conversations with women they use the same devices to try to solve their problems. I suspect that in conversations with their superiors men use what has been regarded as women's conversational style. The underlying issue here is likely to be hierarchy, not simply gender. Socially-structured power relations are reproduced and actively maintained in our everyday interactions. Women's conversational troubles reflect not their inferior social training but their inferior social position.

Reprinted from Howard Giles, Peter Robinson and Philip Smith (eds), *Language: Social Psychological Perspectives* (Oxford: Pergamon Press, 1980).

Dominance and difference

Chapter 19

Deborah Tannen

THE RELATIVITY OF LINGUISTIC STRATEGIES: RETHINKING POWER AND SOLIDARITY IN GENDER AND DOMINANCE

Introduction

IN ANALYZING DISCOURSE, MANY RESEARCHERS operate on the unstated assumption that all speakers proceed along similar lines of interpretation, so a particular example of discourse can be taken to represent how discourse works for all speakers. For some aspects of discourse, this is undoubtedly true. Yet a large body of sociolinguistic literature makes clear that, for many aspects of discourse, this is so only to the extent that cultural background is shared. To the extent that cultural backgrounds differ, lines of interpretation and habitual use of many linguistic strategies are likely to diverge. My own research shows that cultural difference is not limited to the gross and apparent levels of country of origin and native language, but also exists at the subcultural levels of ethnic heritage, class, geographic region, age, and gender. My earlier work (Tannen 1984, 1986) focuses on ethnic and regional style; my most recent work (Tannen 1990) focuses on gender-related stylistic variation. I draw on this work here to demonstrate that specific linguistic strategies have widely divergent potential meanings.[1]

This insight is particularly significant for research on language and gender, much of which has sought to describe the linguistic means by which men dominate women in interaction. That men dominate women is not in question; what I am problematizing is the source and workings of domination and other interpersonal intentions and effects. I will show that one cannot locate the source of domination, or of any interpersonal intention or effect, in linguistic strategies such as interruption, volubility, silence, and topic raising, as has been claimed. Similarly, one cannot locate the source of women's powerlessness in such linguistic strategies as indirectness, taciturnity, silence, and tag questions, as has also been claimed. The reason one cannot do this is that the same linguistic means can be used for different, even opposite, purposes and can have different, even opposite, effects in different contexts. Thus, a strategy that seems, or is, intended to dominate may in another context or in the mouth of another speaker be intended or used to establish connection. Similarly, a strategy that seems, or is intended to create connection can in another context or in the mouth of another speaker be intended or used to establish dominance.

Put another way, the 'true' intention or motive of any utterance cannot be determined from examination of linguistic form alone. For one thing, intentions and effects are not identical. For another, as the sociolinguistic literature has dramatized repeatedly, human interaction is a 'joint production': everything that occurs results from the interaction of all participants. The source of the ambiguity and polysemy of linguistic strategies that I will explore here is the paradoxical relationship between the dynamics of power and solidarity.

Theoretical background

Power and Solidarity

Since Brown and Gilman's (1960) introduction of the concept and subsequent elaborations of it, especially those of Friedrich (1972) and Brown and Levinson ([1978]1987), the dynamics of power and solidarity have been fundamental to sociolinguistic theory. Brown and Gilman based their framework on analysis of the use of pronouns in European languages which have two forms of the second person pronoun, such as the French *tu* and *vous*. In English the closest parallel is to be found in forms of address: first name versus title–last name. In Brown and Gilman's system, power is associated with nonreciprocal use of pronouns; in English the parallel would be a situation in which one speaker addresses the other by first name but is addressed by title–last name (for example, doctor and patient, teacher and student, boss and secretary, building resident and elevator operator). Solidarity is associated with reciprocal pronoun use or symmetrical forms of address: both speakers address each other by *tu* or by *vous* (in English, by title–last name or by first name). Power governs asymmetrical relationships where one is subordinate to another; solidarity governs symmetrical relationships characterized by social equality and similarity.

In my previous work exploring the relationship between power and solidarity as it emerges in conversational discourse (Tannen 1984, 1986), I note that power and solidarity are in paradoxical relation to each other. That is, although power and solidarity, closeness and distance, seem at first to be opposites, each also entails the other. Any show of solidarity necessarily entails power, in that the requirement of similarity and closeness limits freedom and independence. At the same time, any show of power entails solidarity by involving participants in relation to each other. This creates a closeness that can be contrasted with the distance of individuals who have no relation to each other at all.

In Brown and Gilman's paradigm, the key to power is asymmetry, but it is often thought to be formality. This is seen in the following anecdote. I once entitled a lecture 'The Paradox of Power and Solidarity.' The respondent to my talk appeared wearing a three-piece suit and a knapsack on his back. The audience was amused by the association of the suit with power, the knapsack with solidarity. There was something immediately recognizable in this semiotic. Indeed, a professor wearing a knapsack might well mark solidarity with students at, for example, a protest demonstration. And wearing a three-piece suit to the demonstration might mark power by differentiating the wearer from the demonstrators, perhaps even reminding them of his dominant position in the institutional hierarchy. But wearing a three-piece suit to the board meeting of a corporation would mark solidarity with other board members, whereas wearing a knapsack in that setting would connote not solidarity but disrespect, a move in the power dynamic.

The Ambiguity of Linguistic Strategies

As the preceding example shows, the same symbol – a three-piece suit – can signal either power or solidarity, depending on, at least, the setting (for example, a board meeting or student demonstration), the habitual dress style of the individual, and the comparison of his clothing with that worn by others in the interaction. (I say 'his' intentionally; the range of meanings would be quite different if a man's three-piece suit were worn by a woman.) This provides an analogue to the ambiguity of linguistic strategies, which are signals in the semiotic system of language. As I have demonstrated at length in previous books (see especially Tannen 1984, 1986, 1990), all linguistic strategies are potentially ambiguous. The power–solidarity dynamic is one fundamental source of ambiguity. What appear as attempts to dominate a conversation (an exercise of power) may actually be intended to establish rapport (an exercise of solidarity). This occurs because (as I have worded it elsewhere) power and solidarity are bought with the same currency: The same linguistic means can be used to create either or both.

This ambiguity can be seen in the following fleeting conversation. Two women were walking together from one building to another in order to attend a meeting. They were joined by a man they both knew who had just exited a third building on his way to the same meeting. One of the women greeted the man and remarked, 'Where's your coat?' The man responded, 'Thanks, Mom.' His response framed the woman's remark as a gambit in a power exchange: a mother tells a child to put on his coat. Yet the woman might have intended the remark as showing friendly concern rather than parental caretaking. Was it power (condescending, on the model of parent to child) or solidarity (friendly, on the model of intimate peers)? Though the man's uptake is clear, the woman's intention in making the remark is not.

Another example comes from a letter written to me by a reader of *You Just Don't Understand: Women and Men in Conversation*. A woman was at home when her partner arrived and announced that his archrival had invited him to contribute a chapter to a book. The woman remarked cheerfully how nice it was that the rival was initiating a rapprochement by including her partner in his book. He told her she had got it wrong: because the rival would be the editor and he merely a contributor, the rival was actually trying to solidify his dominance. She interpreted the invitation in terms of solidarity. He interpreted it as an expression of power. Which was right? I don't know. The invitation was ambiguous; it could have 'meant' either. I suspect it had elements of both. In other words, it was polysemous.

The Polysemy of Power and Solidarity

If ambiguity denotes meaning one thing *or* another, polysemy denotes meaning one thing *and* another – that is, having multiple meanings simultaneously. The question 'Where's your coat?' shows friendly concern *and* suggests a parent–child constellation. The invitation to contribute a chapter to a book brings editor and contributor closer *and* suggests a hierarchical relationship.

One more example will illustrate the polysemy of strategies signalling power and solidarity. If you have a friend who repeatedly picks up the check when you dine together, is she being generous and sharing her wealth, or is she trying to flaunt her money and remind you that she has more of it than you? Although the intention may be to make you feel good by her generosity, her repeated generosity may nonetheless make you feel bad by reminding you that she has more money. Thus, both of you are caught in the web of the ambiguity of power and solidarity. It is impossible to determine which was her real motive, and whether it justifies your response. On the other hand, even if you believe her motive was purely generous, you may nonetheless feel denigrated by her generosity because the fact that she has this generous impulse is evidence that she has more money than you, and her expressing the impulse reminds you of it. In other words, both interpretations exist at once: solidarity (she is paying to be nice) and power (her being nice in this way reminds you that she is richer). In this sense, the strategy is not just ambiguous with regard to power and solidarity but polysemous. This polysemy explains another observation that initially surprised me: Paules (1991) reports that waitresses in the restaurant where she did ethnographic field work were offended not only by tips that were too small, but also by tips that were too large. The customers' inordinate beneficence implies that the amount of money left is insignificant to the tipper but significant to the waitress.

Brown and Gilman are explicit in their assumption that power is associated with asymmetrical relationships in which the power is held by the person in the one-up position. This is stated in their definition:

> One person may be said to have power over another to the degree that he is able to control the behavior of the other. Power is a relationship between at least two persons, and it is nonreciprocal in the sense that both cannot have power in the same area of behavior.
>
> (255)

I have called attention, however, to the extent to which solidarity in itself can be a form of control. For example, a young woman complained about friends who 'don't let you be different.' If the friend says she has a particular problem and the woman says, 'I don't have that problem,' her friend is hurt and accuses her of putting her down, of acting superior. The assumption of similarity requires the friend to have a matching problem.

Furthermore, although Brown and Gilman acknowledge that 'power superiors may be solidary (parents, elder siblings)' and 'power inferiors, similarly, may be as solidary as the old family retainer' (258), most Americans are inclined to assume that solidarity implies closeness, whereas power implies distance. Thus Americans regard the sibling relationship as the ultimate in solidarity: 'sister' or 'brother' are often used metaphorically to indicate closeness and equality. In contrast, it is often assumed that hierarchy precludes closeness: employers and employees cannot 'really' be friends. But being linked in a hierarchy necessarily brings individuals closer. This is an assumption underlying Watanabe's (1993) observation, in comparing American and Japanese group discussions, that whereas the Americans in her study saw themselves as individuals participating in a joint activity, the Japanese saw themselves as members of a group united by hierarchy. When reading Watanabe, I was caught up short by the term 'united.' My inclination had been to assume that hierarchy is distancing, not uniting.

The anthropological literature includes numerous discussions of cultural contexts in which hierarchical relationships are seen as close and mutually, not unilaterally, empowering. For example, Beeman (1986) describes an Iranian interactional pattern he dubs 'getting the lower hand.' Taking the lower-status position enables an Iranian to invoke a protector schema by which the higher-status person is obligated to do things for him or her. Similarly, Yamada (1992) describes the Japanese relationship of *amae*, typified by the parent–child or employer–employee constellation. It binds two individuals in a hierarchical interdependence by which both have power in the form of obligations as well as rights vis-à-vis the other. Finally, Wolfowitz (1991) explains that respect/deference is experienced by Suriname Javanese not as subservience but as an assertion of claims. [. . .]

Similarity / Difference

There is one more aspect of the dynamics of power and solidarity that bears discussion before I demonstrate the relativity of linguistic strategies. That is the similarity/difference continuum and its relation to the other dynamics discussed.

For Brown and Gilman, solidarity implies sameness, in contrast to power, about which they observe, 'In general terms, the *V* form is linked with differences between persons' (256). This is explicit in their definition of 'the solidarity semantic':

> Now we are concerned with a new set of relations which are symmetrical; for example, *attended the same school or have the same parents* or *practice the same profession*. If A has the same parents as B, B has the same parents as A. Solidary is the name we give to the general relationship and solidarity is symmetrical.
>
> (257; italics in original)

The similarity/difference continuum calls to mind what I have discussed elsewhere (Tannen 1984, 1986) as the double bind of communication. In some ways, we are all the same. But in other ways we are all different. Communication is a double bind in the sense that anything we say to honor our similarity violates our difference, and anything we say to honor our difference violates our sameness. Thus a complaint can be lodged: 'Don't think I'm different.' ('If you prick me, do I not bleed?' one might protest, like Shylock.) But a complaint can also be lodged: 'Don't think I'm the same.' (Thus, women who have primary responsibility for the care of small children may be effectively excluded from activities and events at which day care is not provided.) Becker (1982: 125) expresses this double bind as 'a matter of continual self-correction between exuberance (that is, friendliness: you are like me) and deficiency (that is, respect: you are not me).' All these formulations elaborate on the tension between similarity and difference, or what Becker and Oka (1974) call 'the cline of person,' a semantic dimension they suggest may be the one most basic to language; that is, one deals with the world and the objects and people in it in terms of how close (and, I would add, similar) they are to oneself.

As a result of these dynamics, similarity is a threat to hierarchy. This is dramatized in Harold Pinter's play *Mountain Language*. Composed of four brief scenes, the play is set in a political prison in the capital city of an unnamed country that is under dictatorial siege. In the second scene, an old mountain woman is finally allowed to visit her son across a table as a guard stands over them. But whenever she tries to speak to her son, the guard silences her, telling the prisoner to tell his mother that it is forbidden to speak their mountain language in the capital. Then he continues:

GUARD

. . . And I'll tell you another thing. I've got a wife and three kids. And you're all a pile of shit.

Silence.

PRISONER

I've got a wife and three kids.

GUARD

You've what?

Silence.

You've got what?

Silence.

What did you say to me? You've got what?

Silence.

You've got *what?*

He picks up the telephone and dials one digit.

Sergeant? I'm in the Blue Room. . . . yes. . . I thought I should report, Sergeant. . . I think I've got a joker in here.

The Sergeant soon enters and asks, 'What joker?' The stage darkens and the scene ends. The final scene opens on the same setting, with the prisoner bloody and shaking, his mother shocked into speechlessness.

The prisoner was beaten for saying, 'I've got a wife and three kids.' This quotidian statement, which would be unremarkable in casual conversation, was insubordinate in the hierarchical context of brutal oppression because the guard had just made the same statement. When the guard said, 'I've got a wife and three kids. And you're a pile of shit,' he was claiming, 'I am different from you.' One could further interpret his words to imply, 'I'm human, and you're not. Therefore I have a right to dominate and abuse you.' By repeating the guard's words verbatim, the prisoner was then saying, 'I am the same as you.' By claiming *his* humanity and implicitly denying the guard's assertion that he is 'a pile of shit,' the prisoner challenged the guard's right to dominate him. Similarity is antithetical to hierarchy.

The ambiguity of closeness, a spatial metaphor representing similarity or involvement, emerges in a nonverbal aspect of this scene. In the performance I saw, the guard moved steadily closer to the prisoner as he repeated the question 'You've got what?' until he was bending over him, nose to nose. The guard's moving closer was a kinesic/proxemic analogue to the prisoner's statement, but with opposite effect: he was 'closing in.' The guard moved closer and brought his face into contact with the prisoner's not as a sign of affection (which such actions could signify in another context) but as a threat. Closeness, then, can mean aggression rather than affiliation in the context of a hierarchical rather than symmetrical relationship.

The relativity of linguistic strategies

The potential ambiguity of linguistic strategies to mark both power and solidarity in face-to-face interaction has made mischief in language and gender research, wherein it is tempting to assume that whatever women do results from, or creates, their powerlessness and whatever men do results from, or creates, their dominance. But all the linguistic strategies that have been taken by analysts as evidence of subordination can in some circumstances be instruments of affiliation. For the remainder of this chapter I demonstrate the relativity of linguistic strategies by considering each of the following strategies in turn: indirectness, interruption, silence versus volubility, topic raising, and adversativeness or verbal conflict. All of these strategies have been 'found' by researchers to express or create dominance or subordination. I will demonstrate that they are ambiguous or polysemous with regard to dominance/subordination (that is, power) or distance/closeness (that is, solidarity). Once again, I am not arguing that these strategies *cannot* be used to create dominance or powerlessness, much less that dominance and powerlessness do not exist. Rather, my purpose is to demonstrate that the 'meaning' of any linguistic strategy can vary, depending at least on context, the conversational styles of participants, and the interaction of participants' styles and strategies. Therefore the operation of specific linguistic strategies must be studied more closely to understand how dominance and powerlessness are expressed and created in interaction.

Indirectness

Lakoff (1975) identifies two benefits of indirectness: defensiveness and rapport. Defensiveness refers to a speaker's preference not to go on record with an idea in order to be able to disclaim, rescind, or modify it if it does not meet with a positive response. The rapport benefit of indirectness results from the pleasant experience of getting one's way not because one demanded it (power) but because the other person wanted the same thing (solidarity). Many researchers have focused on the defensive or power benefit of indirectness and ignored the payoff in rapport or solidarity.

The claim by Conley, O'Barr, and Lind (1979) that women's language is really powerless language has been particularly influential. In this view, women's tendency to be indirect is taken as evidence that women don't feel entitled to make demands. Surely there are cases in which this is true. Yet it can also be demonstrated that those who feel entitled to make demands may prefer not to, seeking the payoff in rapport. Furthermore, the ability to get one's demands met without expressing them directly can be a sign of power rather than of the lack of it. An example I have used elsewhere (Tannen 1986) is the Greek father who answers, 'If you want, you can go,' to his daughter's inquiry about going to a party. Because of the lack of enthusiasm of his response, the Greek daughter understands that her father would prefer she not go and 'chooses' not to go. (A 'real' approval would have been 'Yes, of course, you should go.') I argue that this father did not feel powerless to give his daughter orders. Rather, a communicative system was conventionalized by which he and she could both preserve the appearance, and possibly the belief, that she chose not to go rather than simply obeying his command.

Far from being powerless, this father felt so powerful that he did not need to give his daughter orders; he simply needed to let her know his preference, and she would accommodate to it. By this reasoning, indirectness is a prerogative of the powerful. By the same reasoning a master who says, 'It's cold in here,' may expect a servant to make a move to close a window, but a servant who says the same thing is not likely to see his employer rise to correct the situation and make him more comfortable. Indeed, a Frenchman who was raised in Brittany tells me that his family never gave bald commands to their servants but always communicated orders in indirect and highly polite form. This pattern renders less surprising the finding of Bellinger and Gleason (1982, reported in Gleason 1987) that fathers' speech to their young children had a higher incidence than mothers' of both direct imperatives (such as 'Turn the bolt with the wrench') *and* implied indirect imperatives (for example, 'The wheel is going to fall off').

The use of indirectness can hardly be understood without the cross-cultural perspective. Many Americans find it self-evident that directness is logical and aligned with power whereas indirectness is akin to dishonesty as well as subservience. But for speakers raised in most of the world's cultures, varieties of indirectness are the norm in communication. In Japanese interaction, for example, it is well known that saying 'no' is considered too face-threatening to risk, so negative responses are phrased as positive ones: one never says 'no,' but listeners understand from the form of the 'yes' whether it is truly a 'yes' or a polite 'no.'

The American tendency to associate indirectness with female style is not culturally universal. The above description of typical Japanese style operates for men as well as women. My own research (Tannen 1981, 1984, 1986) suggests that Americans of some cultural and geographic backgrounds, female as well as male, are more likely than others to use relatively direct rather than indirect styles. In an early study I compared Greeks and Americans with regard to their tendency to interpret a question as an indirect means of making a request. I found that whereas American women were more likely to take an indirect interpretation of a sample conversation, Greek men were as likely as Greek women, and more likely than American men *or women*, to take an indirect interpretation. Greek men, of course, are not less powerful vis-à-vis women than American men.

Perhaps most striking is the finding of Keenan (1974) that in a Malagasy-speaking village on the island of Madagascar, women are seen as direct and men as indirect. But this in no way implies that the women are more powerful than men in this society. Quite the contrary, Malagasy men are socially dominant, and their indirect style is more highly valued. Keenan found that women were widely believed to debase the language with their artless directness, whereas men's elaborate indirectness was widely admired.

Indirectness, then, is not in itself a strategy of subordination. Rather, it can be used either by the powerful or the powerless. The interpretation of a given utterance, and the likely response to it, depends on the setting, on individuals' status and their relationship to each other, and also on the linguistic conventions that are ritualized in the cultural context.

Interruption

That interruption is a sign of dominance has been as widespread an assumption in research as in conventional wisdom. One rarely encounters an article on gender and language that does not make this claim. Most frequently cited is West and Zimmerman's (1983) finding that men dominate women by interrupting them in conversation. Tellingly, however, Deborah James and Sandra Clarke (1993), reviewing research on gender and interruption, do not find a clear pattern of males interrupting females. Especially significant is their observation that studies comparing amount of interruption in all-female versus all-male conversations find more interruption, not less, in all-female groups. Though initially surprising, this finding reinforces the need to distinguish linguistic strategies by their interactional purpose. Does the overlap show support for the speaker, or does it contradict or change the topic? I have explored this phenomenon in detail (Tannen 1994: chapter 2), but I will include a brief summary of the argument here.

The phenomenon commonly referred to as 'interruption,' but which is more accurately referred to as 'overlap,' is a paradigm case of the ambiguity of power and solidarity. This is clearly demonstrated with reference to a two-and-a-half-hour Thanksgiving dinner conversation that I analyzed at length (Tannen 1984). My analysis makes clear that some speakers consider talking along with another to be a show of enthusiastic participation in the conversation, of solidarity, creating connections; others, however, assume that only one voice should be heard at a time, so for them any overlap is an interruption, an attempt to wrest the floor, a power play. The result, in the conversation I analyzed, was that enthusiastic listeners who overlapped cooperatively, talking along to establish rapport, were perceived by overlap-resistant speakers as interrupting. This doubtless contributed to the impression reported by the overlap-resistant speakers that the cooperative overlappers had 'dominated' the conversation. Indeed, the tape and transcript also give the impression that the cooperative overlappers had dominated, because the overlap-aversant participants tended to stop speaking as soon as another voice began.

It is worth emphasizing the role of symmetry, or balance, in determining whether an overlap becomes an interruption in the negative or power-laden sense. If one speaker repeatedly overlaps and another repeatedly gives way, the resulting communication is unbalanced, or asymmetrical, and the effect (though not necessarily the intent) is domination. But if both speakers avoid overlap, or if both speakers overlap each other and win out equally, there is symmetry and no domination, regardless of speakers' intentions. In an important sense, though — and this will be discussed in the last section under the rubric of adversativeness — the very engagement in a symmetrical struggle for the floor can be experienced as creating rapport, in the spirit of ritual opposition analogous to sports. Further, an imbalance can result from differences in the purpose for which overlap is used. If one speaker tends to talk along in order to show support, and the other chimes in to take the floor, the floor-taking overlapper will tend to dominate.

Thus, to understand whether an overlap is an interruption, one must consider the context (for example, cooperative overlapping is more likely to occur in casual conversation among friends than in a job interview), speakers' habitual styles (for example, overlaps are more likely not to be interruptions among those with a style I call 'high involvement'), and the interaction of their styles (for example, an interruption is more likely to occur between speakers whose styles differ with regard to pausing and overlap). This is not to say that one cannot use interruption to dominate a conversation or a person, but only that it is not self-evident from the observation of overlap that an interruption has occurred, was intended, or was intended to dominate.

Silence Versus Volubility

The excerpt from Pinter's *Mountain Language* dramatizes the assumption that powerful people do the talking and powerless people are silenced. This is the trope that underlies the play's title and its central theme: By outlawing their language, the oppressors silence the mountain people, robbing them of their ability to speak and hence of their humanity. In the same spirit, many scholars (for example, Spender 1980) have claimed that men dominate women by silencing them. There are obviously circumstances in which this is accurate. Coates (1986) notes numerous proverbs that instruct women, like children, to be silent.

Silence alone, however, is not a self-evident sign of powerlessness, nor volubility a self-evident sign of domination. A theme running through Komarovsky's (1962) classic study of *Blue-Collar Marriage* is that many of the wives interviewed said they talked more than their husbands: 'He's tongue-tied,' one woman said (13); 'My husband has a great habit of not talking,' said another (162); 'He doesn't say much but he means what he says and the children mind him,' said a third (353). Yet there is no question but that these husbands are dominant in their marriages, as the last of these quotes indicates.

Indeed, taciturnity itself can be an instrument of power. This is precisely the claim of Sattel (1983), who argues that men use silence to exercise power over women. Sattel illustrates with a scene from Erica Jong's novel *Fear of*

Flying, only a brief part of which is presented here. The first line of dialogue is spoken by Isadora, the second by her husband, Bennett. (Spaced dots indicate omitted text; unspaced dots are a form of punctuation included in the original text.)

> 'Why do you turn on me? What did I do?'
> Silence.
> 'What did I do?'
> He looks at her as if her not knowing were another injury.
> 'Look, let's just go to sleep now. Let's just forget it.'
> 'Forget what?'
> He says nothing.
>
> . . .
>
> 'It was something in the movie, wasn't it?'
> 'What, in the movie?'
> '. . . It was the funeral scene.. . . The little boy looking at his dead mother. Something got you there. That was when you got depressed.'
> Silence.
> 'Well, *wasn't* it?'
> Silence.
> 'Oh come on, Bennett, you're making me *furious*. Please tell me. Please.'

The painful scene continues in this vein until Bennett tries to leave the room and Isadora tries to detain him. The excerpt certainly seems to support Sattel's claim that Bennett's silence subjugates his wife, as the scene ends with her literally lowered to the floor, clinging to his pajama leg. But the reason his silence is an effective weapon is her insistence that he tell her what's wrong. If *she* receded into silence, leaving the room or refusing to talk to him, his silence would be disarmed. The devastation results not from his silence alone but from the interaction of his silence and her insistence on talking, in other words, the interaction of their differing styles.

Researchers have counted numbers of words spoken or timed length of talk in order to demonstrate that men talk more than women and thereby dominate interactions. (See James and Drakich 1993 for a summary of research on amount of talk.) Undoubtedly there is truth to this observation in some settings. But the association of volubility with dominance does not hold for all settings and cultures. Imagine, for example, an interrogation, in which the interrogator does little of the talking but holds all the power.

The relativity of the 'meaning' of taciturnity and volubility is highlighted in Margaret Mead's (1977) discussion of 'end linkage,' a concept developed jointly by Mead, Gregory Bateson, and Geoffrey Gorer. The claim is that universal and biologically constructed relationships, such as parent–child, are linked to different behaviors in different cultures. One of their paradigm examples is the apportionment of spectatorship and exhibitionism. In middle-class American culture, children, who are obviously the weaker party in the constellation, are expected to exhibit while their more powerful parents are spectators. (Consider, for example, the American child who is prompted to demonstrate how well s/he can recite the alphabet for guests.) In contrast, in middle- and upper-class British culture, exhibition is associated with the parental role and spectatorship with children, who are expected to be seen and not heard.

Moreover, volubility and taciturnity, too, can result for style differences rather than speakers' intentions. As I (Tannen 1984, 1985) and others (Scollon and Scollon 1981, Scollon 1985) have discussed, there are cultural and subcultural differences in the length of pauses expected between and within speaking turns. In my study of the dinner conversation, those who expected shorter pauses between conversational turns began to feel an uncomfortable silence ensuing while their longer-pausing friends were simply waiting for what they regarded as the 'normal' end-of-turn pause. The result was that the shorter pauses ended up doing most of the talking, another sign interpreted by their interlocutors as dominating the conversation. But their intentions had been to fill in what to them were potentially uncomfortable silences, that is, to grease the conversational wheels and ensure the success of the conversation. In their view, the taciturn participants were uncooperative, failing to do their part to maintain the conversation.

Thus, silence and volubility cannot always be taken to 'mean' power or powerlessness, domination or subjugation. Rather, both may imply either power or solidarity, depending on the dynamics discussed.

Topic Raising

Shuy (1982) is typical in assuming that the speaker who raises the most topics is dominating a conversation. However, in a study I conducted (Tannen 1994) of videotaped conversations among friends of varying ages recorded by Dorval (1990), it emerged that the speaker who raised the most topics was not always dominant, as judged by other criteria (for example, who took the lead in addressing the investigator when he entered the room?). In a 20-minute conversation between a pair of sixth-grade girls who identified themselves as best friends, Shannon raised the topic of Julia's relationship with Mary by saying, 'Too bad you and Mary are not good friends anymore.' The conversation proceeded and continued to focus almost exclusively on Julia's troubled relationship with Mary.

Similarly, most of the conversation between two tenth-grade girls was about Nancy, but Sally raised the topic of Nancy's problems. In response to Nancy's question 'Well, what do you want to talk about?' Sally said, 'Your mama. Did you talk to your mama?' The ensuing conversation focuses on events involving Nancy's mother and boyfriend. Overall, Sally raised nine topics, Nancy seven. However, all but one of the topics Sally raised were

273

questions focused on Nancy. If raising more topics is a sign of dominance, Sally controlled the conversation when she raised topics, although even this was subject to Nancy's collaboration by picking them up. It may or may not be the case that Sally controlled the conversation, but the nature of her dominance is surely other than what is normally assumed by that term if the topics she raised were all about Nancy.

Finally, the effect of raising topics may also be an effect of differences in pacing and pausing, as discussed above with regard to my study of dinner-table conversation. A speaker who thinks the other has no more to say on a given topic may try to contribute to the conversation by raising another topic. But a speaker who was intending to say more and was simply waiting for the appropriate turn-exchange pause will fell that the floor was taken away and the topic aggressively switched. Yet again, the impression of dominance might result from style differences.

Adversativeness: Conflict and Verbal Aggression

Research on gender and language has consistently found male speaker to be competitive and more likely to engage in conflict (for example, by arguing, issuing commands, and taking opposing stands) and females to be cooperative and more likely to avoid conflict (for example, by agreeing, supporting, and making suggestions rather than commands). (Maltz and Borker [1982] summarize some of this research.) Ong (1981:51) argues that 'adversativeness' is universal, but 'conspicuous or expressed adversativeness is a larger element in the lives of males than of females.'

In my analysis of videotapes of male and female friends talking to each other (Tannen 1994), I have begun to investigate how male adversativeness and female cooperation are played out, complicated, and contradicted in conversational discourse. In analyzing videotapes of friends talking, for example, I found a sixth-grade boy saying to his best friend,

> Seems like, if there's a fight, me and you are automatically in it. And everyone else wants to go against you and everything. It's hard to agree without someone saying something to you.

In contrast, girls of the same age (and also of most other ages whose talk I examined) spent a great deal of time discussing the dangers of anger and contention. In affirming their own friendship, one girl told her friend,

> Me and you <u>never</u> get in fights hardly,

and

> I mean like if I try to talk to you, you'll say, 'Talk to <u>me</u>!' And if you try to talk to me, I'll <u>talk</u> to you.

These examples of gendered styles of interaction are illuminated by the insight that power and solidarity are mutually evocative. As seen in the statement of the sixth-grade boy, opposing other boys in teams entails affiliation within the team. The most dramatic instance of male affiliation resulting from conflict with others is bonding among soldiers, a phenomenon explored by Norman (1990).

By the same token, girls' efforts to support their friends necessarily entail exclusion of or opposition to other girls. This emerges in Hughes' (1988) study of girls playing a street game called four-square, in which four players occupy one square each and bounce a ball into each other's squares. The object of the game is to eliminate players by hitting the ball into their square in such a way that they fail to hit it back. But this effort to 'get people out' is at odds with the social injunction under which the girls operate, to be 'nice' and not 'mean'. Hughes found that the girls resolved the conflict, and formed 'incipient teams' composed of friends, by claiming that their motivation in eliminating some players was to enable others (their friends) to enter the game, since eliminated players are replaced by awaiting players. In the girls' terms, 'getting someone out' was 'nice-mean,' because it was reframed as 'getting someone [a friend] in.' This dynamic is also supported by my analysis of the sixth-grade girls' conversation: Most of their talk was devoted to allying themselves with each other in opposition to another girl who was not present. So their cooperation (solidarity) also entails opposition (power).

For boys power entails solidarity not only by opposition to another team, but by opposition to each other. In the videotapes of friends talking, I found that all the conversations between young boys (and none between young girls) had numerous examples of teasing and mock attack.[2] In examining preschool conversations transcribed and analyzed by Corsaro and Rizzo (1990:34), I was amazed to discover that a fight could initiate rather than preclude friendship. In the following episode, a little boy intrudes on two others and an angry fight ensues. This is the way Corsaro and Rizzo present the dialogue:

> *Two boys (Richard and Denny) have been playing with a slinky on the stairway leading to the upstairs playhouse in the school. During their play two others boys (Joseph and Martin) enter and stand near the bottom of the stairs.*
> *Denny:* Go!
> *(Martin now runs off, but Joseph remains and he eventually moves halfway up the stairs.)*
> *Joseph:* These are big shoes.
> *Richard:* I'll punch him right in the eye.
> *Joseph:* I'll punch you right in the nose.
> *Denny:* I'll punch him with my big fist.
> *Joseph:* I'll-I-I-
> *Richard:* And he'll be bumpety, bumpety and punched out all the way down the stairs.

> *Joseph:* I-I- I'll- I could poke your eyes out with my gun. I have a gun.
> *Denny:* A gun! I'll- I- I- even if-
> *Richard:* I have a gun too.
> *Denny:* And I have guns too and its bigger than yours and it poo-poo down. That's poo-poo.
> *(All three boys laugh at Denny's reference to poo-poo.)*
> *Richard:* Now leave.
> *Joseph:* Un-uh. I gonna tell you to put on – on the gun on your hair and the poop will come right out on his face.
> *Denny:* Well.
> *Richard:* Slinky will snap right on your face too.
> *Denny:* And my gun will snap right –

Up until this point I had no difficulty interpreting the interaction: The boys were engaged in a fight occasioned by Joseph's intrusion into Richard and Denny's play. But what happened next surprised and, at first, perplexed me. Corsaro and Rizzo describe it this way:

> At this point a girl (Debbie) enters, says she is Batgirl, and asks if they have seen Robin. Joseph says he is Robin, but she says she is looking for a different Robin and then runs off. After Debbie leaves, Denny and Richard move into the playhouse and Joseph follows. From this point to the end of the episode the three boys play together.

At first I was incredulous that so soon after their seemingly hostile encounter, the boys played amicably together. I finally came to the conclusion that for Joseph picking a fight was a way to enter into interaction with the other boys, and engaging him in the fight was Richard and Denny's way of accepting him into their interaction – at least after he acquitted himself satisfactorily in the fight. In this light, I could see that the reference to poo-poo, which occasioned general laughter, was the beginning of a reframing from fighting to playing.[3]

Folklore provides numerous stories in which fighting precipitates friendship among men. One such is attributed by Bly (1990:243–4) to Joseph Campbell's account of the Sumerian epic, *Gilgamesh*. In Bly's rendition, Gilgamesh, a young king, wants to befriend a wild man named Enkidu. When Enkidu is told of Gilgamesh,

> his heart grew light. He yearned for a friend. 'Very well!' he said. 'And I shall challenge him.'

Bly paraphrases the continuation: 'Enkidu then travels to the city and meets Gilgamesh; the two wrestle, Enkidu wins, and the two become inseparable friends.'

A modern-day academic equivalent to the bonding that results from opposition is to be found in the situation of fruitful collaborations that began when an audience member publicly challenged a speaker after his talk. Finally, Penelope Eckert (personal communication) informs me that in her research on high school students (Eckert 1990) she was told by boys, but never by girls, that their close friendships began by fighting.

These examples call into question the correlation of aggression and power on one hand, and cooperation and solidarity on the other. Again the cross-cultural perspective provides an invaluable corrective to the temptation to align aggression with power as distinguished from solidarity. Many cultures of the world see arguing as a pleasurable sign of intimacy. Schiffrin (1984) shows that among lower-middle-class men *and women* of East European Jewish background, friendly argument is a means of being sociable. Frank (1988) shows a Jewish couple who tend to polarize and take argumentative positions, but they are not fighting; they are staging a kind of public sparring, where both fighters are on the same team Byrnes (1986) claims that Germans find American students uninformed and uncommitted because they are reluctant to argue politics with new acquaintances. For their part, Americans find German students belligerent because they provoke arguments about American foreign policy with Americans they have just met.

Greek conversation provides an example of a cultural style that places more positive value, for both women and men, on dynamic opposition. Kakava (1989) replicates Schiffrin's findings by showing how a Greek family enjoy opposing each other in dinner conversation. In another study of modern Greek conversation, Tannen and Kakava (1992) find speakers routinely disagreeing when they actually agree, and using diminutive name forms and other terms of endearment – markers of closeness – precisely when they are opposing each other[5] These patterns can be seen in the following excerpt from a conversation that took place in Greece between an older Greek woman and myself. The woman, whom I call Ms Stella, has just told me that she complained to the police about a construction crew that illegally continued drilling and pounding through the siesta hours, disturbing her nap:

Deborah: Echete dikio.
Stella: Ego echo dikio. Kopella mou, den xero an echo dikio i den echo dikio. Alla ego yperaspizomai ta symferonta mou kai ta dikaiomata mou.
Deborah: You're right.
Stella: I am right. My dear girl, I don't know if I'm right or I'm not right. But I am watching out for my interests and my rights.

My response to Ms Stella's complaint is to support her by agreeing. But she disagrees with my agreement by reframing my statement in her own terms rather than simply accepting it by stopping after 'I *am* right.' She also marks her divergence from my frame with the endearment 'kopella mou' (literally, 'my girl,' but idiomatically closer to 'my dear girl').

The following conversation is also taken from Tannen and Kakava (1992). It is, according to Kakava, typical of her family's sociable argument. The younger sister has said that she cannot understand why the attractive young woman who is the prime minister Papandreou's girlfriend would have an affair with such an old man. The older sister, Christina, argues that the woman may have felt that in having an affair with the prime minister she was doing something notable. Her sister replied,

> Poly megalo timima re Christinaki na pliroseis pantos.

> It's a very high price to pay, Chrissie, anyway.

I use the English diminutive form 'Chrissie' to reflect the Greek diminutive ending -aki, but the particle re cannot really be translated; it is simply a marker of closeness that is typically used when disagreeing, as in the ubiquitously heard expression 'Ochi, re' ('No, re').

Conclusion

The intersection of language and gender provides a rich site for analyzing how power and solidarity are created in discourse. But prior research in this area evidences the danger of linking linguistic forms with interactional intentions such as dominance. In trying to understand how speakers use language, we must consider the context (in every sense, including at least textual, relational, and institutional constraints), speakers' conversational styles, and, most crucially, the interaction of their styles with each other.

Attempts to understand what goes on between women and men in conversation are muddled by the ambiguity and polysemy of power and solidarity. The same linguistic means can accomplish either, and every utterance combines elements of both. Scholars, however, like individuals in interaction, are likely to see only one and not the other, like the picture that cannot be seen for what it is – simultaneously a chalice and two faces – but can only be seen alternately as one or the other. In attempting the impossible task of keeping both images in focus at once, we may at least succeed in switching from one to the other rapidly and regularly enough to deepen our understanding of the dynamics underlying interaction such as power and solidarity as well as gender and language use.

Notes

1   I use the term 'strategy' in its standard sociolinguistic sense, to refer simply to a way of speaking. No implication is intended of deliberate planning, as is the case in the common parlance use of such expressions as 'military strategy.' Neither, however, as Gumperz (1982) observes, are linguistic strategies 'unconscious.' Rather, they are best thought of as 'automatic.' That is, people speak in a particular way without 'consciously' thinking it through, but are aware, if questioned, of how they spoke and what they were trying to accomplish by talking in that way. This in contrast to the 'unconscious' motives of Freudian theory about which an individual would be unaware if questioned. (For example, most men would vigorously deny that they want to kill their fathers and marry their mothers, but a strict Freudian might claim that this wish is 'unconscious.')

2   Some examples are given in Tannen (1990). Whereas the boys made such gestures as shooting each other with invisible guns, the girls made such gestures as reaching out and adjusting a friend's headband.

3   Elsewhere (Tannen 1990:163–5) I discuss this example in more detail and note the contrast that the boys fight when they want to play, and the girl avoids disagreeing even when she in fact disagrees.

4   Sifianou (1992) independently observes the use of diminutives as solidarity markers in Greek conversation.

Reprinted from Deborah Tannen, *Gender and Discourse* (Oxford: Oxford University Press, 1994).

Chapter 20

Aki Uchida

WHEN 'DIFFERENCE' IS 'DOMINANCE': A CRITIQUE OF THE 'ANTI-POWER-BASED' CULTURAL APPROACH TO SEX DIFFERENCES

A 'cultural' approach to sex differences[1]

IN THEIR ARTICLE PUBLISHED 1982, anthropologists Maltz and Borker suggested a framework for examining the differences in speech between American women and men.[2] This framework has attracted many researchers to this day, and the influence can be most clearly seen in the works of Tannen (1986, 1990a, 1990b, 1990c), which directly apply and advocate this approach. This framework adopts the view that sex difference is culture difference, that cross-sex communication is cross-cultural communication.[3] Women and men 'come from different sociolinguistic subcultures'; specifically, because the rules for informal interaction are acquired during the period of childhood and adolescence when girls and boys socially interact and play primarily with peers of their own sex, women and men 'learn to do different things with words in a conversation' (Maltz and Borker 1982: 200).

This 'difference/cultural' approach is based on Gumperz's (1982) framework for studying problems in interethnic communication. Members of different cultures will bring their own assumptions and rules of communication and apply them in intercultural encounters to understand what is going on. Differences in such assumptions and rules will result in asynchrony in the flow of conversation and misinterpretation of each other's intention, which tend to be negatively attributed to the personality of individuals or cultural stereotypes. Maltz and Borker maintained that the same thing happens in communication between the sexes. Women and men carry over to their adulthood the conversational patterns they learned from interacting with their same-sex peers during childhood, and the differences between these patterns creates conflict and misunderstandings when they try to engage in a friendly female–male conversation. Problems of sex differences are, therefore, primarily caused by this cross-cultural miscommunication.

This cross-cultural view has been considered by its proponents and by some linguistic theorists as presenting an alternative to the explanation for sex differences in speech behavior in terms of power, commonly regarded as the 'dominance or power-based' approach. The position taken by the cross-cultural view is that dominance and power have little to do with the explanation of sex differences, because the differences – although their outcome may be male dominance – exist without any intention on the part of the males to dominate. '[E]ven if both parties are attempting to treat one another as equals, cultural miscommunication results' (Maltz and Borker 1982: 200). The cross-cultural approach, compared with the dominance approach, allows us to account for the miscommunication without casting blame on either sex (Tannen 1990b).

But how adequate is this assessment? There seem to be two points regarding this position of using a two-culture framework that are worth questioning. Both stem from the practice of dichotomizing the two concepts of *dominance* and (cultural) *difference*. My first argument is that the proponents of the difference/cultural approach, as well as theorists who perceive a dichotomy of two opposing views of sex differences in speech, are falsely assuming that every study including the concept of power and male dominance in its analysis could be categorized under the dominance approach. My second, and more important, point is that it is a mistake to separate power and culture of women and men – and to assume that the two are independent constructs, much less that one would sufficiently explain any sex difference. It is not only wrong on the part of the difference/cultural approach to underestimate the effects of power structure and dominance; it is harmful. These two points are discussed in the rest of this article. [. . .]

Cultural differences between women and men: an overview

Maltz and Borker (1982) delineated some features that they suggested differentiate the speech behaviors of American females and males, behaviors that have been acquired by each sex from interacting with same-sex peers during childhood. In the following, I briefly discuss the main cultural differences between women and men that the proponents of the difference/cultural approach propose.

Relying on studies of children's interaction through play in same-sex peer groups, Maltz and Borker contended that American girls and boys differ in the following aspects in the way they use language: Girls learn to create and maintain relationships of closeness and equality, to criticize others in acceptable ways, and to interpret accurately the speech of other girls (1982: 205), whereas boys learn to assert one's position of dominance, to attract and maintain an audience, and to assert oneself when other speakers have the floor (1982: 207). This shows a pattern similar to that suggested by Gilligan's (1982) work on sex differences in moral development. Indeed, more recent analyses of children's and adolescents' talk with same-sex friends also show sex differences consistent with these patterns (Eckert 1990; Goodwin 1988, 1990; Johnson and Aries 1983a; Sheldon 1990; Tannen 1990a, 1990b, 1990c). The notion that children's socialization with peers is accomplished through interacting primarily with those of the same sex is supported by the observation that children show a strong tendency to group and interact exclusively with same-sex peers. This is reported by Maccoby (1986), who also referred to girls and boys as forming their own culture as a result of this segregation.

Children's speech patterns also seem to match the patterns heard in same-sex conversation of American adults. A review of the increasing literature on women's discourse suggests that the interaction style learned in childhood is carried over to adulthood. Studies of women's joke-telling (Jenkins 1986), bathroom graffiti (Bruner and Kelso 1980; Cole 1991; Davies 1986), gossip (Jones 1980; that of British women, Coates 1988), women's talk with friends (Aries and Johnson 1983; Johnson and Aries 1983b) and in academic settings (Treichler and Kramarae 1983) all support the claim that women's friendly talk is, in general, 'interactional, relational, participatory, and collaborative' (Treichler and Kramarae 1983). Women's speech seen in this light is said to include: more back-channeling or minimal responses used to signal the fact that they are listening, more personal and inclusive pronouns such as *you* and *we*, and more signs of interest and attention (Maltz and Borker 1982; Tannen 1986, 1990ab, 1990c; Treichler and Kramarae 1983). These strategies can be heard as serving the function of cooperation and collaboration essential in the type of discourse in which women engage, which Tannen (1990c) termed 'rapport talk' as opposed to 'report talk', which calls for different norms of interaction, and in which, according to Tannen, men primarily participate.

Therefore, judging from same-sex interaction patterns, it seems legitimate to say that women and men have at least *some* different cultural rules for friendly conversation (Maltz and Borker 1982). However, as we have seen, these differences were mostly found through the comparative analyses of same-sex conversations. The difference/cultural approach to female–male communication does not stop there. The next step is to analyze what happens in communication between the sexes; that is, when the members from different cultures come together to interact as social equals.

Problems in the cross-cultural approach to cross-sex communication

The difference/cultural approach suggests that women and men will interpret each other's behavior according to their own rules for friendly interaction.

Thus, if miscommunication occurs, it can be explained in terms of the cultural differences. This is where I find the first problem with this approach – it assumes that same-sex rules will directly be carried over to mixed-sex interaction. But neither Maltz and Borker nor Tannen offered any empirical evidence that women and men will indeed use the same rules to interpret their conversation partner's behavior regardless of their sex. Tannen (1986, 1990c) only provided anecdotes that imply that women will seek the same supportive response, or rapport talk, from their husbands as they receive from their female friends and that they will feel hurt or frustrated if they are instead answered with jokes or advice. Tannen (1990c) also gave her own reactions to girls' and boys' talk when she was analyzing their video-taped interaction for her study (1990b) and compared them with the reactions reported from men. Tannen found the girls' talk appealing and cute, which she noted was typical of women, whereas the boys' restlessness and mocking made her nervous. On the other hand, she found that men thought of the boys' energy and poking fun as cute, whereas they did not like the girls' behavior of sitting so still and showing obedience to the experimenter. So she concluded: 'Boys and girls grow up in different worlds, but we think we're in the same one, so we judge each other's behavior by the standards of our own' (1990b:254).

This statement sums up the gist of the cross-cultural miscommunication view, and it seems to be too critical a claim to make without some results from a more systematic observation offered as support. How accurate is it to say that we would see the context as the same, and therefore the norms of interpretation as the same, whether the interaction was between partners of the same sex or of a different sex? It may be possible for the sex of one participant to greatly affect the topic, genre, key, rules of interaction, and norms of interpretation in a speech event (Saville-Troike 1989). In their study of conversation content between same-sex friends, Aries and Johnson found that women would talk with their close friends about things they would not with their husbands (Aries and Johnson 1983; Johnson and Aries 1983b). It seems unlikely that the sex of the conversation partner would affect the topic but not the standards by which they judge her or him. Also in Tannen's example of judgmental difference between women and men on girls' and boys' behavior, if by chance the girls had behaved like the boys (being restless, teasing and putting each other down, 'challenging' the experimenter's authority, etc.), would men have interpreted that as 'cute'? We have certain standards for judging people in general, and this may be developed through our living in the world of our own sex, but we also have certain standards for judging females and males, quite separately from what we have learned through our interaction with same-sex peers.

The framework of cross-sex communication as cross-cultural communication seems too simplistic, mainly because no matter how much time children spend interacting with their same-sex peers, they are not completely segregated from the other sex. While they are learning the rules for friendly conversation from their peers, they are also open to the pattern of interaction of their opposite-sex peers, to that between their parents, and to other various conversations, real or fictional. They internalize the culturally prescribed sex-role stereotypes, learning how girls and boys are supposed to differ in the ways they behave and interact. They would not be in the same situation as 'real' intercultural encounters, say, between Japanese and American autoworkers assembled to work in the same plant, where each member had not been truly exposed to the other's culture prior to the encounter.

Moreover, there seems to be a problem in the use of the term *cross-cultural* itself. This term implies a static approach that 'can only lead to lengthy lists of comparative differences between countless cultures; the results of which are impossible to digest or apply in any meaningful way' (DeFrancisco 1990a:2). The cross-cultural view of sex differences in talk can lead us to compare the differences between females and males on isolated variables of speech (e.g., how conversation involvement is expressed and interpreted). If we take this approach, there would be nothing important to note about women's communication unless a comparable difference from men's is found, and vice versa. From this standpoint, the issue of female–male communication becomes relevant only if we assume that these differences are static and constant and will directly be carried over from same-sex conversation. However, communication between members of different cultures involves more than interpreting each other according to one's own rules and miscommunicating. Especially regarding the interaction of women and men in the United States, the approach must be an 'intercultural' one, which 'encourages a focus on how these apparent cultural differences are derived from complex fabrics of cultures' (Sugimoto 1991). More precisely, ' "Cross-cultural" communication involves observing, comparing and analyzing one culture from the viewpoint of the other. It might be called the "observer" approach. In contrast, "intercultural" communication might be called the "participant" approach and can be "characterized by intense involvement on the part of the participant" ' (Harms 1973:41, cited in Sugimoto 1991:1).

The intercultural approach views communication as a more dynamic process of adapting and negotiating and creating new meanings, in which the participants would adjust and modify their rules in response to each other. The cross-cultural view neglects the individuals' ability to take the other's perspective and adapt their speech to the listener. It also ignores the effect of social norms, such as our sex-role expectations, of our sociocultural knowledge of what to expect from females and males in interaction. And it also ignores the fact that a speaker's speech form is affected by the sex of the hearer, although it is not the only factor that creates a difference.

The final thing to note about the difference/cultural approach to sex differences is that, like the dominance/power-based approach, this view also ignores the interaction of race, class, age, and sexual orientation with sex (Henley and Kramarae 1991; Kramarae 1990). Women and men belong to many interconnected social groups in addition to that of their own sex, and an individual is more than just a 'woman' when interacting with others. Maltz and Borker offered their difference/cultural framework to explain 'American men and women' (1982:196), but this generalization neglects the cultural and ethnic diversity, as well as the existence of racial tension in the United States.[4] Tannen (1990c) used her illustrative anecdotes from a relatively homogeneous group: seemingly well-educated, middle-class, heterosexual Americans. It seems strange that although she has elsewhere (Tannen 1984, 1986) analyzed differences in conversational style between Jewish New Yorkers and non-Jewish Californians, which overrode sex differences, these findings are not incorporated into her difference/cultural approach.[5] Here, sex is emphasized as if it is the single major factor that affects conversation, one that could be treated independently of other variables.

The problems of difference and dominance

As noted before, the difference/cultural approach is presented as an alternative to the dominance/power-based approach, stating that power has little to do with what happens in conversation between *socially equal* females and males. This approach, then, will be applicable only with situations where 'women and men attempt to talk to each other as *friends and equals* in casual conversation' (Maltz and Borker 1982:212; emphasis added). This restriction is greater than it may seem. Not too many mixed-sex interactions actually satisfy this condition; besides, who are counted as 'friends' and 'equals' is open to a wide and complex range of interpretation. In any event, the framework cannot be used in contexts where status is involved, such as the classroom (Aries 1987; Treichler and Kramarae 1983), the workplace, communication between doctor and patient, salesperson and customer, mother and son, father and daughter, and even in some cases, between spouses.

Indeed, one may ask: When exactly do women and men interact as equals? It may be tempting to answer that friends would be equal. The difference/cultural approach responds to our need and desire to believe that essentially, women and men are socially equal. However, being social equals can mean two things: being socially equal in principle and being socially equal in reality. The former does not necessarily entail the latter. And when the concept of equality interacts with sex, I suggest that we have two levels to consider – an individual in relation to another individual and a member of one sex in relation to a member of either the same or different sex. Truly social equals must be equal in reality at both levels. And I assert that in cross-sex relationships this is impossible today in US society. As a female, I am seldom socially equal to someone who is male, even when we share other identities such as ethnicity, age, class, and education.

To illustrate, let us take the case of street remarks or unsolicited comments from strangers (Gardner 1980; Kissling 1991; Kramarae 1986b), a common form of mixed-sex interaction where social status is not likely to be so relevant, unless the occupation of either or both parties is obvious. These remarks occur almost exclusively in the form of males addressing females, and this asymmetry itself implies that there is some inequality involved here. Against the addressee's charge of insult or harassment, the addressee can justify himself by saying that it was only a compliment; he was trying to be nice and friendly; and no, of course he had no intention of dominance! But would he have said the same thing to a man? Would he have accepted a similar remark addressed to him by a woman as a compliment or a sign of friendliness? What gives him the right to do this act that cannot be reciprocated? It is the mere fact of his being male and the other being female that does; males and females are not, in this sense, equal.

The problem I find with the difference/cultural approach is that it does not consider this level where male dominance exists regardless of what the individual intends. It sees dominance as something that could be *misinterpreted* as existing in interaction, although not really there. The proponents of the difference/cultural approach state that although men's behavior in cross-sex conversation may seem to exercise dominance, the same behavior functions to show intimacy with male friends; therefore, the male dominance is not intended but a result of cultural difference and miscommunication.

The proponents seem to consider that the lack of intention means that dominance does not really occur. They regard dominance as a matter of interpretation, dominance is seen as being in the same category as evaluative judgements such as 'weakness,' 'passivity,' and 'deficiency,' the difference being only that the latter were how females' behaviors were interpreted according to male norms, whereas the former is how males are interpreted according to female norms. It seems that either the judgmental attribute 'dominating' had been confounded with the act of dominance or the two had been equated. True, one's comments can be falsely interpreted as being dominating without the *intention* to dominate, but dominance occurs or does not occur, regardless of intention. The cross-cultural miscommunication approach *can* explain how and why men's behavior is seen as dominating by women, *can* deny that all men have the *intention* to dominate, and *can* say that the attribute 'men are dominating' is not necessarily true, and these are important issues that had not been adequately raised by the dominance/power-based approach. But it *cannot* say that male dominance does not occur as a mechanism in interaction.

The failure to distinguish *dominance* as a social phenomenon from *dominating* as a judgmental attribute may have occurred because of the following reasons. First, Maltz and Borker themselves had not done any empirical research using the difference/cultural approach to analyze mixed-sex interactions. Their cross-cultural framework was developed relying mostly on works examining same-sex interactions. Second, Tannen, another major proponent of the different/cultural approach, also primarily used studies of same-sex interactions to support her claims. A pattern of inequality and dominance between the sexes is hardly likely to appear in same-sex conversations. It is empirical research on female-male conversation that finds patterns of dominance (DeFrancisco 1990b, 1991; Edelsky 1981; Fishman 1983; Kollock, Blumstein and Schwartz 1985; West and Zimmerman 1983).

Because of US society's patriarchy, males are given the institutional power that in turn reinforces the social system, and this male dominance is guaranteed and maintained through the sexual division of labor. The difference/cultural approach *does* acknowledge the fact that in US society it is men whose talk is valued more and that it is usually women who are labelled negatively (e.g., as 'nags'), punished for their talk, and told to change (Tannen 1990c:15, 31, 75). The reason for this, however, is not pursued, and neither is the effect of this on daily interactions between women and men. If we deny the existence of a hierarchical organization of the sexes, what accounts for the asymmetrical treatment between the language use of women and men? And if we admit that there is a hierarchy, a power structure in the society, it is impossible to claim that it will not affect our everyday interaction. The difference/cultural approach deals with female–male communication as if it existed independently of this structure, as if the immediate context of the conversation was sufficient to fully grasp the meaning of the interaction. To the contrary, it is the sociocultural structure that makes the interaction relevant, and this behavior in turn maintains this structure. The issue here is not whether we cast blame on women or men for problems in communication, but it is whether we recognize that interactions between women and men are operating within a social hierarchy.

The observation of power structure can also be made when we look at the speech patterns acquired by girls and boys through same-sex interactions with peers. Girls' principles of cooperation, collaboration, equality, sharing and relating and showing empathy perfectly coincides with the 'typical' female characteristics: nurturing, supportive, expressive, emotive, friendly, relationship-oriented, and other similar adjectives, which are also associated with 'weakness' and 'powerlessness.' Boys' patterns, on the other hand, involve competing for and holding on to the floor, asserting, challenging, arguing, showing one's dominance and verbal aggressiveness, which are associated with 'powerful' and 'masculine' traits. Tannen's (1990a) own work investigating sex differences in ways conversational engagement was expressed showed results consistent with these stereotypical traits assigned to females and males. Maltz and Borker did not suggest the reason girls and boys learn these specific rules, for example why in girls' interaction it is unacceptable to be 'bossy' and why in boys' they must learn to assert dominance. Socialization *per se* cannot sufficiently explain why gender traits are not symmetrically assigned.

As Cameron, McAlinden and O'Leary (1988:80) pointed out, it is not a coincidence that men can afford to be aggressive and hierarchically oriented conversationalists, whereas women are expected to provide conversational support. Nor does it seem to be a coincidence that men's roles are more likely to be those of the protector, the teacher, the expert, in relation to women (Tannen 1990c). The sexual division of labor shows a pattern that is too consistent with the pattern of dominance to assume that it occurred 'naturally.' The set of prescriptions females and males learn as children follows the culture's norms of how females and males should behave, which, in turn, is in line with the positions in which women and men are placed in the social hierarchy. The sexual division of labor in conversation is not a mere result of cultural differences. The difference, by virtue of its function of creating the expectation that women will naturally try harder to involve men in the talk, whereas men will look aloof and disengaged in the eyes of women, reinforces the pattern that women will (and must) do more work in the conversation than men. If we do not consider why it is the women who are supposed to do more work to show that they are engaged (and are called 'bitches' if they refuse to, are called 'nags' if the job is not done appropriately, but get no credit for doing it right), we are led to justifying this inequality and legitimizing the privilege given to men to toil less in conversation.

Another question arises when we focus our attention on the 'miscommunication,' which is said to be caused by the cultural differences between the sexes. The difference/cultural approach considers the miscommunication as the end result of the female–male interaction, as something problematic for both sexes and as something that can be solved. That is the reason, it is argued, why it is important to make a cross-cultural comparison and come up with a list of differences; for if we understood, or at least became aware of, each other's different ways and assumptions better, we would be able to see the cause of miscommunication and refrain from making negative attributions to individuals (Tannen 1986, 1990b, 1990c). Yet it seems that it is necessary to go a step further from the causal analysis of the phenomenon, to see the *consequences* of miscommunication. The unstated assumption is that, between social equals, miscommunication will produce equally negative results for both parties involved.

But how accurate is this really? Tannen's anecdotal examples of female–male miscommunication (1986, 1990c) give me the impression that women have more to lose from the miscommunication than their male partners. This is so partly because of the very nature of women's and men's 'conversational styles' as Tannen puts it. Take, for example, a situation where a women starts telling her husband about some troubles she had at work (from Tannen 1986). According to her rules of intimacy, she expects her husband to show understanding, reassure her that she is not alone in having trouble, and maybe share his own problems with her. Instead, he, according to his rules of expressing solidarity in conversation, cracks jokes, sidetracks her story, and offers solutions to her problem. She then feels trivialized and thinks he's claiming one-upmanship; he then feels frustrated, not understanding why she got upset. What is the consequence of this miscommunication? She may feel that he does not respect her, he is putting her down, he is insensitive, too logical and rational, and so on. He, on the other hand, may feel that she cannot deal with the problem by herself, does not understand humor, is unreliable or irrational because she says she has a problem but does not want any advice. These attributions made to each other are quite consistent with the negative stereotypes of men and women, but according to the cultural norms that value logic and rationality, her judgement of him does not imply that he is inferior to her, but his judgement of her does imply that she is to him. In addition, the person who actually gets his needs fulfilled, as Troemel-Ploetz (1991:495) pointed out, is the man – who 'solved a problem and presented his solution,' who 'did what he needed to do,' whereas the woman 'did not get what she needed in her situation.'

For women, in addition to these psychological damages, there are more materialistic concerns involved in the outcomes of the miscommunication. In US society, it is usually the men who are in control of the resources – who make more money, have more physical power, are in a more authoritative or a higher social position – thus it is more likely to be men who can reward or punish women for their behavior.

If miscommunication is no one's 'fault' and is something that can be analyzed as mutual misunderstanding of well meant behavior, why is it that casualties are most often heavier on women than on men? Acquaintance rape and wife abuse could, with the miscommunication approach, be termed as extreme cases of such miscommunication (Henley and Kramarae 1991). Not only are women victims of physical violence, but they are also victims of blame and accusation for 'asking for it.' It would be absurd to say that these were caused by unfortunate misunderstandings between social equals who did not happen to share the same rules for interpreting certain behavior. An analysis of miscommunication must take into consideration who gets what they want, who is punished, who is forgiven, and in what ways – both on the individual level and on the societal level – after the miscommunication. And again, there is the issue of power involved. Whether manifested in the form of conversational rules, cultural values, possession of resources, or social norms, there is institutional power owned only by men that affects the result of miscommunication. Men's power allows them to 'misunderstand' women's meanings without getting penalized for it, and also gives them the right to penalize women for misinterpreting men's behavior. As Henley and Kramarae (1991: 19–20) noted:

> Hierarchies determine whose version of the communication situation will prevail; whose speech style will be seen as normal; who will be required to learn the communication style, and interpret the meaning of the other; whose language style will be seen as deviant, irrational, and inferior; and who will be required to imitate the other's style in order to fit into the society. Yet the situation of sex difference is not totally parallel: sex status intercuts and sometimes contrasts with other statuses; and no other two social groups are so closely interwoven as men and women.

The approach that dismisses this aspect and only focuses on differences has the danger of being used to legitimize blatantly misogynist behavior on the ground that it is a case of innocent miscommunication caused by cultural differences.

Conclusion: treating gender as a social construct

[. . .]

To talk about gender is to talk about women and men as composing socio-cultural groups, and the main force that constructs these two groups as different is the difference in the position they are placed in within the social hierarchy. If *difference* and *dominance* are treated as different perspectives of looking at sex, we will only get two different pictures from two different angles. We would not be able to get a holistic, multidimensional view. Difference and dominance (and there may be other dimensions) should be seen as simultaneously composing the construct of gender.

The problem of how to conceptualize gender has so far been dealt with in most language research in a too simplistic way. This comes from a super-ficial view of sex – the categories of females and males are seen as prelinguistic variables (Kramarae 1986a) biologically assigned to individuals at birth – and a failure to recognize that gender is in fact a social construct (Kessler and McKenna 1978; Kramarae 1986a; Rakow 1987). We do not become socialized as females or males because we were born female or male. At birth we are assigned to one or the other gender according to our genital organs, but after our initial gender assignment is made, how we are treated and raised is not dependent upon whether we have a vagina or not (a fact that is not obvious under usual circumstances) (Kessler and McKenna 1978). We learn female rules because we are socially labeled 'female' (from how we are dressed and addressed, etc.) – through the process of 'sex catego-rization' (West and Zimmerman 1987) – and we become female through learning and obeying those rules. West and Zimmerman (1987: 126–7) main-tained that gender is 'a routine, methodical, and recurring accomplishment' and that it is 'the activity of managing situated conduct in light of norma-tive conceptions of attitudes and activities appropriate for one's sex category.' We are *doing* gender (Rakow 1987; West and Zimmerman 1983, 1987) through gendered activity. '[A] person's gender is not simply an aspect of what one is, but, more fundamentally, it is something that one *does*, and does recurrently, in interaction with others' (West and Zimmerman 1987: 140). Thus, regardless of our own intentions, the consequences of our behavior must always be seen in the context of the society that defines gender. In US society's system (as well as in many others), part of being female consists of being the dominated, weaker sex. And the difference between women and men is constructed as a fact to reinforce the construction of gender, meaning that the appropriate doing of gender means the reproduction of 'the institutional arrangements that are based on sex category' (West and Zimmerman 1987: 146).

Gender is one major construct that organizes our world and our social life. It involves all human beings; every individual, after all, cannot escape being categorized as either female or male. But it must also be remembered that gender is so salient *because* it is a *social construct*, something that we do in interaction and not something that is based on nature or biology,[6] And it does not exist independently of other social factors such as region, ethnicity, age, class, sexual orientation, and religion; these elements are constantly in interaction. The issue at hand is not whether we should take the dominance/power-based approach or the difference/cultural approach or both approaches to analyze sex differences in discourse. Rather, it is how we can come up with a framework that allows us to see gender as a holistic and dynamic concept regarding language use – a framework that allows us to see how we, in the social context, are *doing* gender through the use of language.

Notes

1   Throughout this article, I distinguish between the use of *sex* and *gender*. The convention today is that sex is biological and gender is sociocultural (Schlegel 1989). I have used *sex* to refer to the use of female–male dichotomy as a 'prelinguistic variable,' as a 'set category from birth' (Kramarae 1986a). I have used *gender* to signify that the female–male dichotomy is 'man-made' and socially constructed.
2   Hereafter, unless stated otherwise, all reference to women, men, and language will signify women, men, and English used by the majority of those living in the United States.
3   Maltz and Borker (1982) and Tannen's works use 'cross-sex communication' to indicate the interaction between female and male, which they use parallel with 'cross-cultural communication.' However, the term *cross-cultural* must be distinguished from the term *intercultural*, as is discussed later.
4   Therefore, Maltz and Borker's claims should not be extended to females and males who do not belong to the mainstream American culture. However, it is not clear to what extent the general framework of the difference/cultural approach has been regarded by others as universally applicable. It is very often the case that whenever a framework for analysis is presented using American samples, it is assumed to be universal until proven otherwise.
5   In Tannen's analysis of conversation at a Thanksgiving dinner (1984, also cited in 1986), the difference in rules for expressing involvement and solidarity is shown to cause misinterpretation of each other's intention and to lead to the perceived conversational dominance of one group, Jewish New Yorkers, who had more expressive ways of showing involvement. She did not, however, report any sex differences. What then, is the relationship

among the cultural factors that produce these differences such as regional difference, ethnicity, class, age, and sex? Tannen has drawn an analogy between ethnicity and sex, regarding them both as culture in that they produce different conversational styles. But she has failed to address the fact that ethnicity and sex are not mutually exclusive categories. An individual's conversational style is neither a product solely of her or his sex or ethnicity nor can it be adequately analyzed as such.

6   But because one's sex category is the base of doing gender, the social order reinforced by the gendered activity is often thought to reflect 'natural differences' between female and male, which then legitimizes the hierarchical arrangements as being 'natural' (see West and Zimmerman 1987).

Reprinted from *Language in Society* 21, 1992.

New directions: performing gender

Chapter 21

Jennifer Coates

'THANK GOD I'M A WOMAN': THE CONSTRUCTION OF DIFFERING FEMININITIES

THE TWO MOST IMPORTANT THINGS being accomplished in the talk of women friends are *friendship* and *femininity*. Here I want to focus on femininity and on the role of talk in constructing us as gendered beings, as women. (*Femininity* is a problematic word, because of the everyday connotations of the adjective *feminine*. By *femininity* I mean the abstract quality of being feminine (just as masculinity is the abstract quality associated with being masculine): *doing femininity* can be paraphrased as 'doing being a woman'. The latter is a much clearer and less ambiguous way of saying what I mean, but far too clumsy to use repeatedly.)

Most of us spend very little, if any, time thinking about gender, and we are rarely aware of 'doing' (or 'performing') gender. (By 'doing'/ 'performing' gender, I mean presenting ourselves to others as a gendered being.) We take for granted that we are women. But we assume that 'being a woman' is a unitary and unified experience — in other words, we think of ourselves as 'I'/'me'; that is as singular. However, the woman we perform is not the same woman in all circumstances: we have all had the experience of feeling like a different person when we are in a different situation. For example, the 'me' that changes a baby's nappy or mashes a banana for a toddler is a different 'me' from the one who participates in a committee meeting or who poses as a life model at the local art school. Even in the same context we can change if something alters in that context. Liz's anecdote about her friend changing when her husband joined them for a drink is a good illustration of this:

Liz: when I was at the Health Club the other night/ and this girl I went with her husband turned up to have a drink with us in the bar / . and like the whole atmosphere changed when he arrived / <LAUGHS> [. . .] and she changed / she changed / she- she- she suddenly went tense / you know /

We change because different audiences require different performances – and also because we sometimes feel like playing a different role. All kinds of different 'self' are possible, because our culture offers us a wide range of ways of being – but all these ways of being are *gendered*. These possible selves are not different kinds of person, but different kinds of *woman*. Moreover, the alternative versions of femininity available to the woman in my recordings are specific to the so-called 'developed' world at the end of the twentieth century.

A range of femininities

In this section I shall look at a few examples from the conversations to show what I mean by 'doing' or 'performing' femininity, and to give a sense of the range of femininities available to girls and women in Britain today.

The first example comes from a conversation where three sixteen-year-old girls are commenting on the appearance of the fourth, Sarah, who is trying on Gwen's make-up.

[Sarah tries on some of Gwen's make-up]
Gwen: doesn't she look really nice?
Kate: yes /
Emily: she DOES look nice /

Gwen: ⌈ I think with the lipstick
Kate: you should wear make-up ⌊ more often . Sarah /

Gwen: it looks good /   ⌈ Sarah your lips . s- suit lipstick /
Kate: |
Emily: yeah looks ⌊ nice

Gwen: ((I'm saying)) what you said- big lips suit ⌈ lipstick /
Kate: oohh yes / |
Emily: ⌊ you should be

Gwen: yeah / looks good on me /
Kate: ⌈ share it /   yeah /
Emily: ⌊ a model / models have big lips /

Gwen: Sarah you look really nice /
Kate:
Emily:

In this talk, the girls are overtly complimenting Sarah. This is part of the routine support work that girls and women do with each other as friends. At the same time they are co-constructing a world in which the putting on and wearing of make-up is a normal part of doing femininity, and looking nice/looking good is an important goal. In this world, the size of your features – your eyes, your lips – is highly salient, and the fashion model is a significant figure, with high status.

The next example also comes from the talk of younger speakers, girls of fifteen. But they are doing a different sort of femininity. Jessica, Becky and Hannah are talking about a crisis which occurred on the school trip (a trip which Ruth and Claire didn't go on).

[Talking about disastrous time on school trip]

Jess: I can't believe that night / I mean I can't believe ((xx))-

---

Becky: I can't- no I can't believe it either / <u>we were all crying</u> /
<AMAZED>

---

3 *Becky:*   I couldn't be ⌈ lieve it /   everybody ⌈ was /
  Ruth: ⌊ who was crying?
  Hannah: ⌊ everybody /
  Jess: apart from me /

Becky: yeah / <LAUGHING>
Ruth: ((not but)) what were you crying about?
Jess: I was in bed / <LAUGHTER>

Becky: because- ((well)) I was crying because Hannah was crying /

---

6 *Becky:*   Hannah was crying because Ben was um a *sexist bastard*
          /<LAUGHS>
Hannah: <GIGGLES>

Becky: ⌈ and Vicky was crying because Susan was going to be sent home /
Hannah: ⌊ % oh he was REALly horrible to me /%

Becky: and I was crying because ⌈ she never cries /
Clarie: ⌊ did she get sent home?

---

9 *Becky:*   no /
Hannah: and I was crying because Vicky ⌈ was crying /   no /
Claire: ⌊ did she get sent home?

The three friends who are describing what happened agree on the significance of crying. They recount this episode in a tone of amusement, even pride: they seem to be saying 'we're real girls'. The phrase *was/were crying* occurs ten times in all (twelve times if we include those utterances with an elliptted verb, such as *everybody was*, stave 3). The repetition of this phrase functions to emphasize that crying was the key feature of this particular night, and to underline the fact that everyone was involved. Both Becky and Hannah say that they were crying, and they both claim that Vicky was crying. (Jessica, the only one who was not crying, explains, *I was in bed*.) Their reasons for their crying focus on friendship: Becky cried because Hannah was upset; Vicky cried because she thought her friend was being sent home. The only boy mentioned – Ben – was *not* crying: he is one of the reasons that Hannah was crying. Crying is constructed here as a gendered behaviour, something girls do at times of emotional crisis.

Crying is a stereotypical way of performing femininity. This version of femininity continues into adulthood, though, as the next example shows, adult women have some reservations about expressing their feelings in this way.

[Anna arrives from work late and explains why she is upset]

Anna: I just had such a bad week / and then my boss just stood in the office tonight and told me and his deputy that we're both crap managers basically /

Sue: oh /

Liz: oh god /

[. . .]

Anna: I get so angry at myself for crying / but . I wish I could just . ooh! punch him on the nose or something /

Sue: you shouldn't let it get to you /

Anna: ⌈ I know / but-

Liz: ⌊ at least you CAN cry / because I think you should let it out /

Anna: but it's bad / because it ⌈ them think

Sue: makes | I know /

⌊ <GROANS>

Liz: it's when you don't ⌊ cry /

Anna: you're a wimp /

Sue: yeah /

Liz: yeah /

Anna, like Becky and Hannah, talks about an episode that is characterized by strong emotion, which she responded to by crying. Her use of the powerful phrase *crap manager* to describe herself reveals how negatively she has interpreted what her boss said to her. (Later she says glumly, *maybe he's right, maybe I am a crap manager*.) The three friends demonstrate that they share the assumption that if someone significant, such as your boss, is displeased with you, then crying is a 'normal' reaction. But they talk about this reaction with more ambivalence than Becky and her friends. Anna wonders if crying was the appropriate response to her boss. She wonders if she should have punched him on the nose (thus revealing an awareness that anger rather than sadness might have been her chief emotion). Liz supports her in her account of herself, taking the position that it's better to let it out, but Sue's advice is to stay calm (*you shouldn't let it get to you*). Liz implicitly alludes to the gendered nature of crying when she says, *at least you CAN cry*, implying that there are those who can't – men. Anna herself worries that crying is a weak move: it may perform femininity but it also performs power-lessness (*it makes them think you're a wimp*), which is not the impression Anna wants to give to her male boss.

In the next example these same three friends talk about assertiveness training.

[Topic: *Assertiveness course*]
Anna: Linda's going on an assertiveness training course at work /

Anna: ⎡ I ought to go with her /
Sue: ⎣ John's mum   went on one /
Liz: I'd love to go on one /

Anna: assertiveness? =
Sue: = assertiveness / and she said 'I only – I'm only doing it
Liz: I really would /

Sue: so that I can be like you Susan' / I said 'But I'm not assertive' / I mean she's more assertive than anyone I know /

There seems to be an underlying assumption here that assertiveness training is for women: both the people mentioned in association with it are female – Linda from Anna's office and John's mum (Sue's mother-in-law). (However, Sue's claim that her mother-in-law is *more assertive than anyone I know* is ambiguous: does *anyone* refer to all Sue's acquaintances, or just to women she knows?) Both Anna and Liz express positive attitudes to the idea of assertiveness training: they both say they would like to go on a course. Sue is more sceptical. Her statement *John's mum went on one* communicates 'everyone's doing it these days', and her brief story about what John's mother said to her reveals a profound gap between John's mother's reading of Sue as assertive and her own sense of herself as unassertive, with a parallel discrepancy in her sense of her mother-in-law as very assertive and not in need of any training. As women move into more prominent positions in the work-place, we have to juggle with our self-presentation to find ways to perform ourselves as both competent and at the same time feminine. Whether assertiveness is the answer is unclear; certainly the rhetoric that women need some kind of training perpetuates the idea that it is women who don't fit in the public sphere and therefore women who have to change.

The final example is an instance of a woman sharing her sense of achievement with her friends. Janet has been for interview; the following extract shows her responding to her friend's request to 'tell us about it'.

[Janet's job interview]
Meg: did you get your job?
Mary: oh did you go for a job? <HIGH, SURPRISED>

Meg: ((xxxx))
Janet: ((xxxx))
Jen: what job?
Mary: tell us about it /

Janet: I was- four people got interviewed the same day as I did /
Mary: ((four

Ann: hello Bea /
Janet: and they rang me up- that was on the . Tuesday /
Mary: other people /))

<GENERAL NOISE INVOLVING BEA'S ARRIVAL>

Janet: they've still got one more person to interview /⌈ somebody got
Mary: ⌊ what job is it?

Janet: mugged on the day of the inter ⌈view / and so they said they
                                        │ were
Helen: ⌊oh hell /

Janet: interviewing her at the end of last week / cos they couldn't
        not

Janet: interview her just cos she'd got mugged=
Meg: ⌈ so
Bea: = no that would be ⌊ ((very

Janet: =they told me that there was
Meg: anyway they told you that apart from that=
Bea: unfair/))

Janet: only me and her=   =it's external affairs officer for the
Mary: =what job is it?=

Janet: Regional Health Authority=
Mary: =oh I remember / I remember you were- yes/

Janet: it's quite a good job=   =I was really good in this interview
Mary: =yes/
Helen: yes=

Janet: because I was so unbothered about whether I got the job / I think
----

```
Janet: that's the actual ⌈crunch of ⌈the thing=  =it takes the pressure
Helen:                    ⌊ mhm/    ⌊          =mhm=         mhm/
Jen:                                ⌊Meg's told me that/
------------------------------------------------------------------------
Janet:  off you enTIRELy if you-   if you know it's not all or nothing/
Helen:                     yes/
------------------------------------------------------------------------
```

Although the five other women present all contribute in various ways to stretch of talk, Janet's story is the focus of attention. It's important to note that women friends allow each other space not just to complain or talk about problems, but also to talk about successes and feelings of achievement. In this example, Janet asserts that the job is *quite a good job* and that she was *really good* in the interview. This is a much more forceful version of femininity, and the interest that Janet's friends display in the details of her story shows that this story has resonance for them all as potential job-seekers, women who want to succeed in the public world outside the home. At the same time, Janet explains her good self-presentation in terms of not caring about the outcome (because she already has a job). The modesty of this claim balances her description of herself as 'really good'. (Compare this with Sue's denial of herself as being assertive.) The balancing act that Janet carries out here shows that even with close friends, presenting oneself as competent rather than weak or vulnerable has to be done with care; women have to avoid the accusation of 'showing off'.

All these examples, as well as showing female speakers talking *about* issues connected with femininity and self-presentation, also show girls and women *doing* femininity. They present themselves as different kinds of woman, concerned both about their external appearance and about social performance, sometimes more emotional, sometimes more hard-nosed. The talk we do in our daily lives gives us access to these different modes of being, these different versions of femininity. This is because language plays a crucial part in structuring our experience.

Language and the construction of different 'selves'

It would be more accurate to say that *discourse*,[1] rather than language, plays a crucial part in structuring our experience. The whole idea of 'language' is something of a fiction: what we normally refer to as 'language' can more realistically be seen as heterogeneous collection of discourses.[2] Each of us has access to a range of discourses, and it is these different discourses which give us access to, or enable us to perform, different 'selves'. A discourse can be conceptualized as a 'system of statements which cohere around common meanings and values' (Hollway 1983: 131). So, for example, in contemporary Britain there are discourses which can be labelled 'conservative' – that is, discourses which emphasize values and meanings where the status quo is cherished; and there are discourses which can be labelled 'patri-archal' — that is, discourses which emphasize meanings and values which assume the superiority of males. Dominant discourses such as these appear 'natural': they are powerful precisely because they are able to make invis-ible the fact that they are just one among many different discourse.

Theorizing language in this way is still new in linguistics (to the extent that many linguists would not regard analysis in terms of discourses as being part of linguistics).[3] One of the advantages of talking about discourses rather than about language is that the concept 'discourse' acknowledges the value-laden nature of language. There is no neutral discourse: whenever we speak we have to choose between different systems of meaning, different sets of values. This approach allows me to show how language is implicated in our construction of different 'selves': different discourses position us in different ways in relation to the world.

Using the phrase *discourses position us* gives the impression that speakers are passive, are at the mercy of different discourses. But language use is dynamic: we make choices when we speak; we can resist and subvert. Social and cultural change are possible precisely because we do not use the discourses available to us uncritically, but participate actively in the construction of meaning. Talk is particularly significant in our construction and reconstruc-tion of ourselves as women, as gendered subjects. As Simone de Beauvoir said, 'One is not born a woman, one becomes one', and we go on 'becoming' all through life. This is done in many different ways, through all aspects of behaviour, through the way we dress, the way we move, but particularly through the way we talk. Each time we speak, we are saying, 'This is (a version of) me', and, as I've argued, we are also saying, 'I am a woman', because the 'I' / 'me' is always gendered. How this is done has been illus-trated briefly in the opening section of the chapter. In the rest of the chapter I propose to re-examine the conversations of these women friends to explore some of the tensions arising from competing versions of what it is to be a woman, and to pinpoint the resistant discourses available to women today.

Competing discourses

To clarify what I mean by discourse, and to demonstrate how discourses can position us differently in relation to the world, I'll begin by looking at a few brief examples. The first two both come from conversations about mothers. In the first, Meg is talking about the function of funerals:

> *Meg*: I would see it [the funeral] as honouring her memory in some way /

The second comes at a point in conversation when Sue has stated that she phones her mother but her mother never phones her.

> *Sue:* ⌈ ((xx)) I'm not very close to my mother really /
> *Liz:*   ⌊ cos most mothers are a pain in the bum /

In the first example, Meg positions herself as a loving and dutiful daughter. She and her friends discuss whether it would be taboo to miss your mother's funeral. They draw on a dominant discourse where the family is revered and parents are to be honoured, a discourse which upholds the taboo against missing your mother's funeral. The second example represents mothers in a very different way. Here Sue and Liz resist dominant discourses of the family and express feelings which reveal a different picture of mother–daughter relations. This discourse challenges the hegemonic idea that all families are happy and all parents benevolent. We have all probably experienced both positions, and may even hold both views simultaneously. This is possible because of the existence of alternative discourses, alternative ways of thinking about the world.

The next two examples also draw on discourses relating to the family; they both come from conversations about children. In the first, Pat tells Karen about the end-of-term plays at her children's primary school.

> *[Topic: End-of-term school plays]*
> *Karen:* did Peter do his song?   was he good?
> *Pat:*   yes/   he was marvellous/
> --
> *Karen:*   oh the-
> *Pat:*   he was marvellous/ every kid in it was marvellous/
> --
> *Karen:* I think they always are/

The second example comes at a moment in a conversation between Anna, Liz and Sue where they have been talking about a family they all know with difficult children. Their expression of negative feelings about these particular children (*they were ghastly children*) leads them to consider their attitude to children in general.

> *Liz:*   I think is's a- . a fallacy as well that you like every child/
> --
> *Anna:*   no/ . that's right/
> *Sue:*   mhm/   I still quite often don't like
> *Liz:*   cos you don't
> --
> *Anna:*   <LAUGHS>
> *Sue:*   children/ <LAUGHS>
> *Liz:*   actually I think you particularly dislike your own/

Again, we can see the clash between the dominant discourse, which says that children are 'marvellous', and where all mothers take pride in their child's achievements, and an alternative discourse which asserts that not all children are likeable (in fact, some are *ghastly*) and that it is not compulsory for adults to like all children. For women speakers, particularly women who are themselves mothers (Sue and Liz), this is a very subversive discourse. Dominant ideas of femininity (and of motherhood) do not allow for the expression of negative feelings about children. Anna, Sue and Liz support each other in sustaining a radically different view, one which starts with the proposition 'you don't like every child' (Liz, supported by Anna), which moves on to 'I quite often don't like children' (Sue),[4] and then to 'I think you particularly dislike your own' (Liz), a very strong position which directly challenges the idea of women as living, caring, nurturing beings for whom having children is the ultimate experience of their lives.

Finally, her are two examples drawn from talk about the body and appearance. The first arises in a conversation where Pat shows Karen her new sundress and they discuss the new style and whether it makes you look fat.

> [Topic: New sundress]
> *Karen*: you'll look at yourself in the mirror and you'll think 'God I look fat' /

The second example comes in a conversation where Hannah has called Jessica's thighs fat, Jessica has protested at this and Becky (in the role of peace-maker) has insisted that hers are unpleasantly thin (*mine are skinny as a pencil – ugh!*). Hannah then suggests that they would both be happier if Jessica gave some of her fat to Becky.

> [Topic: Size of Jessica and Becky's thighs]
> *Hannah*: well if you think your thighs are fat and you think your thighs are thin / you just scrape off a bit of fat and plaster it on /

Both these examples draw on an ideology which insists that women should maintain their bodies at a size which accords with current fashion (these days, this means slim). Hannah takes up a resistant position in relation to that view, by making fun of Jessica and Becky. Karen and Pat by contrast adopt a discourse which positions them as accepting the dominant ideology. Their conversation is full of references to size and appearance – Karen says later in the same conversation (with reference to some dresses she's seen in the market) *the thing is with them you've got to be ever so skinny I think to wear them*. Moreover, where the ideology by this dominant discourse clashes with reality – in other words, when the perfect body constructed by the dominant discourse doesn't match our actual bodies – we tend to assume that it is we who are at fault. Note who Pat and Karen use laughter to help them deal with the tension produced by the clash between the ideal and the real:

> *Karen*: I've only got about four inches between my bust and my waist /
> *Pat*:   yeah /
> --

Karen: <LAUGHS>
Pat: <LAUGHS> you sound quite deformed <LAUGHS>

These examples give some idea of the conflict surrounding contemporary ideas of femininity. The dominant discourse constitutes women as loving, dutiful (in relation to parents), uncritical (in relation to children), and caring about our appearance, in particular by trying to stay slim. But as some of the examples illustrate, women are not passive in the face of this dominant ideology: we can resist by drawing on alternative discourses where we assert the right to say that sometimes we can't stand our mothers or sometimes our kids drive us mad, or where we mock the dominant view of ideal thigh size.

Competing views of men

The dominant discourses in our society teach us to see ourselves in relation to men. In so far as dominant discourses place men at the centre of the universe, then women are always marginal and only have meaning when fulfilling roles that are significant for men, as mother, as partner, as daughter. In this section I shall look at some of the ways in which women (and girls) talk about men. Our talk about men does powerful work in our construction of ourselves as (certain kinds of) feminine subject.[5] It is certainly noticeable that girls in their early teens start talking compulsively about boys, as part of the negotiation of identity involved in the transition from girlhood to womanhood. I'll begin with two examples from girls in my sample (Emily is sixteen years old, Becky fourteen):

> *[Talking about poster of pop star]*
> *Emily*: what a hunk!

> *[Talking about boy at school]*
> *Becky*: did you really know?   that I still fancied Damien?
> *Claire*:   what?
> *Jess*:   yeah /
> ---
> *Becky*: I was too embarrassed to admit it though /

Adolescent girls relate both to male fantasy figures such as singers and film stars, and to real boys (boys such as Damien, who they go to school with). Emily, in the first of these examples, is more outspoken in her admiration for the man pictured in the poster on Gwen's wall than Becky is about Damien in the second. Where the male in question is known, then there is embarrassment as well as more positive feelings. But both examples draw on vocabulary – *hunk, fancy* – that was not present in the girls' talk a few years earlier,[6] vocabulary which constitutes them as heterosexual feminine subjects.

When the adult women in my sample talk about men in their lives, we find the whole gamut of emotions from love through amused tolerance to anger and contempt. The first two examples both come from the interviews.[7]

> *[Talking about husband]*
> *Jill*:   in a funny way I suppose Roger's my best friend /

> *[Talking about husband]*
> *Mary*: well my partner's my friend you see / [. . .] if you like Dave's my best friend / so- so I feel totally relaxed with him / and [. . .] I look forward to doing more things together /

While Jill and Mary express very positive feelings about their partners, Pat's story about her partner in the next example is more critical. But despite her evaluation of his characteristic behaviour as *dreadful*, her feelings are clearly affectionate rather than hostile.

> *[Talking about husband]*
> *Pat*:   he gives me these little um . notes when he sends me shopping / you ought to see the notes I get with anything that I don't actually . deal with myself / like framing bits or anything like that / you get this long sort of paragraph / which more or less starts with 'Go out of the house / proceed down the road' <LAUGHS> you know /
> *Karen*:   I know /
> --
> *Pat*:   sometimes there's a map of where the shop is / and sometimes there's a little drawing of what the thing ought to look like / and I always play to the gallery by going into the shop and showing them the note / <LAUGHS>
> *Pat*:   ⌈ and they fall ⌈ about/
> *Karen*:   absolutely/ ⌊ why not/ ⌊ about/ that's right/
> --
> *Pat*:   dreadful /

Sue's criticism of her husband in the next example cannot be described as affectionate. But her complaints about the noisiness of his music-making (which is a recurrent feature of her conversations with Anna and Liz) occur against a background where John is seen by all three women as a good bloke, in comparison with men in Anna and Liz's lives. (For example, Anna comments at one point in the discussion of coupledom and relationships: *there's always a voice of reason I think with John, he's- he's very mature like that.*)

[Sue's husband's music gets louder]
Sue: I mean how can you live with this /
Liz: well I know it's difficult when

Sue: ⌈ oh it drives you insane/
Liz: you've got a man around ⌊ but-

The four examples I've given so far are all from speakers who are married. But among the women I've recorded are several who are divorced or separated. The next two examples come from moments in conversation where an estranged or ex-husband is the subject of conversation. (The first of these I'm including deliberately as a warning of the penalties which can be incurred by anyone unwise or unethical enough to record their friends surreptitiously.)[8]

[Discussing Jen's arrangements to get her ex-husband to help with her move to London]
Meg: I mean I shouldn't um rely on him for something as vital as that/

[. . .] <JEN LEAVES ROOM TO ANSWER PHONE>

Sally: your faces when <u>Jennifer said that- that Paul was going to do</u>
Meg: <LAUGHS--

Sally: <u>the move</u>/ .hh <u>I wish I'd got a camera</u> / <LAUGHING> ((it)) was
Meg:---->   <LAUGHS----

Sally: sort of- ((xx)) in total disbelief/   I think the most difficult
Meg: ------>   mhm/

Sally: is- is that when you've loved someone/ you- you half the time
        you forget their faults ⌈ don't you- and still maybe love them/. . .
Meg: ⌊ yeah/

Note the way Meg hedges her critical comments at the beginning of this example, prefacing what she says with *I mean* and then phrasing her utterance in a hypothetical way with *would*. Hedges are necessary as this is a very face-threatening subject. It's also noticeable how protective this group of friends are of one of their number: they clearly think that I (Jen) am acting foolishly in trusting my ex-husband. But Sally avoids outright criticism of me by positioning herself in a discourse where women are viewed as making bad decisions or acting stupidly because their judgement is clouded by emotion. While this discourse provides women with an excuse for bad decisions or stupid behaviour, it positions us as emotional, as nonrational (in contrast with men, who are positioned as rational).

The second of these examples focuses more explicitly on the male: Liz and Sue together describe Liz's husband's behaviour after he left Liz and the two children.

307

[Vindictiveness of estranged husbands]

Liz: I was like terrified/ I thought I was going to ((be)) on the
⌜ streets/
Sue: ⌞ I think he was so horrible as well/

Liz: ⌜ he was not supportive at all/
Sue: ⌞ I mean he was really nasty / but he wasn't even not supportive/

Liz: ⌜ oh he was vindictive/he really want me to suffer/
Sue: he was . vindic ⌞ tive/   yeah/

Liz: ⌜ he really wanted-   yeah/
Sue: ⌞ and his children/that was the thing/his children to go with
----
Sue: it/ oh . horrible/

Here, Sue and Liz explicitly label the man as bad, using words like *horrible, nasty, vindictive*. But at the same time, the man is portrayed as active, the women as more passive: *I was like terrified, he really wanted me to suffer*. And it is only because of Sue's intervention that Liz amends the weaker *not supportive* to the stronger *vindictive*. (Similarly, Becky's words in the example we looked at earlier, *Hannah was crying because Ben was a sexist bastard*, label the boy Ben as bad, drawing on a feminist antisexist discourse, but present Hannah's response as weak.)

The final example comes from the discussion of coupledom analysed in some detail at the end of the last chapter. During the course of this talk, Sue, Liz and Anna ponder whether it is better to be in a couple or independent. Anna comes down on the side of independence:

[Discussing the relative merits of coupledom and independence]

Anna: I just sometimes think I probably never will get married again /
         or never be with anybody again / cos I just love my life on my
         own /

While the women in these examples are positioned in a variety of ways – as women who love men, as women who are critical of men, as women who prefer to live alone – they all share the dominant world view in which heterosocial relations are seen as the norm. In other words, for all these women (and for the girls in my sample) the construction of themselves as feminine involves simultaneously the construction of themselves as heterosocial. As is typical of dominant discourses, this process is virtually invisible: this means that criticism or resistance becomes very difficult. And because my sample contains no women who were lesbian at the time these recordings were made, then a non-heterosocial discourse is not voiced.

Resistant discourses

However, resistance to the androcentric norms of the dominant culture does occur. There is evidence in the conversations that the women in my sample have access not only to dominant (androcentric) discourses but also to resistant discourses, particularly feminist discourses, which offer alternative positions, alternative ways of being a woman. In the final example above, we heard Anna resisting the normative pressures to live as part of a (hetero-sexual) couple. Here are four more examples of women using resistant discourses.

The first draws on a psychotherapeutic discourse which challenges the construct 'the happy family'.

> [Topic: Anna's mother and her sister Diana]
> Anna: but now looking back on it she [A's mother] was really bad to her/
> Sue: mhm/
> Liz: why?
> ---
> Anna: and ⌈Diana says that-
> Sue: ⌊it's funny because your mum holds up the thing
> Liz: I wonder why/
> ---
> Anna: yeah/   ⌈ that's right/ well that's
> Sue: of the happy family quite a lot doesn't ⌊ she?
> ---
> Anna: you have to don't you? that's the ⌈ conspiracy/
> Sue: yeah/   ⌊ that's it/

Anna resists the normative pressures to speak of her family and of relationships between her mother and her siblings in glowing terms. In the conversation preceding this extract she self-discloses to her friends about some of the problems in her family; then, with Sue's support, she goes on to challenge the idea of the happy family and names the discourse that promotes it a 'conspiracy'.

The next example shows how women friends help each other to struggle against prevailing discourses. Helen challenges me – and the discourse I adopt – by refusing to accept my description of recent events in my life.

> [Talking about jobs]
> Helen: you haven't been applying for jobs as well have you?
> Jen: yes/
> ---
> Helen: oh have you?   that's right/ so-
> Jen: there's one at Cambridge/ <LAUGHS>
> ---
> Helen: so have you applied ⌈ for it?   ⌈ oh no but
> Jen: Cambridge! <LAUGHING>   ⌊ oh what hubris/ ⌊ %honestly%

```
Helen:  that's TERRIBLE though isn't it? <HIGH, APPALLED> I mean
Jen:
-----------------------------------------------------------------
Helen: ⌈ you can't imagine any men sitting round/ . saying about their
Jen:   ⌊ oh you mean I'm being ((xx))-
-----------------------------------------------------------------
Helen:  applications that it's hubris/
Jen:                              oh all right/ <MOCK GRUMPY>
-----------------------------------------------------------------
Helen:  you're conditioned to think that/
Jen:
```

Helen draws on a liberal feminist discourse which resists the idea that women and men do things differently or have different abilities. She also draws on the feminist idea that socialization rather than biology determines our sense of ourselves as inferior, arguing that we are socialized to internalize such views – *you're conditioned to think that*. In this brief dialogue we see how friends can challenge each other's views and resist each other's discourses at the same time as supporting each other, since in effect Helen is saying, 'You have as good a right as any man to apply for a job at Cambridge University'. We can accept each other's challenges – and can therefore adopt more radical positions – because we feel supported and validated by each other.

The next example comes from the Oxton group's discussion of child abuse. This discussion, like the one between Anna, Sue and Liz above, focuses on the family, but this time the emphasis is on the tendency to blame the mother when families malfunction.

> *[Discussion of child abuse]*
> Meg: one of the things often said about the incestuous family is that
>   um it's really the mother's fault one way or another / [. . .]
>   I mean I'm so terrified of joining in the blaming of mothers /
>
> [. . .]
> Mary: but I mean so much research is male-dominated / I mean it's
>   just- it's staggering isn't it?

Here we find a group of women discussing a topic which forces them to consider the nature of patriarchy. They struggle to avoid adopting a more conventional discourse on the family and on sexuality, and draw on a feminist discourse to challenge conventional views, explicitly naming *the blaming of mothers* as the construction of a more patriarchal discourse, and using the phrase *male-dominated*, which allies them all with a feminist position which sees male–female relations in terms of dominance and oppression. (But it's interesting to note the presence of the phrase *the incestuous family*, a phrase which does the work of concealing *who* in the family abuses other members of that family, and thus a phrase which clearly serves patriarchal, not feminist, interests.)

The last example comes in a stretch of conversation where Liz and Anna have been telling anecdotes about men in their lives (brothers, ex-husbands) who have let them down or behaved badly.

```
[Talking about the inadequacy of some men]
Anna:  women are just vastly superior/              ⌈ thank god I'm
Liz:                        they ARE / VASTly        ⌊ a superior/
Sue:                        <LAUGHS--------------------------------
------------------------------------------------------------------
Anna:  a woman/ and not like that/
Liz:                      yeah/
Sue:   ----------------------------------------->
```

Anna's statement draws on a radical feminist discourse which claims that, far from being inferior, women are in fact superior. This is a very powerful discourse, since it positions women as being positive about themselves, it allows us to like ourselves and to say things like *thank god I'm a woman*. But Sue's laughter indicates that these three friends make these remarks fully aware of the discrepancy between what they are saying and dominant ideas about women and men. The laughter signals that they can amuse themselves by expressing this view to each other, but suggests that they maybe have doubts about its relevance to their lives in the outside world.

Tensions and contradictions

Given the range of discursive positions available to us, it is not surprising that we present ourselves in talk as different kinds of woman, sometimes more forceful and assertive, sometimes more passive and ineffectual. The clash between different positions produces tensions and contradictions in our talk, where competing discourses came into contact with each other. Earlier brief examples have illustrated that we draw on a range of discourses, but in this section I want to look at a few longer examples to show how different discourses coexist in a single conversation.

First, here's an extract from a conversation between Hannah, Becky, Claire and Jessica when they are fourteen years old. The topic is periods, and at this point they are talking about mood swings.

```
Hannah: everything seemed to be going wrong and everything/
it was horrible/ [ . . . ] it was really horrible
           ⌈ that day/
Jess:      ⌊ but you know when I ⌈ had that really bad . um
Claire:                          ⌊ do you get PMT ((xxx))
------------------------------------------------------------------
Hannah:                                             <LAUGHS>
Becky:                    yeah/ I'm a bitch/ <LAUGHS>        I'm
Jess:     premenstrual tension/
------------------------------------------------------------------
```

Hannah:	so I've noticed/ no-		no but ⌈ some-
Becky:	REally HORrible/	no but-	⌊ so whenever

Hannah:		='Right I might be horrible
Becky:	I'm on my period I say to Hannah um=	

Hannah:	to you but'=
Becky:	='Don't take any notice'/

This passage is part of a more lengthy chain of mutual self-disclosure on the subject of mood swings. The girls in turn tell anecdotes to illustrate how premenstrual tension affects them. Throughout this section of the conversation at least three discourses are simultaneously present: a medical discourse, a repressive discourse, and a more resistant feminist discourse. The friends choose words such as *premenstrual tension* in their talk about their periods; these words are part of a medical discourse. A feminist discourse expressing solidarity and sisterhood is realized through overlapping turns, expressions of agreement, and through the joint construction of text (Becky and Hannah share in constructing the utterance *so whenever I'm on my period I say to Hannah um 'Right I might be horrible to you but don't take any notice'*). The sequence of self-disclosing anecdotes (here we have the end of Hannah's and the beginning of Becky's) involving mirroring and exchange is another feature of this discourse. The third discourse present is a discourse of repression: the girls jointly represent themselves as beings who are *affected*, at the mercy of larger forces, rather than as *agents*, in control of their lives. This is realized through their choice of stative verbs: *was, had, got,* and through the use of negative words such as *horrible* and *bitch*. Through the use of these discourses the girls are simultaneously positioned as having solidarity with each other and as oppressed.

Contradictions are also apparent if we look at a longer extract from the conversation where Anna says, *women are just vastly superior*. The subject of men's inadequacy is part of the larger topic 'Relationships', and follows on from the discussion of the obedient husband and of coupledom. Anna tells a story about the break-up of her last relationship, and complains that men seem to find it hard to understand when a relationship is over. Liz responds with a story about her ex-husband who had come round the previous weekend to help her clear out her loft. She describes wryly how she had 'made a point of it being my loft and my rubbish', so she ends up doing most of the work, and as she leaves for her last trip to the dump she recounts how her ex-husband, now sitting watching football on television, got out a five pound note and asked her to buy him some fish and chips. Her point is that she considers such behaviour appalling (though she does in fact buy his fish and chips). Anna then tells a matching story about her brother (Mark) who had recently come and leaned against the kitchen door, complaining of depression, while she was 'humping twenty-five kilos of cement across the kitchen'. It is at this point that Anna says that women are superior:

```
Anna:  I mean in a way it doesn't upset me things like that any more/
       ⌈ cos I just laugh/ cos I think well .          women are just
Liz:   ⌊ no they don't upset you/ you laugh about it/ yes/
--------------------------------------------------------------------
Anna:  vastly superior/                        ⌈ thank god I'm a woman/ and
Liz:            they ARE/ VASTly               ⌊ superior/
Sue:             <LAUGHS--------------------------
--------------------------------------------------------------------
Anna:  not like that/
Liz:              yeah/
Sue:   --------------------->
```

This leads into a long discussion between the three friends about men and the reasons for some of them being so inadequate. It is this last section that I want to examine in some detail. The three friends move from a radical discourse which is self-affirming, which asserts the value of women, to an oppressive, woman-blaming discourse:

```
Anna:  why though why are boys like that? ⌈ why are they?
Sue:                                      ⌊ it must be ((about having the
Liz:                                                    boys ARE
--------------------------------------------------------------------
Anna:  I mean my mother- my mother and my youngest sister both ring
Sue:   xxx too x apart))
Liz:   like that/
--------------------------------------------------------------------
Anna:  Mark up regularly/ and my- my younger sister Felicity writes to
       him/ and she says . um 'We- Mummy and I are really worried
       about you cos you're so depressed/ and you know if there's any-
       thing we can do just give us a ring'/ and I said to her 'But it makes
       him worse'    =        ⌈ he's been like it since my father died/
Liz:            =yeah/⌊ it feeds it/       yeah/
Sue:            =yeah/
--------------------------------------------------------------------
Anna:  and that's over a year now/      and it all affected us very badly/
Liz:   yeah/                  yeah/
--------------------------------------------------------------------
Anna:  but you know life is to get on with=     =and the more you
Liz:   yeah/                           =yeah=
--------------------------------------------------------------------
Anna:  pander to him being depressed/ and telling him 'Oh poor thing
--------------------------------------------------------------------
Anna:  never mind'=              ⌈ he's going to get worse/
Liz:             = ⌈ the more he'll ⌊ revel in it/      yes/
Sue:             = ⌊ no he loves it/
--------------------------------------------------------------------
```

313

> *Anna:* ⌈ it makes me so cross/
> *Liz:* ⌊ that's right
> -
> *Anna:* and I think in a- in a w- in a way it's women who perpetuate
> that/ it's women who . despise weak men and then just produce
> more
> *Sue:* oh yeah/
> -
> *Anna:* of them/ and say to them you know 'Don't worry darling/ it'll all be
> all right/ and you don't have to-'
> *Sue:* 'I'll look after you'/ <LAUGHS>

Anna, focusing on the particular case of her brother, argues that it is her
mother who is to blame, and generalizes from this that women are to blame
for producing weak men. Liz and Sue go along with this argument. They
add minimal responses as well as more substantive forms of agreement;
they also jointly construct utterances with Anna: Anna's *the more you pander
to him . . .* is completed by Liz with *the more he'll revel in it*, and Anna's *it's
women who . . . say to them . . . 'Don't worry darling it'll be all right'* is completed
by Sue with *'I'll look after you'*. Liz then develops this woman-blaming theme
as follows, introducing the notion of the 'strong' woman.

> *Liz:* it's probably because everybody's- if he's had strong women in the
> -
> *Anna:* it probably is/ ⌈ it probably-
> *Sue:* oh god/ yes/ ⌊ that's right/
> *Liz:* house/ and other people- and other people have
> made ⌊ decisions
> -
> *Anna:* ⌈ yes/ it's awful I know/ I do appreciate that/ I mean
> *Liz:* FOR him ⌊ you see/
> -
> *Anna:* I'm quite bombastic/ <SUE EXITS TO GO TO LOO>

At this point, Anna starts to blame herself rather than her mother for his
brother's weakness. She includes herself in the category 'strong women' with
her apologetic statement *I'm quite bombastic*. This switch from mothers to
themselves is continued by Liz, who starts to talk about her worries about
her own son, who is away at boarding school.

> *Liz:* I worry that I'm too strong/ that's the rea- one of the reasons I
> -
> *Anna:* ⌈ yes/
> *Liz:* sent Dean away/ [. . .] because um I'm strong/
> and he ⌊ leans on me
> -
> *Anna:* Mark does it/ I mean ⌈ I- I pay all the bills/
> *Liz:* for decisions/ ⌊ yeah/
> -

Anna: when they won't give us an overdraft/ I negotiate the building
      society when they won't⌈ lend us m-   the amount-
Liz: ⌊ well that starts   from being
- -
Anna: =it does/ it does/ yeah/ but at the same time . I just
Liz: very young=
- -
Anna: think if I don't do it/ HE's not going to do it/ and then that's
      ⌈ more worry back on me because it's not being done/
Liz: ⌊ but you-   yeah/   and you- you-   you'd have to
- -
Anna: yeah/ it's easier to
Liz: do it for yourself anyway/ so you do it/
- -
Anna: do it for both of you/

In the above passage, Anna and Liz collude in a view of themselves as strong
and therefore potentially dangerous to males who live with them. They then
collaborate in arguing that they are forced to be active and competent because
if they weren't, things wouldn't get done and they would be the ones to
suffer. Having worked themselves into a position where they feel they have
a good reason for taking responsibility for the bills and the mortgage, Liz
initiates a more positive move by asserting that women are normally
prevented from realizing how easy it is to run your own life – to deal with
the *bills and mortgages and everything else.*

Liz: but it's a myth you know/ I wish a lot of women would realize
      that it's a complete and utter myth/ . this- this being on your
      ow- I mean . when I was first- when I was first thrown out
      there on my own if you like/ I was bloody terrified/ bills and
- -
Anna: yeah/   but how much have you learnt since you
Liz: mortgages and everything else/   but-   but yeah
- -
Anna: first ((xx))
Liz: but once you get on with it there's nothing-   there's .
- -
Anna: there's nothing ⌈ to it really/
Liz: ⌊ there's nothing to it/

This last section of their talk about women's competence and men's incom-
petence represents a dramatic shift of position. Here, rather than bewailing
her competence, Liz is celebrating it. And rather than claiming that women
as a group are powerful and dangerous and produce weak and damaged men,
she argues that women are prevented from understanding how easy it is to
be independent (though she doesn't name *who* is responsible for preventing
this). She feels strongly that women should be given the information
they need – and thus, she implies, should have the right to be competent
autonomous people in their own right. This bit of talk ends with the

triumphant repetition of the phrase *there's nothing to it* by both Liz and Anna. So we see Liz and Anna (with Sue in the earlier part) holding the contradictory positions that (*i*) boys and men are inadequate; (*ii*) women are superior to men; (*iii*) it's good to be a woman; (*iv*) women are too strong; (*v*) women are to blame for men's inadequacy; (*vi*) women have to be strong / competent because otherwise nothing would get done; (*vii*) running a house is easy; (*viii*) women are misled into thinking it's difficult.

At the heart of these contradictions is ambivalence about being 'strong'. These women friends are positioned by a patriarchal discourse to see strength as incompatible with femininity and somehow bad, even dangerous. Simultaneously, their exposure to resistant feminist discourses means they also have a sense of strength as good, as part of a different type of femininity, a femininity which is distinct from masculinity but not inferior to it. The problem seems to be that they find it hard to sustain the latter, feminist position: their assertions that they are strong trigger anxiety about weakness in men. In other words, they fall back onto a world view that sees all relationships in hierarchical terms, so if one group is strong, the other group must be weak (or less strong), and if men are weak, that is somehow women's responsibility.

Women's anxiety about our strength is closely related to our ambivalence about power. I've chosen the final extract to show a woman using a more powerful discourse. Meg, in the next example, starts to talk about her experience on an interview panel. This follows on from Janet's story about her recent interview for a job. But where Janet was telling a story where she, the protagonist, was an interviewee, Meg chooses to tell a story where she is in the powerful position of being one of the interviewers. There are several discourses present in the extract, but I want to focus on two: a powerful professional discourse, and a sexist patriarchal discourse.

> *[Topic: Interviews]*
> *Meg:* we did the interviews for the- [. . .] you know I'd been shortlisting/ and there were twenty-four and um inCREDibly well-qualified/ and the twenty-four that applied for er nine places. all had um good degrees in psychology/ I mean and some of them had . M- MPhils and DPhils and um .hh PhDs. you know they were very well qualified/ and . all- virtually all of them had done some . proper ongoing research into child abuse or-
> *Mary:* what's the course?
> the M- it's called the MClinPsychol/
> ---
> *Meg:* it's the qualification I did/⌈masters in clinical⌈psychology/
> *Mary:*   ⌊yes/   ⌊mhm/
> ---
> *Meg:* um . anyway we interviewed them on two days running/ Thursday and Friday/ and ((something)) really funny thing happened/ . one was an extremely pretty girl that's doing . um er er- what's the

diploma? a- a- a Master's in Child Development at Newcastle with Professor Newton/ and she got a SPLENdid reference from Professor Newton/

Jen: you used to have Professor

Meg: ⌈ yeah/   yeah/   but s- and saying things
Jen: Newton ⌊ didn't you?
Helen: did you? mhm/

Meg: like- can't remember the girl's name/ Nicola I think/ saying um you know 'She's academically u- u- unimpeachable/ she's absolutely superb/ she's also an extremely nice girl/ and she's . the sort that joins in well at the party/ and is always- has al- always there- er also there for the washing up'/
      <LAUGHTER>

Meg: that was a nice little domestic note/ anyway um-
Helen: they wouldn't

Meg: ⌈ well there WAS
Helen: have said that about a bloke⌈ ((xx))/
Sally: ⌊ I was going to ⌊ say/

Meg: that/ um . anyway during the interview um . it went okay/ . um she's- she's the sort of- she has a very pleasant manner/ and she answered quite competently/ and at the end/ um David Blair said to her . um 'You've been working with autistic children'/ she's done two special projects with autistic children/ [. . .] he said to her . um 'Do you believe um there's any relationship between dyslexia and autism'?/ and she absolutely panicked/ <AGHAST> and it was TERRible for us
Bea: heavens/
Helen: mhm/

Meg: to watch/

Meg presents herself here as a competent professional. This is done in part through the use of specialized vocabulary such as: *short-listing, clinical psychology, reference, dyslexia, autism*, and abbreviated terms: *MPhil, DPhil, MClinPsychol*, which assume in-group knowledge. It's also done prosodically, with the rhythm and stress patterns of phrases like *she got a SPLENdid reference from Professor Newton* carrying powerful signals about social class and educational level which are readily understood by British English speakers. Meg also accomplishes professionalism through her presentation of herself as someone with agency, a doer, not a person who is done to: *I'd been short-listing; it's the qualification I did; we interviewed them* . . . which is implicitly contrasted with the young woman interviewee who is presented as *an extremely pretty girl* who has a *very pleasant manner* and who *answered quite competently*.

The presentation of the young interviewee is derogatory: Meg's description of her doesn't just accomplish power; it also accomplishes the oppression of women. Not only is the young woman called a 'girl' (thus reducing her to non-adult status), but she is described in terms of her appearance, which is clearly irrelevant to the situation. Later, Meg repeats Professor Newton's reference with approval, though its allusion to the young woman's willingness to wash up after parties is blatantly sexist. Meg initially describes this as *a nice little domestic note*, and it is only when Helen challenges this position with the comment *they wouldn't have said that about a bloke* that she concedes there might be a problem with this aspect of the reference.

It seems as though women like Meg – women who were among the first to take on more senior positions in professions like law and medicine and psychology – can only adopt a powerful role if they also take on the patriarchal values that normally accompany such power. So Meg's self-presentation here illustrates the tensions associated with doing femininity and power at the same time: Meg succeeds in doing power, but at the same time she presents herself as colluding in an ideology that denigrates and trivializes women. The crux of her story to her friends is that a very talented young woman panicked in her interview – in other words, the younger woman lost all claim to competence by contrast with the calm professionals on the panel. Meg's self-presentation works in part because of the contrast between herself – calm, competent, professional – and the young woman who panics.

On the other hand, there are features of her talk which undermine the discourse of power. She hesitates or says *um* and *er* frequently, as well as stammering and repeating her words. She has brief lapses of memory when she appeals for help to her friends – *what's the diploma?*. She also includes hedges in her account – *you know, I mean, sort of*. In part, these 'lapses' are designed to reduce distance between herself and her addressees: as I've said in earlier chapters, women friends avoid playing the expert where possible. But these features of Meg's talk also accomplish a femininity that is not powerful, that needs help and support. This latter aspect of her talk demonstrates how problematic it is for us as women to claim power for ourselves.

Conclusion

As the examples in this chapter have illustrated, there is no single unified way of doing femininity, of being a woman. In the contemporary developed world, many different versions of femininity are available to us. Different discourses give us access to different femininities. More mainstream discourses position us in more conventional ways, while more radical or subversive discourses offer us alternative ways of being, alternative ways of doing femininity. We are unwittingly involved in the ceaseless struggle to define gender: as Chris Weedon puts it, 'The nature of femininity and masculinity is one of the key sites of discursive struggle for the individual (1987: 98).

The meaning of 'Woman' has changed through time, and at any given time it will vary – between, for example, meanings associated with more madonna-like images of femininity and meanings associated with more whore-like images. There is no such thing as a 'woman'; the meaning of 'woman' will depend on which discourse the word occurs in. 'Discourses do not just reflect or represent social entities and relations, they construct or "constitute" them; different discourses constitute key entities [such as 'woman'] . . . in different ways' (Fairclough 1992: 3–4). What 'being a woman' means at this moment in late twentieth-century Britain is a site of struggle, with dominant ideologies being challenged by more feminist ones.

It seems to me that the talk we do with our women friends is particularly important in terms of our sense of ourselves as women, because in our talk we collaborate in constructing a shared view of what constitutes womanhood. We also support each other in resisting particular versions of femininity and in preferring others, and we help each other (consciously or unconsciously) to reconcile conflicting or contradictory femininities. We do this as part of the ongoing work of doing friendship.

Notes

1   The term discourse is particularly associated with the work of Michel Foucault. For further discussion of Foucault's theories of discourse, see Fairclough (1992) and Weedon (1987).
2   For further discussion of these ideas, see Lee (1992) and Gavey (1989).
3   The analysis of linguistic texts in terms of discourse is associated with the branch of linguistics known as critical linguistics and with the work of Norman Fairclough – see in particular Fairclough 1992.
4   At the time this conversation was recorded, Sue had gone back to college as a mature student to train as a primary school teacher.
5   The term *subject* as used here pulls together three different strands of thought, one more political (we are not free but *subject to* the power of others), one more philosophical (we are thinking *subjects*, sites of consciousness) and one more grammatical (sentences have *subjects* – they are what the sentence is about). The word also gains meaning from its opposition to *object*, even though, ironically, the two words are often very close in meaning. Here, for example, it would be equally true to say 'our talk about men does powerful work in our construction of ourselves as feminine objects'. Showing how women are *objectified* in patriarchal discourses has been one of the goals of feminist discourse analysis.
6   I can say this with confidence about Hannah and her friends, since I have recordings of them since they were twelve. But although I knew Emily when she was twelve, I only recorded her with her friends when they were sixteen, so I have no definite proof that her language changed.
7   There are few good example of positive talk about significant males in the conversational data. This could be because one of the chief functions of

women's friendly talk is to allow us to talk about our anxieties and problems, and about our triumphs in the outside world. Ongoing good
relationships do not seem to be a salient topic of conversation.

8 It had not crossed my mind that I might have to leave the room during
recording. On this particular occasion I had to go and answer the phone,
and my friends started to talk about me after I had left the room. I have
only listened to the first few seconds of this talk, as it seems to me that
I have absolutely no right to know what they said in my absence.

Reprinted from Jennifer Coates, *Women Talk* (Oxford: Blackwell, 1996).

Chapter 22

Kira Hall

LIP SERVICE ON THE FANTASY LINES

W‌HEN THE DEREGULATION OF THE telephone industry co-occurred
with a number of technological advances in telecommunications in
the early 1980s, American society witnessed the birth of a new medium for
linguistic exchange – the 900 number. On the fantasy lines, which generate
annual revenues of more than $45 million in California alone, women's
language is bought, sold, and custom-tailored to secure caller satisfaction.
This high-tech mode of linguistic exchange complicates traditional notions
of power in language, because the women working within the industry
consciously produce a language stereotypically associated with women's
powerlessness in order to gain economic power and social flexibility. In this
chapter, I refer to research I conducted among five women-owned fantasy-
line companies in San Francisco in order to argue for a more multidimensional
definition of linguistic power, one that not only devotes serious attention to
the role of sexuality in conversational exchange but also recognizes individual
variability with respect to women's conversational consent.

The linguistic identification of women's language as 'powerless' and
men's language as 'powerful' has its origins in early readings of the work of
Robin Lakoff (1975), who argued in *Language and Woman's Place* that sex
differences in language use both reflect and reinforce the unequal status
of women and men in our society. After identifying an array of linguistic
features ideologically associated with women's speech in American English
– among them lexical items associated with women's work; 'empty' adjectives such as *divine, charming,* and *cute;* tag questions in place of declaratives;
hedges such as *sort of, kind of;* and *I guess;* intensifiers such as *so* and *very;*

and hypercorrect, polite linguistic forms – Lakoff suggested that the association of indirect speech with women's language and direct speech with men's language is the linguistic reflection of a larger cultural power imbalance between the sexes. Her treatise, packaged beneath the unapologetically feminist photograph of a woman with bandaged mouth, has inspired two decades of heated debate among subsequent language and gender theorists. A number of feminist scholars have argued that Lakoff's identification of women's language as culturally subordinate serves to affirm sexist notions of women as deviant and deficient, and sociolinguists steeped in Labovian empirical argumentation have dismissed her claims altogether as quantitatively invalid.

I have no desire to reopen the academic wounds of what remains a divisive subject among language and gender theorists, but a discussion of my research on the discursive fictions produced by phone-sex employees in San Francisco would be incomplete without reference to Lakoff's early description of 'women's language.' The type of language that these employees consider sexual, and that for them is economically powerful, is precisely what has been defined by language and gender theorists since Lakoff as 'powerless.' The notion that behavior that is perceived as powerless can, in certain contexts, also be perceived as sexual may be old hat to anthropologists and sociologists, but language theorists have yet to address this connection explicitly. The very existence of the term *sweet talk* – an activity that, in the American heterosexual mainstream, has become associated more with the speech patterns of women than with men – underscores the ideological connection between women's language and sexual language. By taking on the outer vestments of submissiveness and powerlessness, or, rather by appropriating the linguistic features culturally associated with such a posture, the female 'sweet-talker' projects a certain sexual availability to her male listener so as to further her own conversational aims. Her use of this discursive style, which in its sexualized duplicity might more appropriately be dubbed the *Mata Hari technique*, is itself powerful; the speaker is not the naïve, playful, and supportive interactant her male audience has taken her to be but a mature, calculating adult with a subversive goal in mind. Perhaps in an effort to underscore this very duplicity, Kathleen K. (1994), author of a recent book on her experiences as a phone-sex worker in the Pacific Northwest, chose the title *Sweet Talkers: Words from the Mouth of a 'Pay to Say' Girl*.

In this chapter, I address the superficial conflict in the use of submissive speech for reasons of power. The adult-message industry has enjoyed considerable financial success during the past decade, grossing well over $3 billion since its national debut in 1983. As fear of the AIDS epidemic and the accompanying interest in safe sex spreads throughout the culture at large, the demand for women's vocal merchandise promises to expand into the next millennium. The growing success of this discursive medium in the marketplace calls for a new interpretation of the place of women's language in contemporary society. Its easy marketability as a sexual commodity and the profits it reaps for the women who employ it suggest that the study of cross-sex linguistic exchange must acknowledge the more subversive aspects of conversational consent.

[. . .]

Fantasy and the Telephone

The telephone, as a medium that excludes the visual, allows for the creation of fantasy in a way that face-to-face interaction cannot. In the absence of a visual link, the speaker is able to maintain a certain anonymity that can potentially allow for a less self-conscious and, in the appropriate circumstances, more imaginative presentation. On the 900-lines, where the sense of anonymity is of course heightened by the fact that the two interactants have never met, callers must construct their conversational partner visually. Once they have created such a representation, they have already entered into a fantasy world of sorts, and the construction of any additional representations is facilitated by this entry. Although the majority of communication studies in the 1970s support the assertion that the telephone's lack of visual access restricts individual expression, it seems that today's users find that this lack in fact encourages creativity – a change of attitude that might explain the dramatic increase in phone-related devices, among them answering machines, cellular mobile telephones, cordless telephones, dial-up teleconferencing facilities, and electronic mail, not to mention the numerous varieties of 900 to 976 services. Even though the telephone has been around for more than a hundred years, it is only in the past twenty years that the system has undergone what G. Fielding and D. Hartley (1987:11) refer to as 'explosive growth,' both in quality and scope. The advent of telephone deregulation in the United States and the increasing availability of the mobile telephone have prompted telecommunication theorists like Frederick Williams (1985:191) to argue that the telephone is shifting 'from a "home" or "business" based communications link to an individual, personal based one.' This shift is nowhere more apparent than in the advertising strategies of the telephone industry itself, which regularly appeals to the personal, private, and expressive contact that it affords. With just one thirty-second AT&T telephone call, clients can find a long-lost friend, pacify a weeping mother, or 'reach out and touch' that special someone. Perhaps it is not so strange after all to see advertisement after advertisement on late Saturday-night television for 'romance lines,' 'friendship lines,' 'party lines,' 'psychic lines,' 'teenage date lines,' 'therapy lines,' and 'confession lines.'

Adult-message services have clearly capitalized on this shift as well, appealing to the private and expressive nature of the medium in their own advertising strategies. The company Call Girls offers 'live conversation with a personal touch,' Linda's Lip Service declares that it is 'friendly, personal, and unhurried,' and ABC International features 'completely private, one to one, adult conversations.' Most services appearing on the back pages of *Hustler*

and *Penthouse* advertise their numbers visually – with pictures of naked women in provocative poses talking on the telephone – but an increasing number of services are advertising themselves verbally, perhaps in an effort to represent a more personal, involved, and creative relationship between seller and consumer. The company Terry's Live Talk, for instance, advertises its number in the form of a typewritten letter, urging its readers to call its 'very personal' service and concluding with the intimate salutation 'Love XOXOXOXOXO.' The service Nicole Bouvier, which reserves an entire page in *Penthouse* for its letter of advertisement, opens romantically with a reference to the senses, equating phone talk with touch, smell, and taste and shunning the need for sight altogether: 'My love, it doesn't matter if you can't see me. You can touch me . . . smell me . . . taste me . . . and then you will *know* and always *remember* me.' Still other services choose to imitate the written format of the newspaper personals, listing prose descriptions of their fantasy-line operators (which are presumably fictional because most employers have never met their employees face-to-face) in an effort to set their employees apart from the generic phone-sex model.

Dial-a-porn clients use a medium that is intensely public, with one line potentially servicing as many as fifty thousand calls an hour in an anonymous fashion, in order to engage in a subject matter traditionally thought of as intensely private. The unnaturalness of this interaction must be rectified by the fantasy-line performer, who presents herself through a unique mixture of public and private discourse. Lakoff (1990), differentiating genres of discourse with reference to these two dimensions, argues that participants in private discourse tend to express themselves with shared allusions, jointly created metaphors, and telegraphic references, promoting feelings of intimacy and trust. Participants in public language, on the other hand, because they cannot count on shared allusions, tend to express themselves in an explicit, concrete manner so that the larger public can understand. Because the fantasy-line operator has never met her male client, she clearly lacks the frame of reference necessary for private conversation; instead, she must create a feeling of intimacy by evoking a frame of reference that the majority of her male callers will understand and be familiar with – namely, that of male pornography. Within this rather limited field of discourse, she and her client are able to express themselves with the shared allusions, jointly created metaphors, and telegraphic references necessary for private communication, however stereotypical they may be.

For fantasy to be effective, it must somehow parallel reality, and if its intended audience is the culture at large, it must necessarily prey on certain cultural perceptions of what the ideal reality is. To sell to a male market, women's prerecorded messages and live conversational exchange must cater to hegemonic male perceptions of the ideal woman. The training manual for operators of 970-LIVE, a male-owned fantasy-line service based in New York City, instructs female employees to 'create different characters' and to 'start with one the resembles the ideal woman' – as if this is a universal, unproblematic concept. To train women to fulfill this ideal, the manual gives additional details on how to open and maintain conversations while preserving 'professionalism':

> *Create different characters:*
> Start with one that resembles the ideal woman. Move on to bimbo, nymphomaniac, mistress, slave, transvestite, lesbian, foreigner, or virgin. If the caller wants to speak to someone else, don't waste time being insulted. Be someone else. You should be creative enough to fulfill *anyone's* fantasy.

> *To start a conversation:*
> 'What's on your mind?' 'What would you like to talk about?' 'What do you do for fun?' 'What are you doing right now?'
> Remember: Never initiate sex. Let the caller start phone intimacy.

> *Ways to keep callers interested:*
> Tell them crazy fantasies: Jell-O, honey, travel, ice cream, lesbian love, orgies. If conversation stays clean, tell them an interesting story: movies, TV, books, etc. Make it sound like it really happened. *Insist* that it happened.

> *Professionalism:*
> Do not talk to *anyone* besides a caller when talking a call. Always be bubbly, sexy, interesting, and interested in each individual caller. Remember, *you* are not your character on the phone.
> (Reprinted in *Harpers Magazine*, December 1990, 26–7.)

What makes the ideal woman from a verbal point of view is reminiscent of Pamela Fishman's (1978) definition of *maintenance work*: encouraging men to develop their topics by asking questions (*What's on* your *mind: What would* you *like to talk about? What do* you *do for fun?*), showing assent (*Always be bubbly, sexy, interesting and interested in each individual caller*), and listening (*Don't talk to* anyone *besides a caller when taking a call*). Because the conversation will be meaningless unless it in some way approximates the male caller's under-standing of reality, what becomes critically important to its success is for it to 'sound like it really happened' – for the woman to '*insist* that it happened.' This realization, coupled with the fact that many clients may be calling the lines in response to the increasing threat of AIDS, has even led some companies to practice 'safe phone sex.' The number 1-900-HOT-LIPS, for instance, which advertises as a 'steamy safe-sex fantasy number,' has all of its fantasy-line oper-ators 'carry' – in the verbal sense, that is – condoms and spermicides to their vocal sexual encounters. The suggestion that an interactant might need to practice safe sex over the telephone wires is of course ludicrous; by overtly referencing this practice in its advertisement, however, the message service suggests that there is a very real physicality to the medium and simultaneously alludes to its inherently 'safe' nature.

The Prerecorded Message

The language promoted in the trainer's manual is precisely the kind of
language sold by the prerecorded services – language that, through extensive detail and supportive hearer-directed comments, presents a certain
reality. The two-minute prerecorded message reproduced below in 1 is played
daily on a national fantasy line that advertises as 'girls, girls, girls.' The
speaker is unquestionably the perfect woman: she loves to shop, she wears
feminine clothes, she likes to look at herself in the mirror, and
she lies in bed half the day fulfilling male fantasies.[1]

1 oo::f:: – i'm so ((in breathy voice)) <u>exci</u>ted. – i just got a <u>hot</u> new job.
   (0.8) well, – ((in slight Southern accent)) I've been bored lately. .hh –
   i live in a small town and my husband travels a lot, (0.5) i have lots of
   time on my hands. – .hhh of course, i've always managed to stay busy.
   (0.4) lots of girlfriends, you know, – ((whispered)) i love to <u>shop</u>, – i
   ((laugh)) ^<u>pract</u>^ically live at the mall it seems, but still-.hhhh (2.0) <u>any</u>-
   way. – this friend told me about this job i can do at <u>home</u>. – all i need
   is a <u>phone</u>. – and a lusty imagination. ((laugh)) yeah, you've got it – .hh
   i'm doing <u>h::ot</u> sexy phone calls these days. (0.5) i <u>really</u> get into it <u>too</u>.
   – .hhh i love that sexy hot fellows from all over the country call me and
   enjoy my ((whispered)) voice and my fantasies. (0.4) i like to <u>dress</u> the
   part too. – i went to my favorite lingerie ((in hoarse, breathy voice))
   store, – victoria's secret? – and bought <u>s::a</u>tin bikinis, <u>l::a</u>cy thong
   underwear, – a tight black corset – and fishnet stockings, (1.0) ((in lower
   voice)) and a <u>dangerous</u> pair of <u>red</u> ((whispered)) <u>spiked heels</u>. ((smack))
   – <u>um</u>hmm::::: .hhh – <u>then</u>. when i'm in a dominant mode? .hh i have this
   leather g-string and bra and thigh-high boots. – ooh <u>baby</u>. ((giggle)) (0.5)
   when i dress up and look in my mirror, ((slower, breathy voice)) i – get
   – so – <u>crazy</u> .hhhhh I just can't wait for that first ca::ll. (0.6) <u>then</u>, – i
   assemble all my favorite little (0.3) <u>toys</u> all around me, (0.4) lie back on
   my big bed with <u>s::at</u>in sheets .hhhh (1.0) and live out my fantasies with
   some my<u>sterious</u> stranger .hhhhhhh oo:::::h <u>hearing</u> those voices. .hh –
   those excited whispers and moans, ((in breathy voice)) u::h, it gets me
   so- .hhhh – well, – you know. (2.0) then (0.5) i just go <u>wi::ld</u>, – i have
   <u>so</u> many great <u>idea::</u>s. – they come fa::st and furious, (in hoarse voice))
   oo::h, i can't get enough. -.hh each call makes me hotter, – i just keep
   going, <u>over</u> and <u>over</u>, ((grasping)) ^<u>o:h</u>^ – .hhh <u>yea:h</u> <u>baby</u> do it <u>again</u> –
   ^oo^:::f, hhhhhhh – <u>well</u>. (2.0) I <u>love</u> my workday – ^<u>but</u>^ – by the time
   I put in a few hours on the phone? – i'm so re<u>la:xed</u> hh, – and when my
   husband gets home ((smack)) – <u>oo</u>::h – he gets the treatment. – he lo:ves
   it. – .hh but (1.0) shhh. ((whispered)) don't tell. – it's <u>our</u> secret.

In the absence of a visual link, this ideal is created solely through language
(as the speaker herself says, 'All I need is a phone and a lusty imagination').

She begins by constructing a visual image of herself with words popularly thought of as feminine: *girlfriends, lusty, lacy, lingerie, satin,* and *secret.* Her voice is dynamic, moving from high-pitched, gasping expressions of pleasure to low-pitched, breathy-voice innuendoes. Although this is unidirectional discourse, she makes it quite clear that she would be an admirable conversational partner in any female—male dyad — she 'just can't wait for that first call' so that she can respond supportively to all those 'voices' and 'excited whispers.' Additionally, she sets up her monologue so as to establish an exclusive intimacy with her absentee partner, referring to their conversational relationship as a passionate 'secret' that should be kept from her husband.

Particularly telling is what happens at the end of this fantasy, when the speaker's verbal creativity comes to represent the sex act itself: *I have so many great ideas. They come fast and furious — ooh, I can't get enough!* An equation of the spoken word with the sex act is a common element in such messages, a fitting metaphorical strategy given the nature of the exchange. Often in the beginning of the fantasy scenario, the speaker will be reading a book at a library, selling encyclopedias door to door, or taking a literature course at the local college. By the end of the scenario, swayed by the voice and intellect of the suitor in question (who is often identified with the caller so as to bring him directly into the fantasy), she has discarded her books, her encyclopedias, and her academic pretensions for the bedroom.

In a fantasy reproduced below, for example, the speaker projects the persona of a young college student who is obsessed with her English professor. Having established the power imbalance inherent to this scenario — she, the eager coed; he, the aloof, self-involved intellectual — the student develops a preoccupation with her professor's voice, describing how it repeatedly 'penetrates' her during lectures:

2 ^hi. — my name's vicky^, — and i <u>guess</u> i'm in <u>deep</u> trouble in one of my <u>class</u>es at college. (1.5) ((whispered)) it's my english professor. — he's got me <u>cra::</u>zy, (0.5) and i think I'm losing my <u>mi:nd</u>, — he's really (0.4) not handsome or anything, — it's the way he talks, (1.0) his voice gets deep inside me where it counts, — turns me to jelly, (1.5) i sit at the front of the class, — and i just can't seem — to keep ^<u>still</u>^, (1.5) i remember the first day, i wore jeans and a sweater. (0.5) and my long blond hair up in a bun. (0.6) i felt pretty studious, — but the moment i started <u>listening</u> to him, i knew i was gonna <u>change</u> — all — that. (2.0) and the next session, i showed up in the <u>short</u>est mini-skirt i could find. (0.5) ^i'm real tan^ ((in breathy voice)) and in <u>real</u> good shape. (0.5) and i <u>knew</u> i looked pretty good in that mini-skirt. — i wore a silk blouse that ((slowly)) <u>should</u> have had his eyes riveted on me, — instead — he hardly ^<u>no</u>^ticed, (1.0) ^o:::h^ I was getting so ^<u>cra::</u>^zy. (2.0) well — after a few weeks, — the weather changed and it got <u>real</u> hot, — so i started wearing shorts and this <u>great</u> little halter

top, (1.5) i know i looked okay, because guys in the class were stum-
bling over themselves to sit next to me. – but my professor – there
he was, just a few feet away, and hardly a ^glance^. (1.0) and still I go
back to my dorm room and lay in my bed, and dream about that voice,
((in breathy voice)) <u>all</u> of me responds to it, (2.0) ((sigh)) hhhhh it's
as if he's penetrated me, ((slowly)) <u>reached</u> the <u>depths</u> of my <u>soul</u> and
<u>won't</u> let go. (1.0) i dream about the moment – when we'll be alone,
– maybe it'll be after class, (1.5) maybe it'll be a chance meeting at a
coffee shop or something, but when that moment comes, (0.5) i know
i'm going to tell him what he <u>does</u> to me, – and i don't think he'll be
surprised, – because i ^<u>think</u>^ he already knows.

The speaker begins the fantasy by establishing that she is attracted to this
particular professor not because of his physical appearance but because of the
'way he talks': *His voice gets deep inside me where it counts, turns me to jelly*.
After several unsuccessful attempts to impress the professor by relaxing her
studious stance and gendering herself with the appropriate apparel, the
speaker goes back to her dorm room so that she can at the very least 'dream
about that voice.' She concludes the fantasy by exclaiming, rather emphatically, that she becomes powerless before the sound of it: *All of me responds
to it, it's as if he's penetrated me, reached the depths of my soul and won't let go.*
Although in this particular text it is the speaker, not the hearer, who is the
owner of the fantasy, the one-sided nature of the created exchange (that is,
even though the coed talks incessantly in the hopes of attracting her
professor's attention, he fails to offer her any individualized verbal acknowl-
edgment) parallels the real-life interaction between operator and client. The
caller, unable to respond to the emotional desires of a prerecorded voice,
easily assumes the role of the coed's nonresponsive superior.

As this scenario nicely illustrates, the reality presented on the message
line presents an interactive inequality between the sexes, portraying men as
dominant (penetrating, powerful, intellectual) and women as submissive
(penetrated, powerless, emotional). To have a successful conversation, the
fantasy-line recording must affirm this inequality, for it is essential to
the frame of male pornographic discourse. Rosalind Coward (1986), with
reference to visual pornography, argues that although images of women are
never inherently pornographic, they necessarily become so when placed
within a 'regime of representations' (i.e., a set of codes with conventionally
accepted meanings) that identify them as pornographic for the viewer. The
captions and texts that surround such images identify them explicitly as figures
for male enjoyment, affirming the differential female-as-object versus male-
as-subject. In vocal pornography, because there is no visual link, this
differential must be created through voice and word alone. The fantasy-line
operator has been assisted, of course, by the many advertisements in adult
magazines that have already situated her within this frame, but she must still
actively assume a submissive position in the conversation. In the telephone

advertisement below, for example, offered by a message service as a 'free phone-job sample,' the speaker sells the number by highlighting this very inequality:

3 ((in quick, low breathy voice)) baby I want you to listen closely, – dial 1-900-884-6804 <u>now</u> for <u>hard</u> love, – for <u>tough</u> love, – for girls who <u>need</u> <u>men</u> to <u>take</u> con<u>tro::l</u>. – dial 1-900-884-6804, – for women who aren't afraid to say what they <u>rea</u>::lly want, – for girls who need <u>powerful</u> men to open their deep desires, dial 1-900-884-6804, and go all the way. (0.5) <u>deep</u> into the secret places for a fantasy experience that just goes <u>on</u> and <u>on</u> and <u>on</u>, – dial 1-900-884-6804, and get a girl who wants to give <u>you</u> the ultimate pleasure, 1-900-884-6804, ((quickly)) just half a dollar a minute, forty the first. (0.5) <u>now</u> i can tell <u>you</u> everything, now i can give you everything you want, <u>all</u> you desire, i can do it now, i <u>want</u> to, i <u>have</u> to, ((giggle)) dial 1-900-884-6804.

In a low, breathy voice, the operator explains that the women who work at this particular company will provide the 'love' (which is here overtly sexualized with the modifiers *hard* and *tough*) if the caller provides the 'control.' They are women who need 'powerful men to open their deep desires'— who not only *want* to submit and give their callers 'the ultimate pleasure' but '*have* to' do so.

Certain types of work structures, particularly those that involve women in typically feminine jobs, require female employees to perform emotional labor for their bosses. As Catherine Lutz (1986, 1990) and other anthropologists have pointed out, such divisions follow from the way emotion has been constructed along gender lines within Western society, so that men are expected to be rational and women emotional – a construction that has effects on women's language and on societal perceptions of what women's language should be. What is noteworthy with respect to the present discussion is the way in which fantasy-line operators consciously appropriate ideologies of emotional language and sexual language (which are not always entirely distinguishable) in order to intensify the perceived power imbalance. As one fantasy-line operator explained, 'My job is kind of a three-conversation trinity – one part prostitute, one part priest, and one part therapist.'

Interviews with San Francisco Fantasy-Line Operators

The eleven women and one man interviewed for this study, all residing in the San Francisco Bay Area and working for services that advertise to a heterosexual male market,[2] were aware of the recent feminist controversy over pornography and were highly reflective of their position within this debate. Each of them had reinterpreted this debate within the vocal sphere, perceiving their position in the linguistic exchange as a powerful one. Their positive attitude may have much to do with the fact that in San Francisco, many of the adult message services are women-owned and -operated, with a large percentage of employees identifying themselves as feminists and participating actively in organizations such as COYOTE, Cal-Pep, and COP – political action groups established for the purpose of securing rights for women in the sex industry. For these individuals, many of whom are freelance artists, fashion designers, graduate students, and writers, work on the telephone brings economic independence and social freedom. To them, the real prostitutes in our society are the women who dress in expensive business suits in the financial district, work fifty hours a week, and make sixty-five cents to a man's dollar. They understand the adult-message industry as primarily a creative medium, viewing themselves as fantasy tellers who have embraced a form of discourse that has been largely ignored by the women of this sexually repressed society. Moreover, they feel a certain power in having access into men's minds and find that it empowers them in their everyday cross-sex interactions.

Before embarking on this study in 1991, I informed the San Francisco Sex Information Hotline of my project and asked for assistance in locating phone-sex workers who might be interested in being interviewed. Over the next few months I spoke with twelve people, including nine 'call-doers' (as fantasy makers are sometimes called), two managers, and a woman who is co-owner of one of the oldest phone-sex companies in the United States (K. G. Fox). Most of the interviews were conducted anonymously by phone because many of the participants did not wish to have their names publicized. Approximately half of the interviewees allowed me to record our interviews over the telephone. The race, age, sex, and sexual-orientation backgrounds of the operators I spoke with were roughly equivalent to those of employees working for women-owned and -operated services in San Francisco.[3] Six of the employees I interviewed were heterosexual, three bisexual, and three lesbian; eight were European American, two Latino, one African American, and one Asian American. The employees who granted me interviews ranged in age from twenty-three to forty-six; they were generally from middle-class backgrounds, college-educated, and supportive of the industry. Many of these women had sought employment with women-owned services in reaction to the poor treatment they had received from various men-owned services in the city, among them the financially successful Yellowphone.[4]

At the beginning of each interview I explained that I was writing an article on the phone-sex industry from the point of view of its labor force; only at the end of the interview did I disclose my particular interest in language use. The female participants all believed that both the antipornography feminism of Andrea Dworkin, Sheila Jeffreys, and Catharine MacKinnon and the pro-freedom feminism of Susie Bright prioritize an issue that most of the women in this country – because they suffer from serious economic and social oppression – do not have the privilege of debating. The most important issue to the women I interviewed is not whether pornography is oppressive or whether women's sexuality is repressed but, rather, how they, as a group, can mobilize for a better work environment so that the job they have chosen will be as nonoppressive as possible. They spoke of the need for a sex-workers' union, for health-care benefits, and for approval from people working outside the industry. Each of them chose her or his line of work initially for the economic freedom and social flexibility it offered. Like the fantasy-line operators quoted in excerpts 4 through 6 below – who variously identify themselves as *militant feminist, humanist,* and *feminist most definitely* – they regard the issue of sexual oppression as comparatively unimportant to the other types of economic and social oppression they have suffered.

4 Yes, in one word, the reason I got involved in this work is Reaganomics. It doesn't filter down to people like me. I'm an artist. I refuse to deal with corporate America. I'm an honest person. I have integrity. I work hard. There's no place in corporate America for me. . . . About a year and a half ago when the economy really started to go sour, I started thinking, well, I'm going to have to get a part-time job. I looked around at part-time jobs and it was like, you want me to dress in $300 outfits when you're paying me six bucks an hour? Excuse me, but I don't think so. And I saw an ad in the *Bay Guardian* for a fantasy maker, and I thought about it for months, because I had an attitude that it was really weird and I was concerned that I would end up really hating men, and finally it got down to, well, you can go downtown and spend a lot of money on clothes, or you can check this out.

5 I moved out here a couple of years ago from Ohio, and one of the main reasons I moved out here is so I could still be as strange as I am and do a job. I have piercing – body piercing, facial piercing – and I have tattoos, and I'm an insurance adjuster. And I wanted to come out here and get the piercings, and I'd been having to wear make-up over the [tattoo] ring on my finger, and that kind of thing. And I thought, well, god, San Francisco! If I can't get away with it there, then where can I? Well, I couldn't get away with it here either – not in the financial district. So I started watching *SF Weekly* and the newspapers, and I originally went to a company called [deleted]. And they told me it was a chat line and there'd be a few fantasy calls and not to be surprised by that. And oh boy, I was like, yeah, this is great money, I love it! And so I said sure. And that's basically how I got into it.

6 For me, I can work at home, I can make my own hours. If I want to take off and go on vacation on last minute's notice and be gone for a month, I can do that and know that my job is there. And I like that flexibility and I like the idea of not really having a boss to answer to. In some ways,

it's powerful and in some ways it's definitely not. [We're] people who are sort of marginalized, [there's a lot] that we don't have access to — like health care. It's like forget it, you get sick and you don't have insurance. We don't have any kind of union. I think it would be great if we could have some kind of sex workers' union. So it's a mixed bag, but I guess for me, in light of what the options would be for me to make a living at this point in time, it seems like the best thing I can do for myself. Definitely one of the best compared to the options I see out there, I'm pretty damn lucky with what I'm doing. Because I've tried to have a few sort of semi-straight normal jobs and I didn't cut it very well. I don't deal very well with authority, especially if I feel like the person is not treating me with the respect that I deserve, and that I'm not getting paid what I deserve for the quality of work that I'm putting out- like I have to dress a certain way that I'm uncomfortable in.

All three women have balanced the patriarchal oppression found in corporate America against the patriarchal oppression in a capitalist enterprise like pornography and have opted for the latter (although they made it quite clear that the women-owned services treat them much more kindly than those owned by men, especially with respect to advertising technique).[5] The first of these women entered the industry for economic security in a reaction to 'Reaganomics,' but the other two did so primarily for social flexibility. When the final operator speaks of the phone-sex industry as a *mixed bag*, she is not referring in any way to the sexual subordination that such a job might require of her but, rather, to the subordination required by a society that has marginalized her line of work: she has no benefits, no sex workers' union, no societal support.

Because the income of these women is entirely dependent upon verbal ability, they are very conscious of the type of language they produce and often explain specific linguistic qualities that make their language marketable. The features that make the prerecorded message persuasive are the same features that these operators choose to emphasize in their live-conversation exchanges: those that have been defined by linguists working in the area of language and gender as powerless. They explained that they make frequent use of feminine lexical items, incorporate intensifiers into their conversation whenever possible, regularly interrupt their narrative with questions and supportive comments, and adopt a dynamic intonation pattern.

One operator, a thirty-three-year-old European American heterosexual who calls herself Rachel, pointed out that 'to be a really good fantasy maker, you've got to have big tits in your voice.' She clarified this comment by explaining that she creates sexy language through lexical choice, employing 'words which are very feminine':

7 I can describe myself now so that it lasts for about five minutes, by using lots of adjectives, spending a lot of time describing the shape of my

tits. And that's both – it's not just wasting time, because they need to build up a mental picture in their minds about what you look like, and also it allows me to use words that are very feminine. I always wear peach, or apricot, or black lace, or charcoal-colored lace, not just black. I'll talk about how my hair feels, how curly it is. Yeah, I probably use more feminine words. Sometimes they'll ask me, 'What do you call it [female genitalia]?' And I'll say, well my favorite is *the snuggery*. . . . And then they crack up, because it's such a feminine, funny word.

Rachel initiates conversation on the fantasy lines by creating a feminine image of herself through soft words like *curly* and *snuggery* together with nonbasic color terms such as *peach, apricot,* and even *charcoal* instead of black – a creation markedly reminiscent of Lakoff's (1975:9) early assertion that women are thought to use 'far more precise discriminations in naming colors' than men. Another operator, a European American self-identified butch bisexual whom I will call Sheila, defines what makes her language marketable as an intonational phenomenon. When she explains that she 'talks in a loping tone of voice' with a 'feminine, lilting quality,' she alludes to a vocal pattern identified by Sally McConnell-Ginet (1978) two decades ago as characteristic of women's speech:

8 I feel like definitely the timbre of my voice has a lot to do with it. I don't know, the ability to sound like, I hate to say it, feminine and kind of that lilting quality, and to sound like you're really enjoying it, like you're turned on and you're having a good time. I think that has a lot to do with it because they're always telling me, 'Oh yes, you have such a great voice! God, I love listening to your voice!' I think that's a big part of it, it's just the sound of the person's voice. Some people will tell you that they really like detail and lots of description, and so I can provide that too. But I think so much of it is the way that you say things, more than what you're actually saying. That's kind of funny, you know – sort of an inviting tone of voice.

A third operator, Samantha, a manager of a San Francisco company established in 1990 by a woman and her male-to-female transsexual partner, emphasizes the maintenance work she uses to engage her male callers in a more collaborative exchange, mentioning that she tries to draw out shy callers with supportive questions and comments ('I stop a lot to say things like, "Oh, do you like that?" You know, that kind of thing. I try to get them to talk as much as I can, because some of these people would sit here and not say one word. And if I get one of those, from time to time I say, "Hello? Are you still there?" '). K. G. Fox alludes to the importance of maintaining this conversational attentiveness when she explains, 'You got to be in the moment, you got to pay attention, you go to keep it fresh. It's a performance and you have to stay in time with your audience. After all, it's really a one-person show.' To make the fantasy effective, then, these fantasy makers consciously cater to their clients by producing a language that adheres to a popular male perception of what women's speech should be: flowery, inviting, and supportive.

Even though an attentive and nurturing discursive style seems to be the primary posture adopted by the women I interviewed, many of them additionally explained how they embellish this style by incorporating more individualized linguistic stereotypes of womanhood, particularly those of age and race. Samantha, for instance, makes her voice sound 'sexy' by performing four different characters: (1) herself, whom she calls Samantha; (2) a girl with a high-pitched eighteen-year-old voice who fulfills the 'beach bunny' stereotype; (3) a woman with a demure Asian accent whom she calls Keesha; and (4) a dominating 'older woman' with an Eastern European accent whom she calls Thela. That these performances serve to approximate linguistic stereotypes rather than reflect any particular linguistic reality is underscored by Sheila in her discussion below; she identifies the irony in the fact that European American women are more successful at performing a Black identity on the phone lines than African American women are:

9 Most of the guys who call are white, definitely, and for them talking to someone of a different race is exotic and a fetish, you know. So it's really weird. They have this stereotypical idea of how, like, a Black woman should sound and what she's gonna be like. So frequently, we'd have women who were actually Black and we'd hook them up, and they wouldn't believe the woman, that she was Black, because she didn't <u>sound</u> like that stereotype. So conversely, what we had to do – I remember there was this one woman who did calls and she had this sort of Black persona that she would do, which was like the total stereotype. I mean, it really bugged me when I would hear her do it. And the guys loved it. They <u>really</u> thought that this is what a Black woman was!

Sheila's irritation with her colleague's performance points to the restrictive nature of the discourse; operators must vocalize stereotypes that cater to the racist assumptions of their clients. Because the vast majority of male callers request European American women, Sheila explains that operators must also know how to sound 'white' on the telephone. That women of color are often more successful than white women at doing so is underscored by the remarks of a second manager I interviewed, who acknowledged that 'the best white woman we ever had here was Black.' Certainly this is a very different realization of ethnic 'passing' than that discussed by Mary Bucholtz (1995), whose interviewees overtly resist such stereotypes, voicing their own assertions about their identity rather than affirming the expectations of the observer. On the fantasy lines, in contrast, we have the somewhat unusual situation of speakers being able to perform others' ethnicities more 'successfully' than their own. This fact not only points to the strength of stereotyping in the realm of fantasy but also demonstrates the inseparability of race and gender in the public reception of an identity.

This inseparability is particularly evident in the phone-line performances of Andy, a thirty-three-year-old Mexican–American bisexual who poses as a female heterosexual before his male callers. As with the women interviewed for this study, Andy finds that his conversations are well received when he projects a cultural stereotype of vocal femininity: not only is he attentive to the desires of his unsuspecting caller, but he also projects a 'soft and quiet' voice.

10 Believe it or not, it's important to them that you're basically in the same mood as they are, that you're enjoying it too. So if you can sound like you <u>are</u>, then that's the better, that's <u>a</u>lways the better. And the other thing I've found over the years is it's better to sound soft and quiet than loud and noisy . . . if you're a woman. . . . [It's] better to sound ((whispered)) soft, you know, softer. ((in natural voice)) You know, like whispering, rather than ((in loud voice)) OH HO HO HO, ((in natural voice)) really <u>loud</u>, you know, and <u>scream</u>ing. 'Cause basically you're in their ear. And physically that's a very strange thing also. Because with the phone, you know, you <u>are</u> in somebody's ear.

To convince callers of his womanhood, Andy style-shifts into a higher pitch, moving the phone away from his mouth so as to soften the perceived intensity of his voice. This discursive shifting, characterized by the performance of the vocal and verbal garb associated with the other sex, might more appropriately be referred to as *cross-expressing*. The parallel between such an undertaking and the more visual activity of cross-dressing becomes especially apparent in the excerpt below, when Andy performs a European American woman whom he calls Emily:

11 So here, I'll give you the voice, okay? Hold on. (4.0) ((in high pitch, soft whisper)) Hello. (2.0) Hello? (2.0) How are <u>you</u>? (1.5) This is *Emily*. ((in natural voice)) See? It's more – it's more nostrily. I higher the phone – I lift the phone up. Right now I'm just talking regular but I do have the phone lifted up higher. . . . And then I lower my vocals (3.0) ((inhales, then in slow, high, breathy voice)) Hello::. Hi::. ((gasps)) Oh <u>yes</u>! (0.5) I'm <u>so</u> horny right ^<u>no</u>^::w. . . . ((in natural voice)) It's funny how I've actually taped myself and then played it back, and it's actually <u>two</u> <u>separate</u> voices.

Andy's use of the term *the voice* for his female persona is telling. On the phone-sex lines, person and voice are indistinguishable, with the latter coming to substitute for the former. He begins the conversation by tailoring it to his interactant's state of mind (*Hello. Hello? How are you?*), even before offering up his own name. The phone receiver itself becomes an extension of his vocal apparatus, as he moves it away from his mouth and simultaneously lowers his voice so as to achieve the varied pitch range he associates with European American women's speech.

But female heterosexuality is one of the few constants in Andy's cast of phone-sex characters. He presents himself variously as Asian, Mexican, African American, and Southern, catering to the desires of individual callers. As with his performance of women's language, he garnishes his speech with features hegemonically associated with particular ethnic groups.

12 And then when I put the other little things into it, like – if I want an Oriental, then I have to put a little – you know, then I have to think Oriental sort of ((laughs)) and then it comes out a little bit different. Well it's – for example, okay – (1.0) ((in alternating high and low pitch)) hull^o^::. ^hi^i:::, ^how are^ you::? This is Fong ^Su^u:. ((in natural voice)) See? Then you give them like – I think like I'm ((laughs)) at a Chinese restaurant, and I'm listening to the waitress – you know, take my order or something. And then the Hispanic is more like ((clears throat, in high breathy voice)) He:llo:::, this is Ésta es Amelia, cómo estás? (.hhhhh) o:::h lo siento bien, (1.0) rica. ((in natural voice)) Then I think I'm like watching Spanish dancers or Mexican dancers – you know, with their big dresses? ((sings)) da:: dadada da:: dadada- the mariachis. (1.5) And then the Black is a little bit – you know, on and on it goes. [My black name is] Winona-Winona. Like from the Jeffersons? No, I mean – not the Jeffersons, it was uh – the one guy, Jay-Jay? I can't remember the show name, but anyways the sister was named Winona or Wilona or something like that. And then there's the Southern sound, you know, and then like I say, there's a British sound and a French sound. For the Southern woman I'll use, like, Belle, ((laughs)) something Belle. ((laughs)) Oh, I play right up to it sometimes. . . . You definitely have to use ((in slow Southern accent, with elongated vowels)) a Sou:::thern a::ccent. ((laughs, in natural voice)) Absolutely, that has to come through. Shining. So that's a real concentrator, I have to really – you know, be really quiet.

Andy models his Asian persona on a submissive waitress, adopting a quiet voice that serves to highlight the inequality between himself and his conversational master; his voice, perhaps in attempted imitation of a tonal language, moves back and forth between two distinct pitches. His Mexican voice, in contrast, which he models on a flamboyant Spanish dancer, is more overtly sexual; with breathy inhalation and emphatic pronunciation, he manages to eroticize a number of very common Spanish expressions. Because the success of the interaction depends on the middle-class white male caller's ability to recognize the fantasy frame, the operator's language tends to recall dominant instead of localized gender and race ideologies – ones often deemed highly offensive by the group to whom they are ascribed.

Yet the fantasy maker, while admitting the often degrading nature of such an enterprise, nevertheless views her employment of this language as powerful and identifies her position in the conversational exchange as superior. The operators who participated in the study reported that they are completely in control of each conversation: they initiate and dominate the conversational exchange; they are creators of the fantasy story line and scenario; they can decide what kind of fantasies they will entertain; and they can terminate the conversation with a simple flick of the index finger. Indeed, Natalie Rhys (1993), a phone-sex worker in San Francisco who recently wrote about her experiences in the book *Call Me Mistress: Memoirs of a Phone Sex Performer*, comments that the real victims in the exchange are the customers, who feed their time, energy, and money into a noncaring enterprise that exploits them: 'To the workers, pornography is a job no more exciting than any other job. To the owners and managers, it's a business. Both feel superior to the customers. If this attitude seems calloused, consider that it's difficult to have much respect for someone when the only contact you have with him is when you're exploiting his neediness. You might have compassion for him, but not respect' (119).[6]

In accordance with this outlook, most of the women I spoke with described their work first and foremost as artistic. Sheila calls herself a *telephone fantasy artist*. Rachel, whose self-definition is reproduced below, describes what she does for a living as *auditory improvisational theater on the theme of eros*:

13 I'm a good storyteller. A lot of what I do is wasted on most of these people. They're not bright enough to know some of the words I use. And then about every fifteenth call is one that makes it worthwhile. Because it's someone who will go, 'God, you're really good at this! You really use language well! This is fun! I was expecting this to be really weird, but you're cool!' I have a large vocabulary. I read a lot and I'll use other words. I don't own a television. I think that's a big part of my greater command of language than the average human being. And since I've gotten into this, I've also decided that if I'm going to be a storyteller, I'm going to study more about storytelling. I've listened to Garrison Keillor for years, and in the last year or so, I've taped him several times and listened for the devices that he's using to be a more effective storyteller.

This particular operator has written erotica for a number of years and identifies herself primarily as a *good storyteller*. She explains that she actively incorporates storytelling techniques into her own fantasy creations, imitating Garrison Keillor of *Prairie Home Companion*, as well as a number of other well-known storytellers. She and the other fantasy makers would often jokingly refer to themselves as *phone whores* and their switchboard operators as *phone pimps*, but they did not perceive the conversational exchange as representative of any particular asymmetrical sexual reality. Like the woman in this excerpt, who mentions her 'large vocabulary' and her 'greater command of language than the average human being,' the operators interviewed felt that they were so superior linguistically to the average man who called the service that male power was just not an issue. The only exchanges they did perceive as asymmetrical, and in which they consequently did not like to participate, were those domination calls where the male caller overtly restricted their freedom of expression by limiting their feedback to a subservient *yes sir* and *no sir*. Many of the women refused to take these calls altogether, although one operator did say that these low verbal expectations did at least allow her to get a lot of dishes done.

Still, the same fantasy operators would readily admit that they had to subdue their own creativity in order to please a comparatively uncreative audience. The fantasy maker above who considers herself a storyteller, for instance, explained that her linguistic creativity makes her less popular than some of the other fantasy operators because she often refuses to adopt the expected 'stupid, pregnant, and dumb' voice:

14 If I'm in a surly mood and I get a call from a guy who sounds like he just let go of his jackhammer and graduated with a 1.2 average, you know, I have a hard time with those guys. I mean, they need love too, but jesus! Dumb people bug me. . . . It's hard to realize that you're a lot smarter than whoever it is you're dealing with, and number one, if you're really bright then you won't let them know it, and number two, if they do figure it out, then you're in trouble, because they don't like it, especially if it's a man. I mean, that's just the way it is. Girls are supposed to be stupid and pregnant, or just dumb, so that the testosterone type can get out there and conquer the world for you, or whatever it is that they do. . . . I'm approaching this from the angle that I want to be a better storyteller, I want to increase my linguistic abilities. But that isn't what the average customer wants.

Another operator similarly explained that she had to 'be constantly walking that line' between embracing a sexuality for herself and catering to customer expectations of her sexuality. Interesting in her interview, reproduced in excerpt 15, is that she describes her clients' perception of women's language as a submissive sexual position:

15 I wonder if it really is women's language or is it mostly that we're repeating what it is that the men want to hear and want to believe that women like and think. I think it's more what's in their heads. You know, scenarios where I'm being mildly submissive, even though they don't call it that, and they're like calling me a slut and a horny little bitch. . . . It's a total turn off, I never think of myself that way. And that definitely goes through their heads. . . . So having to sometimes

sort of like repeat their ideas back to them because it's what they want to hear can be a drag. So sometimes it's more my idea than my language and sometimes it's there and it's what they're reading out of these stupid magazines, you know, that they really want to believe women are like. . . . It's interesting to be constantly walking that line where you're trying to make sure they're happy and please them and get them off and at the same time – you know, for me, I want to do my best not to perpetuate all the bullshit that goes on in their minds. It is difficult task sometimes. It's a challenge to come up with ways that you can still turn them on without perpetuating all the bullshit about women that they believe.

She realizes that the male fantasy of female sexuality is so firmly rooted within our culture that even though she tries not to perpetuate it, there is little she can do to dispel it. Her feeling is also shared by Andy. He states that being a man has given him more liberty to speak against such degradation, yet he also recognizes the negative influence such attitudes have had on him as an individual:

16 What I think has bothered me over the years more than anything about it has been the degradation of women that I've had to kind of feel because of the way [men] think and feel towards women – a lot of them. You know, there is a lot of degradation involved and basically it filters over to *you* if you're not careful, and you could yourself either feel degraded or degrade others. [I think I notice this] more than the girls, because the girls are interested, I think, in just pleasing, you know, and trying to do the best they could on the call, whereas I feel that I'm beyond doing good on the call.

Both Sheila and Andy speculated that for the male callers this interactive fantasy was in some sense very real, evidenced by the dismay of those callers who for some reason came to suspect that the voice on the telephone was not the beautiful young blonde it presented itself to be. It seems that although these employees are aware of and wish to break away from the negative stereotypes about women's language and sexuality, they are restrained by their clients' expectations of the interaction, and they must therefore try to strike a balance between employing a creative discourse and a stereotypical one.

Conclusion

What exists on the adult message lines is a kind of style shifting that is based primarily on gender and secondarily on variables of age, class, geography, and race. When on the telephone, the fantasy-line operators in this study, whether Asian American, African American, European American, or Latino, switch into a definable conversational style that they all associate with 'women's language.' Bourdieu (1977) might argue that these women, as 'agents continuously subjected to the sanctions of the linguistic market,' have learned this style through a series of positive and negative reinforcements:

> Situations in which linguistic productions are explicitly sanctioned and evaluated, such as examinations or interviews, draw our attention to the existence of mechanisms determining the price of discourse which operate in every linguistic interaction (e.g., the doctor–patient or lawyer–client relation) and more generally in all social relations. It follows that agents continuously subjected to the sanctions of the linguistic market, functioning as a system of positive or negative reinforcements, acquire durable dispositions which are the basis of their perception and appreciation of the state of the linguistic market and consequently of their strategies for expression. (654)

According to Bourdieu, speakers develop their strategies for expression through their experiences within the linguistic market, a notion that he refers to elsewhere as *habitus*. In their interactional histories (e.g., at school, in the family), the female fantasy-line operators have received positive reinforcement for this particular style of discourse and are now, through additional reinforcement within the workplace, selling it back to the culture at large for a high price. Like examinations and interviews, fantasy-line conversations are situations in which linguistic production is explicitly sanctioned and evaluated. If the operator fails to produce the appropriate discursive style (one that is feminine, inviting, and supportive), she will lose her clients and therefore her economic stability. But for such a style to be so overtly reinforced within this particular medium of discourse, the same reinforcement must exist within the larger public, so that women at a very early age begin to, in the words of Bourdieu, 'acquire durable dispositions' toward this particular strategy of expression.

The question then follows: How can current definitions of linguistic power account for the fact that on the fantasy lines, speech that has been traditionally thought of as 'powerless' suddenly becomes a very powerful sexual commodity? Many authors have followed Penelope Eckert and Sally McConnell-Ginet (1992) in arguing that discussions of gender should be located within particular communities of practice. By studying the local meanings attached to interactions, researchers will develop a more flexible understanding of gender – an understanding that allows for variability of meaning within and among communities. These San Francisco-based fantasy-line operators challenge theories that have categorized women's language as powerless and men's language as powerful. Within the context of the adult-message industry, women have learned that manipulating the female conversational stereotype can in fact be powerful, and sometimes even enjoyable. It potentially brings them tens of thousands of dollars; it allows them to support themselves without having to participate in a patriarchal business structure; it lets them exercise sexual power without fear of bodily harm or judicial retribution. Clearly, there is another dimension to power besides the dichotomy of oppressor—oppressed. To say that all women are powerless in sexual interaction, or to say that all women are powerless when they assume a role traditionally thought of as subordinate in a conversation, denies real women's experience of their situation. The women quoted in this chapter view the success of their exchange in terms of how creative they can be in fulfilling a fantasy. Although they recognize that they often have to perpetuate the girly-magazine stereotype of women to maintain a clientele, they consider the men who require this stereotype so unimaginative that to attribute any power to them in the conversational exchange is ludicrous. This somewhat ironic state of affairs indicates that any theory of linguistic power in cross-sex interaction must allow for a variety of influences with respect to individual consent.

Notes

1   The transcription conventions used in this chapter are adapted from Gail Jefferson (1984):

h	an *h* indicates an exhalation (the more *h*'s, the longer the exhalation)
.h	an *h* with a period preceding it indicates an inhalation (the more *h*'s, the longer the inhalation)
(0.4)	indicates length of pause within and between utterances, timed in tenths of a second
a – a	a hyphen with spaces before and after indicates a short pause, less than 0.2 seconds
sa-	a hyphen immediately following a letter indicates an abrupt cutoff in speaking
(())	double parentheses enclose nonverbal movements and extralinguistic commentary
( )	single parentheses enclose words that are not clearly audible (i.e., best guesses)
[ ]	brackets enclose words added to clarify the meaning of the text
__	underlining indicates syllabic stress
CAPS	upper case indicates louder or shouted talk
:	a colon indicates a lengthening of a sound (the more colons, the longer the sound)
.	a period indicates falling intonation
,	a comma indicates continuing intonation
?	a question mark indicates rising intonation at the end of a syllable or word
ˆaˆ	rising arrows indicate a higher pitch for enclosed words(s) or syllables(s)
...	deletion of some portion of the original text

2   There are a significant number of services that advertise to the gay male market, and still others that advertise to the transgender market; only a limited number of services advertise to women. For a lively analysis of gay male phone-fantasy production, see Miller (1995).

3   Because these services normally hire their employees by telephone instead of in person, precise statistics on employee identity are unavailable. The manager of a company established in 1990 estimated that the employees at her company were equally divided between European Americans and African Americans, as well as between heterosexuals and lesbians. In contrast, K. G. Fox, who has been involved with the San Francisco phone-sex industry since 1981, indicated that San Francisco employees tend to be middle-class white women, college-educated, between the ages of twenty-five and thirty-five; she estimated that 20 to 30 percent of them identify as lesbian and 60 to 70 percent as bisexual or heterosexual.

4   It is quite possible, indeed probable, that the women who did refuse me interviews felt more negative about the industry; for a less optimistic account, see Danquah (1993). Still, the perceptions of the phone-sex workers I interviewed in San Francisco are strikingly similar to those of the twenty operators interviewed by Simakis (1990) for the *Village Voice*, who, for the most part, speak positively about their experiences in the industry.

5   The advertising strategies chosen by the men-owned services tend to be much more pornographic and sexually degrading to women than those chosen by the women-owned services. As one manager explained of her own company, 'Since there's a woman owning it and another woman managing it, even though we advertise in *Hustler*, we have probably the most tasteful ads in it. The model has on a bikini-type thing, long blond hair, and she's not showing anything. But the rest of them are like, open wide! So there's a little class in it. And [the last four digits of] our number is KISS. So it's presented a little softer, a little nicer.' The advertising strategies used by K. G. Fox's company are often subtle as well; one of the company's most successful ads was nothing more than a photograph of a telephone with the phrase *SEX OBJECT* underneath.

6   A very different perspective on the power differential between caller and operator is offered by Harry Goldstein (1991) in his short article 'The Dial-ectic of Desire': 'The psychological effects of performing as a tele-sex operator are comparable to, if not more insidious than, being a flesh and blood prostitute, simply because working as a disembodied mastur-bation enhancement device denies the worker all sense of individuality and a large measure of control. . . . Though most operators cling to the illu-sion that they control the call, in reality it is the man at the other end of the line, fingering his Gold Card and stroking himself to glory, who wields the mental paint brush, rendering his Perfect Woman on the blank canvas of the operator's voice' (33).

Reprinted from Kira Hall and Mary Bucholtz (eds), *Gender Articulated* (London: Routledge, 1995).

Further reading for part three

(full publication details are given in the bibliography)

THE MOST EASILY ACCESSIBLE sources for feminist work on gendered linguistic behaviour have tended to be edited collections of essays. The essays such collections include are usually heterogeneous (both in subject matter and in quality), so judicious use of contents pages and indexes is recommended to readers consulting them.

Three influential collections published before 1985 are: *Language and Sex: Difference and Dominance* (Thorne and Henley 1975); *Women and Language in Literature and Society* (McConnell-Ginet, Borker and Furman 1980); *Language, Gender and Society* (Thorne, Kramarae and Henley 1983). All of these come from the US, and all contain at least a couple of pieces which have since become much-cited 'classics'. Slightly later collections include *Women and Language in Transition* (Penfield 1987); *Language, Gender and Sex in Comparative Perspective* (Philips, Steele and Tanz 1987), which as its title suggests does not confine itself to the English language, and *Women in Their Speech Communities* (Coates and Cameron 1988); the first two are American, the last is British. Some influential articles dating from the 1980s have recently been collected in *Gender and Conversational Interaction* (Tannen 1993).

In the last few years, several collections have appeared in which contributors pursue what I have glossed in this volume as 'new directions'. These include *Gender Articulated* (Hall and Bucholtz 1995); *Rethinking Language and Gender Research* (Bergvall, Bing and Freed 1996) and the first collection to deal specifically with men's language as a gendered phenomenon,

Language and Masculinity (Johnson and Meinhof 1997). Another new departure (not the first volume on the subject but probably the first which comes from a mainstream academic publishing house and is therefore widely accessible) is *Queerly Phrased* (Livia and Hall 1997), which is subtitled *Language, Gender and Sexuality.*

The 'dominance v. difference' debate crops up in a number of the collections cited above, but for more extended arguments readers are directed to other sources. The classic statement of the 'difference' position is an article by Maltz and Borker (1982), 'A cultural approach to male–female misunderstanding'; Deborah Tannen's position, which she established in her popular works *You Just Don't Understand* (1990) and *Talking from 9 to 5* (1995), is clarified and defended in the introduction to *Gender and Discourse* (1994), a volume which collects together all her published scholarly essays on language and gender. An extended argument against the 'difference' approach, as well as against the kind of 'deficit' model represented by Robin Lakoff's early work, can be found in Mary Crawford's *Talking Difference* (1995), while Janet Holmes's *Women, Men and Politeness* (1995) draws on aspects of both 'difference' and 'dominance' approaches.

Many useful observations on these issues are made in Susan Gal's article 'Speech and silence' (1991), a shorter version of which appears under the title 'Language, gender and power: an anthropological review' in Hall and Bucholtz's *Gender Articulated*. Another anthropologically-oriented article which has been influential, since it proposes the important idea that language does not reflect gender difference *directly* at all, is Elinor Ochs's 'Indexing gender' (1992).

The sociolinguists of gender (not quite the same as feminist linguistics, but the two things overlap considerably) has produced a number of accessible introductory texts, such as Jennifer Coates's *Women, Men and Language* (1986) and David Graddol and Joan Swann's *Gender Voices* (1989). Joan Swann has also written a book about the development of gendered linguistic behaviour, *Girls, Boys and Language* (1992), which is of particular interest to teachers and others who work with children and young people. An introduction written primarily for feminists, as opposed to linguists, is my own *Feminism and Linguistic Theory* (Cameron 1985/1992).

Finally, Jennifer Coates has edited a reader titled *Language and Gender* (Coates 1997). It is narrower in its overall scope than this one, but more comprehensive in its coverage of the subject to which it is devoted, namely the sociolinguistic study of gendered speech behaviour. It includes many notable publications of the 1980s and 1990s.

Bibliography

Editor's note

All bibliographical references are to the edition cited in the reprinted text to which they relate. However, where I am aware of a more recent/accessible location for the piece cited I have indicated it at the end of the reference, thus: [also repr. in . . .]. In some instances, where a work exists in UK and US editions with different dates and publishers, I have given details of both; the main reference is to the edition cited in the text (this usually reflects the nationality of the author who cited it), while the other appears in parenthesis: author and title information should be taken to apply to both. A date enclosed in square brackets indicates first publication where this is significant. For instance, 'Beauvoir, S. de (1972 [1949]) *The Second Sex*' indicates that this work first appeared in 1949. The details given refer to the 1972 Penguin edition in English translation, but it's important to make clear that the book wasn't written in the 1970s.

Works Cited in the Text

Althusser, L. (1971) *Lenin and Philosophy and Other Essays*, London: Verso.

Archer, J. (1978) 'Biological explanations of sex-role stereotypes: conceptual, social and semantic issues', in Chetwynd, J. and Hartnett, O. (eds) *The Sex Role System*, London: Routledge & Kegan Paul.

Aries, E. (1987) 'Gender and communication', in Shaver, P. and Hendrick, C. (eds) *Sex and Gender*, Newbury Park, CA: Sage.

Aries, E. and Johnson, F.L. (1983) 'Close friendship in adulthood: conversational content between same sex friends', *Sex Roles* 9:1183–96.

Atkinson, D. (1987) 'Names and titles: maiden name retention and the use of Ms', *JAPLA* 9: 56–83.

Bardwick, J.M. and Douvan, E. (1977) 'Ambivalence: the socialization of women' in Stein, P.J., Richman, J. and Hannon, N. (eds) *The Family: Functions, Conflicts and Symbols*, Reading, MA: Addison-Wesley.

Baron, D. (1986) *Grammar and Gender*, New Haven: Yale University Press.

Beauvoir, Simone de (1972 [1949]) *The Second Sex*, trans. H.M. Parshley, Harmondsworth: Penguin Books.

Becker, A.L. (1982) 'Beyond translation', in Byrnes, H. (ed.) *Contemporary Perceptions of Language: Interdisciplinary Dimensions*, Washington DC: Georgetown University Press.

Becker, A.L. and Oka, G.N. (1974) 'Person in Kawi', *Oceanic Linguistics* 13: 229–55.

Beeman, W.O. (1986) *Language, Status and Power in Iran*, Bloomington: Indiana University Press.

Bell, R.P., Parker, B.J. and Guy-Sheftall, B. (eds) (1979) *Sturdy Black Bridges: Visions of Black Women in Literature*, Garden City: Anchor/Doubleday.

Bellinger, D. and Gleason, J.B. (1982) 'Sex differences in parental directives to young children', *Sex Roles* 8: 1123–39.

Berger, P. and Luckmann, T. (1972) *The Social Construction of Reality*, Harmondsworth: Penguin Books.

Bergvall, V., Bing, J. and Freed, A. (eds) (1996) *Rethinking Language and Gender Research: Theory and Practice*, London: Longman.

Blicksilver, E. (ed.) (1978) *The Ethnic American Woman*, Dubuque: Kendall/Hunt.

Bloomfield, M. and Newmark, L. (1967) *A Linguistic Introduction to the History of English*, New York: Knopf.

Blumenthal, J. and Warriner, J. (1964) *English Workshop: Grades 9,10,11,12*, New York: Harcourt, Brace and World.

Bly, Robert (1990) *Iron John: A Book About Men*, Reading, MA: Addison-Wesley.

Bodine, A. (1975) 'Sex differentiation in language', in Thorne and Henley (eds).

Bolinger, D. (1975) *Aspects of Language*, New York: Harcourt Brace Jovanovich.

Bourdieu, P. (1977) 'The economics of linguistic exchanges', *Social Science Information* 16(6): 645–68.

Bremner, S., Caskey, N. and Moonwomon, B. (eds) (1986) *Proceedings of the First Berkeley Women and Language Conference*, Berkeley, CA: Berkeley Women and Language Group.

Britton, J. (1975) *Language and Learning*, Harmondsworth: Penguin Books.

Brown, R. and Gilman, A. (1960) 'The pronouns of power and solidarity', in Sebeok, T. (ed.) *Style in Language*, Cambridge, MA: MIT Press.

Bruner, E.M. and Kelso, J.P. (1980) 'Gender differences in graffiti: a semiotic perspective', in Kramarae, C. (ed.) *The Voices and Words of Women and Men*, Oxford: Pergamon.

Butturff, D.L. and Epstein, E.L. (eds) (1979) *Women's Language and Style*, Akron, OH: University of Akron.

Byrnes, H. (1986) 'Interactional style in German and American conversations', *Text* 6(2): 189–206.

Cameron, D. (1985) *Feminism and Linguistic Theory*, London: Macmillan [2nd edn 1992].

—— (1995) *Verbal Hygiene*, London: Routledge.

—— (1998) 'Gender, language and discourse: a review', *Signs: Journal of Women, Culture and Society*, Summer.

Cameron, D., McAlinden, F. and O'Leary, K. (1988) 'Lakoff in context: the social and linguistic functions of tag questions', in Coates and Cameron (ed.).

Campbell, J. (1964) *The Masks of God: Occidental Mythology*, New York: Viking.

Chalmers, A. (1978) *What Is This Thing Called Science?*, Milton Keynes: Open University Press.

Chelin, P. (1991) 'Inconsistencies in the *Toronto Star* and its 1990 style guide', unpubl., York University.

Cixous, H. (1976) 'Le sexe ou la tête', *Les Cahiers du GRIF* 13: 1–16.

—— (1980/81a) 'The laugh of the Medusa', in Marks and de Courtivron (eds).

—— (1980/81b) 'Sorties', in Marks and de Courtivron (eds).

Coates, J. (1986) *Women, Men and Language*, London: Longman.

—— (1988) 'Gossip revisited: language in all-female groups', in Coates and Cameron (eds).

—— (1996) *Women Talk: Conversation Between Women Friends*, Oxford: Blackwell.

—— (ed.) (1997) *Language and Gender*, Oxford: Blackwell.

—— and Cameron, D. (eds) (1988) *Women in Their Speech Communities: New Perspectives on Language and Sex*, London: Longman.

Cole, C.M. (1991) 'Oh wise women of the stalls . . .', *Discourse & Society* 2: 401–11.

Conklin, N.F. (1973) 'Perspectives on the dialects of women', paper presented to the American Dialect Society, Ann Arbor.

Conley, J.M., O'Barr, W.M. and Lind, E.A. (1979) 'The power of language: presentational style in the courtroom', *Duke Law Journal* 1978: 1375–99.

Coote, A. (1981) 'The nature of man talk', *New Statesman*, January 2.

Corsaro, W. and Rizzo, T. (1990) 'Disputes in the peer culture of American and Italian nursery school children', in Grimshaw, A. (ed.) *Conflict Talk*, Cambridge: Cambridge University Press.

Council of Ontario Universities (1988) *Employment Equity for Women: A University Handbook*, Toronto: COU.

Coward, R. (1986) 'Porn: what's in it for women?' *New Statesman*, June 13.

Crawford, M. (1995) *Talking Difference*, London: Sage.

Curme, G.O. (1931) *A Grammar of The English Language Vol III* (Syntax), Boston: DC Heath.

Danquah. M.N-A. (1993) 'Hanging up on phone sex', *Washington Post*, June 13: C1.

Davies, C.E. (1986) 'The anonymous collective conversations of women's graffiti', in Bremner, Caskey and Moonwomon (eds).

DeFrancisco, V.L. (1990a) 'Integrating gender issues in the intercultural communication classroom: moving beyond the "variable" approach', presented at the 13th conference of the Organization for the Study of Communication, Language and Gender, Reno.

—— (1990b) 'Response to Pamela Fishman: a qualitative study of ongoing interactions in heterosexual couples' homes', presented at Speech Communication Association convention, Chicago.

—— (1991) 'The sounds of silence: how men silence women in marital relations', *Discourse & Society* 2: 413–23.

Dorval, B. (ed.) (1990) *Conversational Coherence and its Development*, Norwood, NJ: Ablex.

Doyle, M. (19

Dubois, B.L. and Crouch, I. (1987) 'Linguistic disruption: he/she, s/he, he or she, he-she', in Penfield (ed.).

Dunant, S. (ed.) (1994) *The War of the Words: The PC Debate*, London: Virago.

Eagleton, M. (ed.) (1986) *Feminist Literary Theory: A Reader*, Oxford: Blackwell [revised edn. 1996].

Eckert, P. (1990) 'Co-operative competition in adolescent "girl talk" ' , *Discourse Processes* 13: 91–122.

Eckert, P. and McConnell-Ginet, S. (1992) 'Think practically and look locally: language and gender as community-based practice', *Annual Review of Anthropology* 21: 461–90.

Edelsky, C. (1981) 'Who's got the floor?' *Language in Society* 10: 383–421 [also repr. in Tannen 1993].

Edwards, E.R. (1903) *Etude phonétique de la langue japonaise*, Leipzig.

Ellis, H. (1974) *Man and Woman: A study of human secondary characteristics*, New York: Ayer Co Pub Inc.

Ellman, M. (1968) *Thinking About Women*, New York: Harcourt Brace [also London: Virago, 1979].

Evans, B. and Evans, C. (1957) *A Dictionary of Contemporary American Usage*, New York: Random House.

Fairclough, N. (1992) *Discourse and Social Change*, Cambridge: Polity Press.

Fasold, R. (1988) 'Language policy and change: sexist language in the periodical news media', in Lowenberg, P. (ed.), *Language Spread and Language Policy*, Washington DC: Georgetown University Press.

Felman, S. (1975) 'Women and Madness', *Diacritics* 5 (Winter), 2–10 [also repr. in Warhol, R. and Herndl, D.P. (eds) (1991), *Feminisms: An Anthology of Literary Theory and Criticism*, New Brunswick, NJ: Rutgers University Press.

Fielding, G. and Hartley, P. (1987) 'The telephone: a neglected medium', in Cashdan, A. and Jordin, M. (eds) *Studies in Communication*, New York: Blackwell.

Fishman, P. (1978) 'Interaction: the work women do', *Social Problems* 25: 397–406.

—— (1979) 'What do couples talk about when they're alone?', in Butturff and Epstein (eds).

Foucault, M. (1972) *The Archaeology of Knowledge*, London: Tavistock.

—— (1978) *The History of Sexuality*, London: Allen Lane.

Fowler, H.W. (1926) *A Dictionary of Modern English Usage*, New York: Oxford University Press.

Frank, F. and Treichler, P. (eds) (1989) *Language, Gender and Professional Writing*, New York: MLA.

Frank, J. (1988) 'Communicating "by pairs": agreeing and disagreeing among married couples', unpubl., Georgetown University.

French, C.W. (ed.) (1987) *The Associated Press Stylebook and Libel Manual*, Reading, MA: Addison-Wesley.

Friedrich, P. (1972) 'Social context and semantic feature: the Russian pronominal usage', in Gumperz, J. and Hymes, D. (eds) *Directions in Sociolinguistics*, Oxford: Blackwell.

Gal, S. (1991) 'Speech and silence: the problematics of research on language and gender', in M. di Leonardo (ed.) *Gender at the Crossroads of Knowledge*, Berkeley, CA: University of California Press.

Gardiner, J.K. (1981) 'On female identity and writing by women', *Critical Inquiry* 8.

Gardner, C.B. (1980) 'Passing by: street remarks, address rights and the urban female', *Sociological Inquiry* 50: 328–56.

Gavey, N. (1989) 'Feminist poststructuralism and discourse analysis', *Psychology of Women Quarterly* 13: 459–75.

Gilligan, C. (1982) *In a Different Voice*, Cambridge, MA: Harvard University Press.

Gleason, J.B. (1987) 'Sex differences in parent–child interaction', in Philips, Steele and Tanz (eds).

Globe and Mail (1990) *Globe and Mail Style Guide*, Toronto.

Goldstein, H. (1991) 'The dial-ectic of desire: for women at the other end of the phone sex line, some fantasies ring painfully true', *Utne Reader*, March/April: 32–3.

Goodwin, M.H. (1980) 'Directive-response sequences in girls' and boys' task activities', in McConnell-Ginet *et al.* (eds).

—— (1988) 'Cooperation and competition across girls' play activities', in Todd, A. and Fisher, S. (eds) *Gender and Discourse: the Power of Talk*, Norwood, NJ: Ablex.

—— (1990) *He-said-she-said: Talk as Social Organization Among Black Children*, Bloomington: Indiana University Press.

Goodwin, M.H. and Goodwin, C. (1987) 'Children's arguing', in Philips, Steele and Tanz (eds).

Government of Canada (1984) *Report of the Royal Commission on Equality in Employment*, Ottawa.

Graddol, D. and Swann, J. (1989) *Gender Voices*, Oxford: Blackwell.

Graddol, D., Leith, D. and Swann, J. (eds) (1995) *English: History, Diversity and Change*, London: Routledge.

Greenough and Kittredge, (1901) *Words and Their Ways in English Speech*, New York: Macmillan.

Grice, H.P. (1957) 'Meaning', *Philosophical Review* 66: 377–88.

—— (1967) William James Lectures, Harvard University.

Grimshaw, A.D. (1973–4) 'On Language and society: Parts I and II', *Contemporary Society* 2.6: 575–83; 1: 3–11.

Gumperz, J. (ed.) (1982) *Language and Social Identity*, Cambridge: Cambridge University Press.

—— (1982) *Discourse Strategies*, Cambridge: Cambridge University Press.

Gumperz, J. and Levinson, S. (eds) (1995) *Rethinking Linguistic Relativity*, Cambridge: Cambridge University Press.

Haas, M.R. (1964 [1944]) 'Men's and women's speech in Koasati', in Hymes, D. (ed.) *Language in Culture and Society*, New York: Harper and Row.

Hall, K. and Bucholtz, M. (eds) (1995) *Gender Articulated: Language and the Socially Constructed Self*, London: Routledge.

Halliday, M.A.K. (1985) *An Introduction to Functional Grammar*, London: Edward Arnold.

Hanscombe, G. and Smyers, V. (1987) *Writing For Their Lives*, London: The Women's Press.

Henley, N. (1977) *Body Politics: Power, Sex and Non-verbal Communication*, Englewood Cliffs, NJ: Prentice-Hall.

—— (1987) 'This new species that seeks a new language', in Penfield (ed).

Henley, N. and Kramarae, C. (1991) 'Gender, power and miscommunication', in Coupland, N., Giles, H. and Wieman, J. (eds) *'Miscommunication' and Problematic Talk*, Newbury, CA: Sage.

Henry, V. (1879) 'Sur le parler des hommes et le parler des femmes dans la langue chiquita', *Revue de linguistique* 12: 305.

Henry, W.A. (1991) 'Upside down in the groves of academe', *Time* 137(13): 66–9.

Herring, S., Johnson, D. and diBenedetto, T. (1995) 'This discussion is going too far!' in Hall and Bucholtz (eds).

Hiatt, M. (1977) *The Way Women Write*, New York: Teachers' College Press.

Hoffman, E. (1989) *Lost in Translation: A Life in a New Language*, New York: Penguin Books.

Hollway, W. (1983) 'Heterosexual sex: power and desire for the other', in Cartledge, S. and Ryan, J. (eds) *Sex and Love: New Thoughts on Old Contradictions*, London: The Women's Press.

Holmes, J. (1993) 'Women's talk: the question of sociolinguistic universals', *Australian Journal of Communication* 20(3): 125–49.

—— (1995) *Women, Men and Politeness*, London: Longman.

Horner, A. and Zlosnick, S. (1990) *Landscapes of Desire: Metaphors in Modern Women's Fiction*, Hemel Hempstead: Harvester Wheatsheaf.

Hughes, L.A. (1988) '"But that's not *really* mean"': competing in a cooperative mode', *Sex Roles* 19 (11/12) 669–87.

Hull, G.T., Scott, P.B. and Smith, B. (eds) (1982) *All The Women Are White, All the Blacks Are Men, But Some of Us Are Brave: Black Women's Studies*, Old Westbury, NY: Feminist Press.

Hymes, D. (1961) 'Linguistic aspects of cross-cultural personality study', in Kaplan, B. (ed.) *Studying Personality Cross-culturally*, New York: Harper and Row, 313–60.

Irigaray, L. (1985) *This Sex Which Is Not One*, trans. C. Porter, New York: Cornell University Press.

Jackson, S. (1992) 'The amazing deconstructing woman', *Trouble & Strife* 25: 25–31.

Jacobs, G. (1996) 'Lesbian and gay male language use: a critical review of the literature', *American Speech* 71(1): 49–71.

Jakobson, R. (1971) *Studies in Child Language and Aphasia*, The Hague: Mouton.

James, D. and Clarke, S. (1993) 'Women, men and interruptions: a critical review', in Tannen (ed.).

James, D. and Drakich, J. (1993) 'Understanding gender differences in amount of talk', in Tannen (ed.).

Jenkins, M. M. (1986) 'What's so funny? Joking among women', in Bremner, Caskey and Moonwomon (eds).

Jespersen, O. (1938) *Growth and Structure of the English Language*, New York: Free Press.

Johnson, F.L. and Aries, E. (1983a) 'Conversational patterns among same sex pairs of late adolescent close friends', *Journal of Genetic Psychology* 142: 225–38.

—— (1983b) 'The talk of women friends', *Women's Studies International Forum* 6: 53–61.

Johnson, S. and Meinhof, U-H (eds) (1997) *Language and Masculinity*, Oxford: Blackwell.

Jones, A.R. (1985) 'Inscribing femininity: French theories of the feminine', in Greene, G. and Kahn, C. (eds) *Making a Difference*, London: Methuen.

Jones, D. (1980) 'Gossip: notes on women's oral culture', in Kramarae, C. (ed.) *The Voices and Words of Women and Men*, Oxford: Pergamon.

Jong, E. (1973) *Fear of Flying*, New York: Holt, Rinehart and Winston.

K., K. (1994) *Sweet Talkers: Words from the mouth of a 'Pay to Say' Girl*, New York: Masquerade Books.

Kakava, C. (1989) 'Argumentative conversation in a Greek family', paper presented to the LSA Annual Meeting, Washington DC.

Kalčik, S. (1975) ' "...Like Ann's gynecologist or the time I was almost raped": personal narratives in women's rap groups', *Journal of American Folklore* 88: 3–11.

Kaplan, C. (ed.) (1975) *Salt and Bitter and Good: Three Centuries of English and American Women Poets*, London and New York: Paddington Press.

Keenan, E.O. (1974) 'Norm makers, norm breakers: uses of speech by men and women in a Malagasy community', in Bauman, R. and Sherzer, J. (eds) *Explorations in the Ethnography of Speaking*, Cambridge: Cambridge University Press.

Kelly, L., Burton, S. and Regan, L. (1994) 'Researching women's lives or studying women's oppression? Reflections on what constitutes feminist research', in Maynard, M. and Purvis J. (eds.) *Researching Women's Lives from a Feminist Perspective*, London: Taylor and Francis.

Kessler, S. and McKenna, W. (1978) *Gender: an Ethnomethodological Approach*, New York: Wiley.

Ketchum, S.A. (1979) 'Reflections on meaning and power', presented to the Society for Women in Philosophy, Eastern division, Fall meeting, Ithaca, NY.

Key, M.R. (1972) 'Linguistic behavior of male and female', *Linguistics* 88: 15–31.

Khrosroshahi, F. (1989) 'Penguins don't care but women do', *Language in Society* 18: 505–25.

Kimenyi, A. (1992) 'Why is it that women in Rwanda cannot marry?' in Hall, K., Bucholtz, M. and Moonwomon, B. (eds) *Locating Power: Proceedings of the Second Berkeley Women and Language Conference*, Berkeley, CA: Berkeley Women and Language Group.

Kingston, M. Hong (1977) *The Woman Warrior: Memories of a Girlhood among Ghosts*, New York: Vintage.

Kirby, J. (1746) *A New English Grammar*, Menston: Scolar Press Facsimile.

Kissling, E.A. (1991) 'Street harassment: the language of sexual terrorism', *Discourse & Society* 2: 451–60.

Kollock, P., Blumstein, P. and Schwartz, P. (1985) 'Sex and power in interaction: conversational privileges and duties', *American Sociological Review* 50: 34–46.

Komarovsky, M. (1962) *Blue Collar Marriage*, New York: Vintage.

Kramarae, C. (1986a) 'A feminist critique of sociolinguistics', *JAPLA* 8: 1–22.

—— (1986b) 'Linguistic crimes which the law cannot reach', in Bremner, Caskey and Moonwomon (eds).

—— (1990) 'Changing the complexion of gender in language research', in Giles, H. and Robinson, W. (eds) *Handbook of Language and Social Psychology*, Chichester: Wiley.

Kristeva, J. (1980/81) 'Woman can never be defined', trans. M. August, in Marks and de Courtivron (eds).

Kuhn, T. (1972) *The Structure of Scientific Revolutions*, Chicago: Chicago University Press.

Labov, W. (1972) *Sociolinguistic Patterns*, Philadelphia: University of Pennsylvania Press.

Lacan, J. (1977a) *Ecrits: A Selection*, London: Tavistock.

—— (1977b) *The Four Fundamentals of Psycho-Analysis*, Harmondsworth: Penguin Books.

Lakoff, R. (1972) 'Language in context', *Language* 48: 907–27.

—— (1975) *Language and Woman's Place*, New York: Harper and Row.

—— (1979) 'Women's language', in Butturff and Epstein (eds).

Langer, S. (1976) *Philosophy in a New Key*, Cambridge, MA: Harvard University Press, 3rd edn.

Lee, D. (1992) *Competing Discourses: Perspective and Ideology in Language*, London: Longman.

Leonard, S.A. (1929) *The Doctrine of Correctness in English Usage 1700–1800*, Madison: University of Wisconsin Studies in Language and Literature.

—— (1932) *Current English Usage*, Chicago: Inland Press.

Leonardi, S. (1986) 'Bare places and ancient blemishes: Virginia Woolf's search for new language in *Night and Day*', *Novel* (Winter): 150–64.

Livia, A. and Hall, K. (eds) (1997) *Queerly Phrased: Language, Gender and Sexuality*, Oxford: Oxford University Press.

Lutz, C. (1986) 'Emotion, thought and estrangement: emotion as a cultural category', *Cultural Anthropology* 1(3): 287–309.

—— (1990) 'Engendered emotion: gender, power and the rhetoric of emotional control in American discourse', in Abu-Lughod, L. and Lutz, C. (eds) *Language and the Politics of Emotion*, Cambridge: Cambridge University Press.

McCawley, J. (1974) Letter to the editor, *New York Times Magazine*, 10 November.

McConnell-Ginet, S. (1978) 'Intonation in a man's world', *Signs* 3: 541–59.

McConnell-Ginet, S., Borker, R. and Furman, N. (eds) (1980) *Women and Language in Literature and Society*, New York: Praeger.

McKnight, G.H. (1925) 'Conservatism in American speech', *American Speech* 1: 1–17.

—— (1928) *Modern English in the Making*, New York: Appleton.

Maccoby, E. (1986) 'Social groupings in childhood', in Olweus, D., Block, J. and Radke-Yarrow, M. (eds) *Development of Antisocial and Prosocial Behavior*, New York: Academic Press.

Maltz, D. and Borker, R. (1982) 'A cultural approach to male–female misunderstanding', in Gumperz (ed.).

Marks, E. and de Courtivron, I. (1980) *New French Feminisms*, Amherst: University of Massachusetts Press [also Brighton: Harvester Press, 1981].

Martin, D. (1976) *Battered Wives*, San Francisco: Glide.

Martyna, W. (1980a) 'Beyond the he/man approach: the case for nonsexist language', *Signs: Journal of Women in Culture and Society* 5: 482–93 [also repr. In Thorne, Kramarae and Henley (eds)].

—— (1980b) 'The psychology of the generic masculine', in McConnell-Ginet *et al.* (eds).

Mead, M. (1977) 'End linkage: a tool for cross-cultural analysis', in Brockman, J. (ed.) *About Bateson*, New York: Dutton.

Mhlophe, G. (1987) 'The Toilet', in Malan, R. (ed.) *Being Here: Modern Stories from South Africa*, Cape Town: David Philip.

Miller, C. and K. Swift (1979) *Words and Women: New Language in New Times*, Harmondsworth: Penguin Books.

—— (1980) *A Handbook of Nonsexist Writing*, London: Women's Press [3rd revised UK edition, 1995].

Miller, D.E. (1995) 'Inside the switchboards of desire: storytelling on phone sex lines, in Leap, W. (ed.) *Beyond the Lavender Lexicon: Authenticity, Imagination and Appropriation in Lesbian and Gay Language*, New York: Gordon and Breach Press.

Mills, S. (1995a) *Feminist Stylistics*, London: Routledge.

—— (ed.) (1995b) *Language and gender: Interdisciplinary Perspectives*, London: Longman.

Milroy, J. (1992) *Language Variation and Change*, Oxford: Blackwell.

Mitchell, J. and Rose, J. (eds) (1982) *Feminine Sexuality: Jacques Lacan and the école freudienne*, London: Macmillan.

Moraga, C. and Anzaldua, G. (eds) (1981) *This Bridge Called My Back: Writings by Radical Women of Color*, Watertown, MA: Persephone Press.

Morris, P. (1993) *Literature and Feminism*, Oxford: Blackwell.

Murray, L. (1795) *English Grammar*, Menston: Scolar Press Facsimile.

Mushindo, P.B. (1976) *A Short History of the Bemba*, Lusaka, Zambia: NECZAM.

NCCL [National Council for Civil Liberties] (1983) *The Rape Controversy*, Nottingham: Russel Press.

Norman, M. (1990) *These Good Men: Friendships Forged from War*, New York: Crown.

Oates, J.C. (1986) 'Is there a female voice?', in Eagleton (ed.).

Ochs, E. (1992) 'Indexing gender', in Duranti, A. and Goodwin, C. (eds) *Rethinking Context: Language as an Interactive Phenomenon*, Cambridge: Cambridge University Press.

Ong, W.J. (1981) *Fighting for Life: Contest, Sexuality and Consciousness*, Ithaca, NY: Cornell University Press.

Ontario Women's Directorate (1988) *Employment Equity in the Public Sector: A Survey Report*, Toronto: OWD.

Paule, G.F. (1991) *Dishing It Out: Power and Resistance Among Waitresses in a New Jersey Restaurant*, Philadelphia: Temple University Press.

Paulston, C. (1971) 'Language universals and sociocultural implications in usage: personal questions in Swedish', paper presented at LSA 46th Meeting, St Louis.

Paulston, C. and Featheringham, T. (1974) 'Language and social class: pronouns of address in Swedish', paper presented at LSA 49th Meeting, New York.

Pauwels, A. (1998) *Women Changing Language*, London: Longman.

Pecheux, M. (1983) *Language, Semantics and Ideology*, London: Macmillan.

Penelope, J. (1990) *Speaking Freely*, New York: Pergamon.

Penfield, J. (ed.) (1987) *Women and Language in Transition*, Albany, NY: SUNY Press.

Philips, S.U., Steele, S. and Tanz, C. (eds) (1987) *Language, Gender and Sex in Comparative Perspective*, Cambridge: Cambridge University Press.

Pinter, H. (1988) *Mountain Language*, New York: Grove Press.

Ploss, H. and Bartels, M. (1908) *Das Weib in der Natur und Völkerkunde*, Leipzig.

Poole, J. (1646) *The English Accidence*, Menston: Scolar Press Facsimile.

Poutsma, H. (1916) *A Grammar of Late Modern English*, Groningen: P. Noordhoof.

Pullum, G. (1991) *The Great Eskimo Vocabulary Hoax, and Other Irreverent Essays on the Study of Language*, Chicago: University of Chicago Press.

Questions Féministes Editorial Collective (1980/81) 'Variations on Common Themes', in Marks and de Courtivron (eds).

Rakow, L.F. (1987) 'Looking to the future: five questions for gender research', *Women's Studies in Communication* 10: 79–86.

Rape Counselling and Research Project (1979) *Rape, Police and Forensic Procedure*, London: HMSO.

Rhys, N. (1993) *Call Me Mistress: Memoirs of a Phone Sex Performer*, Novato, CA: Miwok Press.

Rich, A. (1980) *On Lies, Secrets and Silence*, London: Virago Press [US edn. 1979, Norton].

Roberts, P. (1967) *The Roberts English Series*, New York: Harcourt, Brace and World.

Rochefort, A. (1665) *Histoire naturelle et morale des Iles Antilles*, Rotterdam.

Rodriguez, R. (1981) *Hunger of Memory*, Boston, MA: Godine.

Rosen, H. (1972) *Language and Class: A Critical Look at the Theories of Basil Bernstein*, Bristol: Falling Wall Press.

Rubin, J. (1972) 'Language planning offers new insights into the nature of language change', paper presented to the AAA 71st meeting, Toronto.

Russell, D. (1982) *Rape in Marriage*, London: Macmillan.

Sacks, H. (1972) 'On the analyzability of stories by children', in Gumperz, J. and Hymes, D. (eds) *Directions in Sociolinguistics: The Ethnography of Speaking*, New York: Holt, Rinehart and Winston.

Sapir, E. (1970) *Selected Writings in Culture, Language and Personality*, ed. D. Mandelbaum, Berkeley: University of California Press.

Sattel, J. (1983) 'Men, inexpressiveness and power', in Thorne, Kramarae and Henley (eds).

Saville-Troike, M. (1989) *The Ethnography of Communication*, 2nd edn. Oxford: Oxford University Press.

Saxon, S. (1737) *The English Scholar's Assistant*, Menston: Scolar Press Facsimile.

Scheman, N. (1980) 'Anger and the politics of naming', in McConnell-Ginet *et al.* (eds).

Schiffrin, D. (1984) 'Jewish argument as sociability', *Language in Society* 13(3): 311–35.

Schlegel, A. (1989) 'Gender issues and cross cultural research', *Behavior Science Research* 23: 265–80.

Schulz, M. (1975) 'The semantic derogation of women', in Thorne and Henley (eds).

Scollon, R. (1985) 'The machine stops: silence in the metaphor of malfunction', in Tannen and Saville-Troike (eds).

Scollen, R. and Scollon, S. (1981) *Narrative, Literacy and Face in Interethnic Communication*, Norwood, NJ: Ablex.

Seidel, G. (1988) 'The British right's new "enemy within": the anti-racists', in Smitherman, G. and van Dijk, T. (eds) *Discourse and discrimination*, Detroit: Wayne State University Press.

Sheldon, A. (1990) 'Pickle fights: gendered talk in preschool disputes', *Discourse Processes* 13: 5–31.

Showalter, E. (1981) 'Feminist criticism in the wilderness', *Critical Inquiry* 8: 189–206.

Shuy, R. (1982) 'Topic as the unit of analysis in a criminal law case', in Tannen, D. (ed.) *Analyzing Discourse: Text and Talk*, Washington DC: Georgetown University Press.

Sifianou, M. (1992) 'The use of diminutives in expressing politeness: Modern Greek versus English', *Journal of Pragmatics* 17(2): 155–73.

Simakis, A. (1990) 'Telephone love', *Village Voice*, July 17: 35–9.

Smith, F. (1971) *Understanding Reading*, New York: Holt, Rinehart and Winston.

Sorrels, B. (1983) *The Nonsexist Communicator*, Englewood Cliffs, NJ: Prentice-Hall.

Spender, D. (1980) *Man Made Language*, London: Routledge and Kegan Paul.

—— (1996) *Nattering on the Net*. Melbourne: Spinifex.

Steinem, G. (1983) *Outrageous Acts and Everyday Rebellions*, New York: Holt, Rinehart and Winston.

Sugimoto, N. (1991) 'A feminist "click" in pedagogy: a case in intercultural communication', presented to NCWSA Conference, Notre Dame.

Sunderland, J. (ed.) (1994) *Exploring Gender: Questions and Implications for English Language Education*, Hemel Hempstead: Prentice-Hall.

Swann, J. (1992) *Girls, Boys and Language*, Oxford: Blackwell.

Swift, J. (1932 [1735]) 'Thoughts on various subjects', in Eddy, W.A. (ed.) *Satires and Personal Writings by Jonathan Swift*, Oxford: Oxford University Press.

Tallentire, D. (1986) 'Confirming intuition about style using concordances', in Jones, A. (ed.) *The Computer in Literary and Linguistic Studies*, Cardiff: University of Wales Press.

Tannen, D. (1981) 'Indirectness in discourse: ethnicity as conversational style', *Discourse Processes* 4(3): 221–38.

—— (1984) *Conversational Style: Analyzing Talk among Friends*, Norwood, NJ: Ablex.

—— (1985) 'Silence: Anything but', in Tannen and Saville-Troike (eds).

—— (1986) *That's Not What I Meant! How Conversational Style Makes or Breaks Your Relations with Others*, New York: Morrow.

—— (1987) 'Repetition in conversation: toward a poetics of talk', *Language* 63(3): 574–605.

—— (1989) *Talking Voices: Repetition, Dialogue and Imagery in Conversational Discourse*, Cambridge: Cambridge University Press.

—— (1990a) *You Just Don't Understand: Men and Women in Conversation*, New York: Morrow.

—— (1990b/1994) 'Gender differences in conversational coherence', in Tannen 1994.

—— (1990c) 'Gender differences in topical coherence', *Discourse Processes* 13: 73–90.

—— (ed.) (1993) *Gender and Conversational Interaction*, Oxford: Oxford University Press.

—— (1994) *Gender and Discourse*, Oxford: Oxford University Press.

—— (1995) *Talking from 9 to 5*, London: Virago Press.

Tannen, D. and Kakava, C. (1992) 'Power and solidarity in Modern Greek conversation: disagreeing to agree', *Journal of Modern Greek Studies* 10: 12–29.

Tannen, D. and Saville-Troike, M. (eds) (1985) *Perspectives on Silence*, Norwood, NJ: Ablex.

Thorne, B. and N. Henley (eds.) (1975) *Language and Sex: Difference and Dominance*, Rowley, MA: Newbury House.

Thorne, B., Kramarae, C. and N. Henley (eds) (1983) *Language, Gender and Society*, Rowley, MA: Newbury House.

Toner (1977) *The Facts of Rape*, London: Hutchinson.

Toronto Star (1980) *Toronto Star Style Guide*, Toronto.

Treichler, P. and Kramarae, C. (1983) 'Women's talk in the ivory tower', *Communication Quarterly* 31: 118–32.

Tressler, J.C., Christ, H.I. and Starkey, M. (1960) *English in Action*, books 1,2,3,4, Lexington, MA: Heath.

Troemel-Ploetz, S. (1991) 'Selling the apolitical', *Discourse & Society* 2: 489–502.

Tschudi, F. (1979) 'Gender stereotypes reflected in asymmetric similarities in language', paper presented to the APA Annual Meeting, New York.

Verdelle, A.J. (1996) *This Rain Coming*, London: The Women's Press.

Vetterling-Braggin, M. (ed.) (1981) *Sexist Language: A Modern Philosophical Analysis*, Totowa, NJ: Rowman & Littlefield.

Visser, F.Th. (1963) *An Historical Syntax of the English Language*, Leiden: E.J.Brill.

Walker, A. (1980) 'One child of one's own: a meaningful digression within the work(s)', in Sternburg, J. (ed.) *The Writer On Her Work*, New York: W.W. Norton.

—— (1984) *In Search of Our Mothers' Gardens*, London: The Women's Press [US edn 1984, Harvest/HRT].

Ward, E. (1984) *Father–Daughter Rape*, Wellingborough, Northants: The Women's Press.

Ward, W. (1765) *An Essay on Grammar*, Menston: Scolar Press Facsimile.

Watanabe, S. (1994) 'Cultural differences in framing: American and Japanese group discussions', in Tannen, D. (ed.) *Framing in Discourse*, New York and Oxford: Oxford University Press.

Weedon, C. (1987) *Feminist Practice and Poststructuralist Theory*, Oxford: Blackwell.

West, C. and Zimmerman, D. (1983) 'Small insults: a study of interruptions in cross-sex conversations between unacquainted persons', in Thorne, Henley and Kramarae (eds).

—— (1987) 'Doing gender', *Gender and Society* 1: 125–51.

White, R.G. (1880) *Everyday English*, Boston: Houghton Mifflin.

—— (1886) *Words and their Uses*, Boston: Houghton Mifflin.

Whorf, B.L. (1976) *Language, Thought and Reality*, ed. J.B. Carroll, Cambridge, MA: MIT Press.

Wilcox, H., McWatters, K., Thompson, A. and Williams, L. (eds) (1990) *The Body and the Text: Hélène Cixous, Reading and Teaching*, Hemel Hempstead: Harvester Wheatsheaf.

Wilkinson, S. and Kitzinger, C. (eds) (1995) *Feminism and Discourse: Psychological Perspectives*, London: Sage.

Williams, F. (1985) 'Technology and communication', in Benson, T. (ed.) *Speech Communication in the 20th Century*, Carbondale: South Illinois University Press.

Williams, R. (1975) *The Long Revolution*, Harmondsworth: Penguin Books.

Wilson, T. (1553) *Arte of Rhetorique*, Gainsville: Scholars Facsimiles and Reprints [also Mair edition (1909), Oxford: Clarendon Press.]

Witkin, H.A. *et al.* (1962) *Psychological Differentiation*, New York: Wiley.

Wittig, M. (1983) 'The point of view: universal or particular?' *Feminist Issues* 3(2) [also repr. in Wittig, M. *The Straight Mind and Other Essays*, Hemel Hempstead: Harvester Wheatsheaf].

Wolfowitz, C. (1991) *Language Style and Social Space: Stylistic Choice in Suriname Javanese*, Chicago: University of Illinois Press.

Woods, R. (1977) 'Discourse analysis: the work of M. Pecheux', *Ideology and Consciousness* 2 (Autumn).

Woolf, V. (1977 [1929]) *A Room of One's Own*, London: Granada.

—— (1965) *Contemporary Writers*, London: Hogarth Press.

357

Yamada, H. (1992) *American and Japanese Business Discourse: A Comparison of Interactional Styles*, Norwood, NJ: Ablex.

Young, M.F.D. (ed.) (1975) *Knowledge and Control: New Directions for the Sociology of Education*, London: Collier-Macmillan.

Subject Index

ableist language *see* disability
address forms 167–8, 178n, 262
assertiveness training 299

bilingualism 80, 229, 243
black women 5, 6–7, 19, 28,
42–3, 158; *see also* racism,
stereotypes

change in language 13, 128, 136–8, 167,
230–1
children, acquisition of language by 56,
58, 200–2, 242–3; gender differences in
speech of 60, 62, 242–3, 274–7, 282–3,
287
class 5, 62, 100, 101–2, 248, 261, 284,
338
computer-mediated communication, *see*
Internet
colour terms, 244–5, 333
consciousness raising 169–70
cooperation as feature of women's talk
203, 274–5, 282

deficit model of women's speech 216
disability 18, 158, 160
discourse 84, 112–14, 198 200, 301–5,
318–19
domestic violence, *see* violence against
women
dominance v. difference debate 14–15, 43,
217–18, 261–79, 280–92, 344

écriture féminine ('feminine writing') 30,
66–70, 73, 76, 208; *see also* style,
'woman's sentence', writing
essentialism 15–18, 218

feminism, liberal 158, 161, 162, 310; radical
156, 311; socialist 84, 101, 112–14

gay men 19, 245, 342n
gender, as grammatical category 84–5,
119, 120–3; as performance 17, 219–22,
295–301, 333–9; as social construct
15–16, 290–1

Names Index

Languages Index

LANGUAGES INDEX